Renate J. Mayr

Belize:
Tracking the Path of Its History

Acknowledgements

First and foremost I am deeply indebted to Univ. Prof. Mag. Dr.
Franz Mathis for his most valuable help in getting this book
published.

To Dr. Patric Kment a heartfelt thanks for his advice and support
and for taking excellent care of the layout.

I am also grateful to Mag. Richard Kisling and the team of the
LIT Verlag for making this book possible.

In Belize, whole-hearted thanks are due to Greg Smith, a friend of
many years, Solie Arguelles and all those who have inspired me
and I am unable to mention here for lack of space.

My special thanks go to all those friends who lent me an ear when
it was most needed and took the time to read through the tricky
passages.

Finally, I would like to express my sincere gratitude to my
husband for his assistance with the digitizing of the maps and
cartographic material, his help in proof-reading, as well as his
encouragement and understanding.

Renate J. Mayr

Belize:
Tracking the Path of Its History

From the Heart of the Maya Empire
to a Retreat for Buccaneers,
a Safe-Haven for Ex-Pirates and Pioneers,
a Crown Colony and a Modern Nation

LIT

Cover (photographs) and maps © by the author

Bibliographic information published by the Deutsche Nationalbibliothek
The Deutsche Nationalbibliothek lists this publication in the Deutsche
Nationalbibliografie; detailed bibliographic data are available in the Internet at
http://dnb.d-nb.de.

ISBN 978-3-643-90481-2

15mm

A catalogue record for this book is available from the British Library

©LIT VERLAG GmbH & Co. KG Wien,
Zweigniederlassung Zürich 2014
Klosbachstr. 107
CH-8032 Zürich
Tel. +41 (0) 44-251 75 05
Fax +41 (0) 44-251 75 06
E-Mail: zuerich@lit-verlag.ch
http://www.lit-verlag.ch

LIT VERLAG Dr. W. Hopf
Berlin 2014
Fresnostr. 2
D-48159 Münster
Tel. +49 (0) 2 51-62 03 20
Fax +49 (0) 2 51-23 19 72
E-Mail: lit@lit-verlag.de
http://www.lit-verlag.de

Distribution:
In the UK: Global Book Marketing, e-mail: mo@centralbooks.com
In North America: International Specialized Book Services, e-mail: orders@isbs.com
In Germany: LIT Verlag Fresnostr. 2, D-48159 Münster
Tel. +49 (0) 2 51-620 32 22, Fax +49 (0) 2 51-922 60 99, E-mail: vertrieb@lit-verlag.de

In Austria: Medienlogistik Pichler-ÖBZ, e-mail: mlo@medien-logistik.at
e-books are available at www.litwebshop.de

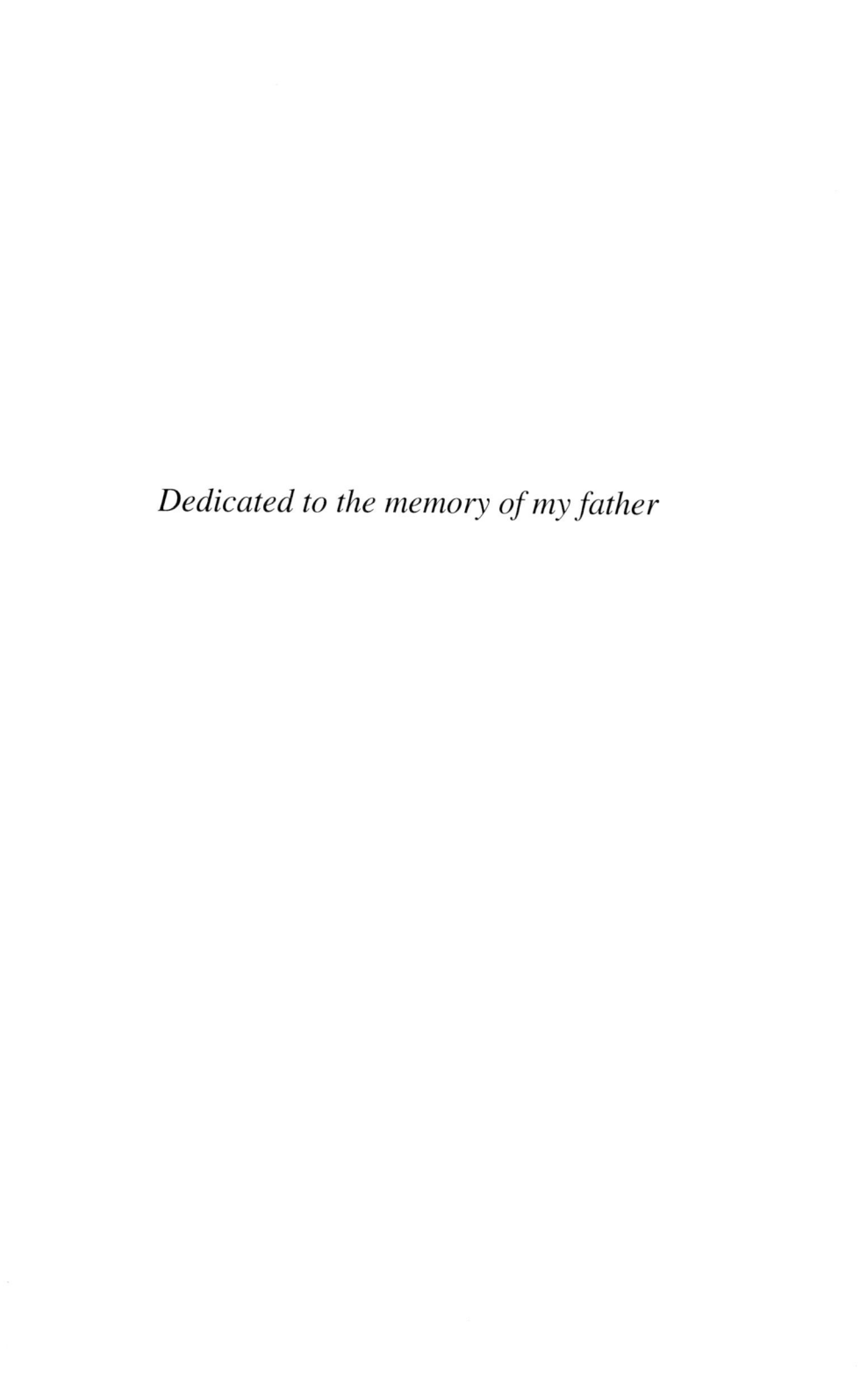

Dedicated to the memory of my father

Contents

Chapter Five: The Bay Settlement in the 19th Century

Chapter Six: From Crown Colony to Independence to Modern Belize

List of Maps and Enclosures

List of Tables

PREFACE

My interest in Belize awoke during regular visits to the then British colony in the late 1970s when residing in Central America. Little did I realize that what had started as a simple desire to find out more about the peculiar history of this country would lead to unexpected depths and would prompt me to embark on a journey that was to last a life time.

After several more sojourns in Belize my research began to take shape in earnest and culminated in a Ph.D. I received from the University of Innsbruck for a thesis on the socio-economic history of Belize.

The present book is directed primarily towards an interested general readership. Given the broad spectrum and the long time span covered it is meant to be a historical survey and not an in-depth analysis of any specific period in the trajectory of the history of Belize. I should also clarify that this book does not pretend to be a scholarly work in the proper sense. Therefore it does neither include specialist discussions nor strictly follow the pattern of formal research methodology.

The book also intends to give answers to why Belize came to be an English-speaking enclave perched between Spanish-speaking countries. I shall aim to explain why the Spanish were never able to colonize present Belize, why its colonization pattern was so unusual and why its diplomatic status remained ambiguous for more than two centuries until it became an official British crown colony in 1862 and finally an independent nation in 1981.

The digressions on the history of the Mosquito Shore and Providence Island I considered relevant to discuss the role these regions may have played for the emerging Belize. Influenced by my holding an M.A. in English and Hispanic philology and my passion for etymology, special attention is given to the various languages spoken in Belize as well as etymology.

INTRODUCTION

For many years, the region that was to become Belize was the heart of the Maya empire. Although, at the time of conquest, the Maya in present-day Belize did not suffer to such a dramatic extent as was the case in the neighbouring regions, subsequent developments in the wider Mesoamerican sphere did affect the "Belizean" Maya to a considerable degree. Nevertheless, they succeeded in retreating into the recesses of the jungle, where, despite various missionary activities, a strong Maya resistance was formed. The last Maya stronghold was finally forced to surrender as late as 1697.

Although the Spanish made several attempts, they were never able to colonize present-day Belize. Thus, they indirectly paved the way for English and Scottish buccaneers/ex-buccaneers to form a permanent settlement on the Belizean coast, where they soon started to cut logwood, a much sought-after source for textile dyes. According to the Spanish, who continued to claim sovereignty over the region and prohibited the setting up of a formal government and the establishment of commercial agriculture, the woodcutters (the "Baymen") were to exploit the timber resources of the area and then move out.

But history was to take a different course. European demand for logwood, and later mahogany, led to the development of a British settlement, the Bay Settlement, the nucleus of the future colony of British Honduras. Until the Treaty of Paris in 1763 the British woodcutters had operated outside the British imperial system. In the process of extracting timber, an enclave economy with a peculiar socio-economic system was created. In order to meet the growing demand, labour from Africa had to be imported and these slaves formed the basis of the settlement's future demographic development.

For two and a half centuries the economy of the Bay Settlement, a British colony in all but name, was focused on the profitable timber trade – first logwood then mahogany – and was in the hands of a powerful local merchant elite.

The entirely export-orientated timber industry, a poorly developed domestic market – partly due to the insecure and abnormal diplomatic status, a lack of infrastructure and the continuing ban on agriculture imposed by the Spanish – and the prevailing pattern of land tenure were the major impediments for the development of a peasantry.

In 1862, after several petitions from the settlers, Britain was finally willing to formally recognize its *de facto* colony. Neglected for centuries by colonial powers and almost by chance, the Bay Settlement became the crown colony of British Honduras.

Mahogany continued to dominate the economy until the 1950s with agriculture playing only a marginal role. From the 1960s onwards, efforts to diversify the colony's economic base have been moderately successful.

Belizean independence was formally declared as late as 1981. Among the reasons for the delay were continuous territorial threats on the part of Guatemala, who claimed to have inherited rights from Spain, to invade the territory.

Belize is a constitutional monarchy and a member of the Commonwealth. Since independence, Belize has experienced a massive influx of Central Americans. It may be seen as an irony of history that although the Baymen have successfully thwarted Spanish claims for almost two centuries, from 1980 to 2013 the percentage of Spanish-speaking people of Hispanic origin has increased by almost 70%. Today, close to 50% of Belizeans are Mestizos/Latinos.

Belize covers an area of 23,000 km². In 2000, it had a population of 240,000. The population estimate for 2013 is 335,000 and up to 350,000 with a population density of only approximately 14,5 inhabitants per km². However, on agricultural land the population density is as high as 360 per km² and the country's population growth rate of approximately 2,21% (2010 estimates) is the highest in the region.

Chapter

One

The Greater Area of Present Belize in Precolonial Times

Before colonization, the territory occupied by the Maya was divided into three main areas:

- The **Northern Maya Lowlands** in the entire Yucatán Peninsula.
- The **Southern Maya Lowlands** in today's Belize, the area of Guatemala's Petén and Lake Izabal, the Mexican provinces of Chiapas and parts of Tabasco and the north-west corner of Honduras.
- The **Maya Highlands** in Mexico's Chiapas province and in the highlands of Guatemala and El Salvador and **the Coastal Plain** along the Pacific Coast of Guatemala and parts of El Salvador.

As can be seen on Map 1, the far north of Belize was part of the Northern Maya Lowlands and the rest of what is now Belize belonged to the Southern Maya Lowlands.

1. Outline of Maya History

For a general description of the epochs of Maya history the following terms are used. In view of the fact that recent archaeological evidence is constantly providing new insights, the traditional conceptions of Maya chronology have become more dynamic and dates are considered to be approximate only.

- PRE-CLASSIC: applies to the time span from 2000 B.C. – A.D. 250. The most important Pre-Classic sites in today's Belize are Cuello, Santa Rita, Cerros, Colha, Altun Ha and Lamanai.

- CLASSIC: applies to the period between A.D. 250 – A.D. 900

The most important Classic sites are:

In Belize: Caracol, Colha, Altun Ha, Xunantunich and Lubaantun

In Guatemala: Tikal, Uaxactún, Quiriguá and Piedras Negras

In Mexico: Palenque, Bonampak, Yaxchilán, Uxmal, Kabáh and Cobá in the provinces of Chiapas and Yucatán

In Honduras: Copan

The longest Maya road known, the "Camino Real" from the Gulf of Mexico to Lake Petén Itzá in the Central Petén in present Guatemala, is approximately 100 km long and was built in the Classic period.

- POST-CLASSIC: dates from A.D. 900. Among the most important Post-Classic sites are:

In Belize: Lamanai and Tipu

In Yucatán: Chichén Itzá and Mayapán

In Guatemala: Tayasal and Seibal

The Post-Classic can be further divided into the:

RE-ADJUSTMENT OR RENAISSANCE PERIOD of Northern Yucatán, the NEW EMPIRE OR LEAGUE OF MAYAPÁN and ends with the

SPANISH CONQUEST of Mexico in 1521

But Maya History does not "end" with the Spanish conquest. To complete the framework, we must add the

- COLONIAL ERA, from 1521 – 1821 and the

- MODERN PERIOD, from 1821 to the present day.

At the end of the Late Classic Period (towards A.D. 900) the Maya started suffering heavy demographic losses especially in the Southern Lowlands, i.e. the Central Petén and the adjacent regions of the interior of Belize. As the many unfinished buildings suggest, construction activities must have ceased virtually from one day to the other.

Scientists have propounded many theories in the attempt to explain this phenomenon and the subject has generated much controversy. Among the various hypotheses put forward until now, we can basically distinguish between two main groups: The one that blames the collapse of the Classic Maya on ecological disturbances and the one that makes political conflicts responsible for it.

In the first case natural exhaustion of the soil or prolonged droughts might have been one reason for a possible insufficiency and/or failure of the agricultural resources to provide subsistence. The lack of regularly available water supplies alone would certainly have been a good reason for a temporary abandonment of a site. In addition there is also a possibility that plagues of different origins may have caused the decline in the population. Bishop Landa's account,[1] our main historical source on Maya culture and written as early as 1566, tells us that in between two "visits" by the Spaniards

> there was also a plague of locusts for five years, so great that no green thing was left and such a famine ensued that they [the Indians] fell dead on the roads ...

There is every reason to believe that much of his descriptions might also be valid for the Classic Period in general and that such famines could easily have occurred at the beginning of the 10th century. Assuming this to be true, undoubtedly, famines must have been a contributing factor to the mysterious population decline.

Social conflicts, such as an internal uprising of the common people against the dominating aristocracy, clashes between political factions and/or invasion of neighbouring tribes belong to the second group of possibilities: During the Late Classic Period more pressure was added to the Maya of the Southern Lowlands. With an increased exploitation of the major riverine waterways such as the Usumacinta River in present Guatemala's Petén, they came into contact with other Maya or Amerindian groups of possibly more advanced commercial and ceremonial centres in Northern and Central Mexico.

If these "foreign" contacts had stimulated the cultural and religious activities of the Maya in the Southern Lowlands positively, the course of history

---

1   Landa (1978: 24)

would have been very different. But evidence suggests that the effects were to the contrary, triggering a series of negative events which led to the gradual disintegration of the old, traditional social and political order. In this sense, demographic factors can be seen as both a cause and an effect of this collapse. A cause, because a decline in the population led to the inability to produce the huge workforce needed to cultivate enough maize to sustain the population, and an effect, because the worsening conditions of life then gave rise to massive emigration to the Northern Lowlands, with the result that the Southern Maya Lowlands consequently suffered from a rapid demographic decline.

In the Northern Maya Lowlands (i.e. present Yucatán and parts of Northern Belize), in the 10th and 11th centuries the Maya civilization flourished again and in the 13th century it experienced another renaissance period. It was, however, in a very different form: Due to the fact that by the late 10th century internal disturbances had become so significant, the Classic Maya had no other option but surrender to the Toltecs, a military race of non-Maya speech from Central Mexico. Over time, the Maya of Northern Yucatán amalgamated with the Toltecs with the result that the religious, ceremonial and artistic emphasis of the Classic Maya was changed, ultimately leading to the emergence of a more military orientated, secular culture.

At this stage it must be emphasized that the region of present Belize and its adjacent lowlands in the Petén was never completely abandoned, as it has often been stated, and that "collapse" does not imply total standstill. Despite massive emigration to the north, villages in the Southern Lowlands were not deserted all of a sudden and the theory of a total abandonment of the area seems difficult to support: Recent archaeological research is yielding substantive proof of the intermittent occupation of several Maya settlements in the north of present Belize beyond the conquest. And throughout the 16th and 17th centuries it was in the north-western and western regions where the headquarters of the Maya resistance force was situated. The Spanish *never* succeeded to penetrate this region until as late as 1667.

In sum, and in my opinion, the most plausible explanation for the causes of the decline of the Classic Maya civilization seems to be the theory that economic and political re-arrangements, together with certain ecological conditions, gave rise to large scale emigration, thus shifting the activities from the Southern to the Northern Lowlands. Archaeologists continue to discover ancient Maya sites in the Southern Maya Lowlands and it is believed that further findings may shed more light on the mysterious decline of the Classic Period. Until then, the abundant explanations offered by scientists will remain hypotheses only.

2. Ancient Maya Settlements in Present-Day Belize

It is now widely agreed that the area today known as Belize was, in the Pre-Classic and Classic Period, the very heart of the Maya Empire. This was for a variety of reasons, the main one being that the territory offers a considerable amount of resource diversity. Whereas in the Central Petén and Yucatán area the landscape is largely uniform, in Belize, we can distinguish between four distinctive geomorphological features. All of them are suited for settlement in one way or another and especially the lowlands in the northern part of the country offer fertile agricultural lands. The offshore barrier reef along with 170 cays and several atolls, although not so advantageous for settlement, not only provided a great diversity of marine habitats but also enabled a safe passage inside the reef which was vital to Maya economy and exchange patterns. This natural diversity of the area that is now Belize has had direct consequences for its occupational history.

Let us now briefly turn to the widely discussed population figures, one of the most controversial issues surrounding the Lowland Maya Classic civilization. Scholars have speculated that the area of present-day Belize including the adjoining lowlands in Guatemala's Petén region may have supported as many as close to one million inhabitants. However, at this point, it is important to place emphasis on the fact that these figures are mostly based on archaeological findings only. Therefore, from a historical point of view they do not provide sufficient basis to be able to draw reliable conclusions about actual figures.

Irrespective of the above, the question keeps arising how the Maya could have sustained a heavily populated area, especially by practising the traditional "slash and burn" farming method?[2] In favourable soil conditions it seems theoretically possible that the Maya were temporarily able to sustain the dense population, whereas in less advantageous conditions, such as throughout most of the Yucatán Peninsula, it seems very unlikely.

On the other hand however, one cannot but wonder how the large populations surrounding the biggest city states, for example Caracol in Belize or Tikal in the Petén, could *not* have starved with this system? Even with an excellent soil, how could the "slash and burn" method have provided enough staple for such a dense population?

---

2   In order to maintain the fertility of the soil the plots (traditionally known as *milpa*) where maize, beans, chili peppers, squash etc. are cultivated have to be shifted every two to three years. Before re-using plots for plantation they are cleared by burning tree stumps and cutting down any vegetation. This method, however, can be practised in reasonably favourable soil conditions only.

Archaeological studies might provide possible clues because evidence of remains of other agricultural methods indicates that Maya farmers had knowledge of alternative farming techniques.[3] Based on the assumption that more advanced techniques were practised, the existence of terraces, irrigation, and drainage systems as a means to reclaim swamps must have made a significant contribution to the effort to raise the production capacity of Maya agriculture.

The classic site of **Caracol** in Southern Belize is believed to have been a heavily populated city. Data collected from more recent excavations at this site have led archaeologists to conjecture that as a result of an elaborate city planning system, urban Caracol may have maintained a population of over 115,000 people in the Late Classic Period around A.D. 700.[4] Again, this estimate is only supported by archaeological findings. These population figures cannot be based on historical accounts or facts and will therefore always have to remain an issue of contention.

As far as the settlement of the area of present-day Belize is concerned already during the Pre-Classic, the fertile lowland areas in Northern Belize in the vicinity of **Cerros** were a favoured region for the founding of early, primitive agricultural settlements. One could even go as far as to say that it is not a co-incidence that this region was to host modern Belize's first serious attempts to promote agricultural plantations approximately 2000 years later. Cerros, which was entirely surrounded by a canal that delivered water to the fields outside the settlement, was an important centre for regional authority and commerce as early as 300 B.C.

Apart from fertile land, the proximity of rivers played an important role for choosing a site for settlement. The important Pre-Classic location of **Cuello**, the oldest Maya site in the country so far discovered, was within reach of a major river, which provided convenient transport to the coast and guaranteed the supply of marine resources which played a big role in Middle and Late Pre-Classic subsistence.

The offshore cays of Belize, as mentioned, did not play a major role for permanent settlement. Nevertheless, the cays, especially Ambergris Cay and Moho Cay (presumably the site of modern Belize City), were important trans-shipment points for the transportation of resources and objects (for example cult items such as shell jewellery and other ornaments valued greatly for status differentiation) to the coast and the interior and vice versa. The strategic position of Ambergris Cay was ideal. It was one of the many natural stopovers on the coastal trade route in both directions. As can be seen on Maps 2 and 3,

---

3   Cf. for example Guderjan (1993:13)
4   Cf. for example Chase and Chase (2007:60, 2008:103–108)

Ambergris Cay used to be the southern tip of the Xcalac Peninsula in Southern Yucatán. In order to open a trade route the Maya had created the cay artificially by digging a canal (present Boca Bacalar Chico canal) across the Xcalac Peninsula. The importance of both the cays in the transport system as well as other aspects of Maya exchange economy and trade routes will be discussed presently.

Many Pre-Classic sites within the area of Northern Belize were able to sustain a reasonably high population well into the Late Classic Period. Evidence from the Post-Classic location of **Lamanai** in the interior suggests a strong settlement, although not continuously, even far beyond the Spanish Conquest. Lamanai was occupied longer than almost any other Maya site (except for Tipu) from about 1500 B.C. to at least A.D. 1650. **Santa Rita**, near present Corozal, in Northern Belize was a powerful community since 2000 B.C. It became the capital of the province of 'Chactemal' and was given the same name. Santa Rita continued to be an important trading centre until well after the late Post-Classic. **Tipu**, a Post-Classic site in the upper, middle Belize area, was highly populated until 1707, when the Spanish finally succeeded in forcibly removing this Maya stronghold to Lake Petén Itzá in the Central Petén.

These facts show us that some sites of Belize are to be considered exceptional in the sense that they do *not* conform to the pattern of the Late Classic demographic decline and eventual disintegration of the Classic Maya civilization. The unique resource diversity of this small stretch of land and the advantages of the offshore cays may have given the Maya an extra bonus and may have made them less vulnerable to certain disturbances with all its fatal consequences.

3. Maya Society

Much of today's knowledge of Maya society is based on speculation and the fragmentary information received from the reconstruction of ceremonial and public building of ancient Maya sites.

Ancient Maya society was a strongly marked class society. During the Pre-Classic (until A.D. 250) the foundations for the later development of the social institutions and kingdoms were laid and from the Early Classic Period (from A.D. 250 onwards) social status groups were already in existence.

Maya population was not homogeneous. Many different subgroups formed cultural and political units with a territorial ruler at the top. Although the religious aspects of the community were in the hands of a shaman, called *Chilan*, who received messages which then had to be interpreted by the priests, the image of Maya society controlled by an elitist theocracy dedicated chiefly to religious affairs within isolated city states is not accurate. The ruler resided in the respective capital of each territorial unit, a form of mini-state. He was supported by the products of his own land, which he leased to other members of the community in exchange for tribute. In this context it is important to point out that, contrary to popular beliefs, the Spanish have not introduced the idea of tribute-paying in the Americas, they only modified the system according to their needs.

Maya society was not a peaceful one. Inscriptions and wall paintings on Classic monuments serve as a testimony for the continuous inter-tribal conflicts over boundaries and lineage honour. For the Maya, blood had a special ceremonial significance and was spilled as a sacrifice for the Gods. As depicted on several stelae and wall paintings (for example at major Early Classic sites such as Bonampak situated in the Mexican state of Chiapas close to the Guatemalan border) bloodletting rituals were an important part of Maya society. Victims for the bloody rituals were sometimes also members of the foreign aristocracy who were captured on the many raids into enemy territory. They had their hearts torn out with a knife whose sharp blade was carved out of obsidian stone or were beheaded, a much used form of sacrifice.[5]

The above outline given on Maya society is intended to be rudimentary only. To go into more details on this subject as well as on the various intellectual achievements of the Maya in the field of mathematics, astronomy, hieroglyphic writing, art etc. would be far too complex for the present purposes.

Let us now take a look at the eating habits of the Maya. The basic staple was maize grown on the *milpa*. Apart from maize, squashes, chili peppers, root crops, and fruit trees were also cultivated. Archaeobotanical evidence of carbonized plant remains for example recovered at Cerros in Northern Belize actually prove the consumption of maize, beans, chili peppers, mamey, cacao, and passiflora seeds.[6] To balance the low intake of protein, beans, snakes, worms, *iguanas* (lizards), the occasional crocodile, deer, peccary, rabbit, agouti, opossum, paca, fox, wild pigeon, and partridge as well as marine products such as estuarine and reef fish, turtles, manatees, sea snails and shells were also consumed. However, there seem to have been considerable dietary differences between status groups: On the one hand archaeological evidence from burial sites suggest the presence of marine products in the diet and on the other skeletons show symptoms of anaemia, which scholars trace to a nutritional imbalance

---

5   Landa (1996[1598], XVIII and XXVIII) regarded these and other rituals as *borracheras* (bouts of drunkenness) and *sacrificios y mortificaciones crueles*.

6   Scott L. Fedick, "The Economics of Agricultural Land Use and Settlement in the Upper Belize Valley" in MacAnany (1989: 215–254)

caused by the heavy consumption of maize.[7] This seems to indicate that the catchers and/or preparers of marine products were not the consumers and that the elite class may have had fish, turtles, manatees, and other marine products on the menu whereas the ordinary class did not. Meat and milk from domesticated animals was not put to use. Vegetables and fruit trees such as papaya, custard apple, avocado, sapodilla, and breadfruit trees were also cultivated and fermented juices were made out of the agave and maguey plant, which yielded additional vitamin C. In times of drought much-needed nutrition could be obtained from many spices and several kinds of wild fruit.

The Maya version of "hot chocolate" must also have provided an extra amount of nutrition. Thanks to an extensive planting of cacao trees in Northern Yucatán, in present Belize along the drainages of the Sibun, Sittee and New River, and on the highly fertile volcanic slopes of Guatemala's Pacific Coast, the Maya were able to consume a chocolate drink. It was made out of a mass obtained from the ground nibs of the fermented, dried and roasted seeds of the cacao tree. Cocoa mass was used to prepare a beverage as well as an ingredient in foods. For the drink, the chocolate mass was well beaten with water to achieve a thick frothy consistence.

At that time drinking chocolate was not custom practice for all classes. In pre-colonial times, the system of cacao production was simply not efficient enough to supply the quantity needed to make it a popular drink for the general public. Moreover, cacao beans were also used as currency until well beyond the Spanish conquest and therefore were much too precious to be processed into a few drops of a luxury beverage. The habit of consuming chocolate was more customary among the ruling class who also used it for ceremonial purposes. Whereas the ruling class added vanilla, chili pepper, and *achiote* (a natural red colorant used also for flavouring) it is assumed that the poorer people – provided that they were able to have access to the basic ingredients – enriched it with young maize to give it extra bulk for nutrition.[8]

As far as the origin of the term "chocolate" is concerned this has been a subject of debate for many decades. Despite the fact that it is, admittedly, far beyond the scope of these pages I would very much like to sort out the vast

---

7   K. Anne Pyburn, "Maya Cuisine: Hearths and Lowland Economy" in MacAnany (1989:325–346)

8   The earliest evidence for cacao consumption in Mesoamerica comes from the Pre-Classic site of Puerto Escondido near the mouth of the Río Ulúa in Honduras (as early as 1150 B.C.) and Colha in Belize (between 1000 and 400 B.C.) where archaeologists found residues of theobromine, a chemical substance of cacao, in ceremonial pottery. At the Early Classic site of Río Azul in Guatemala's northern Petén region cacao traces found in a tomb date from around 400 A.D.

number of possible derivations proposed. Therefore, I ask the reader to bear with me for the following etymological digression:

While it is undisputed that the term "chocolate" entered the English language via Spanish, the question of *how* it came into Spanish is less straightforward and eminent scholars have competed with one another for conclusive theories.[9] Although the most cited explanation is a Nahuatl etymology I am much more inclined to lend credence to well-founded suggestions for a linguistic source based on Mayan languages.

The most plausible Nahuatl etymologies are:

1. *Chocolate* is a derivation from the Nahuatl **chocolātl** (meaning 'bitter water'), from *xococ* ('bitter' or 'sour') and *ātl* ('water' or 'drink').

2. Other theories claim that the original word for the cold chocolate beverage was the Nahuatl **cacahuātl** (from 'cacao water'), from *cacaua* for cocoa.

Maya etymologies gain even more in importance especially if we consider that the Spanish preferred to have their drink the Maya way, i.e. heated rather than cold, which was the Aztec variation. The Spanish may indeed have adopted a Maya rather than Nahuatl terminology although it remains unclear whether or not Nahuatl may have been the lending language.

Of the many possible Maya etymologies

3. the Kakchiquel *čokola* (meaning 'to drink chocolate together') and the K'iche' *chokuā*, possibly as a derivation from *chokol or chokoul (meaning 'hot')* and *"a"* from *haa* ('water') seems the most convincing.

4. A more recent etymology is based on the assumption that the Spanish coined a Nahuatl/Maya hybrid taking the Yucatec Maya *chokol* for 'hot' combining it with the *ātl* ('water' or 'drink') from Nahuatl.[10]

---

9 The question whether the Spanish term *chocolate* has its origin from the early Mixe-Zoquean language *kakawa* for cacao (thus possibly referring to a borrowing from the Olmec language as early as approx. 1000 B.C.) or was adopted from the Oto-Mangean (for example *tzokolate, chikula(t), sikula),* the Uto-Aztecan language family (Nahuatl) or from the Mayan languages continues to be a controversial subject.

10 Cf. Santamaria (1959: 412–413), Dávila Garibi (1939) and Coe and Coe (1996: 119)

5. Finally, another hypothesis revolves around ancient recipes for a beverage which is said to have contained the seeds of the *ceiba* tree (*pochotl)* plus the seeds from the cacao tree (*cacahuatl).*[11] In many Mayan languages the term for cacao contains the root **kaka,** for example *ka:ka:w* in colonial and modern Q'eqchi', *kakaaw* in K'iche', *ka:kow* in Kakchiquel, or *cūkwaʼ* in modern Yucatec Maya.

It does seem possible that the term *chocolate* used by the Spanish developed as a result of a phonological misspelling of *pocho-cacahua-atl* (beverage/water made out of *pochotl* and cacao, then corrupted by the Spanish into *chocahuatl* and ultimately *chocolate*. On the other hand, given the fact that the root **kaka** describes a frothy brownish beverage, it is very likely that its usage could have been culturally inacceptable to the Spanish. However, the fact that several Mexican/Spanish terms containing the root **caca** have survived to the present (such as *cacahuate* for 'peanuts' or *cacalote* for 'popcorn' among others) does give this etymology considerable credibility again and shows us that it cannot be ruled out altogether.

4. Maya Economy and Trade Routes

The greatest asset of Maya economy was the large workforce available. Only with such a large labour supply, a wealthy and diversified economy could have been achieved and sustained. Among important branches of Maya economy were the manufacturing of tools, ritual artefacts, craft items, jewellery out of obsidian, flint and jade, the extraction of salt, the fishing industry, the widespread trade including the necessary transportation in order to market the various commodities.

Maya economy was supported by high tax revenue resulting from a strict taxation system that was very heavy on the individual. Government officials of each mini-state were in charge of collecting the tribute from private people or the entire community and households were only allowed to keep their yearly allowance of maize. Apart from the bare necessities for subsistence, other produce such as honey, salt, limes, chili, seeds, beans, firewood, clothing, feathers, incense, wax-bees, precious stones, deer and manatee hides, jaguar skins, dyes, or in short, whatever commodities a particular region could offer, were collected. After the tribute was paid, the "export department" was put in charge of dispatching the goods to areas with demand.

---

11 Cf. Corominas (1980) and De Silva (1995)

Maya economy was based on barter trade. The basic food items such as maize, beans, and chili, were measured in cubic units and, provided there was no food shortage, exchanged on usually a one to one basis. The value of other commodities was usually quoted in cotton mantles, which were standardized with regard to size, quality and exchange rate – for example a piece of jaguar skin was worth a fixed quantity of cotton cloth. Articles such as copper and stone axes, shells and shell beads, feathers and other ornaments more or less had fixed values in terms of cacao and were used as barter. The concept of money was not in existence and cacao beans were used as a coinage instead.[12] The usage of cacao beans as currency was widespread among the travelling merchants, especially since the beans were of relative light weight and of no bulk. In remoter parts of the Southern Lowlands and the Central Guatemalan Highlands cacao survived as a currency until the mid-nineteenth century.

The region that is now Belize and Yucatán played an important role in Maya economy and several highly specialized "industrial centres" existed. In today's Northern Belize for example, archaeologists found evidence for the existence of several important manufacturing centres (see Maps 2 and 3).

Colha in the province of Chactemal was a significant Late Pre-Classic to Late Classic industrial centre for the production of high quality chart tools which were much treasured for export. Fifteen kilometres south of Colha was the important craft centre of Altun Ha where deposits of green obsidian were found. Since obsidian is of volcanic origin and does definitely *not* occur in the limestone based lowlands in the vicinity of Altun Ha, it shows that it must have been carried to Altun Ha and other production centres (such as for example Santa Rita further north) for the purpose of workmanship. For this reason, archaeologists speculate that most pieces of fine workmanship of obsidian artefacts (such as crescent rings, portraits of men and various animals and prismatic blades) found in the highlands of Guatemala were fully worked lowland imports. If we decide to support this hypothesis, it would mean that the craft centre of Altun Ha must have imported obsidian as raw material which was then fashioned by craftsmen in the local workshops and re-exported back to the highlands.

The province of Chactemal was also famous for its apiculture, producing large quantities of honey, also a major export product to the highlands. At this stage it is important to mention the highly developed Maya fishing industry and the working of tortoiseshell, the products of which found its way inland by a well-organized transportation system, as can be seen on Map 2. Northern

---

12   For exchange rates for weights and measures of cacao in relation to beans for example see MacLeod (1973:70).

Yucatán was an important manufacturing centre for different articles made out of *henequen* (a fibre won from *maguey*, a native plant of Yucatán) and exquisite textiles made out of cotton.

From the above we can deduce that the industrial specialization of this region must have played a major role in supporting Maya economy.

One of the main sectors of Maya economy was the carrying out of widespread trade. An enormously wide assortment of merchandize existed and in order to obtain a better picture of the extent of Maya trade a listing of the most important items will be given below. The presence of markets in the highlands continues to be strong to this very day, whereas in the lowlands they hardly exist. Based on the assumption that the tradition of markets has changed little since the ancient days, one wonders whether markets in the lowlands ever existed to the same degree as in the highlands. If this was indeed the case, we may be able to conclude that goods must have been transported from the lowland areas to the highlands because the chances for marketing were higher there. Among the wide range of trade goods exchanged in the highland markets were:

- **Tools and artefacts** made out of copper, flint, obsidian, jade: for example copper axes (the predecessor of the modern steel *machete*), or flint spears for the hunting of turtles and manatees
- **Grinding implements:** essential for grinding corn and chili pepper, made out of lava and other volcanic stones; still in use today
- **Clay pottery**
- **Worked shell:** in the form of pendants from both the Pacific and the Atlantic
- **Shark teeth:** perforated for pendants
- **Stingray-spines** for sacrificial purposes in bloodletting rituals
- **Quetzal feathers** for adornment
- **Plumage** of other birds such as toucan, hummingbird, parrot etc.
- *Ocote:* small wooden sticks from the pitch-pine, used as lanterns for outdoor illumination and for fire making
- **Pelts, hides, fur:** of the jaguar, rabbit, manatee and other animals as a symbol of rank
- **Tortoise-shell**
- **Honey and wax:** wax was used for ceremonial purposes; the Maya did not know the use of candles
- **Incense:** *copal,* a superior quality of aromatic resin obtained from a variety of tropical trees; still in use today

- **Basic Foodstuffs:** maize, chili, salt, beans, *huisquil* (a variety of courgettes or zucchini), salt, palm hearts, live animals (*iguanas,* snakes, worms etc.), wild vanilla, lime etc.
- **Textiles:** fine cotton garments, loin cloths, *huipiles* (colourfully embroidered, hand woven blouses still used by modern Indian women and girls, with different designs for every region)
- *Henequen* **products:** bags, ropes, hammocks made out of a fibre from the *maguey* plant
- **Rubber**
- **Palm products** for example the leaves of the *cohune* palm tree, used for fire fans and thatching huts
- **Natural dyes** such as *achiote,* which was used to stain the body for ceremonial purposes and for giving flavour and a red colour to food (for the latter purpose *achiote* is still in widespread use today)
  - *Cochineal:* a blood-red dye, unique to Central America and Mexico produced from the dried female insects *Coccus Cacti,* cactus-eating insects which live on the *nopal* tree. As much as approximately 70.000 insects were needed to obtain half a kilogram of dye.
  - **Indigo** for all shades of blue
  - **Logwood** for fine blacks
- **Bark cloth** for making paper and for sacrificial purposes
- **Slaves** used as labourers and/or for religious sacrifice were also an important trade "item".

According to historical records Maya trade was not only intense but also widespread, as depicted on Map 3. Generally speaking, we can distinguish between two types of trade, inland trade and sea borne trade. According to well-known historical accounts of the time in relation to Maya trade[13] freights consisted of cotton mantles, *huipiles,* loin cloths with multicolour designs, small copper axes, and large quantities of cacao beans among other articles. The sources state that cargoes must have originated in Yucatán and were southbound for the Valley of Ulúa in Honduras.

From these historical fragments it can be safely concluded that Maya maritime trade was well organized and carried out on a fairly large scale. Hernán Cortés before starting his expedition into the Mexican interior[14] tells us of sea-faring merchants being familiar with the coastline of Tabasco and coming around the northern tip of Yucatán down to the shores of Honduras. Map 3

---

13   Cf. for example Oviedo y Valdés (1959) and Las Casas (1951)
14   Cortés (1971:339–40)

shows possible and reconstructed inland routes, the Tabasco and Honduras coastal routes as well as Moho Cay (present Belize City), Ambergris Cay and the Bay of Chetumal area which served as an ideal stop-over and was easily reached by using the Bacalar Chico canal. Several connecting inland routes in the form of paths or riverine waterways or the combination of both left from the vicinity of Cerros in the Bay of Chetumal and from several ports of call along the Belizean coast.

It is highly possible that the offshore cays of Belize played a crucial role in the coastal trade. First, and in addition to Altun Ha and Colha on the mainland, they were the location of important manufacturing centres, namely Moho Cay, Ambergris Cay and Wild Cane Cay. With the purpose of shedding more light on possible trade activities in that region specialised analyses of archaeobotanical remains have been carried out.

An example of how goods were transported over long distances is obsidian: Trace elements of obsidian have been obtained at various excavation sites in order to be able to determine the sources of obsidian.[15] The results of these tests may point to the Guatemalan Highlands as the principal source for obsidian. More precisely the area northwest of present Guatemala City, the site of El Chayal a short distance further east and the source of the Río Motagua (situated in the highlands between present Quetzaltenango and Chichicastenango). Since obsidian definitely does not occur on the cays and judging from the high obsidian density in the trace elements, it becomes less far-fetched that obsidian may, indeed, have been transported all the way from the highlands to the manufacturing centres on the Belizean cays.

However, in this context it is important to point out that whereas, on the one hand, archaeobotanical research provides relatively substantiated evidence of a huge diversity of trade goods, it hardly allows us to draw conclusions about the actual intensity of trade as such.

Notwithstanding the above, archaeological analyses may point to the fact that the offshore cays, apart from being manufacturing centres, could also have been important redistribution centres. In this case, Ambergris Cay, the largest of the cays, must have played a crucial role in the exchange system because its strategic position made it an ideal entrepôt. It seems likely that the list of trade items trans-shipped on Ambergris Cay consisted of mainland goods, either highland exports transported to the coast on land routes or down the Río Motagua (mainly raw jade, obsidian, flint, lava grinding stones and pottery) and lowland exports (for example worked jade artefacts, finished flint and ob-

---

15   See Heather McKillop, "Coastal Maya Trade: Obsidian Densities at Wild Cane Cay," in MacAnany (1989:17–56)

sidian tools, fruit and vegetables, cacao, spices, dyes, animal skins and hides, fur, plumage, honey and wax, tobacco, rubber, *henequen* products such as bags, ropes, hammocks, palm products, reef and estuarine fish, worked shell for jewellery and ornaments, sting ray spines, sharks' teeth, tortoise shells). Products that originated in Honduras and were shipped northbound along the Belizean Coast most likely were pottery, feathers, dyes such as *cochineal* or indigo, cacao and tobacco to name only a few.

It is also highly possible that salt, immensely needed on the mainland and collected off on the island of Cozumel (in the north-eastern corner of Yucatán) as well as in the lagoons on Ambergris Cay, was supplied by coastal Maya traders inland via the main riverine routes, thereby linking important communication and redistribution centres such as Altun Ha or Cerros with Maya centres in the Petén. Likewise, salt from the same source could have been shipped up the Río Motagua to highland areas where it was in great demand, despite the fact that the highlands were also supplied by salt extracted on the Pacific Coast.

Coastal trade and the exploitation of the riverine waterways was a vital element in the Maya exchange pattern, especially if we consider the hardships involving the usage of land routes. For example, seasonal climatic changes presented great difficulties and paths traversing large jungle areas and regions easily drowned and were rendered practically useless during the rainy season. But thanks to the possibility of using the main rivers as alternative routes, business operations were able to operate throughout the year. As illustrated on Map 2, the New River, the Río Hondo and the Belize River were the main trade arteries to reach the Central Petén area until contemporary transportation systems were introduced.

There existed yet another reason for why long distance coastal trade and the use of rivers as trade routes were the better option for transport: It was the fact that the Maya did not have domestic animals as beasts of burden to substitute human carriers. The average load per porter was approximately 25 kg (50 pounds) or 2 *arobas,* an ancient Maya weight unit still in use today. Two strings were fixed leading to the forehead of the *cargador* (porter) at both sides of the load to reduce the weight on the back, a carrying method equally still in practice. If we consider the weight of jade, flint, obsidian, the grinding implements out of lava stone or large quantities of salt, the riverine or long distance coastal trade was certainly much more efficient.,

In the endeavour to obtain more information on how Maya exchange patterns functioned, scholars have gone into considerable efforts to reconstruct possible routes of exchange and a series of interconnecting trade route models were proposed. If we were to follow these hypothetical routes shown on Map 2, for example the first route model would lead from the Central Guatemalan

Highlands via the Río Chixoy to the Río de la Pasión to Seibal and Tikal. From there the route would continue either down the Río Usumacinta to the northern sites, such as Piedras Negras and Yaxchilán as far as the Mexican Coast or go east, down the Belize River or Río Hondo to the Caribbean Coast.

Travelling on a second, and equally hypothetical distribution route, we would start at the site of Kaminaljuyú near present Guatemala City and continue east down the Río Motagua to the Caribbean Sea, change to a coastal canoe, touch the strategically important points of Wild Cane Cay, Moho Cay and Ambergris Cay and head northwards along the eastern coast of Yucatán.

Assuming that with the abandonment of many important sites in the Southern Maya Lowlands at the end of the Classic Period it was not possible to maintain the first route model mentioned above any longer, the fluency of different parts of the long distance trade in general must have suffered severely. But in this case the Maya counted on yet another viable route: Following parts of the second reconstructed route model, the one from the vicinity of present Guatemala City to the Caribbean Sea via the Motagua valley, passing today's Belizean coastline and up to Yucatán. This alternative route could still have guaranteed smooth business operations in the Post-Classic and until well beyond the coming of the Europeans especially that this route also enabled the Maya to make connections with the Pacific Coast.

Map 1: The Maya Empire

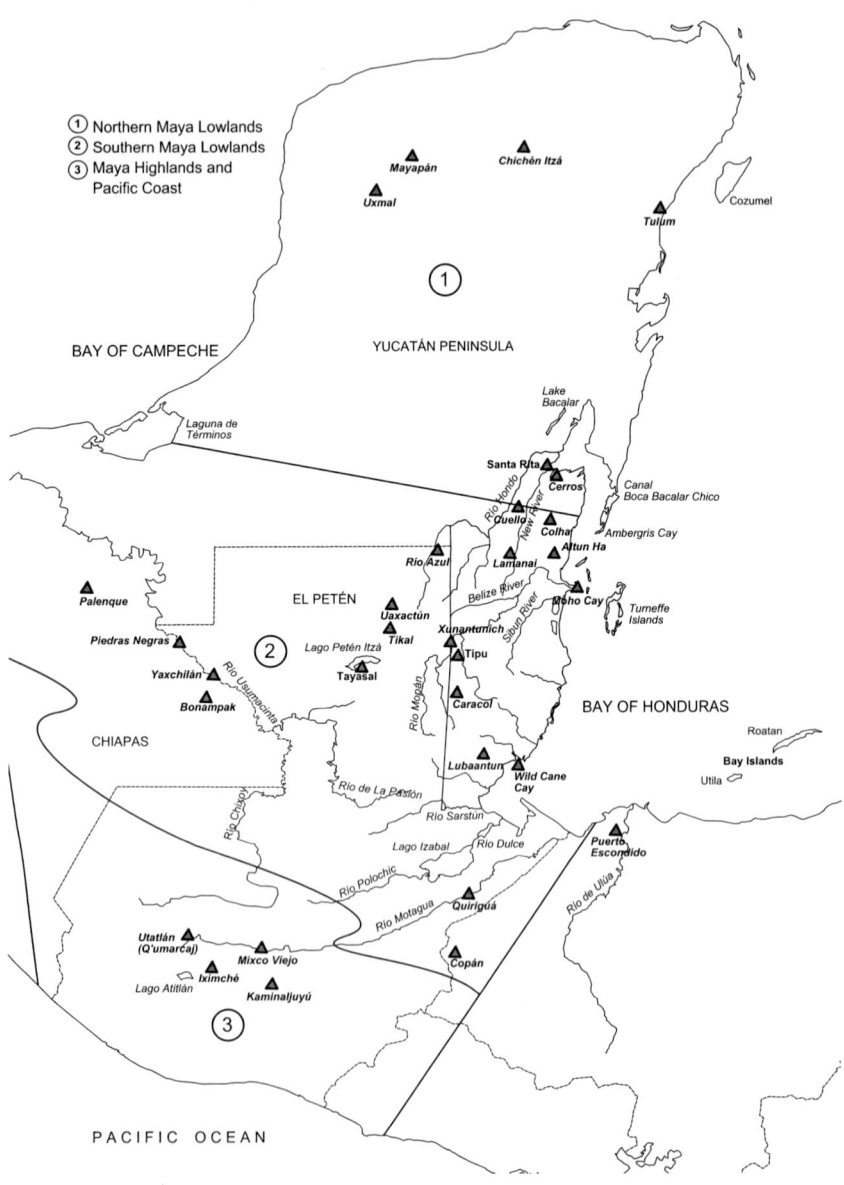

① Northern Maya Lowlands
② Southern Maya Lowlands
③ Maya Highlands and
   Pacific Coast

Mayapán
Chichén Itzá
Uxmal
Tulum
Cozumel

①

BAY OF CAMPECHE
YUCATÁN PENINSULA

Lake
Bacalar

Laguna de
Términos

Santa Rita
Cerros
Quello
Colha
Altun Ha
Rio Azul
Lamanai
Moho Cay

Canal
Boca Bacalar Chico
Ambergris Cay
Tumeffe
Islands

Belize River
Sibun River
New River
Rio Hondo

Palenque

EL PETÉN

Uaxactún
Tikal
Xunantunich
Tipu

Piedras Negras

②

Lago Petén Itzá

Yaxchilán
Tayasal

Rio Usumacinta

Bonampak

Rio Mopán

Caracol

BAY OF HONDURAS

CHIAPAS

Roatan

Rio de La Pasión

Lubaantun
Wild Cane
Cay

Bay Islands
Utila

Rio Chixoy

Rio Sarstún

Lago Izabal
Rio Dulce

Puerto
Escondido

Rio Polochic

Rio de Ulúa

Rio Motagua
Quiriguá

Utatlán
(Q'umarcaj)
Mixco Viejo
Copán

Lago Atitlán
Iximché
Kaminaljuyú

③

PACIFIC OCEAN

Map 2: Ancient Maya Settlements in Present Belize and Adjoining Lowlands

34

Map 3: Maya Trade Routes

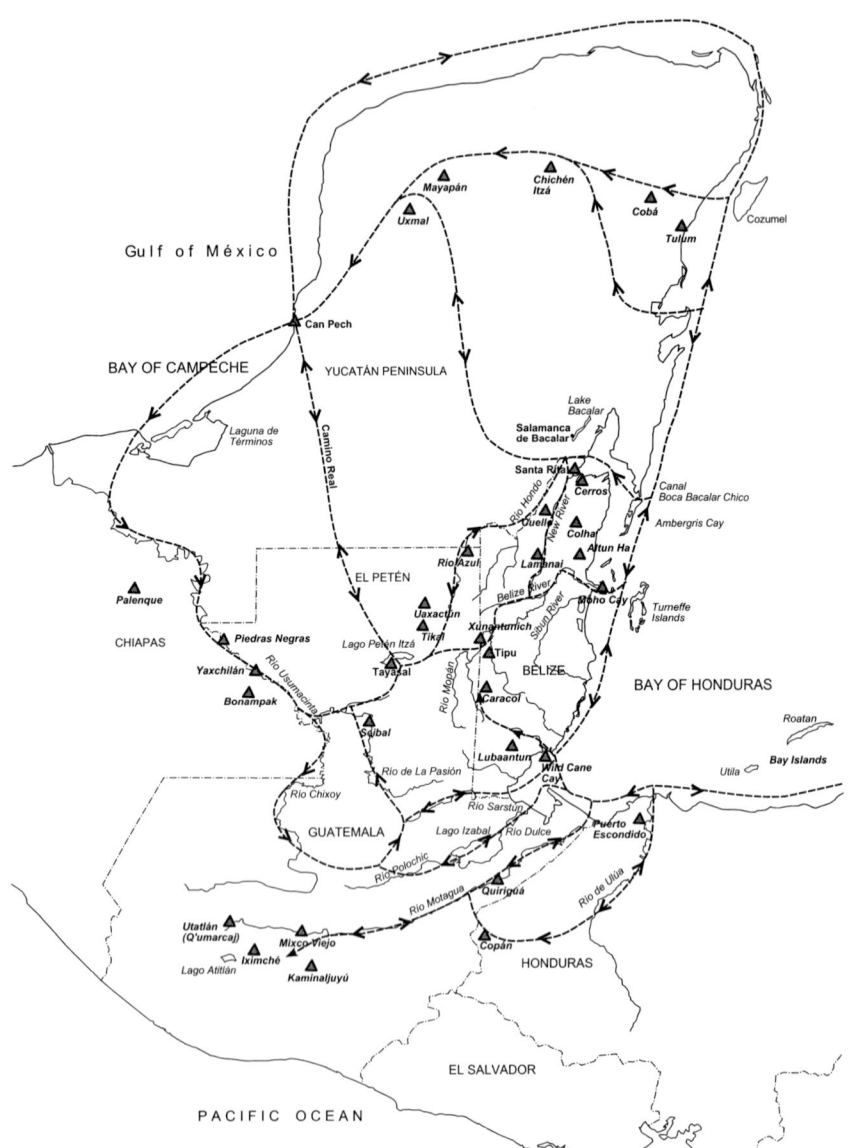

CHAPTER
TWO

THE REGION OF YUCATÁN AND PRESENT BELIZE IN THE 16TH CENTURY

1. First Voyages and Conquest of Yucatán

In order to be able to examine the influence of Spanish colonialism on what is now the territory of Belize, we must turn to the history of the conquest and colonization of Yucatán, for at the beginning of the 16th century, the boundaries had not yet been defined and the territory of modern Belize was considered to be part of the peninsula of Yucatán. Due to a series of historical incidents, the various early waves of Spanish discoveries (see Map 4) left the coast and interior of Belize practically uncolonized.

In 1502 Columbus, travelling south from Hispaniola, touched land at the island of Guanaja, off a Bay which was known for the great depth of its waters, reason for why it was named "Bay of *Honduras*".[1] The vicinity of the Golfo Dulce region and parts of what was to become the Republic of Honduras was called 'Honduras-Higueras'[2]. As far as the region north of the Golfo Dulce (i.e. the future Belize), from the middle of the 17th century onwards, the following terms evolved: "The Honduras Settlement", "The Bay Settlement (in the Province of Yucatán)" or simply "The Settlement".[3] In 1862, this area finally became the colony of "British Honduras". Throughout the first four chapters of this study all the above terms shall be used.

---

1   *"las honduras"*: Spanish for "great depths", from *"hondo"*: deep
2   This was due to the large number of empty calabashes floating in that area. The term *'Higuera'* derives from the Arawak language, the jiguera fruit, which resembles a calabash.
3   Until well into the 18th century the coast was also known as "Cockscomb Coast" named after the Cockscomb Mountain Ridge (the Maya Mountains of present Belize), whose silhouette was, and still is, used as a landmark for sailors.

In 1506 or 1508 Pinzón and Solís anchored in the Bay of Honduras and they were the first explorers to sail west to the Río Dulce and continued north along the Belizean coast. However, they did not go up the Belizean coast all the way but set an easterly course, in order to return to Hispaniola, possibly due to the prevailing northerly winds.

In 1511, a Spanish exploratory mission was shipwrecked between Jamaica and the east coast of Yucatán while en route from Panama to Santo Domingo. Most of the survivors who reached the Yucatán coast were taken as prisoners and enslaved by the Maya Lord of Chetumal. It is known that two of them, Guerrero and Aguilar, survived and remained among the Maya, completely adopting their culture. Guerrero and Aguilar were to play an important role as interpreters in the Maya-Spanish relations years later.

It was not until 1517, when Francisco Hernández de Córdoba discovered Yucatán, that the expeditions – which eventually led to the conquest and colonization of Central America – started in a more organized way.

In the course of the expedition of 1521–1525, which ultimately led to the conquest of the present republic of Honduras, Hernán Cortés led his explorers through the very heart of the Maya empire, traversing dense jungle regions, hitherto unexplored. Cortés passed Tayasal, the capital of the powerful Itzá in the Central Petén, and it is very likely that he crossed parts of what is now Southern Belize before reaching the Golfo Dulce and eventually Honduras in 1525.

In 1527 Francisco de Montejo was officially authorized by the crown to conquer and colonize Yucatán and the island of Cozumel. However, Montejo's ultimate idea was to unite the Yucatán peninsula and the provinces of Tabasco, Chiapas and Honduras, a dream which never materialized. Despite becoming governor and being appointed 'Adelantado'[4] of Yucatán and Honduras-Higueras at one stage, he lost authority over the entire region in 1544.[5]

---

4   Leader of an exploratory expedition or governor of a frontier province. In an agreement with the Crown, the *Adelantado* undertook the conquest of a certain area assigned to him at his own cost and risk and in return, was assigned the title of governor and given hereditary privileges. In some instances however, after the new lands had been brought under Spanish dominion, these powers were declared null and void.

5   As far as the etymology of Yucatán is concerned, at least two of the various theories propounded by the 17ᵗʰ century Franciscan historian López de Cogolludo (1971:I,65) seem plausible: One, in 1511, when Córdoba first arrived at the peninsula and wanted to know the name of a certain settlement, the Indians responded (in Yucatec Maya) '*Mathan cauyi athán*', meaning "I don't understand your words". It is very likely that the Spanish, only hearing the last phonemes, converted '*yi athán*' to Yucatán. The second theory is that the term is a compound created from *Yuca* (the root/plant already known

The fact that Montejo was removed from the position of authority is of considerable importance for the colonization pattern of the future Belize, which by 1524 had already been incorporated in the *Reino de Guatemala* forming part of the province of Verapaz. If Montejo's dreams had come true, the history of Belize would have taken a completely different course. At the end of this chapter I shall summarize the reasons why the Spanish were not able to gain a foothold in Belize, which, in part, was due to Montejo's failure to keep the position of *Adelantado* of Yucatán and Honduras-Higueras.

2. Colonization Efforts in Southern Yucatán and Present Belize

From 1527 onwards, at the time of Montejo's conquest of Yucatán, the northern part of present Belize was the centre of the Chetumal province. To the south lay the recently identified Dzuluinicob[6] province, which extended well into Southern Belize, as shown on Map 5. The western limits of Dzuluinicob most probably ran along the present day border with Mexico and Guatemala. The political centre of this province seems to have been Tipu, a settlement situated in the far west next to the major waterway, the Belize River.

Spanish intrusion upon the Maya began with the early Spanish *entradas*. The 1527/28 *entrada* by Montejo and the one by his lieutenant Alonso Dávila in 1531 were unsuccessful in so far that it was not possible for the Spanish to establish a permanent settlement, a *villa*.

Due to an ironical twist of fate the Spaniards met with unexpected resistance by an Indian army of the region led by Gonzalo Guerrero, the in the meantime completely "mayaized" Spanish renegade and ex-sailor, who was highly

---

to the Spaniards) and the name of a major Maya settlement '*Tolocitán*' where *Yuca* was grown in abundance.

6 With regard to the etymology of the term '*Dzuluinicob*' (or *T's'ul winicob*), meaning "foreigners" or "foreign men", López de Cogolludo (1971[1688]) believed that it was applied to the Spanish conquistadores. However, this is not correct because the term first appeared in the *Probanza* (a detailed description of the conquest for the purpose of giving proof to the right of the claim) of Melchor Pacheco's 1544 conquest of Chetumal, Uaymil and "Dzuluiniques". (Probanza de M. Pacheco, 10.11.1571 in the *Archivo General de Indias*, Seville, Escribanía de Cámara 304B). Since this term was obviously used before the first Spanish *entrada* in 1527, it would not have referred to the Spanish but rather to the third, and southernmost province of Yucatán, which was considered by the Maya in the provinces of Chetumal and Uaymil as a land of "foreign indigenous peoples". Thus, "foreigners" were simply peoples from beyond a civilization they were familiar with.

respected by the Maya lords because of his great military skills. With a cleverly devised strategy, the talented Guerrero and his Indian troops succeeded in defeating the Spaniards before they could conquer the entire area. Of Guerrero, Oviedo y Valdés writes that

> ... *he was already converted into an Indian and was married to an Indian woman [the chieftain's daughter]... and he knew their language and land very well.*[7]

The Spaniards were desperate and even prepared to forgive Guerrero the act of treason

> ... *I beseech you to come to this ship and to help me carry out, through giving me your council and opinions, that which seems most expedient ... [and is] a great opportunity to serve God and the Emperor, Our Lord, in the pacification and baptism of these people ...*[8]

Nevertheless, Guerrero opted to remain faithful to the Indians, pretending that "... as I am a slave I have no freedom [to join the Spaniards] ..."[9] In 1532 Dávila and his men once more made an attempt to re-establish Villa Real, but after trying to hold it for months, they were forced to evacuate the short-lived settlement.

For the Belizean people and scholars studying this particular period in the history of Belize, the question of where exactly the first short-lived Spanish settlement – Villa Real de Chetumal – was, is a very important one, but unfortunately it has not yet been possible to determine its exact location or to ascertain whether it was within the present day boundaries of Belize at all. Despite the fact that historical accounts are vague and could be interpreted in more than one ways, to me there is every reason to believe that ancient Chetumal was *not* within Belizean territory. This subject seems to give rise to much discussion: According to some scholars,[10] historical accounts contain evidence that Chetumal was indeed south of the mouth of the Rio Hondo which would truly place it within present-day Belize. If the above mentioned evidence is correct, the only possible site in Belize could have been the important Post-Classic settlement of Santa Rita Corozal as can be seen on Map 5. This settlement which was

---

7   Oviedo y Valdés (1959[1851–55]: 32–3) cited in Chamberlain (1948: 62).
8   Ibid.
9   Ibid. Chamberlain (1948: 60–68) gives the full account of Guerrero's clever policy.
10   Cf. Jones (1984: 16) and Thompson (1972: 45)

situated near the New River, a major waterway, was a leading trading centre and continued to function until well after the Spanish conquest.

However, the following historical descriptions of Santa Rita Corozal seem to dismiss the above hypothesis: López de Cogolludo states that the settlement was on the shores of the lagoon (… *la laguna en cuya ribera está fundada la villa* …)[11] and Montejo points out that the bay is on one side and [the] lake on the other (… *la bahía está en un lado y la laguna en el otro* …).[12] The fact that the nearest major lake (Lake Bacalar with its lagoon system) is approximately 15 km to the north clearly puts into question the identification of Santa Rita Corozal as the site of ancient Chetumal.

Why were the Spanish so adamant about wanting to establish a permanent settlement on the east coast of Yucatán?

On the one hand the Bay of Chetumal with its fine harbour would have been an ideal second base in the south (especially in addition to the already firmly established Spanish settlements in the west, present Campeche and Merida among others), thus creating ideal preconditions for a successful development of the entire colony. On the other hand, since one of the main reasons for the Spanish coming to the New World was to seek great fortunes, rumours of gold in the lakes, lagoons and rivers of Yucatán led the Spanish to believe that there were abundant gold mines in the provinces of Uaymil (or Guaymil) and Chetumal:

> *Por las noticias y mapa, que de la tierra tenía el adelantado [Montejo], entendieron los Españoles que en la provincia de Bakhalal, que llamaban los Indios de Uaymil y Chactemal, habría minas de oro …*[13]

Despite increased efforts and the hiring of the services of a geologist

> *… un Francisco Vásquez, que tenía gran conocimiento de minas, y a quien prometió el Adelantado trescientos ducados, si descubriera muestras de oro en aquella provincia.*[14]

---

11   See also Dávila's *relación* of 1533 (1864–1884: 97–128) and López de Cogolludo (1971[1688]: 89)

12   Oviedo y Valdés (1959[1851–55])

13   (… On account of information and a map, which the *Adelantado* was in possession of, the Spanish thought that in the province of Bakhalal, which the Indians called *Uaymil* and *Chetumal*, there would be gold mines …). López de Cogolludo (1971[1688]: 88)

14   (… A Francisco Vasquez, an expert in mines and to whom the *Adelantado* promised 300 *ducados* if gold was found in that province …). Ibid.

the Spanish were unable to find gold: «... *y por muchas diligencias que se hicie-ron y diversas catas en la tierra, no se halló oro alguno*»[15]

In 1532, after the abandonment of Villa Real, Dávila had to devise a plan of how to escape the attacking Indians for meanwhile a strong Maya resistance to colonial rule had developed and the region of Southern Yucatán and Northern Belize had started to become known as an ungovernable frontier region. For nearly 200 years the Spanish at Merida failed to control the southern frontier.

Nevertheless, Dávila was determined to continue his search for gold and a place better suited for permanent settlement. He decided to move south in order to try to re-establish the lost Villa Real somewhere along what is now the Belizean coast "... *aquél pedazo que no estaba aún sujetado por los Españoles* ..."[16] and which was still within the jurisdiction of the Adelantado Montejo. In his *relación* Dávila wrote in 1533 that he

> had the firm intention of settling on the first stretch of the coast where a suitable harbour and site would be found, for I had been told ... that beyond the turn of the coast the interior was some- thing very good, land which could be easily pacified, with many good rivers in which gold was found.[17]

The fact that they were not able to establish a new *villa* is crucial to some of the conclusions drawn in the summary at the end of this chapter.

Going south and thereby entering today's territory of Belize, Dávila and his crew deliberately chose the sea-route not only to reduce the likelihood of Indian attacks but also because the journey by land was thought to be impossible:

> ... *nunca se ha visto tal costa en ninguna otra parte, está totalmente inundada del mar por una larga distancia.*[18]

Indian captives, who knew the coast until the Rio de Ulúa in what is now Honduras very well due to the experience gained in Maya long distance coastal trade, served as rowers, guides and interpreters. When food was beginning to get scarce, the Spanish were forced to go inland, with the help of the captive

---

15   (... but despite the effort and the taking of several samples, no gold was found whatsoever), Ibid.

16   (... that stretch of land which was not yet seized by the Spaniards ...), López de Cogolludo 1971:95)

17   Dávila's *relación* of 1533 (1864–1884:14,22)

18   (... Such a manner of coast ... has never been seen or heard of elsewhere, for it is all inundated by the sea for a great distance ...). See Oviedo y Valdés' (1959[1851- 55]:32–8) description of Dávila's voyage

Indians – sometimes up river for several days, in search of cultivated fields and Maya settlements which would provide fresh supplies. According to Chamberlain,[19] who bases his conclusions on Oviedo y Valdés' account, the raids were mostly successful, for large stocks of maize; beans, peppers and honey were stolen. On occasions when raids were unsuccessful, the Spanish still found enough food by collecting wild fruit and palm shoots and consumed marine products such as fish, crabs and turtles.

The lucrative forages inland give us substantive proof that the Belizean territory was settled by a fairly large Maya community. Since it is very difficult to imagine that the Maya were ready to give away their provisions on a voluntary basis, the statement made by the English historian Stephen Caiger

> *… neither the Spanish when they crossed it, or the British when they eventually settled met with any opposition from native tribes …*[20]

seems highly questionable.

The question in how far the important post-Classic commercial centres of Northern Belize were affected by the early Spanish entradas is difficult to answer which is basically due to the scarcity of historical records. Thompson puts forward the theory,[21] which in my opinion is difficult to support, that according to accounts Maya guides deliberately must have led Cortés' army away from Belizean settlements because otherwise their inhabitants would have faced starvation due to the plundering activities of the soldiers. However, archaeological and ethnohistorical research carried out from 1974 to 1980 at the Belizean post-Classic site of Lamanai on the New River provides clear evidence that Maya settlements in the vicinity of Chetumal were strongly affected, if not defeated by the early Spanish entradas.[22]

From the earliest tentative Spanish attempts to settle on the Belizean coast, the colonization pattern of Belize was always strongly influenced by seasonal unfavourable climatic conditions with its unpleasant side effects: In the mid-1700s, when the Bay of Honduras started to become the centre for logwood extraction, this same coast was even more feared for its unwelcoming climate: Atkins when referring to the fierce insects for example complained that "… these vermin are an insufferable plague and impediment to sleep …" and Uring wrote

---

19   Ibid. (1948:120)

20   Cf. Caiger (1951:18)

21   Thompson (1972:62)

22   David M. Pendergast (1981:19–53) "Lamanai, Belize: Summary of Excavation Results, 1974–1980" in *Journal of Field Archaeology,* Vol.8, quoted in Jones (1984:15).

that "… [the mosquito] poisons the blood and leaves a speck as big as a large pin's head, which in two or three days grows rotten …"[23] The mosquito plague surely was a contributing factor to why, during their seven months journey, the Spanish never attempted to stay on shore or remain inland longer than absolutely necessary, let alone for the purpose of just founding the new Villa Real. Dávila and his *cabildo* unanimously decided that the swampy coastal stretch with its many lagoons and the absence of a deep harbour made colonization there highly unacceptable.

After seven difficult months, the Spanish eventually reached the coast of Honduras-Higueras. This region included the Rio de Ulúa valley which was a much more favourable location for colonization than the Belizean coast

> … *a pesar de todas las adversidades llegamos a Puerto Caballos donde inmediatamente discerní que era más adecuado y deseaba colonizar allá … todo el valle era cubierto de árboles de cacao y habitado por innumerables Indios …* [24]

In the meantime, colonization efforts continued to take place on the east coast of Yucatán: In 1544, the father-and-son-team of Gaspar and Melchor Pacheco succeeded in conquering Southern Yucatán and established the Villa of Salamanca de Bacalar (see Map 5) near the Maya settlement of Bakhalar on the shores of Lake Bacalar. The first *encomiendas*[25] were put into operation and in 1544–45, a Spanish expedition was launched to penetrate further south, this time deep into central Belize and the Río Dulce (Lake Izabal) region, for the first time more or less covering today's territory of Belize in its full length.[26]

In 1545 Montejo started with his plans to found a combined trading/military base at Río Dulce. However, this base soon had to be abandoned due to massive protests of the Dominican friars who saw this post as a potential hazard for their way up to Guatemala's Alta Verapaz region and their zealous

---

23   Cf. Atkins (1735:227–28), Uring (1727:358), and Gilbert M. Joseph (1989:10). The hardships of the Belizean climate and how they influenced the economic history of the country shall also be discussed in connection with logwood extraction in Chapter Four.

24   (… despite all the adversities, we arrived at Puerto Caballos [in Honduras-Higueras] where I immediately discerned the suitability of the region for settlement and desired … [to colonize] there … [the valley] is all covered with cacao trees and peopled with innumerable Indians …). Cf. Oviedo y Valdés (1959[1851–55]:32–8) account of Dávila's *relación*.

25   Grant of Indians; first for labour and tribute, later mainly for tribute only.

26   Known only retrospectively from the reports of Juan Garzon's 1569 *entrada* into Dzuluinicob (*Archivo General de Indias*, Seville, Patronato 69–1–10) quoted in Jones (1984:18).

missionary plans to "peacefully" convert the Manche Chol Maya. The friars intervened at court and Montejo was ordered by the Spanish monarch to abandon the Río Dulce base.[27]

Nevertheless, the Pachecos were successful in establishing early encomiendas within the present day boundaries of Belize. According to Jones,[28] and as can be seen on Map 5, the settlement of Chanlacan in the north of present Belize can be identified with almost certainty and possibly the distant Tipu, as far as the upper Belize River area in central Belize, which most likely was the capital of the Dzuluinicob province.

After 1544, however, the Indian response to the early Spanish colonial control on the east coast was soon to be felt. In 18 years, from the first entrada in 1528 to the one by Dávila in 1531 and the brutal conquest of Chetumal in 1544 by the Pachecos, the resistance movement had gained a strong force by moving the headquarters of its leadership from the Spanish controlled Chetumal area to Chanlacan in Belize where, according to colonial sources, "... resided the force of the said province [Chetumal] ..."[29] If this is correct, it would prove that after Dávila's attempted conquest in 1533 the Maya leaders of Chetumal had re-established their provincial capital at Chanlacan in present Northern Belize.

3. Social Consequences of Colonization

At the time of conquest, the territorial units of Yucatán were part of a loosely defined political alliance, whose social organization was already deeply shaken due to a series of internal disturbances. Therefore it is not difficult to explain why the Spanish were welcomed in the beginning.

The first natives the Spanish encountered could theoretically have been members of a temporarily suppressed tribe who saw the well-equipped soldiers as potential allies in their attempts to overthrow a rival and more powerful clan. In 1517 Córdoba named the northern tip of Yucatán, Cape Catoche, because the Indians kept pronouncing the words *"cones catoche"*; meaning "come to our houses."[30] This friendly welcome surely must have paved the way for future, and successful, colonization campaigns. Presumably, it was in this early phase

---

27   Cf. for example Casas (1951[1875]), Landa (1996[1598]), Fuentes y Guzman (1932[1690]) and Cogolludo (1971[1688]).

28   Jones (1990: 44,51)

29   Probanza de Juan Aguilar (1566) in the Archivo General de Indias, Seville, México 244, quoted in Jones (1984: 19).

30   Díaz del Castillo (1958)

that the first Maya allies were won over. Without the co-operation of these allies, the subsequent decisive campaigns would hardly have been as successful as they were and the developments to come would have been significantly delayed. Despite being welcomed in the beginning, the Spaniards were later attacked on several occasions, although the Indians could not compete with the technical advances of the Europeans. Generally speaking, the Indian defence in Mesoamerica was not as organized as was partly the case in other regions of the Americas.

For the Maya population in the provinces of Chetumal and Dzuluinicob, the consequences of both the colonization of Southern Yucatán and the penetration into today's territory of Belize have long been underestimated. Although future Belize did not lie in the centre of Spanish influx (due to the Spanish failure to gain a foothold in Belize) the Maya settlements in Belize have always been strongly affected by the socio-economic consequences of the colonization of Mesoamerica and especially the Yucatán Peninsula. Until approximately the 1980s, the majority of books on Belizean history showed a strong tendency to emphasize only the period of British colonialism. In the following pages and despite the paucity of historical evidence, I shall also endeavour to focus on the repercussions of the Spanish colonial influence upon Belize.

In order to explore some of the consequences of the Maya-Spanish interactions in future Belize, we must be aware of the fact that it is impossible to isolate the area and discuss it separately, since it did not exist politically.

Generally speaking – with the exception of the Manche Chol Maya in Southern Belize, who suffered more severely and due to subsequent ethnic relocations were annihilated to a large degree – the military and missionary penetrations into the Maya territory of Belize never affected the Maya to the same catastrophic extent as was the case in the neighbouring regions of Guatemala and Mexico. The first serious Maya-Spanish interactions in Belize took place when Dávila and his crew were forced to go up river in order to plunder Indian settlements for provisions.[31] If the indigenous population had succeeded in impeding these very first ruthless forages, the crew would have starved and not been able to continue their journey south. The consequent patterns of colonization in Central America would have been considerably different.

As discussed in the previous pages, the major Spanish expeditions came dangerously close to the Belizean post-Classic commercial and cultural centres with the result that they gained easy access to the main communication networks. This, in turn, facilitated the proliferation of the various side effects caused by the Spanish incursions.

---

31   Cf. Chamberlain (1948: 120–24)

3.1. Decline in Population

This subject has given rise to much discussion among scholars who have thoroughly studied the phenomenon of the dramatic decrease of the native population by comparing demographic figures from before and after the conquest and there is little need to dwell on it here.[32] Moreover, demographic figures are considered to be highly controversial due to the lack of accurate counts from the period in question. According to most scholars, the population decline is estimated to lie between 75 and 90 per cent. However, due to the paucity of convincing records, this high percentage will remain largely a matter of conjecture.

Despite the inexistence of accurate figures scholars have widely speculated about possible causes for the massive decline in the native population. To begin with, a huge number of Indian subjects must have lost their lives during and as a consequence of the first decisive battles, since from the start, preconditions for a fair warfare did not exist, due to the technical superiority of the Spanish army. After the bloody conquest of Southern Yucatán by Gaspar and Melchor Pacheco in 1543–44 for example, the population was considerably decimated. According to the Franciscan father Lorenzo de Bienvenida

> *Los Indios huyeron de todo esto y no seguían sembrando su cosecha … todos murieron de hambre … había pueblos de quinientas y de mil casas … ahora uno que tiene cien es grande …*[33]

As a result of this traumatic experience most of the remaining populations of the Maya provinces of Uaymil and Chetumal (see Map 5) started to scatter and moved to the western part of Yucatán, a region with less annual rainfall and a more favourable soil for cultivation. There, they hoped, the healthier climate would provide better chances for a gradual population increase despite the heavy losses. A considerable number of Yucatec Maya fled southwards into the deepest corners of the jungle, entering the unconquered territory of today's Northern and Central Belize, which was an ideal hiding place for the fugitives. Alarmed at the dispersal of a potential workforce, the Spaniards were not slow to apply the methods of *reducción* and *congregación* in order to avoid the ven-

---

32 Cf. for example Borah and Cook (1963), Thompson (1972: 54–61), MacLeod (1973: 70–71) and Jones (1990: 45) among others.

33 (… the Indians fled from all this and did not sow the crops and all died of hunger … there were pueblos of five hundred and one thousand houses … now one which has a hundred is large …). A detailed description of the cruelties committed during the first battles is given in the account of Fray Lorenzo Bienvenida to the Crown in 1548 (1877: 70–80), quoted in Chamberlain (1948: 235).

turing of the Indians into the dense jungle regions and to facilitate to recapture the runaways. Again, the ruthless Pachecos were in charge of these operations inflicting many cruelties on the retrieved individuals and burning down their original settlements.[34]

Another likely reason for the population decline was the *introduction of European-borne diseases:* The Spanish soldiers, inundating the coastal regions and penetrating into the interior, were carriers of pathogens and triggered the devastating pandemics in Mesoamerica,[35] which eventually led to the perishing of large numbers of native people. The Indian populations did not have a natural immunity to fight the imported pathogens nor did they have enough time to develop a certain amount of resistance towards them.

Which were the European-borne plagues introduced by the first Spaniards? Historical records attribute the precipitous population decline to "... measles, smallpox, nasal catarrhs, coughs, bloody stools, haemorrhages and high fevers ..."[36] among others. Some of these symptoms clearly refer to the occurrence of the common cold and influenza, but others refer to intestinal parasites and malaria.[37]

At this stage it is important to emphasize that, contrary to common belief, Mesoamerica was by no means free of local epidemics in the days prior to the conquest. The point I wish to make here is that population loss due to illness cannot only be blamed on the outbreak of plagues introduced from the Old World.

On several occasions prior to the conquest the existence of serious plagues causing severe and widespread famine was reported in the *Annals of the Cakchiquels.*[38] Local epidemics and famine may have led to malnutrition which, in turn, is very likely to have increased susceptibility towards diseases.

---

34   Cf. Chamberlain (1948), Landa (1978) and López de Cogolludo (1971)

35   A detailed list of the major pandemics and local epidemics, which include yellow fever, tuberculosis, pneumonia (pneumonic plague or *dolores del costado)* and typhus (*peste),* is provided by MacLeod (1973: 98–100). For a description of the first outbreaks of yellow fever see *Libro de Chilam Balam de Chumayel* (Mediz Bolio: 1973) and López de Cogolludo (1971: Cap.XIV passim). Oviedo y Valdés (1959, libro 31, cap.6) describes the impact of measles and Bancroft (1883:II.656) quoted in MacLeod (1973) mentions the demographic consequences of smallpox.

36   Oviedo y Valdés (1959[1851–55], 31–6), Fuentes y Guzman (1932) and Landa (1996)[1568]

37   The subject of whether malaria was endemic or introduced by the colonizers, possibly via Africa (cf. Dunn 1965: 386–93) has given rise to much speculation. In my opinion it is extremely likely that malaria, in fact, *was* endemic especially if we consider the ancient Maya system of collecting water in reservoirs. These artificial swamps were ideal breeding grounds for mosquitoes. Cf. also the conclusions drawn in the famous travelling accounts of Stephens and Catherwood (1969) referring to the neighbourhood of Uxmal in Yucatán.

38   An important document written in 1571 containing historical and mythological elements describing the legends of the Kaqchiquel, one of the indigenous Maya people in the

However, an exact identification of the various pre-Colonial diseases is extremely difficult since our knowledge about their existence and pathology is scant and, due to the paucity of convincing evidence, probably will remain so. This most intriguing subject has caused much discussion among scientists and led to a variety of different viewpoints but it would be beyond the scope of this study to go into more detail on this issue.

3.2. Conversion of the Indians

A high percentage of population loss can also be ascribed to the zealous attempts to convert the Indians. The quest for souls, coming third after the hunt for precious metals and land, was one of the major inducements for colonization.

Originally, the *reducciones and congregaciones* were thought to facilitate the handling and "pacification" of the Indians and were highly approved and supported by the colonizers. But when the missionaries started to act independently and without consulting the colonizers, these manipulations were soon seen as a threat to the long term plans the secular orientated Spanish had with the indigenous population. The settlers hoped Indian labour would yield huge profits and secure them a comfortable and life-long income. An increased control of these operations by the friars would have had counterproductive effects. Under the leadership of Fray Bartolomé de las Casas, fervent campaigns were undertaken on the part of the missionaries to protect the Indians from their Spanish masters. As a consequence serious internal conflicts among the Spanish arose. On two occasions, the monastery of Valladolid was burned down causing the loss of many lives. The remaining Indians fled to the forest and the missionaries were forced to go with them.

In 1567/68, well organized *reducciones* deep into Belizean territory were carried out. These forest-areas were completely unconquered as yet, and the Spanish hoped that by resettling the Maya far away from the existing main communication routes it would prove difficult for them to sustain themselves and they would be more inclined to become dependable upon the Spanish. However, their ambitions were thwarted and matters were to develop differently. Within a few years the Maya were to defy the Spanish plans and these regions in Northern and Central Belize were to become, due to their very isolation, the centre of Maya resistance.

In 1618, a major project was launched by the Franciscan order to "spiritually" conquer the Itzá (or itzáes), an independent and powerful tribe inhabiting the

---

mid-western highlands of Guatemala. Cf. Recinos (1953: 115, 143, 156 and 158) and Landa (1978: 24)

shores of Lake Tayasal (Tah Itzá or Petén Itzá, i.e. the area of modern Flores) in the Central Petén (see Map 4). By pacifying the Itzá the friars hoped to gain more control of the southern frontier of Yucatán. On their way to Tayasal, the Fathers Bartolomé de Fuensalida and Juan de Orbita came into contact with the Maya of the Dzuluinicob province in the western part of Central Belize and decided to establish their base at Tipu, a well-populated Maya settlement, located on the Macal River, a tributary of the Belize River. Due to the strategic riverine system (see Map 5), which covered Northern and Central Belize, both the Spanish military and missionaries gained easy access to the interior and were able to select suitable bases. From Salamanca de Bacalar, the last Spanish "fortress" before the wild and ungovernable interior, Tipu could be reached by canoe almost all the way within a few days. However, after a period of very little success both the population of Tipu, with Cristóbal Na as their leader, and other settlements such as Lamanai on the New River became completely indifferent to the evangelization efforts of the brothers of St. Francis. The subsequent frustration of the friars is best described by the Spanish colonial historian Villagutierre who mentions that

> ... after a few years all of them and those of the district apostatized and fled to the forests, leaving the churches burned and the houses destroyed ... [and] they practised their idolatry in the forest to such a degree of sacrilege that their priests, in mockery of the holy sacrifice of the Mass, celebrated heretical masses eating corn tortillas and drinking pozol [in defiance of the Catholic custom of using bread and wine] ...[39]

In response to the question why the Tipu Maya were behaving in such a hostile manner, the most likely reason for this negative behaviour was a previous contact with the Spaniards. This is demonstrated by the full name of the Maya chief: 'Cristóbal' (a Christian first name) and 'Na' (a Maya surname). Consulting 16th century historical records of *entradas* into this region, the only possible incursion could have been the one in 1568 by Juan Garzón who indeed had already been accompanied by a Franciscan missionary and several local Indian allies showing them the way to Tipu and other smaller settlements. From Bishop Landa[40] we know about the cruelties inflicted upon the Indians twenty years previously, and Garzón himself claims that his soldiers captured all the Indians they could find including the *chilam balam* (the native priest and/or

---

39   Villagutierre (1983[1701]: 86)
40   Landa (1996[1598], XV)

prophet) and destroyed temples, idols and books *"de sus antigüedades"*.[41] According to Garzón, the *chilam* had been brought up with friars and could speak Spanish. This may lead us to conclude that some kind of Spanish control had been established at an even earlier date, most likely during and after the very first *entrada* into Belize by the brother Pachecos in 1544.

The Spanish actions described above partly explain the prejudice the Tipu Maya must have felt against the Franciscan Fathers who arrived 50 years later and wanted "nothing else" but convert them. They were forced to be baptised and adopt Christian first names, a custom not previously known among the Maya. Spanish first names such as Gaspar, Diego, Francisco, Cristóbal etc. were simply put in front of the Maya surnames such as Ku, Chi, Dzul, Yam, Chuch etc. Nevertheless since these measures turned out to be only moderately successful, the desperate friars had to ask the Spanish officials for help who succeeded in temporarily bribing the Tipuan *cacique* Can Ek by promising him a tribute exemption. The *cacique* even accepted to be converted because he hoped this would strengthen his political position under a possible future Spanish rule.[42] The intricate social implications of this widely practised procedure will be discussed on the following pages.

Despite the missionaries' fervent efforts lasting for more than two years, the Maya of upper central Belize succeeded in expelling the Franciscans in 1619 and were left relatively undisturbed until 1697, when the neighbouring Itzá were brought within the domain of Spanish colonial control. The missionaries had accomplished virtually nothing and their actions only contributed to the fomentation of anti-Spanish feelings among the Maya of the southern frontier.

Another region strongly affected by the 17th century missionary incursions was the extreme south of today's territory of Belize. The south of present Toledo province was heavily populated by Mopan and Manche Chol Maya (see Map 5)[43] but after several revolts they were finally "pacified" around 1690. Following the example of earlier successful *congregaciones,* for example around the larger, still existing, *reducción* towns of San Luis and Poptún in the Petén, they were herded up and transported to the Guatemalan highlands where they eventually merged with other tribes.

---

41 A detailed *relación* of the three *entradas* by Juan Garzón can be found in the Archivo General de Indias, patronato 69, ramo 1, no. 10; excerpts of this *relación* are quoted by Jones (1990: 48–52).

42 Cf. Jones (1983: 153)

43 The territory of the Mopan and Manche Chol Maya extended from the Moho River in the extreme south of Belize to the Sarstún River (the actual Guatemalan border) to the Sierra de Santa Cruz until the northern shoreline of Lake Izabal en Guatemala.

Southern Belize remained practically deserted until the 19ᵗʰ century when the Black Caribs, exiled from Saint Vincent in the Eastern Caribbean, started to settle there in 1802. From 1880 onwards, descendants of the resettled Mopan from the Petén, who had been displaced previously, together with Kekchi Maya (more recently spelled "q'eqchi") from Alta Verapaz started to repopulate the former Manche Chol territory. While a small number of Mopan Maya succeeded in establishing itself permanently in Southern Belize, the Manche Chol were largely annihilated. This was due to extensive colonial military actions from 1697 onwards and the aforementioned subsequent ethnic dislocations.

3.3. The Development of a New Hybrid Religion and Culture

As it was briefly mentioned above, the Maya political and spiritual leaders were often enticed to convert by promising them certain privileges. However, in many cases it did not take long until the respective members of the Maya elite changed sides again and joined the Indian resistance movement. This was the beginning of an amalgamation of traditional Maya and Christian religious and ritual elements.

Remnants of this new hybrid religion and culture can still be seen in everyday life of the Indian population. Over the years, the contemporary Maya, intentionally or unintentionally, have had to adopt certain elements of European culture in their endeavours to incorporate them into their everyday needs. By following this complicate process of adaptation and transformation and at the same time stubbornly adhering to their own traditions, they have learned to survive. Although it may sound paradoxical at first, in the long term, only by being adaptable will the modern Maya succeed in conserving their identity and survive linguistically and culturally.

As a direct consequence of the efforts to convert the Indian population, in modern Maya communities in Guatemala and in isolated regions in Southern Belize, the present-day observer can still encounter vivid examples of a very flexible religious syncretism.

This is especially noticeable in contemporary Maya dance rituals and other traditional customs which form part of many popular festivities. The European-derived dances are characterized by a strong mixture of traditional Maya and Christian rituals. Examples are *El Baile de Moros y Cristianos, El Baile de Diablos* and the dance-dramas related to the conquest (*El Baile de la Conquista* and *La Danza del Torito* among others). Although these dances, which are decidedly mimetic in character, contain adaptations of mazurka and waltz dance steps, they are not accompanied by string instruments of European origin but rather by medieval tunes played on prehispanic flutes[44] and a large variety of drums. The Maya do use European-style string instruments: homemade violins, guitars, Sicilian-style mandolins and harps. "Maya string music" also includes trumpets, flutes and drums and can be heard during less ceremonial and "normal" festivities, held throughout the year. In addition, the usage of instruments of other origin is also very frequent, for example the *marimba* (the African name for a wooden xylophone with empty calabash resonators provided for each key, thought to have come to the Americas from Southeast Asia via Africa) and the *chirimía* (a wind instrument of Arabic origin and a direct predecessor of the modern oboe).

Another proof of how heathen beliefs and practices with Christian symbols amalgamate is the fact that for the contemporary Maya, certain animals continue to have a symbolic significance. This is, for example, the case with the jaguar ("*el tigre*") and is illustrated in the usage of a special type of altar cloth, called a *palla,* depicting a jaguar. According to a legend, the jaguar*,* as symbol of the night, retrieved a stolen monstrance holding the Eucharistic Host from the depths of the jungle and restored it safely to the church at dawn.

During contemporary Maya ceremonies and Masses, the use of incense is widespread, but, contrary to common belief, this was *not* adopted from the Christians. The burning of *copal,* a hard aromatic resin obtained from selected tropical trees, is an ancient Maya custom.

3.4. Development of a Powerful Resistance Movement – the Role of the Tipu Area in Present Central Belize

The way for a strong indigenous resistance movement was paved at a very early stage: First, because the important post-Classic commercial centres of present Northern Belize continued to function well after the conquest. Secondly, the region did not suffer the dramatic population decline experienced elsewhere. Thirdly, after the early brutal Maya-Spanish interactions the Yucatec Maya, who had been granted refugee status, dispersed southward into the jungle ideal conditions for the development of a Maya underground movement were provided. The interior of present Belize was a perfect strategic location because the existing settlements were mostly at or near the major riverine communication

---

44   Today, a large number of pre-hispanic wind instruments are still in use during any Maya celebration. Their admittedly strident and ear splitting high tones were already very aptly described by Bishop Landa more than five hundred years ago: "*… Un son a los valientes*" (… suitable for the more courageous of ears …)" coming from "*… trompetas largas y delgadas de palos huecos … y flautas de cañas …*" (… long, narrow, hollow trumpets and flutes and recorders made out of reed) Cf. Landa (1996[1568], XXII)

routes, thus facilitating the exchange of intelligence among the various rebel factions along the entire frontier. This also enabled the exiles to communicate relatively easily with other areas.

In 1546/47, only two years after the Pacheco conquest of the Yucatán provinces of Uaymil, Chetumal and Dzuluinicob, the Maya rose in a fierce anti-Spanish rebellion. Nevertheless, from the military base of Salamanca de Bacalar, the last Spanish frontier settlement before the rebellious and ungovernable interior of present Northern Belize and the adjoining Petén region, the Spanish finally succeeded in subduing the rebels, albeit suffering heavy losses. Meanwhile the headquarters of the resistance force had moved to the area of present Central Belize, where the Spanish were less fortunate in their endeavour to pacify the rebels. But after the Spanish succeeded in establishing the *encomienda* town of Tipu (see Map 5), and despite the efforts of a few missionaries, open rebellion broke out, on the entire southern frontier, in present Northern and Central Belize as well as in the neighbouring Petén. Trying to resist the Christianization efforts of the frustrated friars:

> ... *they began to return to their idolatry and after a few years all of them fled to the forests, leaving the churches burned and the houses destroyed ...*[45]

Long phases of alternating rebellion and reconquest followed and needless to say, there was cruelty on both sides. From the first contact with the Franciscans in 1618, on various occasions valuable historical material of the Itzá was burned down. This incident resulted in insults on part of the *cacique* and the subsequent expulsion of the missionaries.[46] When some of the missionaries, in the company of Spanish soldiers, returned to the area in the following year, they were captured and sacrificed by the Itzá. After many unsuccessful attempts to once more penetrate the Tipu area, the governor of Merida decided to send a major military force. Together with 150 Maya allies, Tayasal, the principal city of the Itzá, was finally conquered as late as 1697. The Spanish erected a fortress and by 1707, most of Tayasal's inhabitants were resettled around today's Lake Petén Itzá in the Central Petén. With the capture of the capital of the Itzá, the last independent Maya territory, the conquest of the Maya had been completed.

At this stage it is important to note that the visions of Maya prophets and priests greatly affected the history of this southern zone. In 1618, for example, after having been expelled from Tipu, the Franciscan brothers wanted to continue their efforts by re-establishing abandoned missions in the Central

---

45   Villagutierre (1983[1701]: 86)

46   Cf. López de Cogolludo (1971), vol. II, libro IX, capítulo IX

Petén. The year 1618 coincided with the opening of the *Katun 3 Ahau,* a certain time phase in the sophisticated Maya calendar.[47] The ancient Maya priests had prophesied that there would come the time when they would have to give up the worship of their gods. Therefore the Maya had anticipated the need to plan ahead and arm themselves for the last moments of their history. This decisive date was to take place around *Katun 8 Ahau,* beginning in 1696 or 1697. According to the prophesy there would be a great war, and hurricane rains would be the burden of the *katun* and that this would be the end when they would agree to accept new religious and political arrangements.[48]

But in 1618, the Maya knew the time had not come yet. Therefore, these prophecies greatly influenced and encouraged the Maya rebel movement and indeed resulted in the successful eviction of the friars. Prophesy or no prophesy, fact is that it was precisely in 1697, the beginning of *Katun 8 Ahau,* when the Spanish succeeded in conquering the Itzá and Tipu that the last stronghold of Maya independence in Belize, faded from colonial records.

As mentioned previously, the first Spanish ventures into Maya territory would not have been possible without the help of Indian allies. However, some of these collaborators, who entered the services of the church voluntarily, accepted conversion, the process of hispanization and certain official posts (teachers, substitutes for priest etc.) with the only aim to give assistance to their comrades in the resistance movement, mainly by communicating intelligence. While these allies, some of them also belonging to the Maya elite class, showed a dubious loyalty of the Spanish, they contributed significantly to the formation of a potent, well organized and complex underground network.

After having discussed in detail the important role the Maya resistance played on the southern frontier in present Northern and Central Belize, we can now summarize the following:

The area around Tipu experienced alternating phases of either Maya or Spanish control for more than 150 years and was the most southerly outpost of the Maya resistance force. The Maya town of Tipu, which had developed from the Maya capital of the Dzuluinicob province into a temporary *encomienda* and missionary town and a centre of the resistance force, remained the last Indian stronghold of the southern frontier region. From 1544 until 1697 (1707

---

47   The *katun* cycle was composed of periods of 7.200 days. A full *katun* cycle was made up of thirteen *katuns* or approximately 256 years. For the various interpretations of the *katun* cycles see for example Jones (1990: 325).

48   Cf. López de Cogolludo (1971[1688]), libro II, cap.XI. For a detailed description of the significance of the Maya prophesies in the moulding and activating of the Indian resistance force and the manipulation of the general public see Jones (1990: 146 and 189).

respectively), a strong Maya underground force was able to operate successfully around Tipu. This enabled some of the smaller indigenous settlements
in central Belize to continuously obtain fresh recruits from Yucatec Maya who
migrated south to escape Spanish religious and economic domination.

The long term consequences of this strong resistance were crucial for the
Spanish: Although by 1707 they were already in control of the entire Central
Petén and the once powerful Itzá, it is not an exaggeration to say that because
of the efficiency of the Maya underground movement, the Spanish never succeeded in firmly establishing colonial rule in the territory of today's Belize.

3.5. The Process of Hispanization

From the very early days of colonization, the Spanish settlements were characterized by considerable miscegenation. Due to the scarcity of European women,
it was common among the colonizers to take Maya women as concubines,
sometimes kidnapping them from their homes. During the years to follow,
the Spanish who decided to settle in climatically advantageous regions started
to intermarry with Maya women from the local farming communities. They
formed the basis of the present mestizo population of most of Central America,
especially in the vicinity of the larger cities and towns.

In present Belize, contrary to Yucatán and most other places in Central
America, hardly any hispanization *(mestizaje)* took place during the 16ᵗʰ, 17ᵗʰ
and 18ᵗʰ centuries. This can be ascribed to the fact that the Spanish were never
able to properly colonize the area, as explained previously.[49]

At this stage it becomes important to emphasize once more that if we want
to examine the socio-economic consequences of the colonization of the region
which eventually was to become present Belize, we must take into account that
it is *impossible* to isolate the area. The various aspects of the socio-economic
consequences of colonization and/or colonization efforts respectively always
have to be seen in a much wider geographical context and thus it is more than
legitimate to dedicate a few more lines to the consequences of hispanization.

One of the most noticeable social consequences is that as a result of the hispanization process and in a curious twist of fate, within a few generations the
children of common Spanish and Maya ancestry began to look down upon the

---

49   The mestizo population of modern Belize (according to the 2006 census approximately
     50% of the country's total population), are the descendants of the thousands of mestizo
     immigrants who fled to Belize on account of the *Guerra de Castas* in Yucatán which be-
     gan in the late 1840s. More recently, starting in the late 1970s, a large number of Guate-
     malans and Salvadorans started to come to Belize seeking refuge from the civil wars in
     their own countries.

"pure" Maya and treated them in a way that mirrored the Spaniards' original methods during the contact period.[50] As I have been able to observe on several occasions myself, throughout Central America including most of present Belize, remnants of this behaviour can still be detected in present day 'ladino-indígena' interactions, the intensity varying from one region to the other.[51] The Indians not affected by the process of hispanization were pushed to the poorer and/or remoter highland regions of present Southern Mexico, Guatemala and Southern Belize. The more recent acculturation process of the indigenous population shall be analysed in detail in Chapter Six.

In connection with the hispanization process of the indigenous population the folkloristic concept still exists that it was the Spanish who made the members of each Maya village wear different costumes (*trajes*), so that they would be able to tell them apart easier. However, this theory can be dismissed as erroneous, for, according to historical evidence and as discussed in the section on Maya trade, the cargoes of pre-Colonial Maya canoes already included many different models and styles of Maya clothes, including *huipiles,* a type of embroidered blouse still worn by modern Maya women.[52] The colourful traditional Maya *trajes* with different designs for every village constitute an important ethnographic element and play an important role in conserving Maya identity.

---

50   For a detailed list of alleged prejudices the Spanish had of the Indians such as *"que son haraganes, inclinados al vicio (especialmente a la embriaguez), que no trabajan si no les obliga ..."* (that they are lazy, inclined towards vice (especially drinking), that they do not work unless obliged to ...) cf. for example Martínez Peláez (1973:197–253).

51   The term *ladino* is, contrary to common belief, not a derogatory expression. It is applicable to any individual who adopted 'Latin' culture, speaks Spanish and wears western clothes although the person may even be of pure Amerindian descent. *Ladino* is a cultural, not a racial definition.

52   The vast majority of women in the towns/villages in Guatemala and in isolated regions in Southern Belize, still wear *huipiles,* although, more recently a growing number of women in the Guatemalan lowlands and in the south of Belize no longer use their traditional costumes for climatic reasons, so they say. In general terms, modern Maya women are very proud to wear their beautiful embroidered *huipiles,* with different designs, styles, colours, patterns and even weaving techniques for every village This enables the members of the various communities to differentiate the outfits from one village to another. As with other types of traditional clothes, for example *cortes* (wrap-around skirts) or *fajas* (embroidered belts), *huipiles* may also reveal details of the origin and economic resources of their owner. These traditional costumes express the native, artistic embroidery at its best, giving the owner a certain individual identity, not only within her own community but also in the entire country.

3.7. The Alteration of Ancient Boundaries and Ethnic Dislocations

In the attempt to acquire control over the indigenous populations within the territories controlled by their leaders in a more or less flexible manner, the Spanish imposed a new definition of "territories" by hardly taking into account the already existing boundaries. The Spanish set themselves the aim to execute these re-definitions almost at random, according to their momentary disposition, thereby ruthlessly dismantling the old states and principalities as mentioned above. At the same time they created artificial borders and established new areas of jurisdiction, unfamiliar to the native population.

However, territorial changes were also brought about by the Maya themselves as was especially the case in Southern Mexico, Guatemala and Southern Belize. As already mentioned above, the 17ᵗʰ century *entradas* across the Maya Mountains into Southern Belize, deep into the territory of the Mopan and Manche Chol Indians, reduced their numbers considerably and threatened to throw the remaining members of these tribes off balance. Consequently, they became an easy target for the Q'eqchi' Maya from the Alta Verapaz region in the eastern Guatemalan highlands, who were trying to escape the dangers of being rounded up by Dominican missionaries and started to migrate towards the southeast in direction of what is now Southern Belize. In the course of this process, the Q'eqchi' became more dominant, started to reclaim former Manche Chol territory and absorbed of what was left of its inhabitants. In a wider sense, one of the consequences of the Spanish incursions into eastern Guatemala was that certain parts of Southern Belize were "colonized" by the Q'eqchi' Maya in return, a process which continued until the 1930s.[53]

4. Economic Consequences of Colonization

A large percentage of the early conquerors, and those who followed immediately after them, had their long-term goals clearly in mind: To look for a means of how to extract wealth from the new lands and once found to create an efficient and lucrative export system. As far as the vague reports of gold were concerned, the Spanish soon realized that the rumours were nothing more than gold ornaments in the form of jewels and masks, which they themselves had

---

53 From approximately 1860 to 1930 the Kekchi from Alta Verapaz, this time escaping from oppression by the owners of German coffee plantations, again "invaded" former Manche Chol and Mopan territory in Southern Belize. For a historical overview of the Q'eqchi' and Mopan see Wilk and Chapin (1990:18–20).

confiscated previously. When they found out that, apart from the extensive silver deposits in Mexico and minor ones in Honduras, there were no precious metals in New Spain[54], many of the pioneers abandoned the land granted to them for the more promising Viceroyalties of Nueva Granada and Peru. The colonizers who decided to remain started to look for alternative ways to find a "cash-crop" to replace the non-existent gold and silver. The fact that no gold mines ever existed in Yucatán leads us to assume that the aforementioned confiscated artefacts are evidence of the existence of a well-organized Maya long distance trade.

At first sight it seemed that the only asset of New Spain was the dense native population. Therefore control and organization of the labour force seemed to be of paramount importance, if economic well-being of the colony and a good relationship with the mother-country, i.e. a profitable export trade, was to be achieved. In order to accomplish this, the native economy obviously had to be modified to a considerable degree. Although the Maya were familiar with the concept of export since they had already transported products from where they were cultivated and/or manufactured to areas where there was demand of them, the idea of finding a "cash-crop" exclusively for export was new to the native population. Generally, in the pre-colonial economic system, any surplus from cultivation, production and long distance trade was re-invested into the community and not carried off to distant territories.

4.1. Spanish Interference in Maya Trade and Attempts to Establish a Monetary System

Although there are not enough details known about the trade activities of the contact period to be able to examine in detail the degree to which they were altered in the course of the 16th and 17th centuries, the impact of the conquest interrupted commerce done in the markets and via the trade routes to a considerable degree. From the early days of colonization, Spanish officials and merchants had wanted to take part in the distribution of goods and had taken advantage of the existing Maya trade system.

One example is **cacao**: The Spanish did not hesitate to seize the opportunity and quickly put themselves in charge of the principal export mechanisms, in some cases even redirecting the routes. But they also continued to use the well frequented and safe trading routes inside the protecting barrier reef of

---

54   The Viceroyalty of New Spain included the territories of present-day south-western United States, Mexico, Central America (with the exception of Panama), the Caribbean and the Philippines.

today's Belize for the exportation of cacao from the fertile Rio de Ulúa in Honduras to the main centre of Spanish interest in Northern and Southern Yucatán. The new Villa of Salamanca de Bacalar (established at last in 1544) created new demands and its inhabitants had to be supplied with goods. For example the Spanish commissioned Maya traders from Northern Yucatán to carry products such as cloth and honey to the new Spanish *villa,* in exchange for cacao, either from supplies grown in the provinces of Chetumal and nearby Dzuluinicob (present Northern and Central Belize) or the imported Honduran cacao beans.

This may well have been a continuation of the pre-Columbian form of exchange on the one hand, but on the other, by creating new areas of demand for different goods, the traditional exchange patterns would have become significantly upset.

What were the principal export goods of the Yucatán peninsula and the area surrounding the Bay of Honduras destined for the entire New Spain area as well as the European market? Due to the failure to grow wheat, the native staples **maize, beans, peppers** and **squashes** also became the staple diet of the settlers who started to grow these products in large quantities both for their subsistence and for export. Proper Yucatecan products such as **textiles** made from cotton, natural dyes such as **heart wood** or *palo de tinte* and **cochineal** (producing a scarlet red) soon became highly valued export articles. The Dzuluinicob province also proved suitable for the collection and marketing of **wild vanilla** and the cultivation of *achiote,* a red vegetable dye also used for the flavouring of many dishes. The more enterprising merchants among the colonizers endeavoured to increase the profitability of the relatively small indigenous cacao plantations by assigning extra land, as for example along the drainages of the New River and in the vicinity of Tipu in the centre of today's Belize, to the cultivation of cacao beans for export.[55]

The Chetumal area, in vague geographical terms the north of present Belize including its offshore cays, was also famous for the extraction of **salt,** an immensely important product in Maya long distance trade. The Spanish soon took over the mining of salt along the large natural salt beds on the west coast of Yucatán and on the island of Cozumel. They put themselves in charge of the refining processes and the exportation of the refined product to New Spain and Honduras-Higueras (the vicinity of the Golfo Dulce region including parts of what was to become present Honduras), thus depriving the Maya traders of a substantial source of income. When the Spanish began to interfere in Maya

---

55   Although the chocolate drink and later the compressed form, the bars of *chocolate,* were highly valued in Europe, generally speaking the export figures for Central American cacao were never very high.

trade, especially by shifting the areas of demand, it is highly likely that certain population groups lost control of their traditional trade.

As already discussed the pre-colonial economy was based on barter trade and in most regions cacao beans were also accepted as payment for goods exchanged among the communities. The Spanish aimed at a complete re-arrangement of the Indian barter trade system and not surprisingly, the concept of the value of certain commodities varied greatly between the Indians and the Spanish. In the eyes of the Spanish the Indians, most likely, must have exchanged goods of great value for things of little or no value and vice versa.[56] In an attempt to fix an exchange rate, several measures were introduced. They all failed in the long run and, as a consequence, the Spanish decided to introduce coins in order to replace the cacao beans.

The introduction of coins proved to be more complicated than the Spanish had thought: To start with the conquistadores had only brought with them a limited amount of "cash" of mostly high denominations which could not be used for everyday transactions. Although Cortés had established a mint, the *Casa de Moneda de México,* in 1535 in order to produce coins of lesser denomination, the problem of how to establish a fair and satisfactory exchange rate mechanism remained.[57] Moreover, in several regions of Central America, most likely due to the relatively great distance from the *Casa de Moneda* situated in the capital (today's Mexico City), the shortage of gold and silver coinage of small denominations persisted and Spanish and native merchants alike were forced to re-introduce cacao beans as a substitute for coins. In the long term, the additional use of cacao beans for currency increased their demand and caused a temporary shortage around 1630,[58] consequently boosting production. Cacao beans as currency continued to be used until the middle of the 18th century and in some isolated regions until the 20th century.

---

56 See for example Borah and Cook (1963: 53–75, 24) and Simpson (1950: 46) quoted in Randall (1977: 60,70).

57 For a thorough analysis of the difficulties created by the confusion over the exchange rate see for example Randall (1977: 60,97), Simpson (1950: 46,150,189,197) and Gibson (1964).

58 For example exchange difficulties due to a shortage of cacao beans were reported in: Bishop of Nicaragua to the Crown 1647, Archivo General de las Indias, Seville, 162; quoted in MacLeod (1973: 466).

4.2. The Encomienda System and Its Economic Consequences

In the New World, the *encomienda* system of late medieval Spain[59] was modified and adapted to the needs of the colonists. During and after the early campaigns, the *conquistadores* succeeded in most parts in establishing themselves as the legal successors of the indigenous chieftains, thereby also "inheriting" the right to exact tribute from the Indian population. As a consequence, the Indian and the Castilian tributary system merged and the New World *encomienda* system developed. From the early days of colonization, a very important criterion for a certain region to be considered suitable for colonization was if the chosen area was "… peopled with innumerable Indians …"[60] The settlers envisaged that a large population would contribute to economic success, firstly because it would yield huge profits from tributes and secondly, it could be subjected to forced labour.

In theory, the Indian labourers were protected by contracts defining working hours and forms of payment but these contracts were largely ignored and the workers exploited. When overworking and fatigue began to take its toll, the Indians were very prone to succumb to infectious diseases or die a natural death. As a consequence a shortage of labour was beginning to manifest itself.

From 1680 onwards, in certain regions of Mexico and Central America where there was a sufficient amount of cash crop to provide capital, African slaves were bought and brought into the colony, to help build up the weakened Indian workforce.

The economic consequences of the *encomienda* system were extremely complex and in the long term disastrous for the colonial economy. Again, it is important to bear in mind that as far as the Maya in the region that was to become Belize were concerned, the system affected them much less than those in the areas directly controlled by the Spanish.

The changes in the trade system, especially in the tributary system, were very upsetting to the Indian social and economic structure. In the beginning, the tributes were fixed by the Viceroy and the *Audiencia* and collected in kind in the form of goods the Indians had been accustomed to deliver to their own superiors: Produce such as maize, beans, *mantas* (cloth), cacao beans and other commodities. The Spanish *encomenderos* wanted to standardize the tribute but for several reasons found it difficult to put this into practice. For example they demanded that tax be paid in a more economical form, not just to the liking

---

59 For a discussion of the Castilian form of *encomienda* see for example Chamberlain (1948: 35).

60 Oviedo y Valdés (1959: 32–8)

of the various communities, such as in the form of surplus grains, cacao beans or typical handicrafts of a particular region, but in goods the Spanish were in need of at certain times of the year. This meant that in most cases the Indians had to travel long distances in search of these products which led to significant changes in the local socio-economic structures.

While, on the one hand, these forced journeys must have had a disruptive effect, on the other hand they may also have helped to revive business for the native long distance trade, thereby creating a new group of travelling merchants. But it did not take long until it became difficult to meet the required tributary obligations until it got to the point when the Maya were incapable of delivering the types of goods their Spanish lords demanded, because produce were either not available locally or could not be "ordered" from other regions. When the Spanish started to demand money, they had meanwhile introduced, the situation was further aggravated. For the Maya it was practically impossible to make enough money to meet the tributary quotas they were expected to pay. Over time they had little choice but to leave their villages in order to earn money, for example as seasonal workers on the coastal cacao plantations. Thus, a transformation of society occurred and hitherto stable, socially stratified tribal people were slowly forced to adapt to a mobile and uniform kind of peasantry.[61]

The changed pattern of social and economic life also had beneficial side effects for the Indian population. After 1630, the Audiencia of Guatemala began suffering from an economic crisis owing to the failure of a successful marketing of indigo and the decline of cacao as a cash crop.[62] As a consequence and due to the decline in the cash crops, there was less need now to fill the *repartimiento* demands. For some Indian communities this was their chance to retreat to the original lands and start the process of trying to develop a system which would enable them to be more self-sufficient which, in turn, would help to preserve their traditional culture despite the Spanish influence that was beginning to manifest itself.

The changes in the trade system brought about yet another "beneficial" effect upon the Maya: The development of a kind of clandestine trade with routes passing along the inland riverine routes and shores of present Belize. Especially for salt, cacao, beeswax, cloth, tools, *achiote* and wild vanilla an efficient underground trade was flourishing. Ironically it was the Spanish themselves who started to make good profits from this contraband trade. After the income

---

61 Nash (1966: 58–60,80) quoted in MacLeod (1973:142) summarizes this process.
62 Cf. MacLeod (1973:383).

from tribute declined[63] the Spanish had to modify their commercial activities one way or another and contraband was seen as a viable alternative.

Moreover, the economic position of the new commercial centre of Salamanca de Bacalar was already beginning to weaken and its inhabitants simply began to deliberately avoid paying duties. Some of the inhabitants of the *villa* became successful owners of cacao orchards on the New River in Belize[64] gaining huge profits by dedicating themselves to the clandestine trade in cacao and also salt which was extracted from the ancient salt beds of Ambergris Cay.

4.3. Depression of the Colonial Encomienda System and Its Consequences for Present Belize

Generally speaking the depression can be attributed to a gradual loss of tribute-paying Indians which was mainly because of the following reasons:

First, the drastic loss in population throughout the 16ᵗʰ century caused by plagues and natural disasters, exploitation, overwork, fatigue, bad treatment as well as the repercussions of *reducción* and *congregación* and natural disasters.

Secondly, a considerable number of Maya workers were enticed by the Spanish settlers to come and work on their new farms. In certain areas of Yucatán and Central America, between 1590 and 1630, some privileged Spanish colonists managed to gain titles to tracts of land and aimed to become self-sufficient partly also to avoid the duties imposed by colonial officials as mentioned above. They visited towns less often and retreated to their *fincas* (ranches) and the more enterprising settlers had their hopes high for an alternative cash crop for cacao – cattle raising and indigo growing – which would equally produce rapid wealth.

In search for a new life and new economic opportunities, a large percentage of Yucatecan Maya tribute-payers succeeded in escaping to the frontier region of Southern Yucatán and the present day area of North-western Belize. And because the protecting barrier reef along the coast of Belize was already familiar to them, they eventually reached "Spanish Honduras", the actual republic of Honduras. On these "Honduran" *fincas,* they were, most likely, employed as semi-indebted peons together with an increasing number of Mestizos, the

---

63   Jones (1990:69) mentions that in the 17ᵗʰ century actual tribute income for the inhabitants of the *Villa* of Salamanca de Bacalar was very low and that there were no more than 300 Maya who were to deliver annual payments to their *encomenderos*.

64   Cf. Jones (1990:68).

new class of rurally orientated Spanish had taken with them to make up for the debilitated Indian workforce. In the beginning this new system seemed to be more promising to them than the Spanish *encomienda*, which from the mid-1600s onwards was gradually replaced by the *hacienda* system of landed estates.[65] However, it is important to remember that this settlement pattern did not occur in the area of future Belize, since by that time, no European settlement had taken place there.

Thirdly, *encomienda* Maya increasingly began to escape making their way to the refuge zones in the jungle and forest regions of Central and Northern Belize.

Most of those who decided *not* to go and work on the new estates, equally had to abandon their villages for they were incapable of meeting the excessive quotas due to the economic changes mentioned above. As a consequence, a massive flight to Southern Yucatán and present day North-western Belize took place, most of which was wild and unconquered during the 16th and 17th centuries. Not only was this region an ideal hideaway for the growing resistance movement as discussed above, but also a place of refuge for those individuals or whole communities who were trying to escape from the economic hardships imposed by the extensive amounts of tribute. The missionary Pedro de Mata reported from his general *visita* in 1629 that the Indians from the province of La Pimienta in Central Yucatán (see Map 5) had fled south "… because of the *jueces* (magistrates)," and that they "fear no one, not even ten thousand Spaniards who go to search them out".[66] In a different letter to an official in Northern Yucatán, Juan Ortiz Equiluz mentioned that the flight was so massive that entire towns were left without *caciques* or *alcaldes* (chieftains or principal administrators).[67]

In other words, the continued worsening of the socio-economic conditions in the *encomienda* towns of Southern and Central Yucatán clearly stimulated the growing of a resistance movement. As more and more tax-payers kept leaving Southern and Central Yucatán, the villages there became less capable of meeting the quotas they were required to deliver to the colonists. As a consequence, the pressure on the communities increased and a vicious circle was beginning to develop.

Having analysed the socio-economic consequences of the colonial *encomienda* economy in general terms, we are now able to focus on the immedi-

---

65   The changed system generated a new life-style which, at the same time, produced favourable conditions for the ongoing process of hispanization (*mestizaje*). Cf. MacLeod (1973: 380).

66   Cf. Jones (1990: 197).

67   Ibid.

ate consequences this decadent *encomienda* system had for Southern Yucatán and present Belize.

Apart from an increased back and forth movement of goods and people (especially to and from the region of Spanish Honduras) the economic crisis also provided a very good chance for pirates to establish themselves along the entire Yucatecan east coast and as far down as the Bay of Honduras, thus paving the way for future settlement patterns on the "Belizean" coast. Due to the massive pirate attacks in the area, the colonial administration was forced to provide additional financial resources: This constituted an additional burden for the non-productive colonial tribute economy since fire arms and ammunition had to be financed from the tax revenues. From the mid-1640s onwards, pirates of different nationalities began to terrorize the coast from Bacalar to the Río Dulce attacking the very few, tentatively established, Spanish ports of call as for example the one at the "point of Río Balis".[68] This Spanish *villa,* most likely, was at the very same location where English ex-pirates began to establish their first camp, the beginnings of Belize City.

As a consequence of the corsair attacks on the coast, Spanish control in the interior of Southern Yucatán and today's territory of Belize continued to weaken considerably. In 1648, for example, Salamanca de Bacalar was severely affected by pirate attacks and the remaining inhabitants moved the *villa* to a new location more north to *"un lugar llamado cayos aproximadamente cuarenta leguas a lo largo de la costa en dirección Valladolid."*[69] Thus, the pirates indirectly acted in favour of the Indian population and with the last Spanish "fortress" being destroyed in 1648, Spanish control over the Maya provinces of Chetumal and Dzuluinicob had come to an end.

---

68   In *Auto y relación,*1642 of Diego el Mulato, the Spanish leader of one of these pirate expeditions. Cf. also Jones (1990: 226 ff).

69   (… a place called cayos about forty leagues along the coast in direction Valladolid …) A league is a unit of length – approximately 4 km – referring to the distance that can be covered by walking on foot or horseback in an hour and is still used in many parts of Central America, its exact distance slightly varying from one country to the other. This quotation appears to identify Glovers Reef in modern Belize as a possible site. Cf. López de Cogolludo (1971[1688]: Lib.12, capítulo 12).

5. Summary of the Spanish Failure to Secure Belize

After having examined the pattern of the Spanish colonization of Yucatán and Central America and its consequences for the Maya population, we can reach the following conclusion:

Seen in retrospective and for the various reasons discussed, the Spanish clearly failed to establish firm control over the area that was to become Belize. With the abandonment of the short-lived Spanish settlement of Villa Real de Chetumal in 1532, the Spaniards were not able to re-establish another *villa* further south and the southernmost Spanish outpost of Yucatán remained Salamanca de Bacalar (see Map 5).

What were the main reasons why the Spaniards were not able to secure Belize? First and foremost, it was because the Spanish forces did not succeed in the first stage of their ambitious colonization plan, which was to link the important commercial centres in Northern Yucatán and Campeche with Tayasal, the capital of the Itzá (present Flores in the Guatemalan Petén of today) in order to establish an overland connection between Yucatán and Guatemala.

In 1544, when Montejo lost his authority over the *adelantamiento* of Yucatán and Honduras, the Spanish realized that their hopes of connecting the two provinces would never materialize.

But since the original grant included the Río Dulce area in the far south (see Map 5) the Spaniards decided not to give up and still saw a chance to establish themselves in that region. In 1546–47 a Spanish expedition crossed the Belizean interior to reach the mouth of the Río Dulce, where they installed a combined trading/military base, much to the dislike of the Dominicans. The Rio Dulce area was, at the same time, the port of entry to the Alta Verapaz region (in present Guatemala) which was controlled by the Dominicans and the friars feared that the military base could pose a general threat to their missionary activities. After successful intervention by the Dominicans, Montejo was ordered to abandon the Río Dulce base and in 1549, the Río Dulce area finally came to be a part of the province of Verapaz which, by then, was completely in the hands of the meanwhile totally independent Dominicans.

The fact remains that if Montejo's dreams had come true, the history of Belize would have taken a different course. Having lost both the Río Dulce area and the province of Spanish Honduras, there no longer existed any reason for Montejo's troops to venture south and penetrate what is now Belizean territory. *If* the Spanish soldiers had succeeded in establishing a fortress at Río Dulce and *if* Montejo had succeeded in holding his vast *adelantamiento* to keep the two provinces under one jurisdiction, regular communication between the Villa of Salamanca de Bacalar and the Río Dulce base and down to Spanish Honduras would have increased and, as a result, trading activities would have become more frequent. Many Spanish coastal settlements and ports of call would most likely have sprung up along the present Belizean coast and, as a consequence, it would have been much more difficult, if not impossible, for the English and Scottish ex-buccaneers to settle on this particular stretch of coast. And *if* these ex-buccaneers had not settled there, the boundaries of today's Belize would never have been drawn as they are now. Most likely, a partition of the territory would have taken place and sooner or later the northern part of what is now Belize would have been incorporated into Yucatán and the southern regions would have been ceded to the *Audiencia* of Guatemala.

Due to its ideal strategic location, the Belizean forest and jungle regions developed into a safe hiding place for refugees seeking freedom from the colonial *encomienda* system and the zealous missionaries. Over the years, a potent Maya resistance movement developed, whose members were stoically hiding out using the non-existing border between the Spanish controlled Southern Yucatán and the Belizean interior as a symbolic wall behind which they were trying to keep secret their political plans and their economic, cultural and religious activities.

The Spaniards, on the other hand, were not fully aware of this well organized resistance and underestimated the rebels to a certain degree, especially in the vicinity of Tipu in Western Belize, one of the headquarters of the movement. Tipu was en route to Tayasal in the Central Petén, inhabited by the powerful Itzá, a tribe the Spanish wanted to control but did not succeed to do so until as late as 1697.

There was a great difference between Maya and Spanish philosophy: The Spanish devoted most of their attention to short-term economic successes and were incapable to look beyond their immediate interests. Despite several failures, they kept adhering to their initial manoeuvres and were unable to devise new strategies in order to adapt them to the changing conditions within the Maya society. The Maya on the other hand were concentrating patiently upon their long-term vision. Matters reached breaking point in 1696, when their spiritual leaders called for surrender.

When Tayasal fell to the Spanish forces in 1697, so did Tipu in Western Belize. Over the next years, both the Maya of Tipu and the Manche Chol Maya of Southern Belize, who had suffered more severely from the Spanish incursions, were resettled in several areas in present Guatemala's Petén, especially around Lake Petén Itzá near the former Tayasal, present Flores. Because the Spaniards had relocated the scattered Maya coastal hamlets, first inland and later to the Alta Verapaz region and the Central Petén, the way was now paved for English and Scottish pirates (or "ex-pirates") to occupy an all but deserted coast.

Since the Spanish did not meet with any opposition from native tribes – because they had been practically annihilated previously – it is worth emphasizing that, indirectly, the Spanish paved the way for these ex-pirates to be able to settle on this particular stretch of coast and found a first tentative settlement. Soon the ex-pirates became "respectable part time woodcutters" and started to exploit the vast stands of logwood in the area. This was to be the very beginning of a new era of colonial history.

To a certain degree, the Spanish themselves were responsible for their loss of Belize. The fact that English and Scottish pioneers succeeded in setting up a base on the Belizean coast at all can be seen as a direct consequence of colonial mismanagement and the inability of the Spanish to secure the area that was to become Belize.

68

Map 4: Early Spanish Expeditions

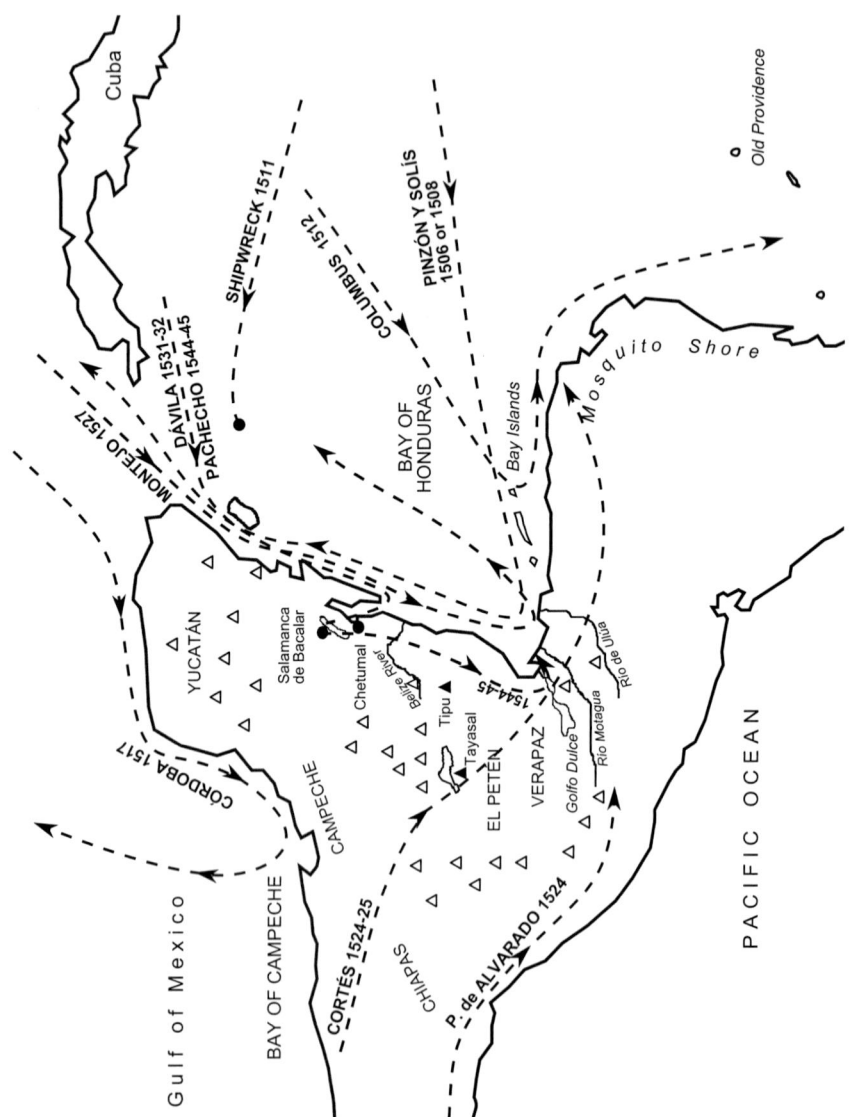

Map 5: The South-Eastern Frontier of Colonial Yucatán (1544–1697)

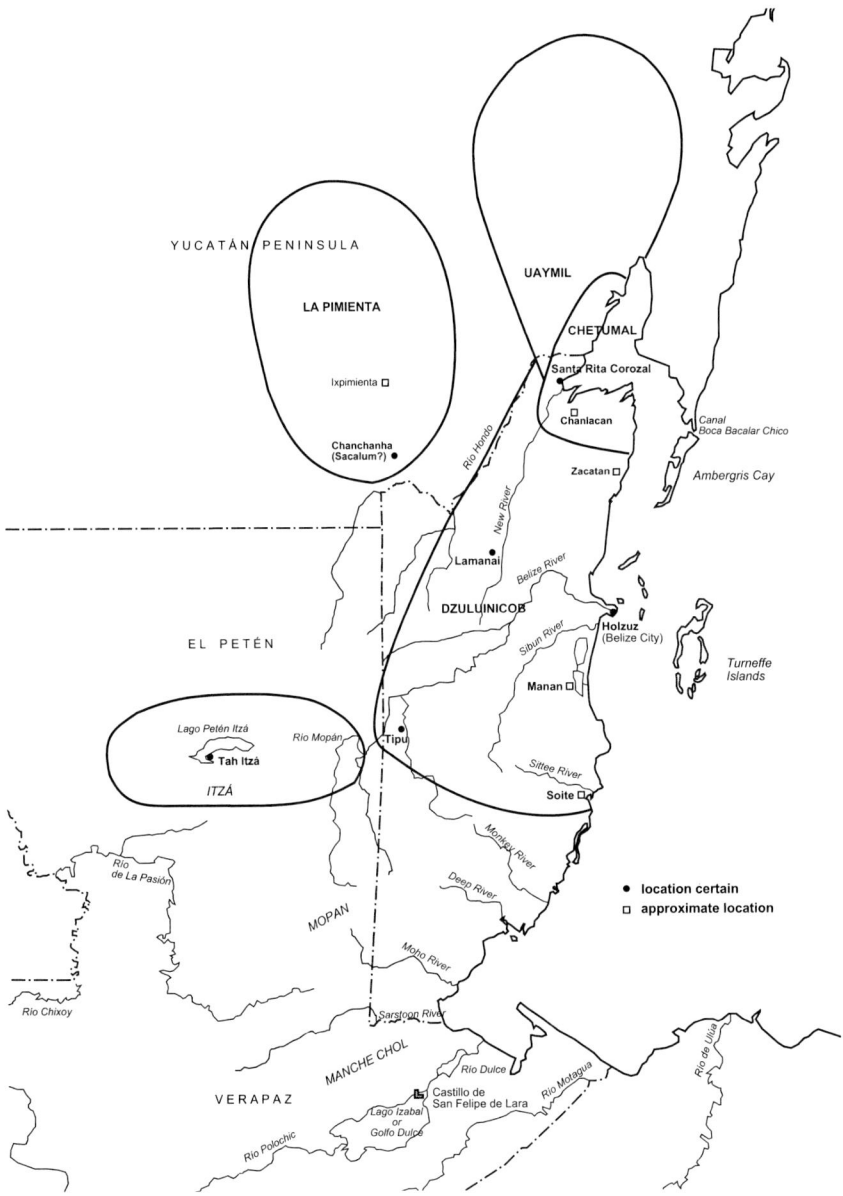

YUCATÁN PENINSULA

LA PIMIENTA

Ixpimienta ☐

Chanchanha
(Sacalum?) ●

UAYMIL

CHETUMAL

Santa Rita Corozal ●

Chanlacan ☐

Zacatan ☐

*Canal
Boca Bacalar Chico*

Ambergris Cay

EL PETÉN

DZULUINICOB

Lamanai ●

Holzuz ●
(Belize City)

*Turneffe
Islands*

Manan ☐

Lago Petén Itzá

Río Mopán

Tah Itzá ●

Tipu ●

ITZÁ

Soite ☐

*Río
de La Pasión*

MOPAN

Deep River

Sittee River

Montoy River

● location certain
☐ approximate location

Río Chixoy

MANCHE CHOL

Sarstoon River

Moho River

VERAPAZ

Río Dulce

Río Motagua

Río de Ulúa

*Lago Izabal
or
Golfo Dulce*

Castillo de
San Felipe de Lara

Río Polochic

Río Hondo

New River

Belize River

Sibun River

Chapter Three

The Bay of Honduras
in the 17th Century

With Special Consideration Given to the History
of Providence Island and the Mosquito Coast

1. A Retreat for Buccaneers and a Safe-Haven
for Ex-Pirates and Pioneers

1.1. Terminology

Pirate is commonly used as a collective term for pirate, privateer (the French *corsair* and Spanish *corsario)*, buccaneer and freebooter alike. Because of their similarity in meaning, they are regularly, and incorrectly, used as synonyms and often cause confusion.

Pirates were bandits from different European countries who made it their business to cruise for robbery on the high seas. They acted without commission from a sovereign nation and without authority from any government. Piracy was considered as a criminal act outside the normal jurisdiction and laws of any country. Pirates' activities were indefensible on any legal ground whatsoever, they were outlaws, were considered as *pessimum genus hominum* and were the enemies of any nation. Even in times of peace, pirates attacked any vessel they encountered, including those travelling under their own country's flag. Not all pirates were men; several notorious female pirates also existed. For example Ann Bonny and Mary Read were female pirates. According to historical records, in order to be able to get on board a ship the lady pirates had to disguise themselves as men.[1]

---

1   Sherry (1986) has humorous stories of what happened when the true identity of these
    women was discovered.

Contrary to pirates, privateers sailed with an official sanction, the "Letter of Reprisal" or "Letter of Marque", given to them by the respective sovereign. In order to obtain this official sanction they had to deliver a certain percentage of the prey. Privateers formed part of naval warfare and whenever European nations were at war with Spain was at war with another European power, pirates of any country were given the chance of becoming lawful privateers. They were given commission to attack and capture Spanish and Portuguese ships and possessions, with the ultimate goal to interrupt and debilitate their overseas trade. The transition from a lawless pirate to a "licensed" privateer and vice versa (for example after the expiring of the privateer's licence) was very common and went smoothly.

Having established the difference between "pirate" and "privateer", we now turn to the third group, "the buccaneers". The term is derived from the French *boucanier*, "the user of a *bucan*",[2] which is a sort of grill used by Carib and Arawak Indians to cure meat. Originally, the name "buccaneer" was given to a group of West Europeans (mostly French Huguenots and British Protestants) who, in the first decade of the 16th century, happened to settle peacefully in north-west Hispaniola, present Haiti, by that time already abandoned by the Spanish. These pioneers lived off the land and by hunting the semi-wild horses, cattle and hogs which had escaped from the former Spanish settlements. Over time they became simple cattle farmers selling hides and meat (also turtle and manatee meat), smoked on the *bucan* to passing ships as a means of sustenance.[3] From 1620 onwards they started to be attacked by the Spaniards and eventually had to flee to the nearby island of Tortuga, off the north coast of Hispaniola.

From there, the Spanish never succeeded to drive them out because the ranks of the buccaneers had meanwhile been joined by a number of adventurers of various nationalities who dedicated themselves to piracy initiating a kind of guerrilla maritime warfare: Runaway bondsmen and castaways from French, English and Dutch ships, "honorary" pioneers and escaped convicts. After 1650, ex-privateers who had converted into pirates also served as reinforcement to the original buccaneers. Soon they had become a very powerful group who extended their operations to the entire Caribbean attacking any vessel they encountered. This conglomerate of individuals developed into private seafarers acting at their own cost and for their own profit. Their ultimate

---

2   In the Carib and Arawak/Taíno language – the native languages of the Caribbean – a *bucan* was a wooden framework of sticks set upon posts, the *barabicu*, which is considered to be the etymology of the English "barbecue".

3   For a detailed history of the original buccaneers see Haring (1910: 66–78 and 113–28).

goal was to destroy Spanish supremacy plundering Spanish treasure fleets (the so-called *"Flotas del Tesoro"*) wherever and whenever they saw a chance to do so. In contrast to the common pirates, buccaneers did not limit their activities to the sea, but also sacked Spanish ports and settlements on *Tierra Firme*, the name given to the present Atlantic coast of Venezuela and Colombia and the Isthmus of Panama.

In order to defend themselves against the retaliations of the Spanish, buccaneers formed a coalition or a community of interests. They were used to live in total freedom and not prepared to subordinate their interests to those of the French authorities of the island of Tortuga and elaborated their own contracts or codes of conduct which ruled everyday life. They formed the "Confederacy of the Brethren of the Coast", a sort of anarchistic society and a perfect example of liberty and revolt at the same time. The members of the brotherhood were expected to abide by the codes of conduct which were based on democratic principles and favoured individual rights and the equitable distribution of profits.[4] Over time, out of this gang of individual adventurers the common freebooter evolved and it did not take long until the two terms started to merge.

The usage of the term freebooter (the source of "filibuster", the meaning of which, however, has lost its connotation to piracy) goes back to the Dutch *vrijbuiter* from *vrij* ("free") and *buit* ("booty") and can be translated with "a rover who pillages and plunders freely".[5]

---

4   Here, I consider it important to emphasize that – contrary to common belief – the existence of a single code which all buccaneers recognized and subscribed to is nothing but a myth. Codes did exist but each ship had its own codes of conduct or articles which were set up by the captains. In principle, the members of the brotherhood were all treated the same and the articles regulated the way crews were to operate and how revenues were to be divided. The main source of reference for details of how the "Brethren of the Coast" were organized is the first hand account of Alexandre Olivier Exquemelin, a passionate and extraordinary narration of the life and custom of the pirates in the Caribbean in the 17th century. Although we have no actual proof, we are given the idea that he was captured by pirates and established himself on the island of Tortuga, where he studied to become a surgeon. He joined the brotherhood and worked as a surgeon on board of the ships of many a famous buccaneer, such as on the one of Henry Morgan. For example in an article drawn up by Henry Morgan it was stipulated what recompense or reward each member ought to have in case of injury. Or, from an article of a certain Captain Roberts it was stated that if any man were to seduce a (white!) woman without her consent, he was to suffer death. Cf. Exquemelin [1678]1993.

5   In my opinion, of several possible etymologies there is only one which seems plausible: under the influence of the Dutch *vlieboot* (small boat) it was transformed to "flyboat" in English, a fast and easy to manoeuvre ship which was used in 16th century Caribbean. Then, the term changed to *flibut* or *filibote* in Spanish and finally, due to a phonetic corruption, it came to mean *filibustero* in Spanish and *flibustier* in French. Hence, free-

The principal aim of examining the "pirate terminology" in its historical context is the fact that during the 17th century, the coast of what is now Belize started to develop into an important retreat for pirates, ex-pirates, ex-privateers, buccaneers and freebooters. The long coral reef straddling the coast offered protection and difficult access for their enemies at the same time.

1.2. European Historical Background of Buccaneering in the Caribbean

During the second half of the 16th century, Anglo-Irish sea-rovers started to venture further south from the strategically ideal ports along the Irish Coast to plunder Spanish treasure galleons returning from the West Indies. When Queen Elizabeth ascended the throne of England in 1558 the rivalry between England and Spain, was already well under way.

This rivalry had its roots largely in religious matters: During the reign of Queen Mary, a Catholic who was married to the Spanish King Philip II, the Protestants feared that she would bring Catholicism to England, something which was to be avoided at any cost. After Mary's death Elizabeth, while openly accepting the courtship of the late Mary's husband Phillip, allowed and even encouraged pirating along the Spanish coast and in the Caribbean. In 1587, as an answer to Spanish claims to the monopoly of trade and colonization in the Americas and as a prelude to the victory over the Spanish Armada one year later, Elizabeth proclaimed her Declaration of Policy, openly questioning the Spanish monopoly

> *The Queen of England understands not why her or any prince's subjects should be debarred from the Trade of the Indies, which she could not persuade herself the Spanish had any just title to by the donation of the Bishop of Rome[6] ... nor yet by any other claim than as they had here and there touched upon the coasts, built cottages, or given a name to a river or cape... and this imaginary property cannot hinder other princes from raiding in those countries or from transporting colonies into those parts thereof where the Spanish do not inhabit.[7]*

thereby openly sanctioning English colonization and piracy in the New World. Soon she could count on a reliable team of expert sailors, such as John Hawkins, Francis Drake and Walter Raleigh who, armed with an official royal decree –

---

booter or *filibustero* is also the source of the modern "filibuster", the meaning of which, however, has lost its pirate connotation.

6   The papal bulls issued in 1493 by Pope Alexander VI granted unlimited rights to Spain.

7   Caiger (1951:20)

the "Letter of Reprisal" or "Letter of Marque" (Spanish *patente de corso*)[8] – set out for the Caribbean waters thus becoming privateers in Her Majesty's service. From the English point of view, the plundering of Spanish vessels became a legitimate trade. In order to obtain the "Letter of Marque", the privateers had to deliver a certain percentage of the prey directly to the sovereign.[9]

The success of both the first sea-rovers and the Elizabethan privateers gradually forced Spain to take measures for the protection of her galleons. From about 1530 they were ordered to sail together, accompanied by a powerful convoy.

Two merchant fleets (the *flotas*) were organized each year, one for Cartagena and Portobelo on Terra Firme and the other going to Vera Cruz in New Spain with an average cruising time of 75 days.[10] With the departure dates and routes more or less fixed by climatic conditions and prevailing winds, the heavy clumsy vessels of these gigantic fleets were an easy target for the privateers who sailed in small squadrons or single ships which were much faster and more easily manoeuvred.

The privateering expeditions were costly and had to be organized well in advance. Joint stock ventures were formed to meet the high expenses since the vessels had to carry provisions for up to 8–12 months. Among the promoters of the expeditions were the London merchants and members of the English gentry and nobility who thought that damaging the King of Spain's empire was a worthwhile undertaking.

In the Caribbean, privateering played an extremely important role:

First, although the region lacked mineral riches, Caribbean ports became way stations for the fleets carrying gold and silver from Peru and Mexico and Caribbean waters soon came to be ideal hunting grounds for prey.

Secondly, after 1630 when the political and economic situation in the Caribbean was gradually but significantly altered privateers became indispensable. In the eyes of the English (but also the Dutch, French and Germans), privateers not only discovered suitable places for colonization and helped to conquer them, but also played a significant role in securing the territorial claims and consolidating the strength of the "new" colonial powers.

---

8   According to 16th century English and German maritime law countries which had declared war on each other had the right to issue these decrees. The holder of such a decree was given official permission and/or order to attack and plunder the enemy at random.

9   For example 17th century records state that in Jamaica 1/15th had to be paid to the English King and 1/10th to the Lord High Admiral, the Duke of York (Pawson and Buisseret 1975:56, mentioned in Sandner 1985:100).

10   Haring (1964:1–56) discusses at length how the fleets were organized and how they were functioning.

As far as the Spanish colonists were concerned, privateering came to fulfil an important additional role. By plundering the Spanish merchant fleets the privateers (and later ex-privateers who had become common pirates or buccaneers) also functioned as traders providing the colonists with products of everyday need. This new type of pirates (or buccaneers), called *herejes luteranos* by the Spanish ("Lutheran heretics", because buccaneering in general was considered against the doctrine of the Catholic faith), supplied the colonists with merchandise which was very difficult and/or impossible to obtain by means of the complicated and slow Spanish fleet system. In other words, by avoiding the *Casa de la Contratación*[11] in Spain and the taxes they would have had to pay, the colonists were able to buy goods directly at a much lower price. Actually, if it had not been for these intermediaries – who were smugglers, slave traders and bandits at the same time – it would have been more costly and more difficult for the Central American and Caribbean market to obtain European products. Consequently, contraband became indispensable for the newly emerging Spanish colonial elite in the Americas.

At the treaties of Madrid in 1667 and 1670 between England and Spain, the English government agreed to contribute to the suppression of buccaneering in return for Spain's ceding to England all its *de facto* territories in the Caribbean not in actual possession of the latter at the time and not in the "possession of any Christian prince".[12] As a consequence, Governor Modyford of Jamaica was sent home in disgrace for his open encouragement of buccaneering and his successors were to carry out a policy of active suppression. However, a definite recession did not occur until approximately 15 years later when Charles II renewed the proclamation offering a general pardon to all who surrendered and showed willingness to start a new life.[13] The passing of the act was also closely related with a growing influence of the merchant class in Jamaica who started to engage in regular legal trade, especially slave trade. They soon found out that regular trade activities were more profitable in the long-term than the occasional contraband ship load from the buccaneers. A similar trend was beginning to manifest itself among the Dutch and French traders. In 1682, Jamaica's

---

11 "House of Commerce" or "House of the Indies", the central trading house and procurement agency for Spain's New World empire from the 16ᵗʰ to the 18ᵗʰ century, situated in Seville and later in Cádiz. It became the instrument of the Spanish crown's policy of control and served as a general overseer of commerce between Spain and its American possessions.

12 As stipulated in 1494 in the Treaty of Tordesillas and in a number of subsequent peace treaties.

13 See Calendar of State Papers, Colonial Series, America and the West Indies, 1685–88, Cos. 1277–78 and Haring (1910: 250–53).

deputy governor, the ex-buccaneer Sir Henry Morgan, who had been pro-buc-
caneering and anti-trade, was removed from office.

Since the buccaneers were no longer able to count on Morgan's and the
merchants' sponsorship and in their frustration of not being able to keep up
and re-establish their lucrative contraband trade, they were forced to retreat
to deserted islands and uninhabited coasts. A preferred region for settlement
was the swampy coastal stretches of Western Yucatán and the entire "Honduran" coast including modern Belize and parts of Nicaragua. There they were
left relatively undisturbed and able to continue to prey upon Spanish treasure
and logwood ships. But attacking Spanish treasure ships was by no means a
"full-time job" and they had to find additional means of how to sustain themselves throughout the year. For example it took not long before the buccaneers
started to cut the wood themselves instead of stealing it from the Spanish who
had been cutting and exporting logwood on the west coast of Honduras and
in the Bay of Campeche for approximately a hundred years. Logwood, a much
valued dye-wood, which grew in stands in the coastal swamps, lagoons and on
the river banks, was much valued in Europe from as early as the mid-1600s.

In the years between 1660 and 1685, buccaneering in the Caribbean was
blooming. Buccaneering was a great hindrance to trade and the major sack-
ings of Spanish cities brought significant hardships upon the nascent Central
American economy. Buccaneering was also seen as an enormous threat to the
growing of smuggling activities: Although buccaneering and smuggling were
closely interrelated and they were often disguises for one another, even for successful smuggling operations a moderate amount of trust was needed, which
was clearly put in danger by ruthless piracy. Strategically important way-sta-
tions and naval passages were haunted by buccaneers and this made smuggling,
not to speak of legal trade, highly dangerous.

Shipping merchandise in general, whether legally or via smuggling, became
such a menace that merchants from the *Audiencia* of Guatemala for example,
had to have their goods shipped overland first, via Nicaragua and the San Juan
River, before using ships all the way to the central depot of Cartagena on modern Colombia's Caribbean coast. Shipping the merchandise with normal-sized
merchant ships on the much shorter route across the Gulf of Honduras and directly up to Havana – the final assembly port for the dispatch of the fleet – was
considered to be highly risky due to the Dutch, French and English buccaneers
hiding and attacking in the ports in the entire Bay of Honduras area.

The constant raids on the ports in the Bay of Honduras forced the Span-
ish to act and withdraw to the interior, using the coastal towns (Santo Tomás,
Omoa, Trujillo in present Honduras and the Golfo Dulce region in present
Guatemala) only for the storage of merchandise which was heavily guarded

during loading and off-loading procedures. Forts were built in various strategic positions, for example the *Castillo de San Felipe de Lara* in 1652, the ruins of which can still be seen on Lake Izabal in Guatemala close to the southern border of Belize (see Map 5). This fortress was built to protect the important commercial route along the ancient Maya trade route from Guatemala's interior and the Pacific region to the Caribbean outlet, the Golfo Dulce.

Especially in the Western Caribbean, buccaneering died very hard. The last great success of the buccaneers was the siege of Cartagena in 1697 but during their return journey most of them were captured by a British fleet which confiscated the buccaneers' booty. Buccaneering continued to become more sporadic, but it was not until the first decades of the 19th century when buccaneering finally came to a standstill.

During the late 16th and 17th centuries the commercial relationship with Spain and the Americas was very complex leaving enough room for the development of subtle nuances between legal and illegal forms of trade.

The Spanish system of trade was not only very complicate and extremely inflexible but soon became decadent altogether. As a consequence regular intervals of the convoy system bound for the Americas started to decrease. If the fleets did arrive, goods were extremely expensive because of high taxes and the charges of various "middlemen", owing to the fact that the vacuum caused by the inefficiency of the system had created new possibilities for foreign merchants.

The initial reaction of the Central American merchants (or Creole[14] merchants) to Spain's inability to replace the degenerated fleet system was to take advantage of the contraband trade conducted by foreign merchants and Spanish "straw men". Then, the next stage of illegality was to eliminate the Spanish at all and to transact business directly with the foreign smugglers in the Caribbean ports.[15] By doing so, exports became more profitable and commodities needed in Central America could be purchased at a much lower price by directly importing them from the foreign smugglers. The beginning of these

---

14   Contrary to common belief, in the Spanish (and French) colonies the term "Creole"/ *criollo* was originally applied to people of "pure" European blood born in the colonies, in contrast to immigrants born in Europe and the indigenous population. In the 19th century the term came to mean the New World natives of mixed European and African blood and their language, a mixture of elements of Pidgin and the respective European language. In the first decades of the 19th century, in North America, the West Indies and the Caribbean Coast of Central America, the term designated a person of mixed Black and European ancestry.

15   For the progression from legal and semi-legal trade to open contraband see for example MacLeod (1973: 351–52).

transactions could be interpreted as the Creole merchants' first tentative attempts to declare economic independence from the mother country.

For the emerging English/Scottish settlement in the Bay of Honduras, the increased smuggling activities were of significant importance. From 1670 onwards, when it was for the first time officially attempted to suppress buccaneering, the entire Bay of Honduras including the Golfo Dulce region and the coast of present Belize became an ideal hiding place for the buccaneers who wished to continue and revive their trade.

1.3. Belizean Waters – A Strategic Hideaway

Although the coastline of Belize did not lie in the direct path of the Spanish commercial fleets, for the crews of smaller vessels it served as a place to shelter and renew supplies from as early as the first decades of the 16th century. In the 17th century the region's natural isolation, its geographical location outside the main shipping routes and the dangerous coral reef running all along the coast and providing access only to those who knew how to locate and navigate the natural channels, were ideal preconditions for the establishment of buccaneer headquarters and refitting ports. During the rainy season, when the lack of wind made boating more difficult, the numerous small coastal inlets, protected bays and cays offered ideal hideaways for the maintenance and repairing of ships.

The offshore cays of Belize and the Bay Islands of Honduras (Roatán, Utila and Guanaja) were one of the principal buccaneer haunts of the time. Legendary captains, such as Cox and Sharp, enjoying open protection from the famous ex-buccaneer Sir Henry Morgan, then deputy governor of Jamaica, were in charge of operations.

A direct proof of the fact that many famous buccaneers of the time must have frequented the area and taken refuge in the Belizean waters at least on one instance can be seen in the etymology of place names: For example Bannister and Goff Cays are said to be named after two English buccaneers. For several cays, a more or less plausible etymology, which takes us back to Dutch buccaneering times and the successful days of the Dutch West India Company when Dutch traders and smugglers anchored at the strategic offshore cays of Belize, can be found: "Cay Bokel" ("Bokel": Dutch for hump or bend), a cay with a small elevation forming part of the Turneffe group, or the domination of the cay "Bluefield Range" which goes back to the Dutch Captain Blauveldt. The name for the present Turneffe atoll accounts for the presence of French (most likely Huguenot) buccaneers on the cays of Belize: A plausible folk etymology for "Turneffe" could be *terre noeve,* a French corruption of the Spanish *tierra nueva.*

Towards the end of the 17th century, in the heyday of the contraband trade, the Belizean waters together with various ports in the Gulf of Honduras (for example Golfo Dulce, Santo Tomás, Omoa and Trujillo) became smugglers' havens. In 1679 for example, a famous raid was made in that region and indigo, cacao, cochineal, tortoise shell, money etc. was stolen from the royal storehouses.[16]

As mentioned in the previous section, after the suppression of buccaneering, instead of robbing the precious logwood cargo from Spanish vessels and mainland depots, the more enterprising adventurers began to come to the Bay of Honduras to cut it themselves. Life in the proper English colonies would have been too dull for the rugged and independently-minded buccaneers who would not have fitted into the tight social structures of an official colony. William Dampier, a 17th century buccaneer and logger who obviously attempts to moderate the negative buccaneering image of the early logwood camps, tells us that "… the more industrious sort of them came hither [to the Bay of Honduras]."[17] Of course, the question arises "industrious" in what way and by whose standards, by those of a crew of honest hard-working men or an energetic band of raiders? Dampier mentions further that there were only two choices: "… either to go to Petit Guavas [present Haiti], where the trade still continued, or into the Bay [of Honduras] to cut logwood."[18]

In the beginning, the wood cutting activities were concentrated in the Laguna de Terminus region in Western Yucatán (see Map 6), where the Spanish had been exploiting logwood for decades. From the Spanish point of view the arrival of English adventurers at the logging sites was a terrible encroachment by her "*decididos enemigos*"[19] ("worst enemies"). The Spanish Mexican historian Calderón Quijano mentions that in

> … *este seguro refugio en la costa yucateca, España se encontraba con que sus más decididos enemigos [los británicos] habían conquistado una posición fuerte en uno de los centros neurálgicos de nuestra estabilidad en el hemisferio americano.*[20]

---

16 For a description of the various buccaneering activities on the Belizean Coast and in and around the Bay of Honduras see Exquemelin (1993[1678]:139), Joseph (1974:19–27), Dampier (1906[1700]:149–179) and Haring (1910:223–26 and passim) among others.

17 Dampier (1906[1700]:50)

18 Ibid.

19 Calderón Quijano (1944:IX)

20 (… in this safe hideaway on the Yucatecan coast, Spain realized that her worst enemies [the British] had been able to conquer a strong position in one of the most neuralgic centres of our stability in the American hemisphere.) Ibid.

The English soon abandoned the Laguna de Términos region, either because they were molested by the Spanish or because the cutting sites were depleted, or both. Then they moved south and down the east coast of Yucatán where new places were discovered by chance as it was the case with the "Honduran" (Belizean) logging areas and ultimately those on the Mosquito Coast. Basing ourselves on historical records,[21] we may estimate that by 1675, between 500 and 700 loggers were operating in the area around Laguna de Terminus and Cape Catoche (see Map 6) and at several logging sites along the "Honduran" (Belizean) Coast.

After the Treaties of Madrid in 1667 and 1670, the shift from buccaneering to logwood cutting and semi-permanent settlement was encouraged by the attempts to outlaw buccaneering. However, "Goin' to the Bay to cut logwood"[22] was a saying which soon became known to the Jamaican governors and British naval officers who were in charge of putting an end to buccaneering as the standard alibi for the continuation of the buccaneering activities in and around the Bay. It meant that woodcutting and buccaneering coexisted for a considerable length of time.

The transition from a buccaneer to a decent logwood cutter was difficult and prolonged and the Belizean waters, together with the first semi-permanent logwood settlements on the mainland, became ideal breeding grounds for the most notorious desperadoes of the time. This is, for example, vividly demonstrated by the existence of a place called "Gallows Point" on Drowned Cay off today's Belize City.

1.4. The Beginning of an English/Scottish Settlement

While buccaneering was still in its heyday a parallel trend towards more permanent settlement in the New World was beginning to manifest itself. One of the motives, apart from trying to achieve economic success, was to escape from the lack of religious tolerance at home. Various trading companies were founded by the English, for example in Virginia and on the Leeward Islands in the Eastern Caribbean. The history of the colonization of these places is well documented, whereas, unfortunately, this is not the case with Belize. The first settlers did not have an inclination to write letters to London, either because

---

21 See for example Dampier (1906[1700]: 46–47,53), Calderón Quijano (1944: 48–66), Burdon (1935: 1–8), Parsons (1954: 11) and Joseph (1989: 9).

22 Dampier (1906[1700]: 53)

they were mostly illiterate[23] and/or concentrated on making a living or for fear their squatting on Spanish territory might be discovered.

The origins of the English/Scottish[24] settlement in the Bay of Honduras are still largely a matter of doubt and conjecture. Some of the earlier historians and authors[25], when dealing with the first settlement of present Belize, consider the possibility that the very first settlers might have been connected to the first English colony in the Western Caribbean: The island of Old Providence, today's Providencia off the Atlantic Coast of Nicaragua.

1.4.1. The Connection with the Providence Colony

Although the immediate beginnings of the settlement in the Bay of Honduras most likely cannot be brought in direct connection with the Providence colony (also called Old Providence), I consider it important to give a survey of its history. In my opinion, the influence the Providence colony had on the Bay of Honduras – and in a more narrow sense the future Belize – is widely underestimated. On repeated visits to the island and after intensive research I have come to the conclusion that developments during the short existence of the Providence colony did affect the emerging English/Scottish settlement in the Bay very strongly. Therefore, I consider the following digression more than justified and I ask the reader to bear with me.

In 1629, the Earl of Warwick, heading a group of the very same venturesome and influential London merchants who organized the colonization of Massachusetts, established "the Company of Adventurers of the City of Westminster[26] for the Plantation of the Islands of Providence or Catalina, Henrietta or Andrea (today's San Andrés) and the adjacent islands lying upon the coast of America [the Mosquito Coast]"[27] and were given a royal patent. In 1631, the first major batch of colonists, mostly eager Puritans, arrived on Providence. They came directly from England on the "Seaflower" and settled on this island

---

23 Here, comparison should be made with the colonizing activities of the Spanish, the documenting of which was mostly in the hands of well-educated friars or missionaries. See also the accounts of Fray Joseph Delgado of 1677 describing his adventures with the ex-buccaneers on the Belizean coast, cf. Dobson (1973: 46).

24 Prior to the Act of Union in 1707, uniting England and Scotland it would be historically inaccurate to call this settlement a British settlement.

25 For example Caiger (1951: 27) and Waddell (1961: 7)

26 In the 17ᵗʰ century the term "adventurer" was used for a person who takes part in a daring venture, an enterprise of a business nature involving financial risk. London at that time consisted of the City of London and the City of Westminster, the seat of parliament.

27 For a detailed study of the colonization of Old Providence refer to Newton (1914), Hampshire (1972: 29–42), Bridenbaugh (1972), Parsons (1985) and Kupperman (1993).

which was in a strategic position close to the routes of the Spanish treasure fleets on the way to Portobelo and Cartagena (see Maps 4 and 6). The Spanish had taken possession of the island, which they named Santa Catalina, as early as 1510, but were never seriously interested in colonizing there. Because of Providence's proximity to the Spanish Main, the colonists were given royal permission to make reprisals against eventual Spanish assailants. The main goal of the zealous Puritans was to establish a model-Puritan colony – as a matter of fact it was the first English colony in the Western Caribbean – with productive plantations, but the experiment proved to be a failure. Although the soil was reasonably fertile on Providence and abundant fresh water sources were available, the planting of cotton, potatoes, vegetables and various fruit trees was not successful in the long-term and the colony's tobacco, although of good quality, did not sell at the expected price at the London market. The settlers also failed to increase productivity and the efficiency of the plantations which was partly due religious motives since they initially objected to employing slaves.

It did not take long until the Puritans, by then aware of their colony being a fiasco and influenced by the pleasant climate, became increasingly lackadaisical and started to forsake their strict religious and moral principles. On several occasions, the Puritan settlers travelled to the Mosquito Coast to explore the possibility of setting up trading posts there. This was to be the beginning of the development of a trade relationship and friendship between the English and the Miskito Indians, one of the indigenous coastal tribes along that coast. The isolation of Providence made communication increasingly difficult and only a minimum amount of money was invested, especially after the London investors too had to admit that the experiment was a complete financial failure. Eventually, the settlers started to engage in illicit trade with Dutch smugglers and to provide shelter and water to the passing buccaneers. This was highly provocative to the Spaniards who began to attack the island from 1635 onwards. As a consequence, instead of employing the colony's labour force to revive the plantations, it was used for building fortifications.

With Providence being constantly attacked by the Spaniards, the character of the supposed "model colony" changed completely. Following a last decisive attack in 1641, after a mere 10 years of existence, the majority of the colonists, approximately 500 men, 40 women and 90 Negro slaves,[28] were taken prisoner and about a hundred men managed to escape to the mainland.

After this last attack on Providence, the English-Spanish relationship deteriorated vehemently. One year later, with the outbreak of Civil War in England, Cromwell came to power and pledged to take revenge. According to a letter

---

28 Cf. Newton (1914: 123)

written by Cromwell to the then commander in chief of Jamaica, the Providence colony would have been an ideal strategic base to carry out Cromwell's "Western Design", the colonization of parts of the Western Caribbean and the continuation of the profitable privateering business against the Spanish.

> *We think and it is much designed amongst us to strive with the Spaniards for the mastery of these seas; and therefore we could heartily wish that the Island of Providence were in our hands again, believing that it lies so advantageously in reference to the [Spanish] Main, and especially for the hindrance of the Peru trade and Cartagena, that you might not only have great advantage thereby of intelligence and surprise, but even block up the same.[29]*

Indeed, the capture of Jamaica in 1655 is partially seen as revenge against the Spaniards for having brought an abrupt end to the existence of the first English colony in the Western Caribbean.

During the following 200 years the island changed hands between famous privateers (such as Francis Drake, Edward Mansfield, Henry Morgan and his Port Royal Privateers, the latter of which made it their base for the famous and victorious attack on the city of Panama in 1671), English and Spanish forces as well as Dutch and French intruders. From the 1750s onwards the English/Scottish settlers returned with a few slaves and started plantations. By 1783, however, the archipelago (San Andrés, Old Providence and Santa Catalina) was again in the hands of the Spanish. After the Convention of London in 1786, the Spanish agreed to resettle the former planters and their slaves on Old Providence and neighbouring San Andrés under the condition that they pledge loyalty to the Spanish Crown and convert to Catholicism.[30] In 1803, Spain assigned the islands of Old Providence and Henrietta (San Andrés) to the Viceroyalty of New Granada. A brief episode with the French adventurer Luis Aury who established Old Providence as his headquarters from which to pursue Central American independence followed. Finally, in 1822, the island was incorporated, for good or for evil, into Colombia and the island's name hispanicized to

---

29 Ibid., p. 323

30 One of these colonists, Francis Archbold, an English captain and slave trader, received a land grant from the Spanish government in 1788 and established a cotton plantation. This was sufficient an incentive for more English/Scottish colonists to arrive, the majority coming from Jamaica. Archbold, Robinson and Newball among others are the prominent surnames on the island even today. To provide the work force for the plantations a larger contingent of African slaves was needed and brought to the island, i.e. the origin of the African-descendant community on present Providencia Island.

Providencia or Providencia Island as it is called by native and Creole speaking islanders.[31]

According to my own experiences and research on Providencia Island, a large percentage of the island's "original population" still consider themselves legitimate descendants of the English/Scottish colonists who were given permission to stay on the island after the Spanish victory in 1641 or re-immigrate from the Mosquito Shore. Until today, the cultural and linguistic characteristics of the islanders of Anglo-Saxon and Celtic descent still differ from those of mainlanders and much effort is taken to conserve identity and traditions.[32]

In 1953, after the neighbouring and much larger island, San Andrés was declared a free port: The so-called "colombianization" was initiated, imposing the predominant Spanish language, religion and cultural expressions. Before that date, Colombia was almost totally absent from the islands, the islanders governed themselves and quite successfully. One consequence of the "colombianization process" was that moral and ethical values of native islanders (*raizales* in Spanish, from *raíz* meaning 'root') had to be adjusted to suit those of the newcomers and a process of adaptation and assimilation of their traditional Anglo-Caribbean culture has now begun. However, islanders are united in the fight to combat the negative effects the "mainlanders" (the "Spanish" as they continue to call them) might have on their own hybrid island culture and try to avoid the total assimilation of the English (Creole) language into the Spanish language. One of their successes is reflected in the Columbian Constitution of 1991 which acknowledges English as the mother tongue of the native islanders establishing both English and Spanish as official languages. Colombian on pa-

---

31 Today, the total population of Providence amounts to approximately 5000 people. They share a blended ancestry which is derived from many different cultures, the Miskito Indians, the English/Scottish, the Spanish, the French and the descendants of Africans as well as mainland Colombians.

32 For example the island's original Creole inhabitants organize traditional dance performances where participants dress in historical costumes. The dances are adaptations from 18th and 19th century European ballroom dances which are said to have arrived on the island in the beginning of the 19th century. Waltz, mazurka, quadrille, polka, the *"schottist"* from Victorian times, but also the *pasillo* (a waltz rhythm from Colombia) form part of many festivities, carnivals and special celebrations. Local music known as "string" is played with violins, mandolins, guitars, accordion, maracas, washtub bass and jawbone. However, a fusion of European and African musical traditions has long begun. Today there is a strong presence of Afro-Caribbean musical elements such as the calypso and *soca* (originally from Trinidad and Tobago), the *mento* (closely related to the Jamaican traditional style of music of the mid-19th century prior to reggae) and the *vallenato* which originated in Valledupar in the northeast of Colombia.

per and claimed by Nicaragua the native islanders consciously cultivate social isolation and cherish insularity to preserve their culture and traditions.

The history of Providence Island serves as an example of an unrealistic and overly ambitious failed colonial undertaking. It remains to be seen whether the native islanders' aim to maintain their identity and achieve sufficient autonomy to be able to define a future of their own will, one day, be more than just a dream.

The main reason for this long digression on the history of the short-lived Providence colony is to draw attention to the fact that, in my opinion, the role Providence Island might have played for the development of the future colony of British Honduras is not given enough credit. However, since the archives of the Providence Island Company do not contain pertinent data on the subject, it is impossible to find out how many of the colonist who succeeded in escaping the island, actually went directly to the "Bay" (the term used for the Bay of Honduras) instead of making a stopover on the Mosquito Coast, called "The Shore" and/or the Bay Islands off present Honduras.

A strong evidence of the presence of Puritans as far north as the Bay of Honduras is provided by the existence of a number of place names of Puritan origin in Southern Belize and the offshore cays in that area. For example the names of the "Gladden" and the "Glory" entrances to the reef seem convincingly enough to point to a Puritan etymology. The sight of the channel could have "gladdened" them, which might indeed be a Puritan expression ("to make glad" meaning "to cheer"). Likewise, "Glover's Reef" goes back to Roger Glover, a member of the Earl of Warwick's company,[33] the first batch of colonists to arrive on Old Providence. The name given to the settlement of "Commess Bight" (or "Commerce Bight Village" on modern maps) also indicates a possible connection to the Providence colony.[34] However, we must bear in mind that although geographical names give us important insights about the colonizing pattern of certain regions, they are of limited historical value and therefore have to be used with caution. In many cases, multiple etymological sources can be found for one place name and, strictly speaking, we also have to take into consideration that a number of place names were merely folk-etymologized.[35]

---

33   Strictly speaking, since there was also a base on Nevis we do not have enough conclusive evidence from which branch of the company Roger Glover actually came from.

34   One of the commissaries of the Providence Company was Captain Camock. Commess' or 'Commerce', in this case is as a corruption of 'commissary'.

35   Cf. Winzerling (1946: 39–47, 81). The etymologies given by the amateur historian are, in my opinion, far-fetched and far from convincing.

In sum, the role the Providence colony played in the development of the future colony of British Honduras is sometimes underestimated. Although if we base ourselves only upon a few place names related to the Puritans, this certainly does not provide enough conclusive evidence for a strong Puritan element among the early settlers of British Honduras. Even if, admittedly, the "Puritan theory" seems convincing, it is impossible to determine exactly if and to what extent the colony of Providence did, in fact, play a major role for the foundation of the Bay Settlement.

Nevertheless, what we do know for certain is that the expulsion, or flight respectively, of the Puritan settlers to the Mosquito Coast and then further on to the Bay Islands, in the long term, strongly affected the development of the colony of British Honduras.

1.4.2. The History and Role of the Mosquito Coast

The territory of the Mosquito Coast, the narrow coastal region between the San Juan River in the south of Nicaragua and Cape Camarón in Honduras, measured about 362 kilometres from north to south. Inland the area varied in width, approximately 64 kilometres. In pre-colonial times this region was inhabited by several tribes of Chibcha Amerindians who resisted Spanish forces during and after the conquest and succeeded in maintaining their autonomy to a certain degree. The Cordillera Central, a mountain chain extending diagonally from Southern Honduras to the San Juan River, formed a natural frontier to put a halt to the advance of Spanish colonization towards the east, south-east, respectively. In the second half of the 17th century, the Miskito Indians or Miskito emerged. According to the most widely accepted hypothesis they evolved from a racial and cultural amalgamation of the Bahwika (a sub-tribe of the Sumu and also called Tawira or Tawahkas) and Europeans and Africans which ultimately resulted in a new mixed ethnic group, the Miskito and Zambo-Miskito.

In order to avoid confusion and because maps and pertinent literature give different denominations and spellings ('miskito', 'miskitu', 'mosquito') we have to analyse the origin of the terms. To start with, I would like to make clear that the terms are, in no way, related to the insect "mosquito", however appropriate it might be. Of a variety of existing theories on the subject I am inclined to lend credence to the following three:

First, 'miskito' could be a derivation of *miskut-upla,* a kind of chieftain of the Bahwika tribe. In fact, it is very plausible that *miskito or miskitu* – which means the people of miskut – could have evolved from the fast pronunciation of this term.

Secondly, it is possible for the term to have developed from 'musket' and/or the Spanish *mosquete,* the firearm. As we shall see below, the Zambo-Miskito received arms in payment for exchanging products with the English. As can be deduced from the first historical accounts English and/or Spanish speakers started to call this native group "musket men" (men/Indians in possession of arms and/or *indios musquetos* or *indios mosquetos).*[36]

Thirdly, the name might be the result of a phonetic corruption of *'muiscas'* to *'moscos'*. In the 16th century a subtribe of the Chibcha people, who inhabited parts of modern Colombia and called themselves 'muiscas', were referred to by the Spanish as 'moscos'. The Spanish might have considered the indigenous people of the Mosquito Coast to be related to this tribe and applied the same name to the Miskito Indians.

The last two theories can be explained by the process of folk-etymology whereby a phonetic change or phonetic transfer of a place name, led to a semantic change.

However hard we try to find a satisfactory explanation, there exists more than one etymology. Each of the above mentioned theories are convincing and, to a certain degree, also conclusive but it is not possible to establish the exact origin of the terms, both for the ethnic group and the region.

As far as the geographical terminology is concerned it can be equally confusing: For example on maps and in literature we come across the terms "Mosquito Coast", "La Mosquitia" or the more modern form "Miskito Coast". In older literature and 19th century treaties, the ethnic group was referred to in English as "Mosquito Indians" whereas older Spanish sources use "Mosquitos-Zambo". In more recent literature the terms "Zambo-Miskito" but also the anglicized versions "Sambu-Miskitu(o)" can be found.

Throughout this book, for the region within modern Nicaragua I shall use "Mosquito Coast" and for the one in the south of present Honduras "Mosquitia". When referring to the ethnic group I have chosen to use "Miskito" and to keep the original Spanish spelling "Zambo-Miskito" (or simply "Zambo"), sometimes also using "Miskito" for both groups to avoid monotony.

The first European contacts with the Mosquito Coast date back to the beginnings of the 17th century. In the 1630s the region was a strategic place for traders, pirates and buccaneers to engage in contraband and to prey on Spanish ships. In 1631 the Puritans from the Providence Company established a first settlement in the vicinity of Cape Gracias a Dios and began to engage in trade with the natives. From 1641 onwards, after the Spanish extinguished the short-lived Puritan colony of Old Providence, the Puritan colonists who succeeded in escaping to the mainland started to found tentative settlements along the coast. Together with the Puritans came their African slaves.

---

36   Cf. For example M.W. (1732)

Apart from the slaves that accompanied the Puritans from Old Providence, the majority of Africans arrived at the Mosquito Coast after having been shipwrecked. Historical references speak of a number of slave ships and different dates but no details are given as to how many actually reached the mainland. The earliest record is of M.W. (author of whom we only know his initials) who mentions that slaves from Guinea managed to escape from a slave ship in 1639.[37] According to two Spanish reports a slave ship shipwrecked off the Miskito Cays either in 1641 or 1652, but both confirm that it was Portuguese.[38] A third Spanish source informs that in 1652 an English slave ship was thrown off-course. Apparently, most slaves escaped and started to live with the Indians in the vicinity of Cape Gracias a Dios.[39] We also know that by 1660 fugitives from Dutch slave ships which stopped in and passed by Trujillo and the Bay Islands had already been present in the Mosquitia in what is now Honduras.[40]

However, the sources do not agree as to how the initial contacts were made. A Spanish report, based on an earlier testimony by a former slave and the reports of missionaries, claims that the Africans violently overthrew the natives and intermarried with their women,[41] whereas Exquemelin who visited the coast in 1671/72 thought that some of the escaped slaves were taken prisoner by the natives.[42] According to these accounts we may be able to go as far as to deduce that after the first hostile encounters friendly relations might have set in which initiated racial and cultural amalgamation:

> *… en ese tiempo contentábanse con vivir bárbaramente entre aquellos gentiles sin aspirar a otra cosa y creciendo su número con la procreación que resultaba de las indias que atraían …*[43]

---

37   M.W. (1732: 284–298)

38   "Bishop of Nicaragua Benito Garret y Arlovi to King, 30 November 1711", in De Peralta (1898: 57–58) and "Informe del Capitán General de Guatemala, Don Pedro de Rivera, del 23 de noviembre del 1742", in ibid, p.121

39   "Informe del Capitán General de Guatemala, Don Pedro de Rivera, del 23 de noviembre del 1742", in De Peralta (1898: 121).

40   Gámez (1939)

41   "Bishop of Nicaragua Benito Garret y Arlovi to King, 30 November 1711", in De Peralta (1898: 57–58)

42   Exquemelin (1993 [1678], part III, chapter VII and VIII)

43   (… at that time they were quite happy living barbarously among these kind people without aspiring to anything else and increasing their numbers by reproducing themselves with the Indian women they tried to attract …). "Informe del oidor Licenciado Don Ambrosio Tomás Santaella Melgarejo, Guatemala, 3 de abril de 1715,", en De Peralta (1898: 78)

The conclusion we may be able to draw is that the process of hybridization occurred slowly and over time. It was intensified whenever favourable circumstances were present, such as the arrival of new contingents of Africans who succeeded in escaping from the slave ships that arrived at the coast at different times and at different places.

The Spanish failure to gain significant influence in the region gave the English *carte blanche* to occupy and found settlements on the Mosquito Coast. Due to the fruitless missionary attempts to found *reducciones,* the Zambo-Miskito as well as the other indigenous tribes were left relatively undisturbed and it was at this time when the first informal alliances with the English were formed.[44] When the Puritan settlers who succeeded in escaping the massive Spanish attack on Providence Island in 1641 went to the mainland, they gradually started to intermarry with the Zambo-Miskito and/or various indigenous coastal tribes. In exchange for "conjugal arrangements", they were given metal tools and arms (muskets) to defend themselves against their common enemy, the Spaniards.[45]

Simultaneously, the assimilation of Africans into the host society begins to consolidate. In the vicinity of Cape Gracias a Dios until La Mosquitia in Honduras the African element becomes more dominant (Zambo-Miskito). This enables us to locate possible sites of shipwrecks more easily but it also reflects the proximity of the first scattered English sugar cane plantations. During the second half of the 18th century the Zambo-Miskito became more dominant with the result that the less mixed Miskito (*"los indios puros"*, called also Bahwika or Tawira Miskito) were forced to resettle more to the south of the Miskito territory.

---

44 Apart from sarsaparilla, indigo, cochineal, logwood, hides and tortoiseshell which were exported to England, the existence of vast natural resources of a fibre called "silk grass" or "Camock's flax" (named after Captain Camock from the Providence Company) seemed to be very promising. It was thought that the fibre would yield a fine sort of flax or linen. After sending samples to London, the fibre was planted with great expectations on Providence (and San Andrés), exported and production of the linen on a large scale was initiated. (Cf. Newton, 1914:148, 168) Nevertheless this experiment proved to be a total failure either due to a lack of interest of the English manufacturers or because they did not have the know-how of extracting the fibre from the rind of the leaf or both. Finally, as stated in a letter of complaint from the Company's directors to the Governor, "… at least on one instance, the fibre served to feed the cattle …" (PRO, I:I:237).

45 From this time onwards Spanish authorities of the Province of Nicaragua increasingly mention attacks by mulattoes o *sambos* and consequently start to identify the Miskito as a different ethnic group with the name of "mosquitos". Cf. for example AGI, Guatemala, 297, 50–61, "Informe de Fray de la Concepción."

Due to the importance the racial and cultural mixture was to assume in the future interactions between the Miskito and the English, at this point it is essential to pay more attention to the process of hybridization which was very complex and manifested itself in many different ways. In simple terms, the Miskito emerged from the interbreeding of Indians of pure blood with Africans and Europeans. However, from now on it becomes much more complicated making it necessary to start differentiating within the group: When the African element is considered to be more dominant, they are called Zambo-Miskito, and when the latter start intermarrying with Europeans, strictly speaking, they would then become Zambo-Miskito, i.e. "mulattoes".

The miscegenation not only initiates the differentiation of the indigenous Bahwika from the other Amerindian subgroups, at the same time also consolidates the economic alliance the Miskito had begun to form with the English in the meantime. In this context it is worth mentioning that the social and economic ties the Miskito and Zambo-Miskito "mulattoes" were able to maintain with the Europeans seem to have been much closer as compared to those the natives of pure blood had with the latter. This makes sense since the offspring of the first group had a European father and an Indian or Zambo mother.[46]

Towards the end of the 17th century the English had established a strong alliance with the Miskito and Zambo-Miskito. In order to strengthen this alliance the English legitimize the Miskito chieftain and nominate him as "King of Mosquitia". From the first decades of the 18th century onwards the Miskito had developed a loosely structured political entity with a Zambo king as figurehead of the state. Control was broken up between the king, a Zambo general and various liaison officers who were in charge of the northern regions of the terri-

---

46 Despite the fact that this subject is far beyond the scope of this paper, I consider it important to add a few comments here: First of all, we must bear in mind that the first Europeans who settled on this coast were individualists who did not have to justify their actions to the colonial powers of the time nor the obligation to fulfil the expectations of official colonizing agencies. They were far away from other people of their own culture and not bound to the rules of conduct of their homeland. Therefore, from the very start, the preconditions for racial mixture were very different, thus facilitating integration in both ways. As far as the Africans are concerned their assimilation was relatively free of conflict and there exists the possibility that this was due to the many similarities between the host society and their traditional African cultures. This may have been one of the reasons why the Miskito, regardless of whether they consider themselves "Miskito of pure blood", "Miskito-mulattoes" or "Zambo-Miskito", emerged as a cultural entity, albeit amalgamated. To complete the picture of the different shades of racial mixture on the Mosquito Coast, miscegenation also took place between white and black (Creole) and white and Indian (mestizo).

tory and an Indian governor and admiral in the south.[47] This political system allowed the Miskito Kingdom to achieve relative stability. For almost 240 years the Miskito were able to maintain their independence, first from Spain, then from the Federation of Central American States and, beginning in 1848 until 1894, from Nicaragua.

The harmonious relationship between the Miskito and the English and the institution of a kingdom was for the benefit of both parties concerned. In view of the fact that maintaining good relations with the kingdom could prove to be useful in the future, the Earl of Warwick of the Providence Company invited the Miskito chief's son to London in 1632. Upon the death of his father he became king initiating the line of hereditary Miskito Kings loyal to the British crown.[48]

For the English the new political and administrative system on the Mosquito Coast proved to be very useful in establishing the first commercial activities on the coast. From 1631 onwards the Puritans from Old Providence started to found settlements on the mainland. They established small plantations of sugar, indigo and coconut, cut logwood and pine, collected other forest products such as chicle (the gum of the sarsaparilla tree and main ingredient in chewing gum) and maintained trade relations with both the indigenous tribes and the Spanish colonies in the interior.

After 1655, the year the English captured Jamaica, the region developed as an important strategic base for all future commercial transactions within Central America. During the reign of Charles II (1661–1685), the Miskito King was once more invited to London and even received in audience at court.[49]

In the 18th century Miskito forces rendered military service to the British on various occasions: To counteract the insurrections of the *maroons* in Jamaica in 1731 and 1795 (the Maroon Wars)[50] and during the American War of Independence when Great Britain succeeded in temporarily securing Florida in 1763.[51]

---

47   Cf. also the accounts of M.W. (1732: 285–290)

48   Cf. the travel accounts of Sloane (1707:xvi-xxvii)

49   Cf. M.W. (1732: 284–298) and Olien (1983: 198–241)

50   The term derives from *cimarrón*, the name given to rebellious runaway slaves who formed independent settlements in the mountainous interior of Jamaica. They are considered to have been the descendants of African slaves and mulattoes who escaped Spanish plantations when Jamaica was captured by the British in 1655. The *maroons* mixed with what was left of the indigenous Arawak and Taino and established free communities maintaining their freedom and independence for generations.

51   Twenty years later, in 1783, Florida once more came under Spanish rule by the Treaty of Versailles.

As far as the Zambo-Miskito were concerned, the formation of an official Kingdom of Mosquitia helped to consolidate their position over the other ethnic groups in the region. From their origin in the vicinity of Cape Gracias a Dios, they dispersed along the entire littoral displacing and subduing other Amerindian groups such as the Paya of present Honduras and the Sumu, Rama and Prinzu of present Nicaragua.[52] Once equipped with arms and having more power in the region, the "Mosqueto Indians" began their raiding campaigns along the Caribbean coast of Central America, from what is now the Belizean coast to Honduras and from Costa Rica to Panama. For nearly 150 years the Zambo-Miskito attacked Spanish held territories and villages of still independent indigenous groups often to rescue Miskito who had been taken prisoners but also to enslave fellow Amerindians in order to sell them as workforce to the British plantation owners in Jamaica.

In 1711, a Spanish report affirmed that there existed "… a population of 5,000 or 6,000 Miskito, of whom 1,000 are capable of bearing arms" and in 1739 it was considered that "… already 2,000 bear arms".[53] By the second half of the 18th century the Miskito Kings had dominion over 10,000 subjects who were obliged to pay tribute.

As to the Spanish, the third party concerned, it was very unfortunate that – despite the fact that they tried to exterminate the Puritan colony on Providence Island in 1641 – the colony had already thrown off shoots on the Mosquito Coast. By 1700, various small English commercial enclaves had been founded along the coast and in Roatán on the Bay Islands off present Honduras.[54] After the first settlement in Cape Gracias a Dios in 1631 followed Bragman's Bluff (Bilwi or Puerto Cabezas), Bluefields and in present Honduras Brewer's Lagoon (Brus Laguna) and Black River (Palacios, near Cape Camarón). In 1655, after

---

52 Some indigenous tribes were absorbed by the Miskito such as the Prinsu from whom the present town of Prinzapolka in Nicaragua derived its name. In their plundering expeditions, Zambo-Miskito raiders also reached the Isthmus of Panama but, according to the accounts of Roberts (Cf. Roberts (1965[1827]: 49–50), were never able to subjugate the Cuna of the San Blas Islands.
  During their armed incursions, Miskito troops also attacked cocoa plantations in Costa Rica and Honduras and a number of Maya villages, for example the one located on Moho Cay near the mouth of the Belize River. Cf. Conzemius (1932: 45,87)

53 "Report of Fray Benito Garret y Arboli [bishop of Nicaragua] on the Mosquito Indians and instructions as to how to reduce them", in De Peralta (1898: 59).

54 The English had already manifested an interest in the Bay Islands in 1638 when a Puritan colony of short duration was founded. For details on the history of the Bay Islands see, for example, Parsons (1954), Sandtner (1985), Floyd (1967), Sauer (1966), Valladares (1939) and Conzemius (1932).

having captured Jamaica, the English for the first time announced their intention to establish a protectorate on the Mosquito Coast.

In the beginning of the 18th century, as a result of the constant threats on behalf of the Spanish, the Zambo king ceded Miskito territory to the British, in exchange for protection from the Spanish. In 1740, the Treaty of Friendship and Alliance was signed and the Kingdom of Mosquitia was officially transformed into the semi-official British Protectorate of Mosquitia. The British dispatched a superintendent from Jamaica who established himself in Black River. Apart from being an advisor to the king, his missions included the codification of laws and land grants but above all laying the groundwork for the establishment of a formal protectorate. The king resided in Sandy Bay, south of present Cape Gracias a Dios. In 1766, 1,500 white people, 4,500 African slaves and 10,000 Miskito were said to have lived on the Mosquito Coast.[55] The Miskito Indians were made business associates and the towns of Black River and Bluefields came to be the most important commercial centres of the coast. Export goods such as sarsaparilla, mahogany, dyewood (indigo, cochineal, and logwood), hides, tortoiseshell, cocoa as well as cattle, turtles and manatees sold as provisions for ships, were exchanged for European commodities: solid iron and iron tools, firearms, crockery, soap, construction wood, fabrics, salt, oil and rum.

In order to guarantee the continuing loyalty of the Miskito kings the British maintained close diplomatic contacts with the kingdom. They started taking care of the education of members of the royal family sending them to Jamaica, British Honduras (Belize) and/or Great Britain or posting British teachers to the Mosquito Coast. So far so good but as stated by the traveller Roberts, in the case of King Frederic Augustus (assassinated in 1824) the education in Jamaica did not seem to have been of much use and

> … it is to be regretted that he did not receive a European education rather than a West Indian. By the former he would have had a fair chance at acquiring correct habits and some idea of order and of the importance of a good government whereas by the latter he became possessed of very little useful information and had an opportunity of engrafting the bad qualities of a European and Creole upon the vicious propensities of the Samboe and the capricious disposition of the Indian by which his life was embittered and his ultimate destruction caused.

King Frederic Augustus is said to have been

---

55 Cf. Gámez (1939:111)

… generally in a state of intoxication … [and his] good resolutions and endeavours at amendment constantly vanished when they were put in competition with the pleasures of the bottle and his other vicious propensities.[56]

Since the initial contact the Miskito adopted English names and have worn European-style clothing. Especially the "royal family" attached great importance to dressing "in true English Gentlemen fashion", according to the descriptions and observations by the traveller Roberts and Young, a trader who resided in the region in the 1830s.[57]

After having taken the above detour we can summarize the following: The Mosquito Coast came to be of fundamental importance for the British, not only for the supply and exportation of natural resources but also as an ideal strategic location for slave trade and the distribution of contraband. Owing to the good relations with the Kingdom of Mosquitia, the British enclaves on the coast (with Black River as headquarters) were able to consolidate as a platform by which Great Britain carried out her commercial transactions to the rest of Central America, North America, Jamaica and Europe and vice versa.

Let us now, at last, turn to the role the Mosquito Coast played for the development of the British settlement in the Bay of Honduras. The first direct contacts with the "Bay" (the name given to the present Belizean coast as opposed to the "Shore", the Mosquito Shore or Mosquito Coast) were initiated approximately between 1700 and 1760, during the boom of the logwood extraction in the Bay. In search for new economic possibilities, a small number of white "shoremen" of Puritan ancestry, accompanied by Miskito women and possibly also a small number of white "shorewomen" and some Miskito men began to migrate to the "Bay" (see Map 7). The Miskito men, being renowned harpooners, proved to be of invaluable help because they were very good at catching turtles and manatees, an important source of protein at the time.

The "Shore" also functioned as a temporary place of refuge for the British logwood cutters in the Bay of Honduras, a historical fact often underestimated: On the two occasions that the loggers were expelled by the Spanish (in 1730 and in 1754) they always had the possibility to go further south until reaching a settlement of their compatriots on the coast. In Black River, the most important British settlement of the time, and situated in present Honduras in the north of the Miskito territory, they found shelter before returning to the Bay where they continued their woodcutting activities.

---

56   Roberts (1965[1827]:148–150)
57   Ibid., p. 76,77 and Young (1842:33)

In the last decades of the 18th century the Spanish started to show an interest in the Mosquito Coast and increased their pressure on the remaining British population along the Mosquito Shore. In 1779, some settlers, accompanied by their Miskito labourers, went to Roatán, only to be driven out from there a few years later in 1783, following the Treaty of Versailles. According to the terms of this treaty, Great Britain not only formally acknowledged the independence of the United States but, among other issues, also agreed to abandon her claims to the Mosquito Coast and evacuate her residents from the British enclaves as well as from Roatán.

In return and as shall be discussed in detail in the following chapter, the Spanish officially authorise the settlement of the logwood cutters in *"la provincia de Yucatán"*,[58] i.e. in parts of the future Belize, between the Río Hondo, New River and Walix River (River Bellese or *Vális en Inglés* as can be seen on Map 8). In the Convention of London of 1786, Great Britain recognises Spanish sovereignty over the Mosquito Coast in exchange for a larger territory concession until the Sibún River. The Spanish, on their part, established the military settlement of San Juan del Norte at the very south of the Mosquito territory at the mouth of the San Juan River, a place which came to be of an immense strategic importance approximately 50 years later. By 1787, the majority of British residents (with the exception of those who recognised themselves to be subjects of the Spanish monarchy) had left the Mosquito Coast.

According to historical material, in 1787 a total number of 2,214 people (including women and children) were relocated in the Bay of Honduras to Convention Town on the Belize River. 537 were free people and 1,677 slaves with a small number of Miskito.[59] The rest of a total of 2,650 evacuees were sent to Jamaica, the Bahamas the Cayman Islands and other British colonies of the time.

At the same time the British were evacuating their subjects from the Mosquito Shore the Spanish made an attempt to settle in the former British enclaves. 1,300 Spanish colonists from Asturias, Galicia and the Canary Isles arrive with the intention of establishing formal settlements in Bluefields, Cabo Gracias and Black River. Three years later a fresh contingent of slaves arrived from Santo Domingo and Cádiz. While the Spanish colonists were decimated by disease within a year, the Africans on the Mosquito Coast began to intermarry with the Zambo-Miskito.[60]

---

58 *"Reales órdenes sobre la evacuación por los ingleses de la Costa de Mosquitos, 25 de agosto de 1783"*, in De Peralta (1898: 213–217).

59 Cf. Col. Lawree to Napean, 26 Jan. 1788, PRO CO 123/6 and *Defence of the Settlers of Honduras …*, (1824: 45–6).

60 Cf. Gámez (1939: 143,162)

By 1800, when it became apparent that the entire shore from Trujillo to Bluefields was ineffectively controlled by the Spanish and not successfully settled by them, the British started to renew their links with the Kingdom of Mosquitia. A gradual influx of British settlers occurred, the majority of them coming from Jamaica, this time settling mostly in the south of the Mosquito Coast. With the British population once more on the rise, the British continued to hold their unofficial protectorate over the kingdom.

From 1787 onwards, the year of the first emigration wave, the "Bay" was considered as the first option for re-settlement of the population of the British enclaves on the Caribbean coast. At last, the descendants of the first Puritan settlers of Old Providence had found a permanent home.

In the first decades of the 19th century, when the position of the future colony of British Honduras had already been sufficiently consolidated, the history of the two regions once more came to be interlinked. On three occasions (in 1818, 1825 and 1845), St. John's Anglican Cathedral in what is now modern Belize was the scene of a pompous coronation ceremony for three successive kings from the Kingdom of Mosquitia. This can be seen as the first step towards paving the way for establishing the Mosquito Coast as an official protectorate and reinforcing the position of the British in Central America.

The Miskito domination of the entire Caribbean coast of Central America and especially the importance the Mosquito Coast had for the development of the future British colony is reflected in the existence of numerous words from the Miskito language in modern Belizean Creole (or Belizean Kriol, a more recent denomination). Whereas a direct influence of the colony of Old Providence can only be confirmed by a very few place names of Puritan origin, in the case of the Mosquito coast we have more conclusive evidence. In fact, it is to the above migration and to future and larger migratory waves that the origins of the occurrence of Miskito words in Belizean Creole as well as the many similarities of grammatical features and lexical forms between the two languages can be traced.[61]

---

61 Although fascinating from the linguistic point of view it is impossible to go into detail here. Nevertheless, I shall mention some of the better known loanwords, which still form part of the everyday vocabulary of modern Belizean Creole. Among the many words I have been able to identify the most important are: *dori* or *duri* (a small dug-out canoe), *waika* (a clearly identifiable ethnic group in Belize, of Miskito ancestry and lighter-skinned than most Creoles, *waawa* (shy, childish, incompetent), *supa* (a certain species of palm tree) and *ibinha* (a kind of wild pig). Cf. Holm (1977:1–17, 1978) and Young (1989:5–8).

The language of the Miskito is a Creole based on the Bahwika and Sumo, native dialects which belong to the Misumalpan branch of the Macro-Chibchan family of languages. The Miskito language shares morphological, syntactical, lexical and

As we shall see in the next chapter, the British were to have an interest in the Shore for many decades to come, until approximately 1850. Between 1823 and 1840 British colonization agencies launched several colonization schemes to be able to re-establish permanent settlements on the Mosquito Coast. However, in the long run, the efforts to attract settlers proved to be unsuccessful. Apart from trying to gain complete control over exports to the rest of Central America and Europe, the ultimate goal of the British was to build an inter-oceanic canal in order to be able to compete with the United States.

In 1843 Great Britain formerly established the Kingdom of Mosquitia as protectorate. Bluefields is declared capital, a consul-general is appointed and the Miskito King proclaims a new constitution. When the possibility of constructing the inter-oceanic canal began to materialize, British troops, "in the name of" the Miskito King, with the help of Miskito forces and in presence of the superintendent of British Honduras, occupied San Juan del Norte, the Atlantic port of the proposed canal. The port is renamed Greytown and a superintendent is appointed. With their interests put in jeopardy, the United States protested and from that moment on decided to support Nicaragua in her claim to the estuary of the San Juan River. This controversy gave rise to the Clayton Bulwer Treaty of 1850 by which Great Britain and the United States were bound "not to obtain or maintain any exclusive control of the proposed canal or unequal advantage in its use". Both parties also agreed that they would not ever "occupy, fortify, colonize or assume or exercise any dominion over any part of Central America" nor make use of any protectorate or alliance (i.e. the Mosquito Coast and the alliance with the Miskito), present or future, to such ends.

Despite the above treaty (and two subsequent ones) both nations were incapable of resolving the controversial issues as to the future of the Mosquito and Great Britain decided to engage in direct negotiations with Nicaragua and Honduras.

In 1859 Great Britain delegated the territory north of Cape Gracias a Dios to Honduras. In 1860, by the Treaty of Managua, the sovereignty of the territory between Cape Gracias a Dios and Greytown was transferred to Nicaragua un-

---

phonological features with the above dialects. At the same time an African, English and German (because of the Moravian missionaries who arrived at the region in the mid-19ᵗʰ century) influence can be traced. With the initiation of the hybridization process between native Indians, Africans and Europeans, the Miskito adopted a contact language or *lingua franca* – the Mosquito Coast Pidgin – which, in turn, started to influence the English based Creole of the African and Creole population on the Caribbean Coast of Central America including modern Belize. At the same time, due to the influence of the Pidgin spoken by the Miskito, the English of the British settlers also started to adopt certain characteristics of Mosquito Coast Creole.

der the following condition: that an autonomous district be assigned to the Miskito people where they were to have the right to govern themselves under the command of a local chief who was to retain a purely administrative authority and the right to grant land titles. The treaty was signed with the understanding that the suzerainty of Nicaragua was "not complete and unlimited but that it is restricted and circumscribed by the right of self-government, conceded to the Mosquito Indians" and did not imply the right to "meddle with the internal affairs … and exercise any jurisdiction".[62] In 1861 Great Britain dissolves her protectorate for good. The Miskito King became hereditary chief and the Miskito territory an autonomous reserve. The power vacuum left by the British, in reality, was soon filled by North American commercial interests. Due to the fact that the Miskito hereditary chief still had the authority of granting licenses for the acquisition of natural resources, logging camps and banana plantations operated by North American companies were established throughout the region. Commerce flourished and the port of Bluefields boomed with steamships regularly arriving from New Orleans.

Since the conclusion of the Treaty of Managua in 1860, differences have existed as to the interpretation of the above treaty; especially with regard to the financial compensation the government of Nicaragua was to pay annually to the Miskito and the articles concerning the continuation of San Juan del Norte as a free port and the right to regulate trade and levy duties on goods shipped by the projected inter-oceanic canal.

New constitutions, institutions and laws were created but it did not keep Nicaragua from meddling with the internal affairs of the reserve and coming into conflict with the local authorities. After the last hereditary chief's death in 1865 the government of Nicaragua simply refused to recognize his successor.

During the years to come Nicaragua and Great Britain were incapable of resolving this abnormal state of affairs and it was agreed that the case be submitted for arbitration to the emperor of Austria and Hungary, Francis Joseph I. The award of 1881 affirmed that the suzerainty of Nicaragua was limited by the Miskito's right of self-government. Furthermore, they would continue to have the right to administer their own economic affairs and retain all rights to their territory's natural resources (precious wood, rubber, chicle gum,[63] coconuts, and moderate findings of gold and silver) and "the most profitable disposal thereof."[64]

---

62 Cf. Treaty of Managua, January 28th 1860, Article I of the draft, pp. 317 ff. and 372 ff.

63 Chicle gum is the gum of the sarsaparilla tree, the main ingredient in chewing gum.

64 Cf. *Award as to the Interpretation of the Treaty of Managua …,* 2 July 1881, Volume XXVIII pp. 167–184, United Nations, 2007. The arbitral decision also ruled in favour of the Mi-

Nevertheless, thirteen years later, in 1894, Nicaragua took complete control over the region. With the aid of a United States military force invading Bluefields, the Mosquito reserve was incorporated into Nicaraguan territory.

As for the Miskito territory north of Cape Gracias a Dios, the border disputes between Nicaragua and Honduras continued until 1960 when the region was officially awarded to the Republic of Honduras by the International Court of Justice.[65]

Coming to the end of this subchapter the main reason for elaborating the history of the Mosquito Coast was to highlight the fact that it is impossible to study the development of the British settlement in the Bay of Honduras without taking into account the influence of the short-lived Puritan colony of Old Providence and the Mosquito Coast.

First and foremost, if the Puritans from the Providence Company had not started to engage in trade activities with coastal indigenous tribes and the Zambo-Miskito, thus laying the foundation for future relations, the British would never have been able to establish an alliance with the Miskito and Zambo-Miskito.

---

skito's right to granting territorial concessions for the exploitation of the products above mentioned "… the utilization of the Mosquito soil can but belong to the Mosquitoes only …" and to "… levy duties on goods that are imported into or exported from their district." As to the payment of the annuity, which was destined for the purpose of improving the social position of the Miskito, Nicaragua was instructed to pay the arrears directly to the hereditary chief. However, the Republic of Nicaragua, who has always interpreted the terms of the Treaty of Managua in a different way, put forward the claim that she never came to exercise full sovereignty over the Mosquito Coast (although, from the beginning, it was stipulated that it was "not complete and unlimited"). Maintaining that whatever relation Great Britain might have with her former protectorate in the future, was to be seen as inadmissible "intervention". This recrimination on part of Nicaragua can hardly be justified since Great Britain is considered to have the right to insist upon the fulfilment of the articles stipulated in favour of those who were formerly under her protection.

65   At present, the Miskito territory is an autonomous region with limited rights and consists of two districts, the *Región Autónoma del Atlántico Norte y Sur* (RAAS and RAAN) and the Reserve of La Mosquitia (or simply La Mosquitia) in Honduras. The Miskito people were never fully controlled by the governments of Nicaragua and Honduras and even today, many Miskito do not identify with "Spanish" Nicaraguans or Hondurans, respectively. The Miskito represent approximately 55% of the total population of the Mosquito Coast followed by English-speaking Creoles (approx. 23% and Spanish-speaking Mestizos (approx. 15%) and a very minor percentage of Garifuna and indigenous tribes. In Honduras, the Miskito population is estimated to be 75,000 concentrated in Brus Laguna and the vicinity of Puerto Lempira. In Nicaragua approximately 67,000 Miskito were registered.

On more than one occasion, the Mosquito Coast served as a pawn of no little value during the negotiating of the territory concessions granted to the future Belize. And it was precisely these newly gained territories that were a decisive factor for the settlement eventually becoming an official British colony. Moreover, the mass return of previously expelled Baymen and the large scale immigration of Shoremen including slaves to the Bay Settlement played an important role in establishing the future colony's society. In sum, owing to the pact the British had with the Miskito King, the Mosquito Coast and British Honduras came to be closely interrelated throughout the 18th century and the first half of the 19th century.

1.4.3. Origin and Structure of the Settlement's Population

After this extensive digression it is time we returned to the second half of the 17th century and the first tentative English/Scottish settlement in the Bay of Honduras. Although we cannot count on actual facts as to the exact origin of the settlement's population, it can be safely concluded that the approximately 300 people who had settled in the Bay by 1670 and were engaged in the cutting and loading of logwood, could impossibly all have been ex-buccaneers. Many of the logwood cutters were honest men, veteran seamen or men who had failed to obtain a suitable occupation offered by the colonial structures at the time, and were in search for a means of gaining a modest income. At the time "Goin' to the Bay" came to be considered an activity which offered good prospects. Although logging was extremely hard work since the men had to work in hot and humid malarial swamps almost all day for several weeks, it was, as Dampier describes "… a Place where a Man through hard work, might have gotten an Estate."[66]

Let us assume that, for example, of the approximate 300 settlers 50% were ex-buccaneers, it still leaves us wondering about the rest of the settlers. The number of people from the first immigration wave from the "Shore" (i.e. the Puritans from Old Providence) was too insignificant to have formed the rest of the approximate total population mentioned. But where did the other of white settlers originate from?

According to the *Archives of British Honduras* the first settlement took place between 1638 and 1650 and the first settlers are said to have been shipwrecked sailors and English pioneers seeking refuge from the Spanish. However, although quoted by most contemporary historians, it is considered unwise to lend too much credence to these archives. They are nothing but a collection

---

66   Dampier (1906[1700]: 45–55)

of material from doubtful local sources and Colonial Office Records, at times poorly edited and summarized by amateur historians.[67]

A fairly convincing, but equally not documented, possibility is the "Wallace theory". The Scotsman Peter Wallace (or Willis) was the leader of a group of mostly English/Scottish buccaneers who were driven from the island of Tortuga by the French in 1640 and who may have gone south and stopped at Providence to help its compatriots in the defence of the colony against Spanish attacks. According to father Charlevoix, a French Jesuit traveller and historian (1682–1761), these buccaneers may then have gone to the Bay of Honduras with the aim of founding a settlement there.[68] But owing to the non-existence of conclusive records – and as the author of the *Archives of Honduras* above mentioned himself admitted – "… the origin of the settlement must therefore be left as a matter of legend and tradition until confirmation of the above accounts [i.e. the Almanacs] can be found".[69] And obviously, since most of the historical documents which served as a basis for the Almanacs have been destroyed by fire and hurricane floods, confirmation is not likely to occur.

It bears emphasizing that the founders of the first settlement, wherever they may have come from, did not have the luxury of selection as the first Spanish group had in 1533. With the possibility still open to move south to places hitherto uncolonized (present Honduras), it was easy for the Spanish to describe the Belizean coast "… as the most undesirable place to colonize …" There can be no doubt that one of the reasons why the English ex-buccaneers were able to settle on the Belizean coast at all a hundred years later, was the fact that this region was the only stretch of coast the Spaniards had no settlements on. Moreover, it is important to note that the first settlers along what is now the Belizean coast acted independently and not influenced by any spirit of imperialistic expansion. Therefore, they had to take what was left, no matter how unpleasant the climatic conditions might have been in that region.

---

67   Cf. *Archives of British Honduras* (Burdon 1935). For the compiling of the archives, Burden uses three volumes of *The Almanacs of British Honduras"*, which are no longer extant. Apart from the fact that these volumes were based on historical records that have long been destroyed (together with most of the Almanacs) they were written almost two hundred years after the supposed first settlement of the Bay Settlement.

68   Cf. Charlevoix (1730:10) and Dobson (1973:51).

69   *Archives of British Honduras* (Burdon 1935)

1.5. The Possibility of the Existence of Maya Settlements

Now that we have tried to find out more details about the early settlement of Belize, the question as to whether or not the area was still populated by the Maya keeps arising. As explained in Chapter One, the Maya were threatened by the Spanish *entradas* throughout the 16th century and according to historical evidence, most Maya hamlets were relocated the Alta Verapaz region and in the Central Petén, both in present Guatemala. Those who escaped Spanish relocation, showed a tendency to abandon the coastal regions and to retreat into the recesses of the jungle.

However, the Spanish were not the only ones attacking the Maya. The fact that in the 17th and throughout the 18th century armed Zambo-Miskito groups raided native Amerindian villages along the entire Caribbean coast, including a Maya settlement at Moho Cay at the mouth of the Belize River near present Belize City provides a different perspective: It would mean that the Spanish colonization efforts *alone* cannot be made responsible for the displacement of the Maya along the Belizean coast, but also the raids of the Zambo-Miskito, a fellow Amerindian group.

According to recent evidence[70] there exists the possibility that in the late 16th century some coastal Maya settlements may have been established along the Belizean coast, most probably under Spanish influence (see Map 5). These settlements may have served as a stopping-off-point for Spanish officials and merchants travelling from Yucatán to the Spanish possessions in Guatemala and Honduras, using the ancient Maya trade routes along the shores of Belize. However, these coastal settlements were largely abandoned in 1638 during a general revolt by the Maya resistance force of Belize, as discussed in the previous chapter.

It is widely assumed that the first settlers (i.e. the conglomerate of shipwrecked sailors, pioneers and ex-buccaneers) began to emerge on the Belizean coast shortly *after* the Maya "disappeared" from that coast, i.e. after 1640. Presuming the above evidence to be substantiated, it would indeed imply that these settlers were likely to have found the coast virtually uninhabited, which clearly must have facilitated the setting up of camps. So far, no accounts whatsoever of possible opposition from the native population have been discovered, which makes us lend additional credence to this theory.

The main reason for the early settlement along the Belizean coast was logwood, a dye-intensifier of high value to the growing textile industry in Europe. As logwood sites were near the coast and at the banks of the New and Belize River, the settlers were mostly concentrated in these regions and there was no

---

70   Cf. Jones (1990: 288)

immediate necessity for them to go further inland. At this stage it is important to emphasize that from the very beginning the first logwood camps were purely export-orientated and at the time, permanent settlement was not even considered. Only in the late 18th century and throughout the 19th century, when the British began to search for mahogany, did the woodcutters start to enter into the forest. This penetration into Maya "territory" did lead to serious socio-economic consequences as we shall analyse in detail in Chapter Three.

In sum, for the exploitation of logwood it was never necessary to penetrate further inland. Therefore, we may assume that during the 17th and most of the 18th centuries, the remaining Maya villages in the more remote parts were left relatively undisturbed by the woodcutting activities on the coast and at the river banks.

Although the above evidence seems very convincing, due to the paucity, unreliability and inaccuracy of the available historical records (the *Archives of British Honduras*), it cannot be verified *if* at the time of the first tentative settlement, the area was indeed unoccupied or to what extent it may still have been populated by "Indians only", "... they [the woodcutters] go to places uninhabited or inhabited by Indians only".[71]

Nevertheless, two things can be safely ascertained: One, within the area of present Belize, there was no large indigenous population to be displaced. Two, no massive or decisive European colonization was ever engaged in that region which could have triggered a direct usurpation of the local population.

After having thoroughly examined the historical background to the early settlement, we may reach a conclusion. As far as the origins of the Bay Settlement are concerned, until the present day, a satisfactory explanation has not come to light. All a responsible historian would be allowed to say is the following: Whoever founded the settlement at the mouth the Belize River, the nucleus out of which the colony began to grow, most likely was also connected with the establishment of a number of smaller logwood settlements along the coast of Belize and on the banks of the Belize River in the second half of the 17th century.

There can be no doubt that after Jamaica had been secured by the English in 1655, the attractiveness of the Belizean coast as an area for potential settlement increased. During the 17th and 18th centuries, English/Scottish subjects were continuously expelled from their enclaves along the Atlantic Coast of Central America until eventually, they all congregated in what was to become the future colony of British Honduras. Until the latter half of the 19th century, the unique and peculiar domestic history of Belize remained strongly interlocked with that of Providence Island, the Mosquito Shore and the Bay Islands.

---

71   Burdon (1935:15)

1.6. Etymology of "Belize"

From the mid-17th century onwards, the English/Scottish settlement near present Belize City became known as "The Bay Settlement", "The Honduran Settlement", "The Settlement in the Bay of Honduras", "The Wallace (or Walix) Settlement", "The Bay" or simply "The Settlement". It was not until 1973, that the country was officially re-named Belize.

As to the origin of the name "Belize", for many decades one of the most accepted etymologies was the traditional colonial view, the so called "Wallace theory" or "Anglo-Hispanic theory". Although this theory turned out to be nothing but a myth, I shall include it in the four etymologies I consider reasonably plausible. However, looking at the theories mentioned below more in detail, none of them seem satisfactory enough to be able to reach a definite conclusion.

1. First of all, in view of the country's historic background, it is obligatory to consider Maya etymologies. Among the most convincing seems to be *"be'lix"* or *"beel-is"*, Yucatec Maya for "muddy waters". One of the earliest records of this toponym dates from 1642 and comes from the account of a Spanish pirate who mentions a *villa* "at the point of Río Balis"[72], the future Belize City at the mouth of the Belize River. Among other documentary evidence for the use of this name is the diary of the Dominican priest Fray José Delgado. In 1677 he travelled along the shore of present Belize and recorded a "Río Balis", the name of which was given to him by an interpretor. In a correspondence to London of 1705 a "River Bullys" is mentioned. In the map annexed to the Anglo Spanish Treaty of 1783 (see Map 8) and the accounts of the voyage of Captain Nathanial Uring of 1790 we find "River Bellese".[73]

   On several Spanish maps (for example from 1785 and 1790) the denominations Walix and Wallix are used. One likely explanation for the appearance of these terms is that English speakers may simply have substituted the Mayan and Spanish "b" with the letter "w". Other maps state "Valis" which goes back to the same etymology. In the Spanish language, for the English "w", two symbols are used, "b" and "v" but only one sound exists. In modern Spanish, orthographic rules exist for the cor-

---

72 In *Auto y relación*,1642 of Diego el Mulato, the Spanish leader of a pirate expedition from Yucatán along the Belizean coast all the way to Honduras. Cf. also Jones (1990: 226 ff).

73 Cf. The Spanish documents quoted by Calderón Quijano (1944: 46–49 and 62)

rect usage of these two symbols but in 17th and 18th century Spanish it was accepted to exchange the letter 'b' for 'v' and vice versa.

According to this theory it would have been the name of a river that gave the country its name. At first sight, this seems quite straightforward but in my modest opinion, two important factors make this theory seem a bit shaky: One is that *"bel'ix"* or *"beel'is"* is a word from the Yucatec Maya and its usage would not have extended as far south as the central parts of present Belize, where the Belize River is situated. The second problem with this theory is that assuming both English and Spanish speakers adopted the Maya "muddy waters" to name the first settlement, this still raises the question why the Maya themselves called this river "Tipu" and not "muddy waters" *("bel'ix or "beel'is)*.

The Maya denomination *"Bal'itza"* (land of the Itzá people) I consider a far less probable etymology. Besides, it would be historically incorrect because the Itzá Kingdom was miles away in the Central Petén.

2. The French *"balise"* and the Spanish *"baliza"*, an anchored or drifting beacon marking the channel to enter the reef, have also been mentioned as possible sources for the name "Belize". Here, the fundamental question arises, why a few hundred would-be settlers of mostly English and Scottish origin (although there might have been a small percentage of French in this group) would have adopted a French or Spanish term to name their camp. Moreover, it is doubtful if such beacons ever existed. They would also have been noticeable by vessels of the Spanish "enemies" which, clearly, would not have been in the interest of the buccaneers hiding inside the protective reef. Seen in this light, the French or Spanish equivalent for "beacon" does not appear to be a credible etymological source.

3. The "Anglo-Hispanic Theory": In the opinion of the Mexican historian Calderón Quijano the name "Belize" evolved from the form the settlement was written at various times on different, predominantly Spanish, maps from the late 17th century and from 1783 to 1790 (see for example Maps 8 and 9).

According to this theory, the followers of a certain Peter Wallace, (the leader of the aforementioned group of English, Scottish and presumably a much smaller amount of French buccaneers driven out of the island of Tortuga by the French in 1640) would have named their first camp at the mouth of the Belize River after their leader. However, there exists a strong argument against this theory and mainly revolves around the unavailability of documentary evidence which would link anyone with the name of Wallace of Willis to the coast of present Belize. The fact that the letter "w" does not exist in the Spanish language may explain the corruption from the English "Wallace" or "Walix" to "Balis". And, as mentioned above, since it was permitted in 17th and 18th century Spanish to use both 'v' for 'b' or vice versa (for example for the only Spanish stronghold in Eastern Yucatán, Salamanca de Bacalar, both spellings Bacalar and Vacalar were frequent[74]), "Valis" was also in use. Spanish letters reporting the locations of encroachment by English/Scottish settlers mention the Belize River, which they take to be the "Wallace River", spelled as follows: *"... Río Bellese, que parece ser el Río Valis."*[75]

If we take a closer look at the different way the term "Belize" was written throughout the centuries (as shown in Enclosure 1), we can see how the Spanish mis-spelling resulting from the mis-pronunciation of "Wallis" or "Wallace" may have changed to "Balis", until finally becoming "Belize".

The above theory has given rise to much discussion. One of the reasons for this debate is that it is regarded as highly unlikely that the mostly British settlers and black slaves of African descent would have adopted a Spanish mis-spelling, rather than choosing to name their new home themselves. This is a view *not* possible for me to share but in any case, since the "Wallace theory" lacks fundamental evidence, it is not worth dwelling on this issue.

4. Last but not least, the possibility of an African etymology should also be contemplated: For example in at least three different atlases, I have come across a town/village with the name of "Belize" spelled exactly as it is today in English (as opposed to "Belice" in Spanish) in Northern Angola, in the province of Cabinda, near the outlet of the Congo River. Since the Congo River was, apart from the Niger and Cross Deltas in present Nigeria, one of the main transportation routes to bring slaves from the interior to the coast, an African etymology seems reasonably probable.

---

74 In 17th century correspondence toand fromt he Crown. In *Archivo General de Indias* (AGI), Sevilla, quoted by Ibid.

75 "... The River Bellese, which seems to be the Valis River ..." Archives of Mexico, 3099, Repercussions of English logwood cutting, Madrid 1757, quoted by Calderón Quijano (1944: 62). Cf. also the Spanish and English documents quoted by Ibid. and the summary of his theories (1944: 46–49).

Throughout various times in the history of Belize, we can detect a tendency to favour one etymology over the other. In the later years of the colonial period, approximately ten years prior to independence, the more imperialistically orientated historians had no desire for the name "Belize" to have a Maya or even an African origin, whereas from 1981 onwards, politicians and the general public have given preference to mostly Maya but also African sources.

The desire to come up with a sound explanation for the origin of "Belize" has always been very strong and in the case of such a peculiar place name it is more than justified. But however strong this desire may be, the fact remains that to this day no satisfactory etymology has come to light. Given that etymology seldom is totally conclusive and in many cases leaves ample room for interpretation, the exact origin of "Belize" will remain a mystery.

1.7. Social Life of the Early Settlers and First Economic Activities

In this section, we shall take a look at the way the first settlers of Belize lived and how they sustained themselves. As already mentioned, the majority of these settlers were English with a strong Scottish element among them.[76]

Logwood cutting was hard work, especially taking into account the hardships of the climate and the labour-intensive method of extraction due to the difficult nature of the terrain. Dampier, an indentured labourer who escaped from a plantation in Jamaica in 1670 to embark upon a far more promising career as a buccaneer, eventually becoming a temporary logger in Campeche and Honduras draws the following picture:

> *The Logwood Cutters are generally sturdy strong Fellows, who will carry Burthens of three or four hundred Weight … they are contended to work very hard.*[77]

---

76 A historical study (Davidson 1979: 49) of the Bay Islands (Roatán, Utila and Guanaja) off present Honduras may explain the domineering Scottish element among the early settlers of Belize. According to the study, the Providence Company – the agency in charge of attracting settlers to come to these islands – assigned Roatán not to an English investor, but to an experienced North American colonist, William Claiborne, who brought only Scottish emigrants from Maryland and Virginia. Throughout my research in Belize and the Bay Islands, I was still able to detect certain Celtic traits in the remaining few all-white, or mostly only lightly creolized, population of Belize as well as Roatán, Utila and Guanaja.

77 Cf. Dampier (1906[1700]: 79–80)

An effective means to compensate the hardships of their cutting and loading activities was drinking. An English merchant, Nathaniel Uring, who was ship-wrecked off the coast of Belize and was forced to spend a considerable time among the ex-buccaneers, "… had a very unpleasant Time living among these People, [a] Crew of ungovernable Wretches …"[78] He describes the woodcutters as a

> … *rude and drunken crew … their chief delight is in drinking until they fall asleep … where there was little else to be heard but Blasphemy, Cursing and Swearing …*[79]

The onset of the rainy season was eagerly awaited by the logging crew. With the channels and rivers being flooded, the logs could be floated easily to the coast. At the peak of the rainy season, the logging activities had to be temporarily interrupted. Armed with large supplies of alcohol, the loggers had bought "when ships come from Jamaica with Rum and Sugar …"[80], they moved their huts to more elevated ground and waited for the rains to clear. Dampier related that during the wet season, life in the logging camps went on but "… three foot under water … "and that alligators were a common threat to the cutters

> *We do frequently meet them … and I have drunk out of a Pond in the dry time, that hath been full of them … they lying with their Heads towards mine as I was drinking, and looking on me all the while".*[81]

Although it may seem that this rugged crew of individualists, the "Baymen", were mostly outlaws or living on the margins of the law, they did abide by some sort of common code of decency. The elemental democratic nature of bucca-neering-life continued to exist among the first settlers, and eventually led to the setting up of primitive political structures during the last years of the 17th century. In the first decades of the 18th century, Public Meetings were held during which all free settlers discussed their common business and defence. Once a year a Magistrate was elected who exercised executive and judicial functions and had to abide by a strict code.[82]

---

78   Uring (1926: 354 – 358)

79   Ibid.

80   Dampier (1906[1700]: 79 – 80)

81   Ibid. p. 74 – 78, 82, 100)

82   Cf. Waddell (1961: 49 – 51)

One of the positive consequences of the buccaneer legacy was that the rough discipline and customs aboard ships were transported to the settlements ashore. The first-hand accounts of the French/Huguenot writer and surgeon Alexander Exquemelin, himself a buccaneer in the Caribbean until about 1674, provide certain evidence that the first primitive political structures and the first Public Meetings in the Bay Settlement must have evolved from the seventeenth century gatherings on board the ships. For example methods of allotting shares in the profit from the logwood business were based on the traditional models of distribution of the plunder:

> *... according to their laws [they] declared what they had; having beforehand made an oath not to conceal the least thing from the public ... Neither does the steward give any greater proportion of flesh or anything else to the Captain than to the meanest mariner. They then agree upon certain articles which are put in writing by way of bond or obligation, wherein they specify what sums of money each particular person ought to have for that voyage ...*[83]

As regards the first economic activities are concerned, the extraction of logwood was, apart from a few rather insignificant agricultural plantations in the south, the only form of land exploitation. The idea of a permanent occupation was, most likely, *not* considered by the early settlers and therefore the land as such was of little value to them, their sole concern being the logwood stands in the forests and along the river banks. When one area was depleted, the cutters moved to the next and the land valued most was that within easy reach of rivers, the only means of transportation. The land on which logwood grew was known as a "location". These cutting sites were acquired by the "system of occupation", in other words simple tenure rules which were drafted by the "Baymen" themselves. "Occupation" merely meant the building of a hut on a particular site. Only in the first decades of the 18ᵗʰ century a more formal code of laws was drafted, the basics of which will be discussed in the next chapter.

Apart from cutting wood, the ex-buccaneers along what is now the Belizean coast also had to devise a marketing strategy, which was, as mentioned, strictly export-orientated, since no domestic market whatsoever existed. The import of logwood into England was officially prohibited because the English were being very sensitive towards the already troublesome diplomatic relations with Spain and did not want to strain them any further.

But the loggers needed to sell their wood and partnerships between the ex-buccaneers in the Bay and English merchants were being formed on both

---

83   Cf. Exquemelin 1993[1678]: 82–117,217)

sides of the Atlantic in order to smuggle the logwood across the Atlantic and launch it on the English market. The Foreign Office vacillated to give the settlers any support or even revoke the royal ban on the import of logwood. However, as a means to reward Court favourites, the Stuart Kings had granted a special patent, which permitted the import of fifty tons of wood per annum.[84]

Needless to say, any quantity exceeding this amount had to be smuggled into England. Due to the economic importance of logwood, the government decided to turn a blind eye on the clandestine imports until after the English Civil War, when Charles II finally revoked the ban in 1662. The full diplomatic and economic repercussions of the beginnings of the logwood trade will be discussed on the following pages and also in Chapter Three.

In the south of today's Belize, the more agriculturally-minded settlers once more tried their luck with the planting of silk grass out of which a useful twine for the manufacturing of fish nets and hammocks was obtained, and the planting of tobacco. Several trading posts or "stands" were established to sell these products but overall, the success of the early plantations was very modest. The names of the present coastal town of Stann Creek (from "stand" and renamed Dangriga in the 1970s), Commerce Bight to the north and a group of cays close by called Tobacco Range, still remind us of these "stands" and the early commercial activities.

2. Consequences of English Occupation

In considering the consequences of the English occupation of Belize in the 17th century, it is important to emphasize that this odd assortment of buccaneers, pioneers and shipwrecked sailors, wherever they may have come from, began to settle the region without any initiative from the English government whatsoever. For the three parties involved, the logwood cutters, the English government and the Spanish, the diplomatic, political, economic and social consequences were serious.

2.1. Disputes over Sovereignty

Although the Spanish had not succeeded in establishing permanent settlements in the area now called Belize throughout the first half of the 16th century, they continued to claim sovereignty over the region. Therefore, the first English/

---

84 Cf. Joseph (1974:16)

Scottish settlers on the Belizean coast had, strictly speaking, never colonized but only occupied Belize and were, in reality, squatting on Spanish territory.

The Spanish, aware of this trespassing, condemned it as "*ataques filibusteros*" (pirates' attacks). But since Spain was going through the worst economic crisis in its history it would not have been capable of devising suitable strategies in order to retaliate on a larger scale. From the Spanish point of view, Calderón Quijano admits that the defence was

> ... *inadecuado, y que se redujo en el mejor de los casos aresistir a los filibusteros en los lugares donde atacaban, sin organizar un plan coordinado para expulsarlos.*[85]

Nevertheless, several attempts were undertaken to expel the English woodcutters from the Bay of Campeche in the Western Yucatán, the main cutting area of the English at the time, but generally speaking, these efforts did not have the desired impact. On the contrary, they encouraged the discovery of new logwood areas as the cutters were escaping towards Cape Catoche and further south on the east coast of Yucatán (see Map 6). The English, being aware of Spain's weakness took advantage of the situation and openly challenged the latter's monopoly over the early logwood trade. When the governor of Jamaica, Sir Thomas Modyford was asked in 1666 about the seriousness of the Spanish attempts to expel the woodcutters he remarked that "... every action gives new encouragements to attempt the Spaniards, finding them in all places very weak ..."[86]

Not until later did the Spanish become fully aware that the cutting of logwood was but a preliminary step to the growing of English settlements in the Bay of Honduras and along the Mosquito Coast. The expelling of the British logwood cutters was largely in the hands of the Governors of Yucatán and Campeche but often they acted independently and not in accordance with the government in Spain.[87]

Here, I consider it important to point out that *if* some of these *gobernadores* (governors) had acted in a different way at certain critical times and *if*, from the very beginning, Madrid had given direct and definite orders to expel the English from the logging settlements on the Belize River and its shoreline, it

---

85   ... inadequate, and for the main part directed only towards the pirates and the places where they attacked without devising a coordinated scheme to expel them. Cf. Calderón Quijano (1944: 46).

86   PRO Calendar of State Papers, Colonial Series, 1661–1668, pp. 359–60

87   Cf. for example Joseph (1974: 12)

would have been very unlikely that the Honduras Settlement would ever have crystallized into a British colony.

Prior to the 1670 treaty of Madrid where Spain ceded to England all its *de facto* possessions in the West Indies, the Governor of Jamaica, Sir Thomas Modyford, had been trying to persuade the government in London to recognize the Honduras Settlement so that it be officially included in the territories belonging to England at the time – and the "Baymen" would be permitted to cut logwood. However, the Foreign Office was apprehensive that such an action would endanger the diplomatic relations with Spain and was indifferent to his plea. In short, the English government was unwilling to properly recognize the settlement, This was very unfortunate for the logwood cutters in the sense that they were not given any support as far as their economic activities and the defence against the occasional Spanish attacks was concerned. Throughout the 17th century, the "Baymen" had to organize their own defence, the offshore cays serving as ideal look-out posts as the name for present "Spanish Lookout Cay" suggests.

Since London was not prepared to recognize the Honduran Settlement, it was *not* included in the Treaty of Madrid in 1670, a rather ambiguous treaty from the start, and therefore did not count as a proper English colony. The fact remains that even *if* the Bay Settlement had been included in one way or another, the name "Honduran" Settlement would always have been prone to create genuine misunderstandings. Compared to most of the more explicitly held English territories at the time, in the Honduran Settlement there were no boundaries defined as yet and the geographical term "Honduras", vague as it was, would, most likely, always have been interpreted in a number of ways.

In the meantime the woodcutters in the Bay, insisting their claim to be legitimate, continued to consciously operate outside English jurisdiction. This in turn was highly disapproved by Spain who officially prohibited the cutting of logwood in 1672.

The Home Government in London pretended to ignore the critical situation altogether but the English Ambassador in Madrid, Lord Godolphin, when asked about his opinions on the trade, suggested that

> … *if the English confined themselves to cutting wood alone, and in unoccupied places remote from Spanish settlements, the king might connive at, although not authorize, their so doing.*[88]

The English did confine themselves to the "cutting of wood alone" and were making huge profits. Between 1671 and 1684, over a hundred vessels entered

---

88   PRO, Calendar of State Papers, Colonial Series, 1669–74, No. 825

the Bay Settlement, shipping directly to England via Jamaica close to six hundred tons per year, and from 1686 to 1691, the trade almost doubled. Due to the presence of North American and Dutch traders in the Bay, the "Baymen" were also able to export dye-wood directly to European ports, via the New England states.[89] Naturally, this new facet of the logwood trade was highly disapproved in England, since the Crown was losing revenue from customs and the traders had to pay import duties.

In 1680, a crew of English loggers was attacked in the Yucatecan logging areas, imprisoned and badly treated by the Spaniards. This time, the warnings were taken seriously and officials attempted to put an end to the woodcutting activities in the Bay. As Governor Lynch from Jamaica wrote in a report to London:

> *I have forbidden our cutting logwood in the Bay of Campeche and Honduras [Belize] your Lordships having justly declared that the country being the Spaniards' we ought not to cut the wood.*[90]

This procedure, however, was a mere formality and although they "ought not to have cut the wood", the cutting and trading of logwood continued to flourish. The issue became even more complex when a number of different interest groups (merchants, traders, independent dyers etc.) involved in the profitable logwood trade in one way or another began to put their views forward. The dye was most important for England's nascent woollens industry of the time "... so essentially necessary in dying our manufactures that it would be of the last and worst consequence to be deprived thereof."[91]

Clearly, at first sight, this state of affairs was not to the advantage of the logwood cutters in faraway Belize. Not only did it affect trade but also every aspect of social life in the settlement, especially with regard to law and order and as far as the forming of a primitive government was concerned.

However, this abnormal diplomatic situation did not only have negative consequences for the "Baymen" and indirectly, it may also have helped them: If the English Foreign Office had recognized the Bay Settlement and if it had been included in the Treaty of Madrid in 1670, the woodcutters would not have been able to have their logwood shipped *directly* to European markets. Moreover, the non-recognition literally forced the settlers to stand on their own feet and

---

89   For more details on the exportation of logwood see Joseph (1989: 7,8)

90   PRO, Calendar of State Papers, Colonial Series, 1681–5, no. 668. Lynch to Lords of Trade 1682.

91   As voiced by a trader before the Board of Trade in 1714, PRO, Calendar of State Papers, Colonial Series, 1714–1715: 59 and 1733: 52.

set up their own governmental body with the advantage that local agendas, and not the interests of colonial rule could be given priority.

At this stage it must be emphasized that although the English government did not support the settlers by recognizing the Bay Settlement as an official English possession, it did intend to monopolize the logwood trade in order to gain huge profits from the trade and customs. For this to be possible, the logwood issue would have had to be incorporated into the complicate system of Trade and Navigation Acts, which controlled the flow of trade to and from English colonies.[92]

But it was exactly here where the problem was rooted: The Honduras Settlement was *not* regarded as an official English colony, neither by the English themselves, nor by the Spanish. If the settlers had been given open protection as English subjects, then the Navigation Acts could indeed have been applied to the settlement, counting then as an official possession of the Crown. But for diplomatic reasons this was beyond the bounds of possibility.

When the English finally did show an inclination towards recognizing the Bay Settlement, the most important issues were:

1. Was the Bay Settlement indeed to be considered as an *actual possession*? The Spanish had considered the other main logwood area, Cape Catoche (see Map 6), *not* in actual possession by the English and therefore saw the English claim to the above region unjustified. As a consequence, the Spanish decided to apply the same strategy to the Honduras Settlement. Spain's main argument was that the area was not in possession but only *exploited* by the English.

2. For this argument to be solved, to the Spaniards the following question was crucial: Had the English settlers indeed formed a proper settlement in the Bay, or were they just scattered wildly around the stands of wood at the mouth and on the banks of the Belize River? Whereas the English naturally had the tendency to be in favour of the first,[93] the Spanish view held it that the British settlers were simply *"... un conjunto de vagos que se rancharon sin sujeción a población ni gobierno ..."*[94]

---

92   The complex Trade and Navigation acts are carefully examined in a thesis by Cook (1927:IV,V) and a summary of his ideas is presented by Joseph 1974:10–11). Cf. also Dobson (1973: 60–61)

93   As for example reflected by the imperialistically-orientated writer Stephen Caiger (1951)

94   (... an idle crowd of vagabonds, who lived in primitive huts, were not established in a formal settlement and had no proper government). In Archives of Mexico City,

These issues continued to put a strain on the diplomatic relations between Spain and England until an official agreement was reached in 1763, at the Treaty of Paris. At last English officials had succeeded in pressing the claim for its subjects to have the right to cut logwood in areas unoccupied by the Spanish the settlement in the Bay finally received a recognized status. England was given usufructuary rights as far as the extraction, loading and marketing of logwood was concerned. Any agricultural activity (with the exception of modest subsistence farming), the setting up of a government or the building of fortifications for defence purposes was strictly prohibited and Spain continued to hold sovereignty over the entire territory. However, the 1763 Treaty of Paris did not solve the controversy for good and the matter was to be raised again and again during the centuries to follow.[95]

On the other hand, and seen in a much wider perspective, the commercial activities of the logwood cutters and the tentative establishment of an English settlement in the Bay of Honduras brought about important consequences for the rest of Central America.

2.2.1. The Bay Settlement – Its Importance for the Central American Merchants

Until the late 1500s, Central America's colonial economy was fundamentally dependent on agriculture, Indian labour and tribute. After the collapse of the *encomienda* economy, some privileged colonists gained titles to tracts of land and a rurally-orientated oligarchy began to develop.[96] Preferred regions for settlement were present west and north Yucatán, Guatemala, El Salvador, central areas of Honduras and Nicaragua and certain Pacific regions. The Yucatecan east coast, the entire coast of present Belize, the Bay of Honduras and the Caribbean coast of Southern Honduras and Nicaragua (the Mosquito Coast or "The Shore") were among the areas in Central America the Spanish did not include in their settlement scheme.

After the boom of the cacao industry subsided (from the 1630s onwards), the economy of the Central American colony started to decline vehemently and the region fell into isolation. Thus, for the Central American merchants

---

1017,14–5–725. The Marquis of Casafuerte to the King, quoted in Calderón Quijano (1944: 64,65).

95 Paradoxically, an agreement was only reached when the profits from the logwood trade had started to decline vehemently, due to a heavy overstocking of the market following excessive trade. For 1768, the price per ton was only £ 4, as compared to a hundred years before when it was £ 25–50. Cf. Table 1 in Joseph (1989: 8).

96 This phenomenon did not take place in Central Mexico and Peru since the major economic base there was the mining industry.

(the "Creole" merchants) it was high time they started to take action. Above all they had to look for an alternative "cash-crop", which would enable them to develop new commercial strategies. Then, in order to sell their produce and bring in European commodities, they had to find a way how to link them with the Atlantic market.

Whatever efforts the Central American merchants might have undertaken, Spain, the mother country, was forced to concentrate on areas from where precious metals could be extracted and was unable to absorb the Central American products and pay an adequate price for them. Spain was going through an economic decline and could literally not afford to send *flotas* to the Bay of Honduras any longer. Because of Spain's inability to revive or replace the degenerate fleet system, for the Central American market serious difficulties of transport arose: The Creole merchants could not bring their produce to the market and Spain was not able to support the colony by providing it with the required European goods. In addition, the heavy trade restrictions imposed by the Spanish King made legal trade extremely difficult and profit margins, if any, very low. On the whole this situation did not encourage the initiative of the Creole merchants. The logical consequence was a trade vacuum was created which was soon to be filled by increased smuggling activities.

Throughout the 17th century contraband trade was flourishing. Markets were overly satisfied and prices began to drop. Inspired by the desire to overcome this precarious situation, and attain economic independence from Spain, the Creole merchants grasped the first opportunity available and started to take part in this illegal trade. Thus, a vicious circle was beginning to form itself: On the one hand, the Creole merchants pleaded with the Spanish King for greater commercial freedom but on the other, in order to solve their market problems, they joined the illegal trade with Spain's enemies buying and selling their merchandise via a well-organized international contraband network throughout the Caribbean. Eventually, the market became so saturated that *if* a Spanish fleet did manage to sail, its ships experienced great difficulty in selling their produce.[97] Obviously, this was very much to the annoyance of the Council of the Indies (*Consejo de las Indias*) in Spain, who was even more reluctant to ease the trade restrictions, therefore not encouraging alternative, and legal, forms of trade.

---

97 In one instance, a period as long as ten years passed without any fleet arriving from Spain. In addition, Spanish traders frequently reported that fleets were unable to sell their cargoes in the Golfo Dulce region and Honduras and had to report heavy losses upon their return to Spain. Cf. Haring (1964:150) and MacLeod (1973:464) and various court records (*expedientes*) in for example *Archivo General de Indias*, (AGI), Sevilla AG/282

In this critical situation the emerging settlement in the Bay of Honduras came to fulfil a vital role for the Creole merchants. On many occasions Central American goods were sent to the Bay Settlement's main port, situated at the mouth of the Belize River. There, they were transloaded and, together with the contingent of logwood, shipped to Jamaica which was the closest large island, providing an ideal base and offering good storage facilities. The advantage was that for the crossings from the Bay Settlement to Jamaica and vice versa, boats which had long been rendered worthless for the journey across the Atlantic could still be used. The cargo was stored at the warehouses in Jamaica until fast and well equipped ships were becoming available for the transatlantic journey, directly to the markets in Hamburg, Amsterdam and London. The same principle applied to commodities imported from Europe. They could be stored in bulk in Jamaica, and, according to demand, were then shipped to the Bay and also to the island of Roatán for further distribution.[98]

We can even go so far as to say that thanks to the facilities provided by the Bay Settlement's ports, Central America was able to leave their subsistence economy behind once and for all. A good example is indigo:

Due to the expanding textile industry in England, a new demand in dye was created and was soon to be fulfilled with indigo from Central America. For the Central American merchants, indigo was the long awaited cash-crop substitute for cacao, which by now had lost its importance as an export product. Thus, the availability of transport facilities for the precious indigo was becoming crucial.

Fortunately for the Central American merchants the English-orientated trading post in the Bay of Honduras offered well organized and reliable transport logistics. The Bay Settlement came to be the ideal place for commercial transactions and increased quantities of Salvadorean indigo were carried to the Caribbean coast and shipped to Jamaica via the Bay Settlement.

For almost 150 years indigo remained a highly valued export product; from the mid-1600s to approximately the 1790s. Other Central American products shipped from the Bay Settlement were sarsaparilla hides and silver from modest silver strikes in Honduras.[99]

Among the cargo transshipped in the main port of the Bay Settlement was also South American silver and South American goods in general, which were brought to the Central American Pacific ports and carried across the Isthmus.

---

98   Cf. also Christelow (1942: 310–13) in MacLeod (1973: 464)

99   Although the exports of Honduran silver were of considerable economic importance they were not on a regular basis. Cf. Clegern (1988: 6).

As regards to imports, a variety of European goods the Central American merchants otherwise would have lacked (for example grains, oil, wine, livestock, horses and technological equipment for agriculture and the weaving industry) were increasingly funnelled through the Settlement's ports.

The increase of trade activities in the Bay of Honduras had a strong effect on the emerging Bay Settlement and caused several socio-economic consequences:

For example, in order to guarantee successful trading operations, it was necessary for some of the logwood cutters to forsake their career as loggers and dedicate themselves at least part time to trading. For the inhabitants of the English enclaves on the Bay Islands (Roatán, Utila and Guanaja), along the Caribbean coast of Southern Honduras and on the Mosquito Coast, the sudden boom in trading was a considerable incentive to move to "The Bay".

As a result of this migration, the population diversity of the settlement began to increase and the initial community of logwood cutters was soon enlarged by traders and agents. As far as the first forms of a primitive government were concerned, a consequence of the increased population diversity was that the making up of rules and regulations became more complicated. For example, now not only the interests of the woodcutters, but also those of other occupational groups, such as traders or fishermen, had to be considered.

3. Summary

We have learned from this chapter that the buccaneers in and around the Bay of Honduras gradually changed their strategy: Logwood raiding almost imperceptibly merged into logwood cutting and a form of semi-permanent settlement. However, from the early days, the economy of the settlement was purely export-orientated and no domestic market existed. The beginning of buccaneering activities in the area had helped to establish the importance of the region, and the news about the "accidental" discovery of new logwood areas stimulated the migration of settlers. Inspired by the substantive profits gained from the first illegal exports of the precious wood, the "Baymen" began to cut wood on a larger scale, but for export only.

However, since Spain continued to hold sovereignty over the region and England was not prepared to recognize the growing settlement as official English territory, serious diplomatic rivalries between England and Spain occurred. Meanwhile, due to the high demand for dyewood created by the growing of the English woollens industry, the cutting operations continued, a fact which was to shape the future destiny of this region.

The first English/Scottish settlers on what is now the Belizean coast and the Bay Islands off present Honduras founded the basis for this region to become a permanent trading post for Central America. Parallel to the increased importance of the region as a source for logwood, the Bay Settlement, due to its strategic location and connections with Northern Europe, began to be used as a trading entrepôt. The availability of the Settlement's ports not only played a significant role for the revival of the critical economic situation in Spanish Central America but also directly contributed to Central America's gaining full economic independence from Spain.

The Bay Settlement was able to maintain its commercial importance as entrepôt until the 19th century. The region as such (i.e. the future British Honduras) remained influential, although to a much lesser degree, for Central America's economy well into the 20th century.

The determining factor leading to a more permanent settling of present Belize undoubtedly was the regions' forests. The immense value of her virgin forests has greatly influenced the "colonization" of Belize, from the days of the first semi-permanent settlement to the final recognition of the territory by the British government.

Map 6: Probable Sites of British Logwood Cutting (1640–1770)

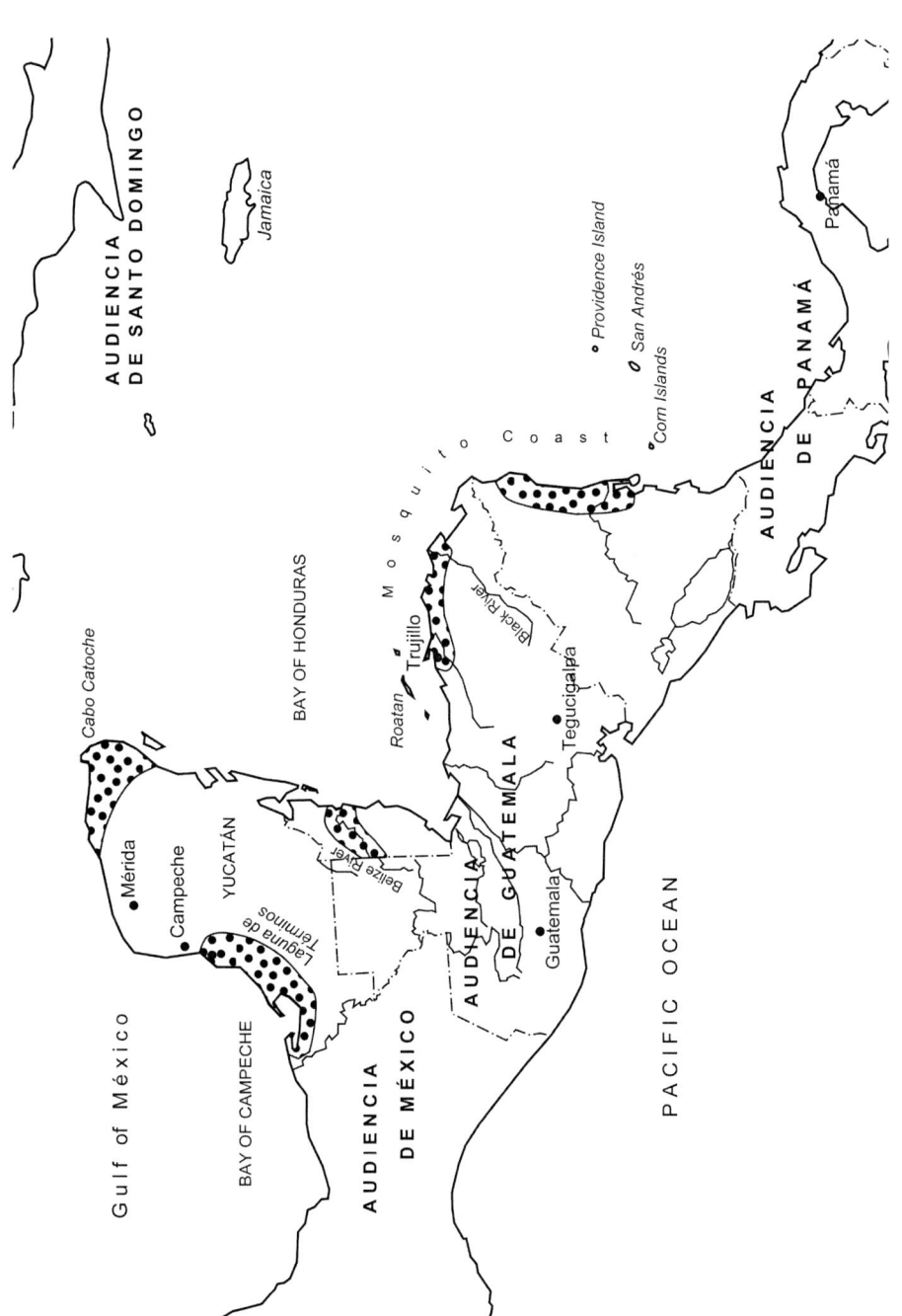

Map 7: The Western Caribbean (Immigration from the Mosquito Coast)

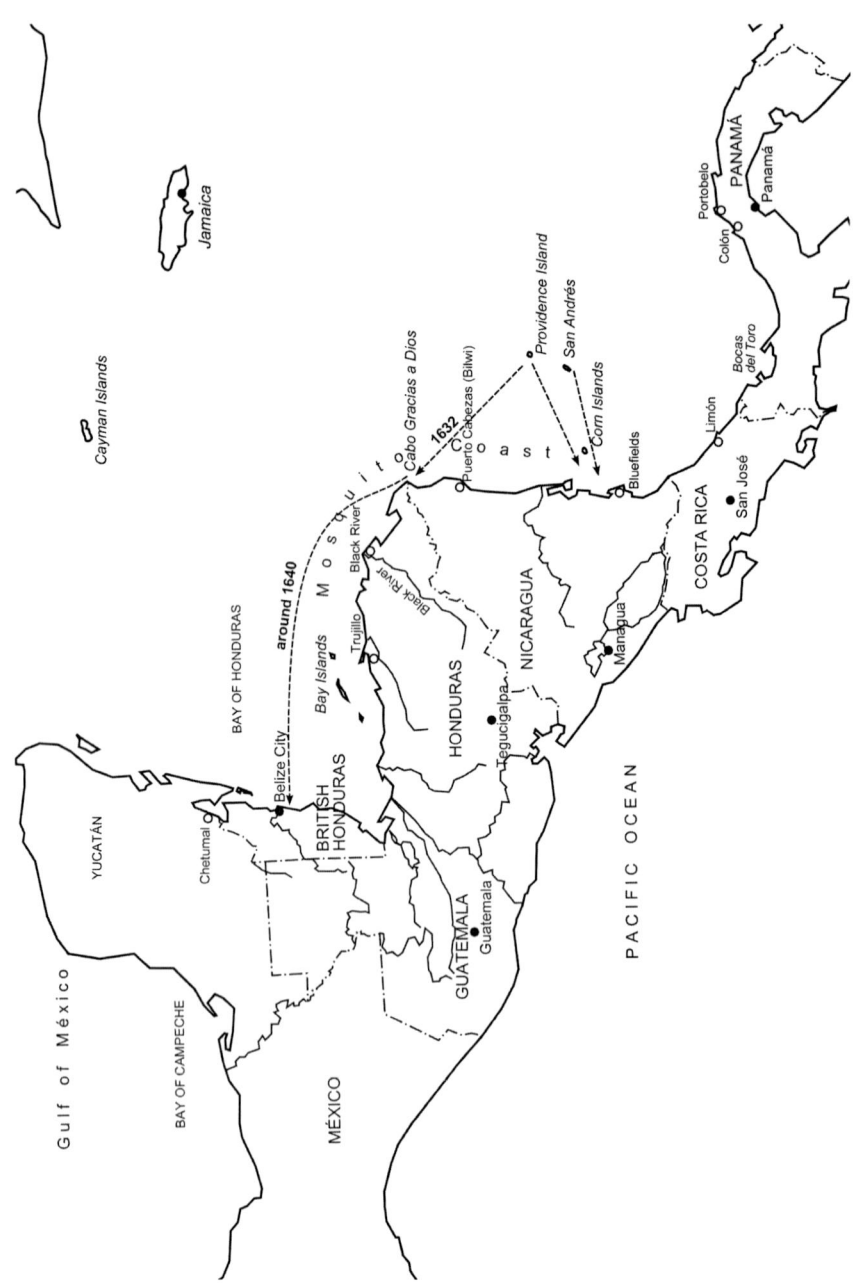

Map 8: Map Annexed to Anglo-Spanish Treaty of 1783

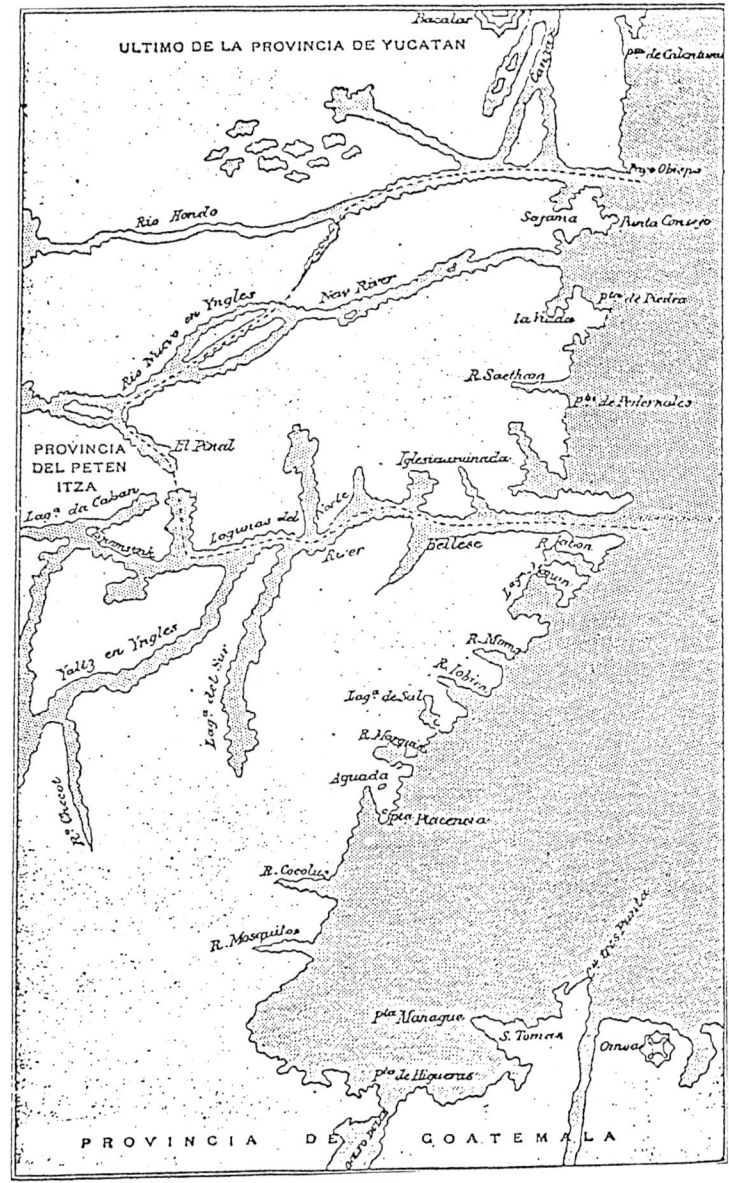

Map 9: Late 17ᵗʰ Century Map

Enclosure 1: Etymology of Belize

Wallixo	Valix,	Baliz,
Wallis	Valis,	Bellie
Walixo	Valix	Bellise
Walis,	Balixo	Belize
Waliz	Balis	

Chapter Four

The Bay Settlement in the 18ᵗʰ Century

In this chapter, and in the subsequent ones, the reader will increasingly encounter a number of different terms for the British settlement in the Bay of Honduras. Since the 16ᵗʰ century, the region that was to become present Belize had generally been known as the "British Settlement in the Bay of Honduras", the "Honduras Settlement", the "Bay Settlement" or simply "The Bay". On maps and in correspondence the Spanish described the Bay area as "Río Vális" or "Walix".[1]

Throughout this work, I have constantly retained these older, English, denominations. From the mid-19ᵗʰ century onwards, and especially after receiving colonial status in 1862, the region was called "British Honduras". The name "Belize" I have mostly chosen to use only when referring to the modern nation of Belize.

The main feature of the British settlement in the 18ᵗʰ century was the beginning of the exploitation of the region's forests. Until approximately 1770, mainly logwood was extracted, subsequently mahogany. Although Britain was not prepared to officially recognize the Bay Settlement and Spain consequently did not include the area in the Treaty of Madrid of 1670, logging operations were thriving. By 1705 the harbour at what today is Belize City, had become an important location for the export of timber.

1. The Extraction of Logwood

Of all the logwood areas shown on Map 6 in Chapter Three, at the beginning of the 18ᵗʰ century, the mouth of the Belize River and its adjacent coastline was the main region for logwood extraction. From approximately 1660 until 1770, logwood was *the* export commodity of the Bay Settlement, which, at that time,

---

1   Both forms are phonetic corruptions of "Wallace", the surname of the Scottish ex-buccaneer.

was far from being a territorial unit; no boundaries had been defined as yet and when referred to in Spanish documents, it was usually considered as part of Yucatán.

In the wider Central American and Caribbean context, however, the economic importance of logwood may always have been slightly overemphasized. Colonial trade figures clearly show that logwood, although being among the main and most valued trade items, was preceded by sugar, rum, cotton, indigo, and ginger.[2] In addition, we may assume that until the British gained the monopoly of slave trade at the Treaty of Utrecht in 1713 (the *Asiento de Negros*, which gave the right to supply African slaves for the Spanish colonies in the Americas), the initially illicit slave trade must also have been more profitable than the logwood trade.

Logwood was mainly used as a dye, producing essentially fine solid blacks and all shades of black and grey, but also purple, violet, bright red and rather impermanent shades of blue and green. In the 1670s, the Europeans had not yet fully mastered the art of dyeing and although the wood was valued highly in Europe, it produced rather fugitive dyeings. Exquemelin wrote in 1678 that the wood would be esteemed

> ... *much more, in case we [the Europeans] had the skill and science of the Indians, who are so industrious as to make a dye or tincture that never changes its colour nor fades away.*[3]

In the course of the expansion of the British woollen industry, the Europeans finally succeeded in producing lasting colours by using logwood as a colorant.

Nowadays, the term "logwood" is not as familiar as it was in the 18th century, and most likely only known to naturalists or historians specialized in colonial history. Therefore, I consider it necessary to briefly explain where it grew, what it looked like, and how it was used as a dye.

Logwood (Campeche wood, Spanish *palo de tinte*) or *Haematoxylum campechianum* is a medium sized, nine to fifteen meter tall, prolific tropical tree. The terrain most suitable for its growth is brackish water near the coast or swampy ground in the vicinity of rivers and creeks. Today logwood still grows on the Yucatán Peninsula, along the Belizean coast, on the cays and in coastal areas of Southern Honduras and Nicaragua (see Map 6) without having to be cultivated. It has a short, crooked trunk, a rough bark and branches twisted into peculiar shapes. Its leaves are oval, similar to those of the laurel, and the

---

2   Cf. Joseph (1974:8) who cites from 18th century export statistics and governors' reports.

3   Exquemelin (1993:134)

wood is heavy and extremely hard. The dye is obtained from the heartwood, which is red in appearance.

The heart of the logwood tree was only one component in the complicated dyeing process. Logwood, like most other natural dyestuffs, had no affinity *per se* for most textile fibres, and if one wanted to dye cotton and/or wool, the material had to be treated with a mordant first. The mordant, a special solution of an aluminium, iron or tin compound, was a fixative to guarantee a proper absorbing of the dye into the fabric. This is the explanation for why logwood was capable of producing such a variety of colours: Reds (in combination with aluminium), browns (on iron), rose-pink (on tin) or fine blacks (on a chromium oxide mordant). In the second half of the 19th century, the discovery of the first synthetic aniline-based colorants led to a decline in the use of all natural dyestuffs and also of logwood. Today it is only used occasionally, and when a natural dye is appropriate, for example for bacteriological and histological stains, tanning hides or to dye surgical nylon black.

In the 17th and early 18th century the extraction methods of logwood, i.e. the actual process of cutting and transporting the wood, although laborious, seems to have been relatively simple and the basic necessities (hatchets, axes, saws, machetes etc.) were brought in from Jamaica. After having chosen a suitable area, temporary camps were set up to gather the most accessible trees, mostly the ones close to the shoreline. The commercially valuable part of the tree was only the heart, which was cut out of both the roots and the lower part of the trunk.[4]

When the shorelines were progressively denuded, the loggers, usually working in small gangs,[5] were forced to go deeper inland to find logwood suitable for cutting. After the bark was stripped off, the wood, at this stage about a mere ten centimetres in diameter, was cut into small logs of approximately one meter in length. The sticks were much easier to handle; they could be bundled together and were left on the ground until the onset of the rainy season. By using floating devices made of palm leaves, the inundated terrain facilitated transportation to the nearest river and on to the coast.

According to Captain Nathaniel Uring, who was shipwrecked sailing from Jamaica in 1720 to fetch a logwood cargo from Belize and was forced to live among the logwood cutters for several months, after the wood had been ex-

---

4   "… we chip off all the white sap, till we come to the heart; and then it is fit to be transported to Europe. After it has been chipp'd for a little while, it turns black; and if it lies in the water it dyes it like ink; and sometimes it has been used to write with …" Dampier (1906[1700]: 57).

5   For example the gang Dampier (Ibid.) worked for were "six in company".

tracted it was shipped to the central storehouses (*barcadares*) near the coast.[6] From there it was sent to England where the bundles of wood were transported to special mills, in order to grind the sticks into a fine dyeing powder.

At this point it is worthwhile mentioning that, according to a historical source, during the 17ᵗʰ and 18ᵗʰ centuries, ecological issues in relation to the cutting of logwood were barely a matter of discussion among the British loggers and traders alike. So far, no records giving evidence of British efforts to replant the logged areas or to cultivate the dyewood as a regular crop in suitable areas have come to light.

If we decide to lend credence to a Spanish source, however, the Spaniards did seem to have given some thought to conservation: When they became aware of the activities of the woodcutters in the "Walix Settlement" or "Río Válix", Don José de Gálvez was ordered to carry out a *visita* in Yucatán and Campeche in 1766. He was asked to study the potentials for the Spanish to regain the monopoly for the exploitation and marketing of logwood and an eventual establishment of a dyeing industry in Spain. As the results of the survey show, on at least one occasion, concern for conservation by proposing the usage of careful and planned cutting techniques was expressed.[7] In the same report the woodcutters of "Walix" were indirectly accused of irresponsible felling and "... *abarrotando el palo como lo hace el inglés*" (... cramming the wood [into the boats], just as the English do ...).[8]

During the first decades of the Bay Settlement's existence, the settlers remained only a couple of hundred and profits from the logwood trade were lucrative. As long as resources were plentiful, it was relatively easy for a logger to claim an area for his exclusive usage and when the timber on one "stand" – or "location" as the logwood areas were commonly known[9] – was depleted, he

---

6   "When they have cut down the Tree, they cut off the Bark and Sap, and then lay it in Heaps, cutting away the Underwood, and making Paths to each Heap, that when the Rains come in which overflows the Ground ... they go with small Canows or Dories and load'em, and carry it to the *Barcadares* ..." (Uring 1926: 354–58).

7   *Informe de José de Gálvez en 1766. Archivos de los Franciscanos en Mérida.* Legajo 23, número II, quoted by Calderón Quijano (1944: 208–211). «*Se podrá cortar sin limitación guardando la prudente economía de no desarraigar los árboles, de que se observe la naturaleza para dar tiempo al retoño, se conserve la espiecie, no volviendo a cortar en una misma parte sino de 12 en 12 años ...*» (The cutting possibilities shall be unlimited provided that precautions are taken not to uproot the trees and respect nature by giving the shoots enough time. In order to conserve the species, after the completion of cutting, a site should be left to rest for 12 years ...)

8   Ibid.

9   In order to be able to claim a new location and establish a camp, unexploited stands had to be *located* first, hence the term "location".

simply moved to an unexploited region. After the logwood stands on the coast had been cleared, it became necessary to shift the cutting operations to regions further inland, thus causing serious socio-economic repercussions for the Bay Settlement as shall be explained in detail in the appropriate section.

By the 1760s, after the Treaty of Paris, when the British were given usufructuary rights to cut timber, the number of settlers had shown a steady increase. Consequently, the competition for land became stronger, although, and according to the terms of the treaty, it was not possible for the settlers to actually possess land. Since permanent settlement was not considered in earnest, land on which logwood (and later mahogany) did not grow was of little value to the early woodcutters.

Land, as such, was only valued in terms of its accessibility. The principal means of transport was the intricate river network of the ancient Maya traders and the rivers were as crucial as the timber stands in evaluating the importance of a particular piece of land. Without easy means of transporting the logs to the coast, timber extraction from the forests would have been virtually impossible at this early stage. The need to regulate the boundaries of the locations became obvious and in 1765 the Baymen agreed to a resolution which would define the methods of staking a claim.[10]

Another important socio-economic consequence of moving the cutting operations further inland was an increased demand for labour due to the changing nature of the cutting. When the woodcutters had to go farther inland in search for logwood, the methods of extraction became more labour intensive and the few Zambo-Miskito from the Mosquito Shore, who had been working alongside the White settlers, did not provide sufficient labour any longer. The settlers who wanted to expand the lucrative trade had to acquire additional supplies of labour. But they were unable to turn to the Maya, since the ones that remained – and were left relatively unaffected by the Spanish *entradas*, the subsequent relocations by the missionaries and possibly also the raids of the Zambo-Miskito – had withdrawn into the very recesses of the jungle. The only other option was to bring in African slaves who were imported directly from Jamaica, thus forever changing the demography of the settlement.

---

10 "First: When a person finds a spot of logwood unoccupied, and builds his hutt the spot shall be deemed his property; and no person shall presume to cutt or fall a tree, or grub a stump, within less than one thousand paces or yards of his hutt ... Second: That no inhabitant whatever shall occupy two works at any one time in any one River. Third: That no inhabitant shall claim a double portion of logwood works, under pretence of a partner, except that partner is, and deemed to be, an inhabitant of the Bay." Minutes of Public Meeting, April 10th 1765 and May 6th 1766, PRO CO 123/5, and "Laws of Honduras 1806–1810"; General Registry, Belize City.

In 1717, when the British were expelled from the Campeche cutting areas, the logwood trade in the Bay Settlement began to gain in importance and to become more lucrative. This expansion of trade meant additional labour force but by now, the settlers were wealthy enough to buy African slaves on the open market. The peak of the logwood trade was around 1756, when the Baymen were selling almost 18,000 tons of logwood per annum.

Over time the, by now very successful, woodcutters had converted into proper timber traders. Whereas the first ex-buccaneers had to devise their own marketing strategy (from approximately 1670 onwards the logging crews sold their wood to traders on Jamaican or New England ships in exchange for rum, sugar, beef and other provisions[11]) only a few decades later, the woodcutters/traders were gaining a huge profit by putting the precious logwood up for sale themselves at the markets in Jamaica, New England and Europe.

Logwood as a dye was essential for the growth of the British cotton industry. By imitating the texture and colours of material imported from India and China by the East India Company, the local industry was developing rapidly. But the ultimate goal was to try and create domestic substitutes in order to gradually replace imports. Without a constant supply of logwood, the development of the British cotton industry would have been significantly delayed, until alternative dyestuffs had been introduced. However, although in Britain, i.e. in Western Europe in general, the manufacture of cotton textiles actually had started and flourished with the importation of tropical logwood, its dye was not *indispensable* for Europe's economic growth of the time. The point I wish to make here is that sooner or later, the cotton industry *would* have grown, with or without the massive imports of tropical logwood.

Between 1749 and 1756, there was a sharp increase in the quantities of logwood exported by the year from the Bay, as can be seen in Table 1. After 1756 prices soon started to drop radically and continuously, because it did not take long until production came to exceed the actual demand (as shown in Table 2). As a consequence, the London merchants started to fill up their warehouses and reduced the price they paid to their suppliers, thus disrupting the entire logwood trade.

The drastic fall in the price paid for logwood was the beginning of a steady downhill trend for the commercial importance of logwood. In the second half of the 19ᵗʰ century less expensive synthetic dyes were introduced and apart from a short revival of the trade towards the end of the 19ᵗʰ century, logwood began to lose its commercial importance on the world timber market. The disruptions

---

11   See Joseph (1974: 31)

and decline of the logwood trade led to serious socio-economic crisis in the Bay Settlement.

Had it not been for the rise in demand of the new forest product mahogany, the very existence of the Bay Settlement would have been seriously threatened.

2. The Extraction of Mahogany

When the price of logwood became depressed the settlers had to find an alternative, the cutting of mahogany. By 1770, mahogany had by far superseded logwood as the principal export commodity and the demand rose sharply. Until the cutting of mahogany was officially permitted in 1786, it was done illegally.

With the expansion of the English luxury furniture industry, the Bay Settlement had acquired a new raison d' être: In 1783 it was reported that "… the mahogany consumed in Great Britain alone, is estimated at ten times the quantity of all the log-wood consumed in Europe."[12] Not only was mahogany highly esteemed by the shipbuilding industry and railroad coach builders, the masterpieces created by the designers and furniture makers Chippendale and Sheraton also made the beautiful and durable timber a much sought after material for luxury furniture. From 1805 to 1846, for example, the mahogany exports from the Bay Settlement more than doubled, as can be seen in Table 3.

The European demand for the precious wood, however, was far from being regular. According to an observer of the time "… a change in the taste for furniture [mahogany] to maple or black walnut would send it [the market] down for years."[13] Consequently, the demand and the prices for mahogany were subject to enormous fluctuations, which is one of the reasons why the settlement's economy was never very stable. Nevertheless, for more than 150 years – from the last quarter of the 18th century until the beginning of the 20th century – mahogany remained *the* principal export commodity.

In the 1930s the mahogany trees within the areas of easy transport to a waterway were becoming scarce. In addition, production costs were rising because the traditional system of animal haulage had become both inefficient and uneconomic mainly because it restricted logging operations to the dry season. This traditional system was in use until after the end of the First World War and was the only method of transportation. Alternative transport facilities were always extremely poor, and there was a complete lack of a cohesive railway or road system. Several projects for the construction of a railway existed but the

---

12   White to Townsend, 10 Feb. 1783, PRO CO 123/2
13   Gibbs (1883:117)

colonists were never successful to persuade the Home Government to help finance the building of a railroad.[14]

As a result of the inadequate transport facilities, the local mahogany industry began to suffer from the competition from Peru and Brazil and the mahogany substitutes from the British possession of The Gambia in West Africa. The industry suffered even more when, in the building of railway coaches and ships, mahogany was gradually being displaced by steel.

3. The Introduction of Slave Labour

The first African slaves brought into the Bay were mostly purchased at auctions in Kingston/Jamaica, but some were also imported from the United States.[15] In the Bay Settlement it was never compulsory to register slaves making it difficult to give precise numbers, dates and types of occupation of the early slave population. By 1745, the slaves already far outnumbered the White settlers and the settlement reportedly consisted of "… a small quantity of People, not exceeding above fifty White Men and about a hundred and twenty Negroes …"[16] Some of the descendants of the Zambo-Miskito (in Belize also known as "Waikas") who immigrated to Belize from the Mosquito Shore were also used as slaves, although the British government was strongly opposed to this practice.

From the 1770s onwards a considerable quantity of Black slaves was imported into the Bay Settlement from Africa. Approximately from 1730 to 1790 the principal sources for the British slave traders were the Niger and Cross deltas in the Bight of Benin and from 1790 to 1807 the Congo and also Angola.

In one of the first censuses taken in 1790[17], names of the slaves recorded include such names as Congo Will, Angola Will, Guinea Sam and Eboe Jack among others. Tribal identification must have persisted until well into the 19th century as an observation by Frederick Crowe, a missionary to Central America, indicates. He reported in 1850 that there were in Belize "Congoes, Nangoes, Mongolas, Ashantees, Eboes and other African tribes."[18] Members of the

---

14 As shall be discussed in detail in Chapter Five, several privately financed, short distance railway tracks existed but mostly only from the cutting sites to the nearest river. The operation of these lines involved the handling of difficult technical constructions and maintenance was costly. The rail lines were dismantled after only ten to twenty years and the two most important ones have had roads constructed on top of the former rail way.

15 See also Henderson (1809: 39) and Bancroft (1887,II: 626)

16 Inhabitants to Major Caulfield, 8 June 1745, PRO CO 137/48 in Bolland (1977: 49)

17 In: "General Return of the Inhabitants …", 22 Oct. 1790, PRO CO 123/9 in Ibid.

18 Crowe (1850: 59)

"Eboe" tribe seem to have been especially well represented in the Bay Settlement: According to the title page of the weekly newspaper "The Royal Gazette" of Jamaica,[19] auctioneers in Kingston offered first choice "Eboe Negroes", as can be seen on Enclosure 2. Members of the Eboe tribe lived in a particular section of the growing settlement at the mouth of the Belize River, the future Belize City. On historical maps, this section was still referred to as "Eboe Town"[20] until the 1850s.

In the 1780s, after the commercial value of logwood had declined on the European market, the Bay Settlement began to face a serious economic crisis and the settlers became more and more indebted to the merchants of Great Britain. The fact that the settlers attempted to compensate the decrease in the value of the dyewood by trying to maximize production meant that slaves had to put in more working hours. Harsh treatment was the consequence and the slaves were becoming increasingly dissatisfied. Here, I wish to emphasize that any harsh treatment of slaves in connection with the exploitation of logwood (and especially later with the extraction of mahogany!) was not so much a consequence of British colonial policy, but rather a result of the local efforts to maximize production and increase profits. The very fact that the Bay Settlement was *not* an official colony as yet, may also have played an important role in the desire and need to boost production, the primary cause for the cruelty towards slaves. The settlers were desperate for the attention of, and the recognition by, the British government. They hoped that *if* the Bay Settlement became prosperous and important enough, London would be more willing to declare it an official British colony, which was in the interest of the majority of settlers.

Fortunately, for both master and slave, the subsequent boom in the export of mahogany eased and soon solved the crisis in the Bay. Conditions were improved and the jobs for the labourers became more secure while at the same time increasing the demand for new labour.

Generally speaking, by far the largest percentage of slaves was employed in the extraction of timber. According to estimates, after 1770 about eighty per cent of all male slaves over the age of ten worked in the timber industry. The slaves who were not suitable for the cutting and transporting of timber were used as boat builders or in the warehouses, where also females and adolescents of both sexes worked. The latter two were mostly employed in the cultivation of provisions for the forest labourers and also worked as domestic servants, the

---

19   "The Royal Gazette" of Jamaica, February 1785 in Calderón Quijano (1944)
20   The Honduras Almanack for 1829 shows a map identifying Eboe Town.

so called "house-negroes". In 1806 there were approximately 1270 male slaves in the settlement, of whom probably 1000 were engaged in the cutting of wood.[21]

According to early censuses, and as can be seen from Table 4, by the middle of the 18th century, slaves accounted for more than seventy per cent of the total population in the settlement, thus far outnumbering the White settlers.[22] As long as it was possible to import slaves, their numbers increased. With the abolition of the slave trade in 1805, the number of slaves in the Bay and their proportion to the rest of the population began to decline vehemently. In the Bay Settlement and the British West Indies, slavery as such was not abolished until 1833.

At this stage it is important to emphasize that abolition alone cannot be made responsible for the decline of the slave population in the settlement; it was rather the consequence of several other factors occurring at the same time:

- **First:** High mortality rates due to the strenuous nature of the work.
- **Secondly:** Restrictions in the ability of the slave population to reproduce itself due to the practice of abortion and the large number of slaves escaping into the neighbouring Spanish-controlled territories.
- **Thirdly:** In the Bay Settlement – and compared to the British West Indies[23] – the rates of manumission were especially high.

Let us now turn to the subject of manumission: While in most slave societies in the West Indies, a slave was theoretically only able to obtain his freedom at his master's will, in the Bay Settlement, a significant difference existed. Because of the seasonal aspect of forestry work, the method most practised was the one that allowed slaves to purchase their own freedom with the money they had been able to save from game and crocodile hunting, fishing and turtling.[24]

---

21 Cf. Leon (1958: 219)

22 These early censuses did not attempt to enumerate the Mayan population whatsoever. First, they had retreated to the forests and secondly, they would for the most part have been outside the then existing boundaries of the Bay Settlement in any case.

23 Cf. Dobson (1973: 155)

24 Especially turtling was an activity of considerable importance to the slaves when off duty from their forest work. Turtling was shared with the poorer White settlers, who generally dedicated themselves to turtling and exporting the shell of tortoiseshell (*carey*). One of the earliest records of tortoiseshell being exported to Europe is a Spanish report of 1790: "*El carey lo proporcionan los pescadores tortugueros … suelen llevar también algunas porciones de carey a Europa …* (Tortoiseshell is provided by the turtlers and a small amount is also exported to Europe …). Report of the state of the export activities from the British establishment at the Walix River, Lucas Galvez to Campo Alange, 8–9–1790,

Another common practice was that the White men established relationships with their "house-slaves" some of whom they manumitted together with their offspring, usually at a symbolic price. The rate of manumission reached its peak throughout the first three decades of the 19th century, especially after the independence of Guatemala in 1821. And since the newly emerging independent Central American republics had already abolished slavery, many slaves were tempted to elope into freedom. As a consequence, from the 1820s onwards, the Bay settlers showed more inclination to manumit their slaves in order not to disturb the equilibrium of the settlement and to prevent the loss of their workforce.

With manumission being constantly on the rise, society was undergoing a rapid change. The major social divisions were not between Black and White any longer but between free and non-free. Not all Blacks were slaves; the 1790 census reported 261 Whites, 371 free-Coloureds[25] and 2024 slaves.

The possession of slaves was by no means only a privilege of Whites. Apart from the main White slave owners, Richard O'Brian, Henry and Edward Jones, William Tucker and Lawrence Meighan among others, "free Men of Colour" were also allowed to hold slaves, "possess" timber locations and engage in the trade.[26] At the end of the 18th century, a coloured man named James Pitt Lawree was even the largest owner of slaves in the Bay Settlement.[27]

Apart from the fact that the White settlers were dependent on slave labour – without which the Bay Settlement's forestry economy could never have been built – slaves also played an important role in the development of a population in the future British colony. Contrary to many other new world countries such as the United States of America, Canada, Brazil, Argentina, Chile, where White settlers alone were able to permanently populate the respective region,

---

Archivo General de las Indias, (AGI), Sevilla, (México 3023), quoted in Calderón Quijano (1944: 368).

25 Census 1790. General Registry, Belize City. In Bolland (1988: 35). The terms "free-Coloureds" or "free People of Colour" were used for freed slaves of mixed African and European ancestry, as opposed to "Black", which meant pure African descent. In the mid-19th century, these terms began to be used when referring to representatives of both categories. From the 20th century onwards, however, Whites and Coloureds alike have shown a strong tendency to use the expression "Coloured people" as a kind of euphemism for "Blacks" and/or "Negroes".

26 The first superintendent of the Bay Settlement, Colonel Despard, describes the Coloureds as "… very intelligent [and possessing] very considerable properties of slaves" (which meant approximately up to 22 slaves each). In: "A Narrative of the Public Transactions …", PRO CO 123/10. Cf. Bolland (1988: 37).

27 Ibid.

in the Bay Settlement, the growth of a population would hardly have taken place without slaves.

For the African slaves in the Bay Settlement the introduction of slave labour brought about a series of important cultural and socio-economic consequences: Among the most immediate ones were the loss of African tradition and language and the beginning of the social discrimination of Blacks. For example until well beyond the emancipation in 1834, political privileges were denied to Blacks and land ownership was not granted to them.

Another far reaching consequence of the introduction of slavery was the miscegenation between Blacks and Whites and the beginning of the creolization process. In the Bay Settlement, the offspring of Black and white unions, of which many were slaves, seemed to have been particularly well represented owing to the relative ease with which they were manumitted. As everywhere in the Caribbean the "coloureds" were regarded as a kind of "buffer caste"[28] and were treated with more respect. This, however, would vary strictly according to where exactly an individual would be placed along the colour-line. To this present day, the distinction of the different bars along the colour-line in relation to the social status of a person, is still made throughout the Caribbean.

3.1. The Slave Policy in the Bay Settlement – Compared to the British Colonies in the Caribbean

Compared to the British colonies in the Caribbean, the institution of slavery in the Bay was very different but unfortunately, due to the peculiar diplomatic status of the settlement and the lack of a proper government, historical material for the 18th and 19th centuries is scarce. Court cases were not recorded regularly and only occasionally was information requested by the British parliament (population estimates, returns of baptisms, marriages, punishments awarded) actually sent to London. Moreover, very few visitors ever reached the area during that time. Those who did, for example the US emissary to Central America, John Lloyd Stephens in 1839, did not penetrate inland, saw little of the conditions in the mahogany camps and, in fact, barely mentioned them. His travel accounts and his general impressions of the settlement, which might have been biased in favour of the slave owners, in any case, do not reveal details as far as slavery was concerned.

Perhaps it was this paucity of records that initially led colonial officers, historians and observers to believe that slavery in the Honduras Settlement barely existed or, if it did, was imposed with such leniency by the settlers that it was

---

28   Cf. Young (1974: 67)

only minimal. For example Caiger claims that "… they [the Baymen] became celebrated for their humanity, indeed their egalitarism, as masters". He even goes as far as to deduce that "mutual esteem, loyalty and even affection" existed between the Baymen and their slaves, and concludes by affirming that "British Honduras was an honourable exception [to the] policy of oppression and inhumanity towards the Negroes … practised in the West Indies in general …"[29]

Historical accounts that seem to actually give prove of the different treatment of slaves in the Bay Settlement came from traders, merchants and commissioners who mostly arrived via Jamaica (the Honduras Settlement – and from 1862 onwards the official colony of British Honduras – was subordinate to Jamaica until 1884). They were all positively impressed when comparing the slave conditions in the Bay to those prevailing in Jamaica and other West Indian colonies. Henderson, who seems to have his information based on actual visits to the timber camps, was one of the first to notice that "… the slaves possess indulgences which are not granted to their condition in any country."[30] Colonel Arthur, who was appointed superintendent in 1816, wrote to the Secretary of State after two years in the colony:

> *Although I came to the West Indies [as]… a perfect Wilberforce as to Slavery, I must now confess, that I have in no part of the world seen the labouring class of people possessing anything like the comforts and advantages of the Slave population of Honduras.*[31]

These and other similar statements succeeded for some time in creating a kind of myth and convinced certain interest groups in England and apologists for colonialism, to believe that in the Bay Settlement, slavery hardly ever existed: "… slavery can hardly be said to exist in the settlement …"[32]

In the Bay Settlement, the treatment of slaves might have been more lenient, but it would be incorrect to assume that there was no cruelty and that all slaves were treated with great humanity by their owners. Suffice to say that therefore, certain parts of the above statements most likely were nothing but romanticized misconceptions of the actual conditions of the time.

Nevertheless, and for several important reasons exposed on the following pages, we cannot but truly admit that the institution of slavery in the Bay was very peculiar, unique and different.

---

29 Caiger (1951: 26)
30 Henderson (1809: 46)
31 Col. Arthur to Lord Bathurst, 7 Nov. 1816, PRO CO 123/25
32 Ibid.

What were these factors that were responsible for creating so essentially different slave conditions which shaped the country's future socio-economic developments?

3.1.1. The Different Nature of "Colonization"

Within a few years after the first settlement, the Baymen, although only been given usufructuary rights to exploit the forest within limited boundaries, came to regard the area as their new home. However, they were not supported by England and had little or irregular contact with the mother country. This was a completely different pattern compared to the sugar planters on the West Indian islands, for example in Barbados and Jamaica. There, once their plantation yielded the expected profit, the planters had the tendency to return to Europe. Attorneys were employed to manage the estates and the planters became absentee landlords, never really identifying with the far away colony.

The settlers/woodcutters in the Bay of Honduras were aware that a successful exploitation of the timber was the only way of making a sufficient income and it is not difficult to imagine why they began to identify with their new home and were consequently more concerned for the welfare of their slaves. The fact that in the Bay Settlement registration for land ownership was not granted until 1858 may also have influenced the settlers to treat their slaves differently since they were their only property. On the large sugar plantations in the West Indies, overseers and attorneys generally were merely in charge of the slaves and avoided any unnecessary interaction with them. All that was expected of the managing attorneys was to achieve rapid and huge profits. There was no need to establish personal contacts and there was relative lack of concern for the slaves' well-being. The Baymen must have understood from an early stage that their future was dependent upon the success of the management of their slaves and this may have led to more personal contact with them.

3.1.2. The Different Nature of Work

18ᵗʰ and 19ᵗʰ century slavery in the Caribbean and in the Americas in general existed mostly in connection with the plantation production-system of sugar and cotton. In the Bay Settlement, slave labour had a different economic function as it was exclusively used for the extraction of timber, first for logwood then mahogany. The different nature of work created by the timber industry modified the organization of slavery as such and, consequently, also the conditions and treatment of the slaves.

The working conditions in a timber camp were different from those in a plantation mainly because the nature of logging required continuous moving from one location to the other. When resources became exhausted in one area, the settlers had to lay claims to new and unexploited locations.

Over the years a number of relatively small production units evolved, situated predominantly along the banks of rivers, creeks and lagoons amidst untouched terrain, both within and outside the concession areas. The "estates"[33] of the Baymen were small, compared to those in the West Indies.

In the Bay Settlement, in order to be able to get the "permission" to cut timber, a settler only had to possess a minimum number of four slaves. When mahogany superseded logwood as the principal export commodity, twenty to thirty slaves per owner was considered "… a very considerable property in slaves …" and at the end of the 18th century only one slave owner existed who was in the possession of 126 slaves.[34] On the West Indian Islands, one or two hundred slaves per estate were not uncommon, and the top slave owners had over five hundred.[35]

For the extraction of mahogany the co-operation between master and slaves was essential. Compared to the extraction methods of logwood, it was a more complicated operation out of which various additional occupations evolved: For example, jobs such as the huntsmen whose task was to climb the tallest trees in order to survey the area at a great distance to discover places where mahogany grew in abundance or the job of the axmen who had to fell the trees from an insecure platform above the ground.[36] Once the tree was felled, other slaves were responsible for the trimming and the clearing of the tracks on which cattle were used to haul the huge trunks to the riverside. All these new professions required both courage and skill, and soon achieved a considerable degree of status among the workforce.

The small size of the production units, the isolation in the forest and the different nature of work, made a constant control of the workforce and the usage of drivers and whippers unnecessary "… the name of Driver is here unknown …"[37] This too contrasted sharply with the practices on the large sugar estates of Jamaica and Barbados.

---

33 In Belize, the term "estate" had a different meaning in comparison to other British colonies of the time: It did *not* exclusively refer to a defined area of land, for example a plantation, but it included both the claims of cutting areas, the "location", *and* the number of slaves a cutter owned. Until 1858, when proper land ownership was given and land registration became compulsory, the size of an "estate" was measured by the wealth of the settler and the number of slaves he possessed.

34 "A Narrative of Publick Transactions …", PRO CO 123/10 mentioned in Bolland (1977: 45).

35 See Williams (1970), Klein (1986) and Brathwaite (1971: 121).

36 Cf. the accounts of Captain Henderson (1809: 47–50).

37 Maj. Gen. Pye to Earl Bathurst, 26 July 1822, *Archives of Belize,* (AB) R.2

In the Bay Settlement, Whites and Blacks alike had to cope with the isolation and dangers in the rainforest. Since only one or two White loggers lived in remote isolation among a crew of healthy, strong, and well acclimatized slaves, it was in the Whites' own interest to treat their work-force well and to establish and maintain a reasonably amicable master-slave relationship. Unlike the West Indies, only a small amount of slaves per camp existed "… the gangs of negroes employed [in a location] consist of from ten to fifty each … "[38], which prevented the spread of solidarity among the slaves, at the same time encouraging teamwork and fellowship in the entire crew.

From the 1770s onwards the mahogany industry – *the* only industry in the Bay Settlement – yielded considerably high profits, and contractors were eager to promote and expand their business. In order to be able to do so, it was vital to secure the supply of labour first. This, however, was not so easy an undertaking. Due to the problem of fugitives labour began to get dangerously scarce and contractors had to agree to offer certain incentives: For example mahogany workers normally were required to work only five days a week, and sometimes only until midday. That way they were free to work for other contractors at the weekend and/or to cultivate subsistence crops ("making plantations"[39]). Moreover, due to the seasonal nature of the work, there were long periods of standstills when the slaves were free to return to the settlement on the mouth of the Belize River and pursue their own interests. Compared to the harsh conditions on the sugar and cotton plantations, the working conditions in the Bay must have seemed very attractive.

But on no account should these somewhat more liberal working conditions lead us to believe that the slaves in the forest had an easy job. According to excerpts published from evidence submitted to the slavery committee of the House of Lords in 1833, work in the timber camps was considered to be "decidedly heavier than the work of a field negro on a sugar estate …"[40]

In this context it is interesting to mention that to this very day several former mahogany camps, now small villages and hamlets mostly in the southern districts of modern Belize, still exist. Meaningful place names such as "Hellgate", "Go to Hell Camp" and "*Salsipuedes*" (Spanish for "get out if you can"), marked on Map 10, speak for themselves and are a testimony of the difficult working conditions in the timber industry at the time.

---

38   Henderson (1809: 47)

39   Belizeans today still use this expression when referring to the cultivation of subsistence crops, such as rice, beans, corn, plantains, pineapples, and melons.

40   From: "Letters from Legion": Second Letter, Anonymous (1833: 16, 116–122) quoted by Young (1974: 69).

3.1.3. The Higher Monetary Value of Slaves

Since the settlers were unable to obtain legal title to land, they had most of their capital invested in slaves. Only the fittest slaves could be used for timber work and buying slaves at the auctions was both costly and time consuming. Not only was the purchasing price very high, the expenses for the slaves' upkeep were also considerable: Most food had to be imported because the few subsistence crops the slaves were allowed to plant, were never enough. Compared to the West Indies, the monetary value of slaves in the Bay was much higher: The problem of runaways was a most important issue and the loggers had to avoid arousing the discontent of their slaves. After the abolition of slave trade in 1805, when it was difficult to obtain a fresh supply of suitable slaves, an overall shortage of mahogany workers was beginning to manifest itself. This, in turn, increased their value even more and the settlers had a vital interest to treat their property well.

Within the forest workforce, the huntsman played a crucial role. The loggers not only depended on the skill and ability of the huntsman to spot virgin forests, but also on his sense of duty and the degree of loyalty towards his master to report the discovery of new stands to his own master, and to not sell the information to possible competitors. Also, while on reconnaissance the huntsman had to be careful so as not to be followed by fellow huntsmen in the service of other White loggers. As can be appreciated, the financial success of an entire logging venture depended on the huntsmen and consequently, the White loggers had an enormous interest in maintaining a balanced relationship with them.[41]

In sum, the institution of slavery in the Bay Settlement contrasted sharply with that of the West Indies and North America because the different nature of colonization (i.e. occupation) and the different requirements and working conditions in the timber industry resulted in the development of an essentially different attitude towards the slaves. This can be seen as a possible reason for why observers in the 18th and early 19th centuries unanimously agreed that slavery in the settlement was less oppressive than other slave-societies of the time.

Given that this phenomenon is, indeed, peculiar to Belize, it becomes necessary to investigate in more detail *if* and to what extent the slaves in the Bay really did receive a more lenient treatment.

---

41 "It not infrequently happens, when the huntsman has been particularly successful in finding a large body of wood, that it becomes a contest with his conscience, whether he shall disclose the matter to his master, or sell it to his neighbour". Henderson (1809: 47–50)

To begin with, the slaves had to be equipped with arms because the extraction methods of timber made it essential for the slaves to possess machetes, cutlasses, axes and knives. Some of the workers also carried guns, not only to defend the camp against wild animals (jaguar, puma, wild pigs, crocodiles, poisonous snakes etc.) but also to provide food, since the economy of the time was strictly non-agricultural and the crops cultivated for subsistence were scarce. Another purpose behind providing the slaves with arms was to help defend both the camps and the settlement against occasional attacks by the Spanish who repeatedly ruined the provision grounds the slaves had been cultivating from the beginning of the 18ᵗʰ century.

In 1786, at the Convention of London, it was again officially forbidden to grow crops even for subsistence and visiting Spanish/Yucatecan officials dutifully had the plantations destroyed. Clearly, this was enough a reason why the Spanish were seen as a common enemy by master and slave alike.

It bears emphasizing that the motive for officially prohibiting any agricultural activities whatsoever was purely political and not economic. The Spanish thought that if the small population of woodcutters and slaves was not allowed to grow crops it would reduce the likelihood of a more permanent British settlement on what still was, officially, Spanish territory. As it turned out these fears proved to be not completely unfounded: Three years later, when Spain eased her restrictions and permitted the cultivation of small plots for the exclusive use of provisions, Rafael Llobet, an official from Bacalar (the southernmost Spanish military garrison and administrative and commercial centre north of present Chetumal in Southern Yucatán), stated in his diary that

> *Casi toda la gente que lo habita es sumamente pobre, tanto que a no haberles S.M.C. [Su Majestad Católica] concedido la gracia de cultivar huertas, sin duda alguna, hubieran abandonado el país …*[42]

From this diary it can be deduced that the Spanish officials based in Yucatán indirectly blamed Madrid for this generosity, which, in their opinion, was responsible for the English not leaving the Bay. Since the Yucatecan officials did not agree with the decisions taken in Spain, they began to take matters into their own hands, and continued to have the camps harassed, particularly those within close reach of the boundaries on the New and Belize Rivers.

---

42   (The settlers inhabiting the coast were extremely poor to the extent that had His Catholic Majesty not generously granted permission to raise provision grounds for subsistence, without any doubt they would have left …) Diary of Rafael Llobet, 1–5–1790, *Archivo General de Indias,* (AGI) Sevilla, (México 3023) quoted in Calderón Quijano (1944: 367).

Let us now return to the question of whether or not the slave population in the Bay Settlement did receive a more lenient treatment. As was reported by several observers (two of which were British superintendents!), by the standards of the time, the slaves were said to have received an especially adequate allowance of food and clothing. For example in 1808 the following account was written:

> ... they are well fed by their Owners, generally receiving seven Pounds of Beef, & six pounds of Flour per week, or in lieu of Flour fifty Plantains; two Gills [equals ½ pint or 300 ml] of Rum per day, & if working in the water, or rain, it is generally increased to three Gills per day ...[43]

In 1816, two years after his appointment, Superintendent Arthur was of the opinion that

> All the Slaves are most abundantly fed by their Proprietors on the best Salted Provisions – Pork generally, at the rate of five pounds per week to each man, with Yams, Plantains, Rice, Flour, Salt, & Tobacco. Every Slave has a Moschetto Pavilion, Blanket, and Sheet found him – also, two suits of Osnaburgh annually.[44]

and in 1823 Superintendent Codd reported rather favourably that

> Here the Negro is well fed, well clothed, and every comfort suiting his station is liberally provided for him ... the best Irish Mess Pork, and good flour, are weekly delivered to him, and if not flour, Plantains which they in general prefer they have the unlimited use of; ... with the addition of rum, tobacco, pipes, a knife, powder and shot and a short Sword constitutes all their wants; ... and I really believe that in no part of the World where slavery exists can the government of them be in a more indulgent form![45]

One of the main reasons for White loggers to treat their workforce well, to keep them reasonably content and to try to form a better relationship between master and slave was the fact that the loggers were very much aware of the easy chances for escape into the neighbouring "Spanish" territories. George Hyde, a wealthy free coloured merchant and slave owner, reported in 1825 that "As pun-

---

43 Gen. Montresor to Gov. Coote, 22 Oct. 1806, PRO CO 123/17
44 Supt. Arthur to Lord Bathurst, 7 Nov. 1816, PRO CO 123/25
45 Supt. Codd to Bathurst, 8 March 1823, PRO CO 123/34

ishments or ill-usage (if ever so deserved) we dare not inflict it, so easy is their retreat to the Spaniards."[46] The settlers were in constant fear of mass desertions which would have led to the ruin of the settlement.

> *... if they were not governed with mildness, kindness and liberality, from the encouragement held out by the Spaniards to desert, and the facility with which they could do so ... the country would be in a moment deserted, and the Settlers ruined.*[47]

Even if the loggers in the Bay Settlement did treat their slaves better than the West Indian and North American planters we need to be aware that the reason for this apparent "mildness, kindness and liberality" was purely selfish in nature and did not stem from a feeling of genuine "comradeship".

Just like in any other slave society, the slaves in the Bay too refused to accept their situation and rebelled. It would be absurd to claim that cruelty did not exist and the slaves worked on a voluntary basis "... slaves in this settlement being so by choice only ..."[48] The available court records containing numerous cases of unjust and/or harsh corporal punishments ordered by the magistrates for minor offences and ill treatment caused to slaves[49] convince us to the contrary. Just as convincing are the later reports of Superintendent Colonel Arthur who, after having been in the colony for some years, had seen enough in order to modify the once favourable opinion he had of the slave owners upon his arrival.[50]

In the Bay Settlement the slaves' reactions to unjust treatment were as strong as elsewhere: An immediate response was the desire to desert and the possibility of escape presented less difficulty than on the West Indian sugar islands because the Bay area had a significant geographical advantage: It was not completely surrounded by sea[51] and there existed permanent and safe hiding places.

---

46 Crowe (1850: 321)

47 In: *The Defence of the Settlers of Honduras ...*, (1824)

48 Supt. Hunter's "Plan of Police", 18 May 1790, PRO CO 123/9

49 See for example: Summary of Court Records 1817–21, f.23, 43 and Col. Arthur to Lord Bathurst, 7 Oct. 1820, PRO CO 123/29 reviewed in Dobson (1973: 153).

50 In 1820, he reported that in camps close to the Belize River some slaves "had been treated with very unnecessary harshness by their Owner, and had certainly good grounds for complaint" and went on to inform London of "the increasing severity and cruelty which is now practised with impunity and that "in many cases the slaves were severely oppressed". Arthur to Bathurst, PRO CO 123/29 in Bolland (1977: 70).

51 An exception was Jamaica, where runaway slaves – the so called Maroons (from Spanish *cimarrón:* "wild") – were able to remain in hiding and establish Maroon communities on

There is substantial evidence from Spanish as well as English records that frequent desertions took place in the Bay Settlement. This may lead us to believe that, in reality, the relations between master and slave most likely were not as harmonious as claimed. After having been neglected for a long time, Spanish documents from the former *Audiencia* of Guatemala kept in the *Archivo General de Centroamérica* in Guatemala City, have now been thoroughly studied and a number of references in relation to Black fugitives from the region that is now Belize who hoped to gain freedom in the Spanish administered regions have been discovered.[52]

Three major escape routes existed:

The first was south along the coastline and on to present Honduras. As early as 1728, a Black fugitive from "Río Vális" was found by a member of the San Felipe garrison on Lake Izabal, near the present day border between Guatemala and Belize. The second route was north across the Río Hondo into Yucatán where the "Spanish"/Guatemalan outposts were willing to offer protection and encouraged the slaves "… to seek freedom, by embracing the Roman Catholic Religion and afford them temptations to elope from their owner.[53] The third, and very popular, way of escape was to use the intricate network of the Belize River into the Petén.

Much to the dismay of the settlers, the neighbouring "Spanish" were all too willing to grant asylum to the fugitives. In the words of a frustrated logger, the "Spanish" deliberately sought to destabilize the settlement's economy by enticing away its labour force:

> There is one circumstance which … serves to discourage our Industry & even threatens the total ruin of the Trade of this Settlement, & that is the Desertion of our Negroes to the Spaniards which increases daily & that of late to such an alarming degree, that no One Man however well-disposed he may consider his Negroes, can think his property safe for a single Night.[54]

When the provinces of Guatemala and Comayagua (present Honduras) gained their independence in 1821 the abolishment of slavery followed in 1829. During this time desertion of slaves to the neighbouring regions (into the Petén and the Honduran coastal towns Trujillo and Omoa) increased even more. The 1826 census had 215 of the total 2410 slaves listed as runaways and other censuses

---

the north side of the island, from which they would keep harassing the search parties.

52 Cf. Feldman (1983: 9–20)

53 Supt. Hunter, 18 May 1790, PRO CO 123/9 quoted in Bolland (1977: 77)

54 Letter from Potts, 28 May 1792, PRO CO 123/13 in Ibid.

indicated that the slave population was reduced by about one half between 1823 and 1835.[55] In British Honduras slavery was not abolished until 1834. After that a transitional period of "apprenticeship" followed which lasted until 1838.

Guatemala seems to have welcomed the runaways as can be deduced from a response to an official complaint to the Petén authorities by the colonial officials across the border where

> ... a town of black people ... had been formed already whose inhabitants had ... emigrated from your Establishment, ... [and who] already enjoyed the privilege of [free] Citizens.[56]

Not all runaways opted for escape into the neighbouring territories, some established independent slave towns in the interior of present Central Belize. For example the name of the present river "Runaway Creek", a tributary to the Sibun River, south of present-day's Western Highway leading from Belize City to Belmopan (see Map 10).

Most telling is also another place names that has survived to the present day and bears witness to these desertions. Close to the border to the Petén in upper Central Belize and also in Northern Belize, villages and entire areas are known by the name of "Spanish Lookout". It remains not quite clear, however, whether these places received their name because runaways were looking out for Spanish assistance, whether they were strategic posts for Spanish troops to spy on the developments in the settlement or were used as lookout places by the English settlers.

From the settlers' point of view, allowing the most rebellious slaves to desert increased the chances of regaining at least temporary stability.

In the Bay, the White settlers were in constant fear that runaways, "instigated by the Spaniards"[57], would team up with those still in the camps and stir up a massive slave revolt. This was mainly for the following reasons: Slaves were the majority, a government and an executive power was non-existent, the vast areas of uninhabited terrain, the remoteness of the timber camps and the limitations as far as communications and transportation were concerned.

Moreover, the slave owners in the Bay were perfectly aware of the successful slave uprisings in other parts of the Caribbean, as was the case in Saint Domingue (present day Haiti). Although slave owners generally thought their slaves to be more "loyal" and "devoted", the effect the revolt in Haiti had on

---

55   Censuses of 1823, 1826 and 1835, General Registry, Belize City
56   Leon Baldison to Codd, 15 Nov. 1823, PRO CO 123/34 in Bolland (1977:78)
57   Codd to Bathurst, 18 Feb. 1825, PRO CO 123/36 in Ibid.

the slaves in the settlement must not be underestimated. For example, in 1791 the settlers decided that a French ship with over two hundred Black rebels on board "should not be permitted to land so infectious a cargo."[58]

Generally speaking, because the favourable geographical conditions facilitated escape, in the Bay Settlement massive slave revolts were never as big a problem as on the West Indian islands. The "Belizean" slaves never seriously considered attempting overtaking the settlement either. But to believe that they did not do so solely out of devotion and loyalty towards their masters would be a little too idealistic. The truth is that in the Bay, there was no immediate need for revolt, when freedom could be obtained relatively easily by disappearing into the forest and crossing the borders of the settlement.

Nevertheless, slave revolts did occur. Small scale ones in 1765 and 1768, and in 1773 the biggest slave revolt in the history of Belize took place. The revolt lasted over five months and a naval force from Jamaica had to be called in for assistance. General chaos reigned in the settlement, the situation in the interior camps was critical and trade in the Bay was at a standstill. The causes for this massive revolt was the economic crisis the settlement experienced during the 1770s, when the settlers endeavoured to compensate the falling prices of logwood by maximizing extraction and exports. During this time, the over two thousand slaves in the settlement had to cope with an increased amount of work and their working conditions were becoming extremely bad.[59]

The institution of slavery in the settlement was different for yet another reason in the sense that slavery was not the *only* means of recruiting labour: From the end of the 18th century onwards, wage workers (mostly Zambo-Miskito Indians and Black Caribs, the latter of which are known today as Garifuna people and are a racial mixture of Carib and Arawak Indians and escaped slaves[60]) could be hired to meet the ever-growing demand for labour. The British woodcutters welcomed these migrants because of the high cost of buying and maintaining slaves.[61] Although these hired labourers were basically free, they were expected to do the same work and accept the same working conditions as the Black slaves, a fact, which in the long term, might also have helped to improve the terms and conditions of the slave population in the Bay.

---

58   James Bartlett to Dyer, Allan & Co, 26 Nov. 1791, PRO CO 123/13 in Ibid.

59   Cf. Burdon (1935,3: 121–24).

60   The Garifuna people (or plural Garinagu) settled on the Caribbean island of St. Vincent. In 1779, they were deported from there to the coastal regions of present-day Honduras and Nicaragua where they eventually joined the Miskito Indians who were travelling up the Mosquito Coast to the Bay of Honduras in search of work. A detailed history of the Garifuna people (Garinagu) shall be given in Chapter Six.

61   Cf. Stone (1990: 24)

3.2. Summary & Conclusion

Slavery in the Bay Settlement was a means of securing labour for the purposes of timber extraction and evolved in a unique way because the requirements of the timber industry were different to those of the sugar and cotton plantations. The slaves had various occupations due to the special working conditions in the forest. The size of the production units was small and master and slave depended on one another while logging.

Initially, slave owners were particularly successful in creating and perpetuating myths of exemplary slave conditions in the Bay of Honduras. Although, according to historical evidence and in comparison to the West Indian islands, the slaves in the Bay indeed seemed to have received a less harsh treatment, on no account should this make us believe that slavery in the Bay Settlement existed to a lesser degree. The numerous evidence of cruelty inflicted, the high number of runaways and the constant fear of rebellions confirm that the slaves' reactions to slavery were as strong as elsewhere. What can be ascertained though is the following: The different working conditions in the timber camps fostered a closer relationship between Blacks and Whites due to common interests, which, to a certain degree, may have helped to reduce the impact of the social consequences of slavery experienced in other slave societies in the Americas.

Without exaggeration we may be able to conclude safely that in the Bay Settlement, the many peculiarities of the institution of slavery created a unique pattern. This phenomenon eventually led to the development of a different society compared to that of the British West Indians Islands and had a great influence on the community's future socio-economic developments.

4. The Shift from Logwood to Mahogany and Its Socio-Economic Consequences

In comparison to logwood, the mahogany tree was much larger, grew farther inland and was scattered over vast forest areas. For the cutting, the extraction, and the transportation of the new timber not only more labour and capital but also more land was needed. These new requirements gave rise to a series of significant and far reaching socio-economic changes, the repercussions of which, in some instances, reached well into the 19ᵗʰ and 20ᵗʰ centuries.

Because the indigenous population of the area had withdrawn into the forest, the only way of solving the growing demand for labour was to import a larger number of African slaves. From the second half of the 18th century, until after the First World War, mahogany felling was done exclusively by hand and the traditional methods of transport were by animal (cattle) haulage and floating the logs down the rivers to the coastal warehouses. As mentioned, this method of transport was extremely labour intensive and no large scale alternatives, i.e. a railway, was ever available in the region.

The increased import of African slaves formed the basis for the demography of the future British colony. With the arrival of the first large slave contingent, the Bay Settlement ceased to be a mere enclave of a few British ex-buccaneers and settlers including their labourers and a temporary stopover for British tradesmen to export wood. By the end of the 18th century, the settlement had completely turned into a Black majority society. As shown on Table 4, in the year 1803, there were approximately 3000 slaves and only 1000 Whites residing in the Bay.

At the Convention of London in 1786, it was agreed that the settlers for the first time would be allowed to extract both logwood and mahogany south of the Belize River under the condition that the British evacuated all her residents from the Mosquito Coast and the Bay Islands. Now, the woodcutters were able to continue with their activities as far as the Sibun River ("The New Limits"), a significant territorial increase, as can be seen on Map 11. The availability of more land led to a growth in production and consequently in the demand for labour which, in turn, increased the demand for population.

Economic activities *not* in connection with the timber industry, such as fishing and turtling, were, however, still forbidden. The settlers were only allowed to use "all the Fruits, or Produce of the Earth, purely natural and uncultivated," but it was prohibited to set up "any Plantation of Sugar, Coffee, Cacao, or other like Articles"[62], erect fortifications or establish a formal government.

In a certain sense these terms were a major impediment for the development of agriculture on a larger scale. The ban on agriculture, together with the increased demand for provisions, may be interpreted as the reasons for the beginning of a colonial dependency on imported foodstuffs which reached its climax in the 19th century.

Apart from a rise in expenses owing to the high costs for purchasing and maintaining a large number of slaves, more capital was also needed due to the more complicate nature of mahogany transportation. For example, it became indispensable that barriers be installed near the river's mouth, so that the floating logs, which had been formed into rafts, would come to a standstill at the riverside or "barquadier". These barriers, called booms, were "large cables placed

---

62   Article three of the Convention of London, 1786

across the rivers at the different eddies or falls, to sometimes [support] more than a thousand logs together ..." [63] The present day village of Burrell Boom on the Belize River, approximately twenty miles from the coast and modern Belize City, still reminds us of these cables.

It did not take long until the high demand for mahogany led to a depletion of the more easily available timber and the Baymen were forced to lay new claims to untouched forest regions, the "locations", much farther inland. While the woodcutters were only a few hundred in numbers, the arrangements they made with each other were by and large adhered to and there were no reports of the existence of major difficulties as far as the occupation of land was concerned. This was soon to change because the increased extraction of mahogany coincided with the British evacuation of the Mosquito Shore in 1787 and the subsequent migration of the former Shoremen to the Bay Settlement, as explained in detail in the previous chapter. Despite the fact that only one quarter of the 2,214 immigrants consisted of White people, competition for land was growing constantly and it was inevitable that this new bunch of immigrants, the White newcomers from the Mosquito Shore (the Shoremen), the Creoles, and the Zambo-Miskito and Black Carib labourers would come into conflict with the old-established Baymen over the rights to claim mahogany locations.

With the increased competition for land, tension among the different groups of White settlers started to grow and it became necessary to regulate the ownership of land by making a number of adjustments to the existing agreements, or "location laws", as they were named by the Baymen. Since the mahogany trees suitable for cutting were relatively scattered (at that time an acre only yielded three marketable trees), a much larger area of land was needed for exploitation and a new scheme had to be worked out how to decide the size of the new locations. The system of claiming land by occupation as such remained the same but after the treaty limits had been extended and the extraction of timber had been officially granted as far south as the Sibun River (see Map 11), a much larger area had now become available for the extraction of timber.

All navigable creeks, rivers and lagoons were open for occupation and it was also agreed that for the larger works inland, a prospective owner should possess a minimum number of ten able negro slaves and servants (presumably the free hired Zambo-Miskito) and that "no person shall possess more than two Mahogany Work in any River, let him be possessed of what number of negroes so ever." [64]

---

63   Henderson (1809: 53–54)
64   "Laws of Honduras, Part I", General Registry, Belize City

In 1781 new location laws were introduced but the controversial issue of proper land ownership and land registration was not dealt with. Although, from a legal point of view, the settlers were actually "in possession" of mahogany works by mere occupation or squatting, the mahogany works were still treated as freehold property which was bought and sold freely. The settlers, being aware of the possible legal repercussions their peculiar land tenure in usufruct would eventually cause, were putting considerable pressure on the superintendents to give them valid titles.

As far as the allocation of the newly conceded lands was concerned, the less well-off settlers among the established Baymen were clearly discriminated. So were the White Shoremen who had been forced to leave the Shore in compliance with the Convention of London. According to orders from the British government, the Shoremen were to be given priority regarding the distribution of the area between the Belize and Sibun Rivers.[65] After all, this territorial increase was gained precisely for the complete withdrawal of the British from the Mosquito Shore. The established Baymen, however, refused to comply with these instructions and just one year after the arrival of the Shoremen, most of the newly conceded lands had come into the possession of a few well established settlers.[66]

In reality, the new location laws, instead of bringing more order and justice into the Bay Settlement, had a contrary effect and only fostered the further monopolization of forest lands.

- **First:** The size of holdings was increased which clearly was *not* an impediment to the monopolization of land.
- **Secondly:** The agreement that a person fulfilling the requirements should be permitted to own up to two works led to significant abuse. In 1779, Superintendent Despard discovered that approximately fifteen men held at least "twelve fifteenths of all mahogany works." This was due to the fact that owners claimed additional land under the name of their servants "by fictitious collusive co-partnerships between masters or owners of slaves and their kind servants."[67]

---

65   Sydney to Despard, 31 July 1786, PRO CO 137/36 in Bolland (1977: 32).
66   "… Messrs Hoare, O'Brien, McAuley, Bartlett, Potts, Meighan, Armstrong, Davis, Tucker and Sullivan and Garbutt … alone possess at least nine parts in Twelve of the present augmented District." Letter from Despard, 31 Oct. 1787, PRO CO 123/6
67   Letter from Despard, 4 March 1788, PRO CO 126/6 quoted by Burdon (1935).

- **Thirdly** and most importantly: The rule that "a gang of at least four able negro men slaves or servants"[68] (and ten for the works extending further inland) was the minimum to work a location in any of the rivers meant that only those who could afford the above amount of slaves were able to acquire mahogany works.

With the above requirements holdings were indirectly reserved for the more well-off settlers/cutters, the latter of which had already begun to form a kind of elite group. This new elite, by re-establishing their London connections from the heydays of the logwood trade, had become very influential. They had also managed to gain significant control of the entire import trade thus exerting a considerable amount of power upon other settlers. In 1788, Colonel Despard reported that the wealthy settlers were

> ... *almost our sole importers, exporters, and retailers, too; and that they had the equity to import, just what served themselves ... keeping the people poor and totally dependent upon them; for they ... set their own price upon their goods ...*[69]

Since the establishment of a formal government was still forbidden by the Spanish, the new settlers' elite was also in complete control of the legislature and judiciary in the settlement. Matters concerning law and order were dealt with in the Public Meeting, an institution invented by the settlers themselves and very peculiar to the Bay Settlement as we shall see in detail in the next subchapter. These meetings were controlled by the influential cutters and their representatives in the Magistracy and the extremely small size of the population allowed the wealthier of the settlers, to hold several offices at the same time.

By holding the monopoly of land ownership this elite group virtually deprived other settlers, both the less well-off among the original inhabitants (small tradesmen, turtlers, fishermen or the employees of woodcutters and import traders) and the newcomers from the Mosquito Shore, of their access to the one and only economic resource of the settlement, the exportation of mahogany. A complaint written by three immigrants from the Mosquito Shore, who, according to the censuses were owners of between twelve and twenty slaves and therefore were not even among the poorer of the immigrants, illustrates to what extent the powers of the old-established Baymen (or the "principal inhabitants" as they were known) was already exercised:

---

68 Ibid.
69 Letter from Col. Despard, 11 Jan 1788, PRO CO 123/6 in Bolland (1988: 44).

A combination hath been formed against us by the former English Inhabitants of the Bay of Honduras ... Many of us were told that if we continued of that opinion, we would soon find ourselves in a very disagreeable situation ... so that we must either conform or leave the Country. The Mahogany works in the new limits we have found all possessed by the former Bay people who claim every spot, where Mahogany is to be cut, under various pretences.[70]

But these complaints were to no avail. Since the British government was still unwilling to assert sovereignty over the territory claimed by the settlers, the logical consequence was that it was also unable to impose authority over the Bay Settlement.

Even the appointment of a new superintendent did not alter the situation. Colonel Arthur, upon his arrival in 1814, was confronted with a number of disputes arising from the peculiar system of "Possession of Land by Occupation". Having been invested with the authority to allocate land within the treaty limits, he made several unsuccessful attempts to weaken the old settlers' monopoly but the elite had already become too powerful and claimed all suitable land on which mahogany could be exploited.

In the 1820s, after several Public Meetings, the land owners unanimously decided that the locations, which, in fact, were only *occupied,* should become freehold property. The system of land ownership by occupation was abolished after long disputes between the settlers and the superintendent, the latter giving title to a number of occupied lands. However, these amended location laws never attempted to regulate the need for proper land registration and the issue continued to give rise to problems until 1859, when the large landowners finally had to have their titles officially registered in the Lands Title Registry.[71]

Owing to the intervention of Superintendent Arthur, unclaimed land in both the Northern District and south of the Sibun River (the "Old and New Limits") became Crown lands. It was further resolved that possible future territory concessions, which were actually granted south of the Sibun River in the middle of the 19th century, were to become automatically Crown lands first, and only later allotted to applicants by means of grants.

Crown lands were productive land as such but mahogany there was said to be of inferior quality and rivers were not ideally situated for transport. Therefore these areas remained mostly idle until 1862, when the settlement became an official British colony. Since by that time, the ban on agriculture was no

---

70   Robert English, Samuel Harrison and Abraham Bull to Supt. Despard, 20 Aug. 1787, PRO CO 123/5 in Bolland (1977: 44).

71   Cf. Ashcraft (1973: 30), Bolland and Shoman (1975: 72–77)

longer valid, the former Crown lands were regarded as potentially valuable land to be used for agricultural activities.

As far as the development of agriculture was concerned, the rest of the suitable land (situated mostly in the Northern District) was unavailable because it was used for commercial mahogany cutting and owned by members of the "forestocracy". In the first decades of the 19th century, when the need for economic diversification grew stronger, it was precisely this monopolization of potentially suitable land that was a major impediment for diversification to take place. The monopolization of land, which had its beginnings in the late 18th century, was to influence the country's efforts for economic diversification for two hundred years to come, well into the last quarter of the 20th century.

In sum, although Superintendent Arthur failed to eliminate the monopoly of land ownership altogether, he did succeed in saving the little of the unoccupied land that was left in the Northern District (Río Hondo to Sibun River) and most of the territory south of the Sibun River (the Crown lands) from being monopolized by the settlers' elite.

Last but not least, another important consequence of the shift from logwood to mahogany was that the woodcutters came in contact with the Maya.

From the late 1770s onwards, when the most accessible timber resources near the rivers and creeks were depleted, the logging crews had to penetrate more into the recesses of the forest in search for additional sources of the valuable timber. These incursions into the forests, especially to Western Belize, invariably brought the loggers into contact with the Maya who, threatened by the Spanish *entradas* of the late 17th century, had retreated into the depths of the forests as a last resort.

In 1779, after the initial major penetrations farther inland and subsequent first encounters, the presence of a few Maya was reported: "The Indians who live near the English are so inconsiderable that it is unnecessary to take any notice of them."[72] But less than ten years later the British were *forced* "to take notice of them", because the Maya had become a major hindrance to the cutting and extraction activities of mahogany. Whereas for the loggers, the traditional Maya slash-and-burn agriculture was an impediment for the extraction of timber, the Maya saw their environment, subsistence, and independence endangered by the logging operations. In short, the reaction of the Maya to this new invasion was strong resistance and, judging by the above document, was underestimated or not expected by the woodcutters.

Although the exact origins or cultural identity of these pockets of Maya cannot be determined, it is highly likely that they came from the environments

---

72   Unsigned letter to Gov. Dalling, 3 Sept. 1779, PRO CO 137/75 in Bolland (1977: 21).

of Tipu, one of the centres of Maya resistance in the 17th century and the various communities around Lake Petén Itzá in present day Guatemala.[73]

In 1788, the first report was made of an "attack of wild Indians"[74] on the New River and four years later an appeal for military assistance was made in order to "… punish the Indians who are committing depredations upon the Mahogany works".[75] In 1807 the settlers solicited "arms and ammunitions for gangs working up the River at Hogstye Bank, who have been attacked by Indians".[76] The reference to two geographical terms, the New River and Hogstye Bank (above of present Roaring Creek on the Belize River), enables us to approximately reconstruct the frontier, as shown on Map 11.

The increasing attacks of the Maya had yet another important impact on the woodcutters. The unexpected violent contact with the remaining indigenous population caused great fears to the few White loggers, who felt themselves placed "entirely at the mercy of the Slave Population."[77] The settlers were scared of the possibility that rebellious slaves and runaways might join the Maya and were alarmed at the outcome of such a co-operation. The fears of an eventual slaves/Maya allegiance proved groundless since no mention was ever made of a Maya participation when a minor slave revolt occurred on the Belize River in 1820.

Despite many attacks upon the timber camps, in the long run, the Maya were not able to put a halt to the invasion of the woodcutters. Although the Mayan population had been very successful in disrupting the expansionistic movements of the woodcutters for approximately thirty years, in the 1820s and 1830s they finally started to retreat farther into the rainforest.

---

73 In relation to the cultural identity of these pockets of Maya, I consider it important to draw attention to the fact that the historian and anthropologist, the late Eric Thompson (1972: 71) failed to differentiate the terms "Maya" and "Indians" when describing the activities of the British woodcutters in the Bay Settlement. This may have led (or may still lead) to a major misunderstanding because, apart from the Maya, a modest amount of Zambo Miskito, who had come as slaves and mercenaries to the settlement in 1787, were also living within the boundaries of the settlement. Therefore, and as Bolland (1977: 22) rightly points out, the statement made by Thompson (1972: 71) "that the British logwood cutters working on the Belize River employed Indians … probably the descendants of the Maya of Tipu culture" must be dismissed as incorrect and is therefore not to be used as source. The Indians to whom Thompson refers were in fact Zambo Miskito and *not* Maya.

74 Thomas Graham: "Journal of my Visitation on Part of the District granted by His Catholic Majesty for the occupation of the British settlers …," 27 Oct. 1790, PRO CO 123/9 and Report from Supt. Despard, 8 March 1791, 123/10 in Bolland (1977: 21).

75 Burdon (1935, II: 58)

76 Ibid. p. 101

77 Minutes from the Public Meeting, 25 Feb. 1817, PRO CO 123/26

Towards the end of the first half of the 19th century, the Maya emerged once more from their hiding places in order to resume their struggle. By that time the settlement had become an official British colony in all but name and plans had been made already for the integration of the Maya into society. As we shall examine in more detail in Chapter Five, the Maya were not in agreement with the terms of their future integration and started to openly challenge colonial rule.

5. Social Changes in the Settlement and the Forming of an Elementary Government

The expansion of commercial activities and the high profits gained from the exportation of timber gradually led to a population increase in the settlement. Population growth, however, was not steady and throughout the 18th century population figures in the Bay fluctuated a great deal.

Among the main reasons for these fluctuations were:

- **First:** Actual Spanish assaults and an ever-present fear of them may have led to a continuous exodus and re-immigration, once the threats were over.
- **Secondly:** It is very plausible that travellers and observers mentioning population figures may have been misled by the seasonal absence of the cutters and their slaves at the inland timber camps.
- **Thirdly:** We must take into consideration that the counting was done with almost no administration involved and therefore these figures could not have been more than mere estimates.
- **Fourthly:** It may also have been difficult to obtain accurate numbers because many people were reluctant to have themselves registered. For example, when Superintendent Despard made a first semi-official attempt to properly enumerate the population in 1790, he reported that the total figure should include "fifty or sixty people more, who did not give their names for [the prohibited] garden grounds".[78]

For the reasons given above only from the 1861 census onwards can population figures be reasonably relied upon. Although the population estimates prior to that date (as shown in Table 5) are bound to be far from reliable, they do serve to indicate demographic changes. In retrospect, these changes can be

---

78   "A Narrative of the Publick Transactions …", PRO CO 123/10 in Bolland (1988: 35).

connected to certain practices in the settlement. For example, the decrease in the amount of slaves and the increase in numbers of the free coloureds and free Blacks reflect the growing rate of manumissions which reached its peak in the years prior to emancipation in 1834. Caution should be used in interpreting 18th and early 19th century population figures since none of them seem to reflect the massive immigration from the Mosquito Shore in 1787, when over two thousand settlers arrived. These immigrants were said to have outnumbered the "principal inhabitants" by five to one which would suggest that the population prior to that date could not have been more than a few hundred.[79]

The new prosperity of the woodcutters affected the general life style in the Bay and in the last decade of the 18th century, the settlement at the mouth of the Belize River began to take shape. The elementary former accommodation was gradually replaced by proper, elegant houses as well as some plantation manors. Although the wealthier settlers may have been well-off in terms of the Bay Settlement, they were not living in the same splendour as the planters on the West Indian sugar islands. In the beginning of the 19th century, according to Henderson, the town already consisted of about 200 houses of which those owned by "opulent merchants, [were] spacious, commodious and well finished".[80]

Prior to the 1790s most of the White settlers were said to have lived on "Cayo Cosina" (renamed St. George's Cay by the British) opposite the mouth of the Belize River, where, as stated in a Spanish account, the climate was said to be more salubrious, especially because the steady breeze offered protection from the numerous fierce flying insects: *"... el único motivo que conduce allí las gentes, es él de la salud."*[81]

The poorer settlers and the slaves less fit for work in the forest showed a tendency to populate abandoned campsites at the river banks in the interior. According to the same Spanish account they lived in a deadly climate surrounded by biting insects of all kinds and their living conditions were miserable:

gentes pobres, o negros esclavos poco útiles para el trabajo, que se mantienen con los plátanos que cultivaban y con la pesca, y la caza, pasando la más

---

79   The fact that none of this is reflected in Table 5 illustrates that these figures must not be overestimated in their value. Cf. letter from Supt. Despard, 23 Feb. 1787, PRO CO 123/5 in Ibid. (27,21).

80   Henderson (1809:13)

81   (… the only motive for people to go there is for reasons of health …) Lucas Gálvez a Antonio Valdéz, 8–10–1789, AGI, México 3108, printed in full in Calderón Quijano (1944:360–1).

desgraciada vida en unas desabridas chozas, bajo de un clima mortífero, y rodeados de innumerables insectos picantes de diferentes especies ...[82]

Most interesting and amusing are the comments the Spanish official Rafael Llobet made in his diary concerning the layout of the principal establishment of the British, now situated on both sides of the mouth of the "Río Walix". Being very different from a "Spanish" town in Central America at that time, the settlement was clearly not to the Spaniard's taste. He criticized that it had neither squares, nor streets, nor order and no symmetry: *"... sin plazas, calles, buen orden y simetría"*. Llobet further noted that there were 138 houses, of which 102 were built of solid timber and, instead of having whitewashed walls as the Spanish-style buildings, were painted in various colours. Moreover, he claimed that all of these houses had a terrace where the people spent their time for most of the year: *"... un corredor ... donde la mayor parte del año se está el dueño pasando."*[83] Llobet also gave a picture of the rest of the population, but he did not specify whether they were Whites or slaves. He pitied these people and mentioned that they had become accustomed to their condition of exclusively living on plantains, *macal,* yuca and other roots.

Llobet's notes also convey the impression that the woodcutters must have engaged in a kind of barter trade, both among themselves and with merchants from outside because, according to Llobet, they hardly ever needed money and exchanged wood or other goods: *"... rara vez necesitan dinero, porque a cambio de palo, o de efectos, se entienden y se componen."*[84] As far as provisions were concerned, basic necessities could be obtained from a small number of retailers. In addition, four shops existed in the settlement from where pieces of pottery, biscuits, gunpowder, shot, canvas, coarse cotton, salt meat, knives, locks, iron tools and needles could be obtained.[85]

---

82   (... poor people or Black slaves who are of not much use for forest work maintain themselves by the plantains they cultivate and by fishing and hunting. They lead a most miserable life, live in primitive huts, under a deadly climate and surrounded by innumerable biting insects of all kinds ...) Ibid.

83   Diary of Rafael Llobet, 1–5–1790, AGI, México 3023, quoted in Calderón Quijano (1944: 366)

84   Ibid.

85   (*Hay cuatro tiendas que en ellas se encuentra loza ordinaria – pero no vajilla completa -, galletas, pólvora, perdigones, bretañas, sarazas bastas, carne salada y otras menudencias como navajas, candados, hierros de campo, agujas etc.*) Cf. Llobet (1790) and "Report of the exports from the British Establishment at Río Walix", from Lucas Gálvez to Campos Alange, 1790 quoted in Calderón Quijano (1944: 366,368).

From the 1740s onwards, due to the increasing commercial activities and the continuous import of African slaves and the free hired Zambo-Miskito labourers, the small enclave community was beginning to create a new society. The carefree, easy going society of the 17th and early 18th centuries had come to an abrupt end.

In order to meet the needs for this new and growing society, it was necessary for the primitive form of government to become more refined and sophisticated. As early as 1738, the original settlers already had established some sort of civic organization: A committee of influential settlers gathered regularly in the so called Public Meetings, the practice of which is said to date back to the basic economic arrangements of the buccaneering times.

In the Public Meeting a number of magistrates were elected who functioned in a semi-judicial as well as in an executive capacity. In addition, the settlers nominated a superintendent from their own ranks, who functioned as liaison with London. This home-made and rather spontaneous form of government was based purely upon the internal needs of the community and not upon the laws and rules of Great Britain. With slight variations it continued to exist until beyond the second half of the 19th century.

Although Britain's policy towards the Bay Settlement remained vacillating, in view of the constant threat of the settlers being eventually dislodged by the Spanish forces stationed in neighbouring Bacalar, London was not at all disinterested in the developments in and around the Bay. An officer, dispatched from Jamaica to the settlement to give a detailed report on the developments there, recommended that a proper legislative body should be formed with the capacity to draw up a constitution based on English law. This advice, together with several petitions from the settlers to establish a formal government, was ignored by the Foreign Office; after all one did not want to provoke Spain and was not prepared to take risks.

In 1765, Britain took a first tentative measure and sent Admiral Burnaby, the Commander-in-Chief of the British navy in Jamaica, to control "the state of Anarchy and Confusion"[86] in the settlement. Trying to ease the situation, Burnaby framed a number of simple laws, known as "Burnaby's Code", which were based upon "The Ancient Usages and Customs of the Settlement" and signed by most of the "Principal Inhabitants."[87] This code did not come near to a constitution but it gave both the institution of the Magistracy and the Public Meeting a vague official recognition. In any case, the settlers saw it as an offi-

---

86 Burdon (1935, I:100–6)
87 Ibid.

cial blessing of their activities and *the* first official step towards giving them a quasi-official status.

The institution of the Public Meeting, whose basic outline was democratic in nature, was unique in the history of British overseas possessions. In the beginning, the meeting was a simple gathering of woodcutters to discuss and regulate general business. From the 1740s onwards, the inhabitants admitted to the Public Meeting had both the right to elect the Magistracy (at that time consisting of a jury of thirteen settlers), and to introduce urgent matters of common interest and requiring an immediate solution. Once a resolution was passed it was put in force as law, provided it was approved by the majority of the members. There were no special qualifications for membership apart from proving ownership of property worth a certain amount.

When the population increased and became more heterogeneous in character due to the growing number of free persons of colour and free Blacks, the criteria for membership had to be revised. As a consequence, it became more difficult for the free coloured and free Blacks to meet the requirements and those who had been able to do so previously, lost most of their rights and were no longer allowed to vote. In the beginning of the 19th century, the requirements were even stricter: Whereas white settlers had to have resided in the Bay for one year, free coloured persons had to show residence of five consecutive years and prove ownership of twice as much visible property as White persons.[88] Nevertheless, even if the rules for the admission of the free coloureds were very discriminatory and almost impossible to meet, the very fact that all free men regardless of colour could, theoretically, be admitted to the Public Meeting was very advanced, especially in comparison to the West Indies.

In the course of time, both the Magistracy and the Public Meeting became controlled by the more influential White settlers who also were the owners of large tracts of land. It was in the interest of this elite to protect and consolidate its rights and powers at the expense of the less affluent White settlers, the free coloureds and the free Blacks. The immigrants from the Mosquito Shore once more complained that the

> ... *former English inhabitants of the Bay of Honduras ... raising themselves into a kind of legislative body, form laws and regulations, and make Magistrates to enforce these Laws ... [which] seem partial and in favour of one set of people, and palpably calculated to enslave another ...*[89]

---

88   Burdon (1935, II: 232)

89   Robert English, Samuel Harrison and Abraham Bull to Supt. Despard, 20 Aug. 1787, PRO CO 123/5

It did not take long until the first superintendent appointed by London, the Irish-born Edward Despard, who had been commissioned with only minimal authority in 1787, came into conflict with the magistrates. But since neither the institution of the Magistracy nor the Public Meeting was recognized by the British government – and was therefore never given any constitutional authority under the British Crown – London did not support the superintendent and he was left to fight for himself. According to London, the major task of the superintendent was merely to enforce the terms of the London Convention and co-operate with the Spanish in destroying the small plantations of subsistence crops. When it came to distributing the newly conceded lands, Despard acted according to the orders he had received from London and was in favour of resettling the immigrants from the Mosquito Shore on certain parts of these lands, thus arousing strong discontent among the "principal inhabitants".

As far as the Magistracy was concerned, Despard soon found himself in a dilemma, because strictly speaking, the institution in its executive as well as semi-judicial function was violating the very terms of the Convention. In fact, the Spanish interpreted the institution of the Magistracy as a provisional form of government:

> ... en la boca del mismo Walix, residía un Cuerpo de 9 Magistrados ... y siendo todo sistema de gobierno en aquel paraje directamente contrario al artículo 7º de la Convención celebrada en 1786 ...[90]

Despard tried to comply with the terms of the treaty and forced the magistrates, whom he described as "a very arbitrary aristocracy",[91] to give up their office. When the situation became critical, open war broke out between the two parties involved. The reactions shown by the influential settlers were massive and they were afraid that the new policy would, eventually, undermine their power. When Despard made plans to facilitate the ownership of land, not only for the newcomers from the Mosquito Shore but also for the free coloured and free Blacks, the landowners, together with their representatives in the Magistracy, took the decision to appeal directly to London for help. The main argument of the old-established settlers was that Despard's intentions would cause a sig-

---

90 (... At the mouth of the same Walix, a corps of 9 magistrates resided and since in this place every form of government is totally contrary to article seven of the Convention of 1786 ..."), Gálvez a Valdéz, 8–10–1789, AGI México 3108, printed in full by Calderón Quijano (1944: 360).

91 "A Narrative of the Publick Transactions ...", PRO CO 123/10 in Bolland (1977: 38).

nificant social upheaval in the settlement and be against the basic principles of law and order

> *It breaks in pieces all the Links of Society, and destroys all Order Rank and Government ... but upon this wild and Levelling principle of Universal Equality, they would become entitled not only to elect Magistrates, but themselves to be elected ...*[92]

These prospects were terrible enough to convince the British Parliament to interfere, reduce Despard's authority to deal with the magistrates and finally have him called back in 1790. Back in England, Despard continued his fervent fight for the "suppressed". The Anglo-Irish rebel was arrested for co-operation in the Irish uprising in 1798 and was finally hanged for treason in 1803 due to his alleged involvement in a plot to assassinate King George III and proclaim a republic.

Despite the first superintendent having been an utter failure (in the eyes of the British) and in response to the ever present danger of the Spanish destroying the Bay Settlement, the Colonial Office decided to continue to appoint superintendents. They all indirectly acted in favour of the established elite and helped to re-establish the old "order" by giving recognition to the magistrates.

The Colonial Office remained adamant in its position and refused to delegate the superintendents with more competence than absolutely necessary. The magistrates were practically the only authority in the settlement and did not refrain from openly challenging the superintendents, whose position remained rather week. According to Superintendent Hamilton, the general standards of the institution were appalling: In 1807 he complained about the bold behaviour of the magistrates[93] who, knowing only too well that the commission issued to the superintendents was too vague and far too general, took full advantage of the hesitant position of the Colonial Office. The struggle for power between the superintendents and the magistrates continued and if we are to lend credence to the opinions the superintendents had of the magistrates "... the most illiterate Men of the worst Characters are placed on the Bench ..."[94], it is understandable why their relationship never improved.

After having examined the general lifestyle in the Bay Settlement and its elementary form of government, we may now summarize the following:

---

92 Memorial from Robert White to Lord Sydney, 21 Feb. 1788, PRO CO 123/6, Ibid.

93 Hamilton to Gov. Coote, 26 Nov. 1807, PRO CO 123/17, Ibid.

94 Arthur to Bathurst, 2 Dec. 1814, PRO CO 123/23, Ibid.

Throughout the 18ᵗʰ and until the first two decades of the 19ᵗʰ centuries the government of the Bay Settlement or Honduras Settlement, as it was increasingly beginning to be referred to, was based upon the "Ancient customs of the Bay". This system of government was spontaneous and rudimentary and consisted of

- a number of magistrates who had a judicial and an executive capacity
- the Public Meeting as a form of legislative assembly and
- a permanent superintendent with limited authority, sent and paid by London.

From 1778 onwards, the form of government in the settlement was characterized by a continuous struggle for power between the magistrates and the superintendents, which did not end until 1862, when the Honduras Settlement was finally recognized as official British colony. Until then, the influential settlers, consisting of the magistrates and the Public Meeting, held executive powers and remained in unchallenged control of their homemade legislature and judiciary.

6. European Diplomatic Rivalries and Their Effect Upon the Settlement

Although the British settlement in the Bay of Honduras may have been only of minor importance for the imperialistic powers of Europe, it cannot be studied in isolation and the wider issues at stake have to be considered.

Throughout the 18ᵗʰ century the fate of the Honduras Settlement was strongly connected to the diplomatic scenario of Europe at the time. Several wars between Great Britain and Spain and the ever changing state of Anglo-Spanish diplomatic relations – which depended largely on whether or not Spain and France were allies – shaped the future developments of the settlement.

During the Spanish War of Succession, Britain supported the French pretender to the Spanish throne and signed peace with France at the Treaty of Utrecht in 1713.[95] In compensation Britain gained the *Asiento de Negros*, an

---

95   Britain, Spain/Austria, and Holland had formed an alleigance against France. The three countries supported the Austrian candidate for the Spanish throne, the Habsburg Archduke Charles, instead of the Bourbon candidate Phillip of Anjou, a grandson of Luis XIV. After the brother of Archduke Charles died, the latter – in the cases of his election

agreement by which Spain granted the monopoly of the Spanish colonial slave trade for thirty years at the rate of 4,800 slaves per year. As a consequence, the contraband activities in and around the Bay of Honduras increased and received a quasi-legal status. The ideally situated ports were convenient places for the refitting of ships and the reshipment of slaves. These activities, together with the timber trade, played an important role in establishing the economic importance of the region.

Due to the fact that Britain had signed the Treaty of Utrecht, she was no longer in favour with Spain who consequently refused to acknowledge any British rights to the Bay of Honduras. Britain, although not willing to officially recognize the disputed areas in the Bay as a British possession, took the local woodcutters' point of view that both the treaties of 1670 and 1713 gave a legal basis for the continuation of the cutting activities. In retaliation, the Spanish mounted several attacks on the Honduras Settlement to dislodge the British from the principal woodcutting areas.

The Spanish assaults in the Bay of Honduras, however, were not the only cause for the growing hostility between the two countries. After the Treaty of Utrecht in 1713, the Bourbon dynasty came to power in Spain and a more reformed economic policy was pursued. Spain began to insist vehemently on her trading monopoly in all parts of the Caribbean: Every attempt was made to put an end to British smuggling activities and Spanish *guardacostas* (coastal guard ships) were ordered to seize all English vessels carrying trade goods coming from a Spanish colony. This came unexpected for the British who had combined the gaining of the *Asiento de Negros* with an increased exploitation of commercial opportunities in and around the Bay, for example by forming a trading company, the "British South Seas Company".

Whereas in former days, the English would have retaliated by giving privateers royal licences for counter-attacks, in agreement with the Treaty of Utrecht it was now endeavoured to settle the matter through diplomatic channels. Again, the undefined status of the Bay of Honduras gave constant rise to problems. While diplomats were conducting negotiations in far off Europe, the crews of the Spanish *guardacostas* were not always up to date with the current diplomatic situation and therefore uncertain whether to take action or not. To exclude all possibility of doubt, Spanish forces in the Caribbean not only began to attack every British vessel they encountered but also to harass the woodcutters in the settlement.

– would have ruled over both the Spanish and the Austrian Empire. Alarmed by these prospects, the British saw the equilibrium of Europe in danger, left the allegiance, supported the French pretender and signed a treaty with France.

Next came The War of Jenkins' Ear (1739–1748), during which Britain was first and foremost concerned with challenging Spain's monopoly of trade and securing her own rights of both trade and sovereignty: The Honduras Settlement was not spared from the repercussions of this war and it did not take long until several Spanish assaults occurred. In 1745, camps along the New River were destroyed and in 1754, Spanish forces attacked from the Petén region despite the presence of military from Jamaica and Roatán.

After a series of diplomatic struggles and the Seven Years War (1756–1763) Britain was in a strong position again. Almost every West Indian island except Saint Domingue was in the hands of the British. Nevertheless, at the Treaty of Paris, which ended the Seven Years War, Britain agreed to restore Martinique and Guadeloupe to France (in return for Canada), and Cuba to Spain. As far as the Honduras Settlement was concerned, for the first time, the Spanish officially authorized the economic activities in the Bay of Honduras. However, the Spanish neither defined boundaries nor mentioned specific geographical names and the respective article of the treaty remained extremely ambiguous and further troubles were predestined.

These troubles soon manifested when attempts were made to temporarily settle the question of boundaries. The Governor of Yucatán ordered the Baymen to confine themselves to cutting on the Belize River only, which, strictly speaking, was in defiance of the aforementioned treaty. The adherence to these restrictions was to prove a major problem because the timber stands on the Belize River had already become exhausted. But since there was a great demand for the timber on the European market, the Baymen ignored these restrictions and began to extend their cutting activities far beyond this provisional and unofficial boundary. On this occasion, London finally saw a reason to interfere; the continuation of its supply of the valuable wood was at stake and precautions were taken by sending a British warship to the Bay. This must have had the desired effect and during the decade to come no Spanish attacks were reported.

When the North American colonies declared war against the mother country in 1776, Britain's streak of successes came to an end. Spain's decision to unite with France and the other European powers and join the "United American States" in their fight for freedom also added a new dimension to the problems in the Bay. Being an ally of France, Spain took advantage of her strong position and once more seized the opportunity to dislodge the British from the settlement. Before the Baymen even knew that war had been declared, a huge Spanish fleet, led by the *gobernador* of Bacalar in person, anchored outside the reef and attacked the small offshore community on St. George's Cay. More than three hundred and fifty prisoners were taken (approximately one hundred White people, forty of mixed colour and two hundred slaves), most of which were shipped to Yucatán and from there to the dungeons in Havana. The rest of the population, which, at the time of the attack had, mostly likely, been working inland, were reported having abandoned the settlement and having arrived on the islands of Roatán and Guanaja (Bonacca) off the Atlantic coast of present Honduras.[96]

With the signing of the peace treaty of Versailles in 1783 (which not only recognized the independence of the United States but also dealt with the ownership of a number of islands in the Caribbean), the boundaries in the Bay Settlement were properly defined (see Map 11) for the first time.

The settlers, however, were not satisfied with these concessions and hundreds of woodcutters with their families and slaves had already started to occupy areas beyond the boundaries, "The Limits". Via their agent in London, several petitions for an extension of these boundaries were made. In 1786 the Baymen finally succeeded, and it was agreed to draw up a supplement to the treaty, the Convention of London. Due to, among other reasons, Britain's success in Gibraltar (whose inhabitants successfully held out during a three year siege) and by her occupation of the Falkland Islands, the British were in a very strong position at the conference table. The petitions for the extension of boundaries, "The New Limits", were granted, with the restriction that neither permanent settlement nor other activities except woodcutting were allowed.

Throughout the reign of Charles III (Carlos III, *el político*) from 1759 to 1788, Spain's policy towards Britain was one of revenge. This was mostly due to the temporary British occupation of the Spanish stronghold Cuba, and the capitulation of Manila (at that time the Philippines were a colony of Spain) before British troops. As far as the Caribbean was concerned, although Britain was in a dominant position, Spain's anti-British monarch only agreed to grant the territory concessions in the Honduras Settlement under the condition that the Mosquito Shore be evacuated of all British citizens, as shall be discussed in detail in the following section.

During the Napoleonic Wars, when Spain joined France against England in the Alliance of San Ildefonso in 1796, once again the area of the Bay of Honduras was seriously affected. The court of Madrid despatched orders to Yucatán to start actions for "*... una expulsión inmediata y eficaz de los colonos ...*",[97] (... an immediate and efficient expulsion of the colonists).

---

96   "An account of the Spanish landing at St. George's Key ...", PRO CO 137/76. White to Lord Shelbourne, 2 July 1782; White to Lord North, 8 April and 11 Dec. 1783, Ibid. 123/2 and Bartlett to Dalling, no date, Ibid. 137/76.

97   Calderón Quijano (1944: 353)

As a consequence, the situation started to become very tense; a state which lasted for two years and was the cause for serious internal disputes and much tension. At the Public Meeting it was even discussed whether to defend or evacuate the settlement at the mouth of the Belize River, but eventually, the majority of settlers voted in favour of defence and preparations for the forming of adequate troops were initiated. In order to assemble enough soldiers for the defence force, Jamaica assisted by sending additional troops[98] and the settlers took the decision to give a considerable number of slaves their freedom. At the same time, the Governor of Yucatán, Arturo O'Neill Tirone,[99] an Irishman in the service of the Spanish, with the help of several ships sent by the Viceroyalty of New Spain and the Captaincy General of Havana, was dedicating himself to preparing a *"... magnífica expedición para la cual no regateó gastos ni esfuerzos"*[100] (... a magnificent expedition for which neither costs nor efforts were spared).

On September 3rd of the year 1798, the Spanish attack on the actual settlement finally began. Historians have written at length about the different strategies of this battle (the Battle of St. George's Cay), making it unnecessary to deal with this chapter of the history of Belize in detail here. For the present purposes, it will be sufficient to say that after a series of brief naval actions and one decisive battle, the Spanish began to retreat:

> *... el contacto de las fuerzas fue violento y rápido, destacando los españoles por su temerario valor en el ataque, y los ingleses por la hábil estrategia con que se defendieron ... [pero] ... vista la imposibilidad de conseguir el objetivo, O'Neill retiró sus fuerzas a Bacalar.[101]*

While credit must be given to the Baymen and their army of approximately 1200 adult male slaves for successfully defending their settlement against such

---

98 Details of this Public Meeting and the preparations in case of a Spanish attack can be found in *Archives of British Honduras*, Burdon (1935, I: 220–52).

99 O'Neill added "Tirone" to his last name because he originally came from the province of Tyrone in present Northern Ireland.

100 Calderón Quijano (1944: 353)

101 (... contact between the two forces was violent and quick, during which the Spanish showed outstanding courage in the attack and the English much skill in the defence strategy ... [but] ... after he realized that it was impossible to defeat the English, O'Neill and his forces retreated to Bacalar.) A complete and detailed account of the battle is given by Humphreys (1987: 85–100), Burdon (1935, I: 120 and passim) and Dobson (1973: 77–8). For a Spanish version see Molina Solís (1913: 342–346) and Calderón Quijano (1944: 394–6).

a strong Spanish armada, the actual significance of the success of the Battle of St. George's Cay was subsequently over-glorified by British observers and superintendents alike.[102] Indeed, comments made by "Spanish" historians seem to reduce the actual merits of the Baymen and their slaves and make us see the Battle of St. George's Cay in a different perspective. For example the Yucatecan historian Molina Solís claims that from the beginning, the large Spanish fleet was too clumsy and lacked a proper leadership and plan:

> *se notó la falta de un general en jefe, militar de talento y experto marino que supiese trazar un plan y ejecutarlo con energía y pericia"*[103]

Moreover, according to Molina Solís, the forces were severely affected by illness

> *... sufriendo la mayoría de la gente en el camino [de regreso a Mérida y Campeche] los horrores de la fiebre amarilla."*[104]

In addition, the advantages of nature, such as the treacherous reef, the narrow and twisted channels around the small cays and the right winds at the right time may also have acted in the Baymen's favour.

For the British settlers and some of the superintendents, the victory over the Spanish fleet signified that the place had been won by conquest and had finally become theirs: "... it may indeed be considered as a Conquered Country".[105] Even if the battle was always overemphasized in its historical importance, in the long run, the Baymen succeeded in gaining the increased attention of the British government. At last, the Honduras Settlement came to be regarded as a British colony in all but name. A permanent British garrison was stationed but the legal status of the settlement was not altered at all. To this very day, a festival is held in Belize annually on September 10ᵗʰ to commemorate the victory over the Spanish fleet. In an ironic twist of fate, it is exactly the descendants of the Spanish troops (i.e. the Mestizo immigrants from Southern Yucatán and the refugees from El Salvador, Honduras and Guatemala who were given asylum

---

102 Such as for example Burdon (1935:I) and Caiger (1951: 95–100), cf. also the various letters from Barrow to Portland, PRO CO 137/101 quoted in Humphreys (1987: 90–98) and the centenary edition of the Colonial Guardian newspaper of 1898 quoted in Ibid.

103 (... there was an absence of a general, talented army officer and expert mariner who would have been able to work out a plan and execute it with skill and energy...), cf. Molina Solís (1913: 342–6)

104 (... on their way back to Merida and Campeche the majority suffered the horrors of yellow fever ...), Ibid.

105 Burdon (1935, I: 274)

and the possibility of immigration in the "safe-haven" of modern Belize) who heartily participate in these festivities.[106]

Throughout the Napoleonic Wars, issues regarding the Honduras Settlement continued to be affected by the state of affairs between Spain and France. Generally speaking, as far as the question of sovereignty and the territorial boundaries of the settlement were concerned, there were no more disputes, neither military nor diplomatic. All negotiations were postponed and the situation continued as determined in the treaties prior to the Napoleonic wars.

7. The Problem of Sovereignty and the Important Role of the Mosquito Coast

Despite the victory over the Spanish fleet in the Battle of St. George's Cay "… esta campaña, en la cual pretenden [los Ingleses] ver el nacimiento de su derecho de soberanía a aquellas tierras …",[107] and the subsequent general opinion by settlers, superintendents and some 19th and 20th century historians that the territory was finally won by conquest, Spain continued to hold firm sovereignty.

This was a very abnormal situation because in reality – and mainly due to the appointment of a superintendent from London – official British involvement in the administration of the area could no longer be denied. The British Colonial Office, however, made it quite clear that the Honduras Settlement remained what it had long been "… a settlement, for certain purposes, in the possession and under the protection of His Majesty, but not within the territory and dominion of His Majesty."[108] Legally, it came to Spain's holding the territory *de jure* and the settlers' holding it *de facto;* an ambiguous situation which continued until the Honduras Settlement officially assumed colonial status. Throughout the 18th century, Britain's sole interest in the settlement lay in

---

106 As I was able to witness for myself, a considerable number of these Mestizos tend to have a complete lack of the historical background to this festival. Those who pretend to have at least some historical knowledge, see the battle as the only basis for the very existence of modern Belize. Despite the existence of a significant amount of tension in race relations in modern Belize, all Belizeans welcome any anniversary mainly as a pretext for taking days off work, joining the celebrations and temporarily forgetting about racial and political issues. To a large percentage of the population, the actual historical background to festivities is of secondary importance.

107 (… In this campaign the English pretend to see the beginning of their sovereign rights to that territory …), Calderón Quijano (1944:354)

108 Parliamentary Act of 1817, 57 Geo.III, C53 quoted by Dobson (1973:79).

claiming her rights to the exploitation of the region's forests while, at the same time, respecting Spanish claims to the land as such.

The problem of sovereignty remained a contradictory issue. Spain insisted that her claim was based entirely upon the Papal bull of 1494 and the subsequent Treaty of Tordesillas between Spain and Portugal, the latter of which supposedly was to settle the respective claims in the New World. In turn, the settlers and the diplomats in charge of the negotiations must have asked themselves the question on what grounds the Spanish were still able to claim sovereignty over a stretch of land they had never been able to occupy from the 16th century onwards? It was inevitable that after 250 years, doubts should arise whether the Papal bull could still be taken seriously or would still be valid at all.

The settlers on their part argued that *because* the place had been populated by their forefathers, exploited and successfully defended, it had rightfully become their homeland. And since they were determined to hold on to it at any cost, they were dependent on the region's sole economic source, the forests.

Although it cannot be denied that the demand for logwood and mahogany created by the European market initially boosted the local forestry industry, at this stage it has to be emphasized that the expansion of the cutting activities as such was *not* initiated by the Europeans in Europe. It was the expatriates in the settlement (woodcutters, contractors, traders, agents etc.), who were looking for an increased and steady income possibility.

When the forest reserves within the territory concessions had become depleted, the woodcutters simply went beyond the boundary limits in search of virgin forest stands. Although these new forest areas were not inhabited by "Spanish" people and there was consequently no resistance (the only people living in and on the fringes of these new areas were scattered pockets of Maya), this violation of boundaries was an open provocation for Spain.

But this was not the first time that the boundaries were ignored. In fact, throughout the period of occupation and from the moment concessions were granted, the boundaries of the areas allocated to the woodcutters were continuously violated and logwood operations were extended west and especially south of the limits. One must bear in mind, however, that there were no expansionistic ideas behind these infringements. The violation of boundaries were primarily made for economic reasons: Since it was still forbidden to engage in agricultural activities, the settlers' livelihood depended exclusively on the extraction and exportation of timber and they saw no other choice but to look for fresh supply beyond the limits. The boundaries were not ignored because land was becoming scarce as a result of, for example, a drastic increase in population. As we have seen, this was not the case: The inhabitants only numbered approximately three thousand including slaves and vast stretches of land within the limits were still available at this time.

After the settlers had been conceded usufructuary rights, they began to feel more confident and showed a stronger tendency to deliberately ignore the boundaries. Although various superintendents tried to enforce the terms of the treaties on behalf of the Crown, "… land was occupied without heed to the limits prescribed."[109]

Only relatively late did the Spanish begin to realize that the violation of boundaries was more than just trespassing, that the settlers' presence was beginning to have a dangerous permanency and that their claims presented actual danger ("… *sus derechos adquieren un carácter de peligrosa permanencia …*"[110]). Finally, the Spanish reacted and made several attempts to drive the Baymen out of the entire territory. Nevertheless, in the long run, the Spanish were not able to do so, a fact which, to this very day, continues to raise basic questions such as:

- Why were the Spanish forces incapable of dislodging these settlements of outlaws *("aquellas poblaciones de bandidos"[111])?* and
- Why did they not erect permanent forts to guard the boundaries, especially after having already made several unsuccessful attempts?

The following factors might partly explain Spain's incapability to secure the territory:

- **First**: From the beginning, Spanish policy towards the Bay of Honduras had been indecisive, which was mainly due to a lack of unity and coordination difficulties between Old and New Spain.
- **Secondly**: The heyday of Spain's power had long passed. After 1713, when the Bourbon dynasty came to power in Spain, her position was temporarily revitalized by gaining a stronger position at the treaties but in a longer term context, it did not alter the situation.
- **Thirdly**: During the earlier times when the various efforts to dislodge the settlers would most likely have been more successful, the Spanish clearly failed to gain control over the area. It seems that, at the time, they were much more concerned about the settlers' religion, and the negative effects the non-Catholics would have on the already converted Indians than about the settlers' trading and smuggling activities in the Bay.

---

109 Burdon (1935, III)
110 Calderón Quijano (1944:181)
111 Ibid.

> ... *los Contrabandistas, se componen por la mayor parte de Judios, Hereges, Luteranos, Calvinistas, Zuinglianos, ... Methodistas, y otra infinidad de Enemigos mortales de nuestra Sta. Fee Cathólica, que porfían en engañar los Corazones de los incautos Yndios ... es de creer que se exterminará la verdadera Religión en aquellos Payses ... del mismo modo como aconteció con las Provincias de Flandes ...*[112]

In a certain sense, the Spanish were short-sighted and, at the time, did not fully comprehend the economic consequences their conceding the British the right to cut logwood would eventually have.

On the other hand, these fears were not completely unfounded: In the 17th century for example, the British had succeeded in forging a strong allegiance with the Zambo-Miskito of the Mosquito Coast who, from that time on, were to prove loyal and faithful friends of the British: "*... según han alcanzado los Yngleses con los Yndios Mosquitos o Zambos en la Costa de Honduras,*" as written in a report sent to Spain in 1770.[113] In actual fact, on various occasions the Zambo-Miskito sided with the British in their fight against their common enemy, the Spanish.

Apart from the Yucatecan Commissioners directly in charge of the Honduras Settlement, the Spanish government possessed only very limited knowledge of its exact geographical location. The truth was that Spain was unsure of its proximity to the Mexican, Guatemalan and Honduran dominions and whether the trespassers presented a real danger to these places or not.

According to Spanish documents, "The Settlement on the Río Walix" was thought to be close to Merida, the provincial capital of Yucatán. In addition, the fact that hardly any geographical distinction was made between the "Bay of Campeachy" (an area in the Gulf of Mexico the British logwood cutters had abandoned as early as 1714) and the Bay of Honduras, reflects the limited knowledge as to the exact location of the "Walix Settlement". When Madrid gave orders to expel the woodcutters from the Bay Settlement, "*... [que] se desalojen los ingleses de las islas y parajes que han ocupado en las vecindades de*

---

112 ... these smugglers to a large degree were composed of Jews, Heretics, Lutherans, Calvinists, Zwinglianists, and Methodists ... and other infinite deadly enemies of our Holy, Catholic Faith ..., it is to be believed that the true religion of these countries shall be exterminated ... just as it occurred in the province of Flanders ...", Report by Don Thomas Southwell, 1770, Bibliotéca del Palacio Real, Madrid, Misc. Ayala, Tomo XVII, No. 2831, Fols.1–25 quoted by Calderón Quijano (1944: 453).

113 (... just as the English had been able to do with the Mosquito Indians or Zambos of the Honduran Coast ...), Ibid.

Campeche ..." [114], the area was still referred to as "the islands and places in the vicinity of Campeche", which was quite a distance away on the other side of the Yucatán Peninsula in the Gulf of Mexico.

The Spanish may have been successful in temporarily dislodging the settlers, but, in their view, they were not able to eradicate "*... el mal de raíz ...*" (the root of the evil). [115] This was mainly because each time the woodcutters were driven out of the territory, prior to 1786, they were able to go south and seek refuge among their compatriots on the Mosquito Coast, where the British had established a Protectorate. From there they would start to repopulate the area and re-assume their former activities once danger had passed.

At this stage it becomes again necessary to turn to the Mosquito Coast. In order to fully appreciate the significant role the Mosquito Coast played for the future colony of British Honduras we once more have to elaborate on additional details of its history.

To begin with, and generally speaking, the allegiance the British had been able to establish with the Miskito Indians served as a tie to the consolidating of British power in the Western Caribbean which ultimately led to a further weakening of Spanish power. Due to the hostility of these allies, the Zambo-Miskito, the Spanish were never able to integrate the Mosquito Coast into the Captaincy General of Guatemala. As far as the status of the Honduras Settlement was concerned, the amicable relationship the British had with the Zambo-Miskito indirectly contributed to the Baymen eventually achieving their goal.

As we have seen in Chapter Three, by 1750 the British were well rooted on the Mosquito Coast. After Cape Gracias a Dios and Black River (present Palacios) were established, Bragman's Bluff (present Puerto Cabezas or Bilwi), Bluefields and Brewer's Lagoon followed. The settlers also founded small plantations of sugar, indigo and coconut, cut logwood and pine, collected other forest products such as chicle [116] and maintained trade relations with both the indigenous tribes and the Spanish colonies in the interior.

While it is true that Britain's main objective in the Western Caribbean was to secure the supply of logwood and mahogany from the British settlement in the Bay of Honduras and her concern for the Mosquito Shore and the Bay Islands came only secondary, the economic and strategic role of the Mosquito Coast (and to a lesser degree the Bay Islands) should not be underestimated.

---

114 (... the English should be expelled from the islands and places they occupied in the vicinity of Campeche ...), Royal cédula of 11 Dec 1724 to the Viceroy, Marquéz de Casafuerte and the Governor of Yucatán, Antonio de Cortaire, quoted in Joseph (1987: 45).

115 Calderón Quijano (1944: 69)

116 The gum of the *sapodilla* tree, which is the main ingredient in chewing gum.

First and foremost, the Mosquito Coast served as a pawn of no little value during the negotiating of the territory concessions granted to the future Belize. At the Convention of London in 1786, where the British asked for the extension of the territory limits, Spain only agreed to the petitions of the British under the condition that the Mosquito Shore and the Bay Islands be evacuated. A mass return of previously expelled Baymen and a large scale immigration of White Shoremen including slaves and Zambo-Miskito soon followed. 2,214 people in total, as mentioned previously, arrived in the Bay Settlement.[117] It was a substantial sum and together with the already existing population of approximately 2,700, these immigrants played an important part in shaping the settlement's future society.

In the years following Britain's official withdrawal from the Mosquito Coast in 1786, her economic interests in the area began to wane. In 1823, however, the year of Central American independence and the formation of the Central American Federation, a revival of British influence on the Mosquito Coast began to manifest itself and for the first time earnest efforts were undertaken to attract British settlers to the Mosquito Coast.

Here, it is worth dwelling on a particularly unsuccessful and tragic re-colonization scheme, the so-called "Poyaisian Land Scheme", a relatively little-known episode in the history of Central America. This venture was one of a number of undertakings by a Scottish charlatan and soldier of fortune Gregor MacGregor,[118] who managed to obtain from the Miskito King a grant to a huge tract of land in the Black River area, in the north of the Miskito territory which included a region called the Poyais, named after a tribe of natives, the Poyer (the present Paya).

As it turned out, this "Poyaisian Land Scheme" was nothing but a massive fraud. "Sir" MacGregor, who took on a false identity and false lineage, proclaiming himself "His Majesty [or *Cacique*] of the Principality of Poyais" and succeeded in interesting a group of merchants in forming a colonization company who started promoting the healthy climate, the fertile soil, the abundant

---

117 Cf. Col Lawree to Napean, 26 Jan 1788, PRO CO 123/6 and *Defence of the Settlers of Honduras ...*, (1824: 45–6)

118 In the years prior to initiating his fraudulent colonization schemes, MacGregor was involved in fighting the Spanish in Florida and South America. In 1817 he led a band of troops to a victory over a Spanish garrison that was in control of an island on the north-eastern coast of Florida. He also took part in the independence movements of Venezuela and the remaining states of the Viceroyalty of Nueva Granada (present Colombia, Ecuador and Panama). Hoping to reap rich benefits, once independence was achieved, British merchants had financed British mercenaries who rendered their services in the struggle for independence and MacGregor was one of them.

crops, the many rich gold mines, the variety of marine resources, the perfect harbour and the friendly natives "… said to be affectionately attached to the British".[119] MacGregor even had special currency printed, the Poyais dollars, and induced many a credulous investor and naive settler, mostly fellow Scots and Irish, to invest and/or make down payments on land they had never seen and to book a passage across the Atlantic to become the first settlers of this New World paradise.

From the beginning, the experiment was ill-fated. In late 1822 the first colonists landed at the mouth of the Black River and selected Brewer's Lagoon as a site for settlement. When the second contingent arrived in early spring of 1823, instead of a thriving settlement they only encountered dense jungle vegetation and some survivors from the first group who informed them of the bitter reality. Many of the second group were professionals who had been promised positions in the civil service of the Poyais country and some colonists had also purchased positions as officers in the Poyaisian army.

To make matters worse, the ship that had brought the second group sailed away without notice, taking with it provisions, arms, merchandise, medicines and construction material. The would-be settlers were now completely left to their fate, although, at one stage, they were temporarily given assistance by the Miskito King. When the puzzled natives started to demand payment for the land they thought the colonists had purchased from MacGregor, it came to light that Poyais currency was bogus money and therefore not accepted.

In the absence of adequate housing and sanitation and with no replenish of supplies, tropical diseases began to take their toll. Abandoned by the colonization company in faraway Britain, the would-be settlers were left completely to themselves, struggling with the hardships of the tropical climate under miserable conditions.

During most of this time, MacGregor, the culprit, remained in Britain, living well off the proceeds of the invalid land sales and continued to distribute "titles of nobility" in his "Poyais Kingdom". He also began to launch similar schemes in France.[120]

---

119 Authentic propaganda to recruit colonists can be found in Anonymous (1838) and Strangeways (1822); the latter of which is believed to be a pseudonym of MacGregor.

120 In France, MacGregor was sentenced to eight months in prison, before he was transferred to Westminster where he was acquitted of his crimes in less than a week. In 1839 – after several modified and equally successful "Poyaisian schemes" – MacGregor retired in Venezuela having married a cousin of Simón Bolívar previously. In Venezuela he requested and received a pension as a general who had helped fight for independence. After dedicating himself to the cultivation of silkworm he died in 1845 and was buried with full military honours.

Fortunately, notice of the settlers' plight had reached the authorities in the Honduras Settlement farther north. Ships were sent to rescue the unfortunates and they were informed that "Poyais" was nothing but a fictional country. Many of the would-be settlers were so weakened that they died upon their arrival. A total of 180 of 250 had perished and the rest was ruined financially. Of the survivors that decided not to settle in the Bay only 50 made it back to Britain alive.[121] For many years to come, the news of the project's failure and the loss of many innocent lives dampened endeavours in Britain to push the colonization of the Mosquito Coast any further.

In Central America, Great Britain now began to see herself as the natural heir to the vacuum left by Spain and throughout the post-independence period diverted her attention from the Mosquito Coast only to expand her commercial influence in the rest of Central America. After all, the British had control of what is now Belize, which was well situated and on the way to strengthen and further expand its already important position as an entrepôt to serve Central American trade with Great Britain and the rest of Europe, as we shall see in Chapter Four.

Meanwhile, on the Mosquito Coast, the handful of remaining British residents wished for a revival of the old British influence. By the late 1830s, the descendants of the first superintendent, the Hodgson family (among others), had started one more campaign to attract immigrants to the district of Black River. The time seemed to be appropriate for there existed significant economic hardship in Britain itself, and politicians were eager to promote emigration to the colonies. The exaggerated propaganda praising the enormous possibilities of the "Poyaisian country", as it was still referred to, was only successful to a limited degree. Despite these, this time well-intentioned, post-Poyaisian colonization ventures, the few colonists who did arrive at the "tropical paradise" were never really able to properly acclimate to the Mosquito Coast whose poor soil, excessively wet tropical conditions, and the almost complete absence of a dry season, were extremely limiting.

Over the years the region of the British Protectorate of the Mosquito Coast lost its commercial and strategic importance and was developing more and more into an isolated coastal stretch, where a conglomerate of adventurers, sailors, merchants, free Blacks and fugitives from Jamaica and other West Indian islands as well as Black Caribs found their place. But, by now, it had become obvious that the area was no longer important enough for this peculiar group

---

121 First-hand accounts of this tragic colonization venture can be found in Sinclair (2004). For background information on MacGregor see Brown (2006) and Arends (1991) among others.

of residents to persuade the British Colonial Office to proclaim the Mosquito Coast a royal colony.[122]

Nevertheless, the British never ceased to keep a close eye on the Mosquito Coast, and with good reason: After the end of Spanish rule in Central America in the 1820s, voices for a revival of the ancient trans-isthmian route and the building of a canal became loud. On the Caribbean side, this route would have followed the San Juan River at the very south end of Miskito territory, the present border between Nicaragua and Costa Rica. The British did not hesitate to grasp this opportunity and it was agreed to let the Mosquito King have an annual allowance of 300 pounds sterling for granting an eventual right of way across territory owned by the Indians, "… otherwise we should lose his friendship, as the Spaniards and Americans are only too anxious we should do".[123] After all – and in comparison with the early activities of the logwood cutters in the Bay of Honduras – greater commercial interests were now at stake.

By pursuing the trans-oceanic canal project across the isthmus, which would have made the San Juan River accessible to commercial liners throughout the year, the British would have been able to not only enter in direct competition with the United States but also fulfil their ultimate goal – to weaken the economic presence of the Spanish in the area once and for all. But time had not come yet for this plan to materialize.

Only with the discovery of gold in California was the strategic position of the Mosquito Coast (and the republic of Nicaragua) for inter-oceanic traffic considered of crucial value. In 1849, the North American millionaire Vanderbilt opened up a route, on which gold prospectors from New York, together with the heavy equipment needed for mining, were transported across the isthmus.

As can be seen on Map 12, the journey was from the Caribbean port of San Juan del Norte (*"del Norte"* because the official former Spanish denomination for the Atlantic was *"Mar del Norte"*) up the San Juan River, over Lake Nicaragua and completing the last 20 km stretch overland until reaching San Juan del Sur (from *"Mar del Sur"* for the Pacific) on the Pacific side where passengers then took ships for San Francisco. Compared to the hardships of transporting passengers and mining equipment over the Rocky Mountains (the North American transcontinental railroad line was not opened until thirty years later!), the journey from New York to the San Juan River, across the isthmus

---

122 Generally speaking, however, the policy the British government had been pursuing in the case of the Mosquito Shore was very important for the evolution of the "Protectorate System" as such, a system which was characteristic for 19th century British informal empire especially in Africa.

123 Burdon (1935, II: 315)

and up to California lasted only 18 days. By 1851 regular services of the Vander-bilt's Accessory Transport Company were in operation.

Due to this revived interest in the building of a trans-oceanic canal, the British foothold on the entire Mosquito Coast, however weak, regained tem-porary importance. Immediately, the British took advantage of their good rela-tionship with the Zambo-Miskito and decided to reclaim the traditional capital of Mosquitia, San Juan del Norte. It would have functioned as port of embarka-tion for the future canal and was renamed Greytown. For many years, San Juan del Norte, which was the southernmost point of the British Protectorate of the Mosquito Coast, remained the gateway to the passage across the isthmus and became the most important Caribbean/Atlantic port for Central America.[124]

Although the British decided to withdraw from the Mosquito Coast and dissolve her protectorate for good in 1856, they did *not* abandon the inter-oce-anic canal project. On the contrary, very enthusiastic and overconfident, the British Foreign Secretary, Lord Palmerston, was even considering a British/American joint venture which he thought would be economically advanta-geous. It is worth citing from his rather vainglorious proposal:

> ... *having the whole American continent occupied by an active enterprising race like the Anglo-Saxons instead of the sleepy Spaniards ... I have long felt inwardly convinced that the Anglo-Saxon Race will in Process of Time become the Masters of the whole American Continent North and South, by Reason of their superior Qualities as compared with the degenerate Spanish and Portuguese Americans.*[125]

This intended joint venture, however, never materialized. In fact, by 1890 North Americans had established banana and sugar plantations on the entire Mos-quito Shore and North American capital controlled almost 90% of the region's commerce.

In 1890 "The North American Maritime Company" actually began to build the canal but after only two years, the company faced serious financial trou-ble. All activities along the trans-isthmian canal across Nicaragua came to a

---

124 Unfortunately, this historical site, was also a strategic point during the Sandinista War. It was evacuated in the early 1980s and almost completely destroyed by heavy bombing and shellfire. The ruins of the former important Atlantic port are now partially sunken and completely overgrown by dense jungle vegetation.

125 Cf. Palmerson to Clarendon, 7 July, 30 Sept., 22 and 31 Dec. 1857 cited in Bourne (1961: 290), Humphreys (1968: 204) quoted in Naylor (1989: 183). In fact, by 1880, the North Americans had established banana and sugar plantations on the Shore and Amer-ican capital controlled almost 90% of the region's commerce.

standstill. Subsequent difficulties between the United States and the Nicaraguan government were responsible for the American Senate giving orders to purchase the bankrupt French Panama Canal Company in 1895. In 1904 the building of the Panama Canal was initiated and any plans to re-open the ancient trans-isthmian route along the San Juan River and Lake Nicaragua were finally removed from the agenda.

The main purpose of elaborating on the Mosquito Coast and its role in the proposed trans-oceanic canal was to prove the importance of the Mosquito Coast for the future development of the settlement in the Bay of Honduras, the emerging colony of British Honduras, present Belize. *If* the Puritan settlers had not established friendly relations with the Miskito Indians in the first place, the expelled woodcutters from the Bay would never have been able to find shelter easily, at least not within relatively close reach of their settlement. Without the existence of the British Protectorate of the Mosquito Coast, the loggers from the Bay Settlement would most likely have sought refuge in Jamaica or gone to the North American colonies. From there, a mass return to the Bay Settlement for the purpose of repopulating the region would, no doubt, have been less likely. As a consequence, the British possessions in the Bay of Honduras, the future Belize, would probably have been populated by people from Southern Yucatán, the Petén and the Río Dulce region and incorporated into Mexico and Guatemala respectively.

From the 17th century onwards, the Mosquito Coast and the Bay Settlement came to be closely interrelated: Throughout the 17th and 18th centuries, Zambo-Miskito mercenaries helped to defend the British settlement against Spanish attacks. In the 19th century the Mosquito Coast was of significant importance for the settlement's forestry industry. In the late 1830s "Honduran" mahogany companies were seeking to extend their cutting operations to the north coast of the Miskito Kingdom and succeeded in persuading the Miskito King to grant them cutting rights on virgin forest tracts, not yet exploited by "Honduran" timber companies.

The final withdrawal of the British from the Mosquito Coast in 1856 facilitated the immigration for the Zambo-Miskito and the region's Black and Creole population into the future colony of British Honduras. Whereas the latter two groups were invaluable labourers for the exploitation of mahogany, the Zambo-Miskito, being expert fishermen and hunters, were employed by the British mahogany companies to hunt, fish or "make plantations".

Finally, *if* the trans-isthmian canal project via the San Juan River on the southern end of the Mosquito Coast had been realized, the British would have been in a very strong position: For example they would have been able to block the entry to the canal in times of trouble. Eventual developments on the Shore could have been easily overseen from the future colony of British Honduras which, apart from already playing an important role in Central American commerce, would also have gained considerable importance as a strategic base. In my opinion, among other reasons, the strategic potentials of the entire Bay area, no doubt, was an important contributing factor for the decision of the British government to finally proclaim the Honduras Settlement an official colony.

Most Belizeans, when discussing the history and development of modern Belize, generally seem to neglect the importance of the Mosquito Coast. As already pointed out in the previous chapter and as the foregoing digression hopefully demonstrates, the historical development of Belize can and must not be studied without taking into consideration the history of the Mosquito Coast.

Having established the crucial strategic position of the Mosquito Coast, we now return to the Bay of Honduras and the core question of *why* the Spanish forces were not able to permanently expel the British settlers.

During the second half of the 18ᵗʰ century, the Bay Settlement/Honduras Settlement had expanded considerably which was the result of several demographic developments, especially the mass relocation of Baymen and the immigration of Shoremen in 1787. Undoubtedly, by that time, it would have been much more difficult for the Spanish to try to evacuate the settlement. In addition, now it even counted on a vague military protection from Jamaica and only a large scale and carefully devised colonization scheme on part of the Spanish would have solved the problems of sovereignty once and for all.

But it was too late for such plans because Spain had already made peace with England "... *una paz cristiana universal y perpetua.*"[126] Any plans for a realization of full scale colonization would have been extremely embarrassing for Madrid since "... *una sincera y constante amistad entre sus Majestades ...*"[127] was proposed in 1763 at the Treaty of Paris. Meanwhile, the Spanish had already devised an alternative strategy: By enticing away the Black labour force in the settlement, they hoped to indirectly weaken its economy. Although runaway slaves did cause temporary upheaval in the settlement, in the long term, these measures turned out to be unsuccessful.

Before coming to the end of this chapter, it is essential to analyse another important aspect in connection with the socio-economic developments of the Bay Settlement in the 18ᵗʰ century. So far it has been implied that the general uncertainty in the entire region, caused by the anomalous diplomatic status,

---

126 (... universal and perpetual Christian peace), Article I of the Peace Treaty, 10–2–1763 quoted in Calderón Quijano (1944:180).
127 (... sincere and constant friendship between Your Majesties ...), Ibid.

had only negative effects for the settlers but, retrospectively seen, it was not the case. This was mainly for the following three reasons:

- **First:** The fact that agriculture was prohibited also had positive effects, albeit for a selected group of settlers only. The wealthier and more influential woodcutters (the local elite) were at the same time also gaining huge profits from the import and distribution of provisions and other basic necessities. They did not have to fear competition from eventual domestic agricultural activities, thus consolidating even more their powerful position.
- **Secondly:** The ambiguous diplomatic status and the fact that the Bay Settlement was not an official British colony as yet, in certain ways also acted in the settlers' favour. For example, the Navigation Acts – which controlled the flow of trade to and from the colonies – could not be applied and as a consequence the settlers were not exclusively tied to Great Britain and were free to engage in trade relations with the United States.
- **Thirdly:** The hesitant position of the British Foreign Office allowed the formation of an administrative and political body relatively free of the influence of colonial rule. This, I believe, was positive for the settlers in the long run, because compared to other British colonies, the Bay Settlement was in a much more advantageous position when negotiations for independence were initiated.

In sum, while the continuous problem of the uncertain diplomatic status may have been a hindrance for achieving the internal equilibrium of the Bay Settlement, it does explain and justify the hesitant position of the British government to not grant official colonial status until 1862. Besides, it cannot be denied that for both parties involved, Great Britain and Spain, the region in the Bay of Honduras clearly lacked in importance in order to agree to withdraw from more valuable possessions elsewhere.

The fact remains that for both powers, the area of the Bay of Honduras simply was not important *enough* for them to be willing to reach an immediate and irreversible agreement.

Enclosure 2: Title Page of "The Royal Gazette", Jamaica 1785

ROYAL GAZETTE.

JAMAICA. PUBLISHED BY ALEXANDER AIKMAN,
PRINTER TO THE KING'S MOST EXCELLENT MAJESTY.

VOL. VII.   From SATURDAY, Feb. 12, to SATURDAY, Feb. 19, 1785.   N° 8.

Advertisements of a moderate Length are inserted for 5s per Week, or 15s per Month.

For Liverpool,
THE SHIP
LADY PENRHYN,

For Liverpool,
THE SHIP
EARL OF DERBY,

For Freight or Charter, to any
port in Great-Britain, Ireland, or America,
THE SHIP
MOLLY,

FOR SALE,
THE SLOOP
MARY,

FOR SALE,
ENDEAVOR,

For London,
THE SHIP
HIBBERTS,

For **CHARLESTON**,

For SALE, on Monday
Eboe **NEGROES**,
by *Coppell & Goldwin*;

FOR SALE,
Eboe Negroes,
By *Coppell & Goldwin*,

To be peremptorily sold

MANBY & SHERRIFF,

Ironmongery & Ship-Chandlery.

London, November 3, 1784.

KING'S BENCH.

FOR SALE,
On Wednesday, the 9th inst.
ON BOARD THE SHIP,
Eboe Negroes;
By *Coppell & Goldwin*.

For SALE, on Monday
Eboe **NEGROES**
by *Coppell & Goldwin*.

Map 10: Historical Place Names in Belize

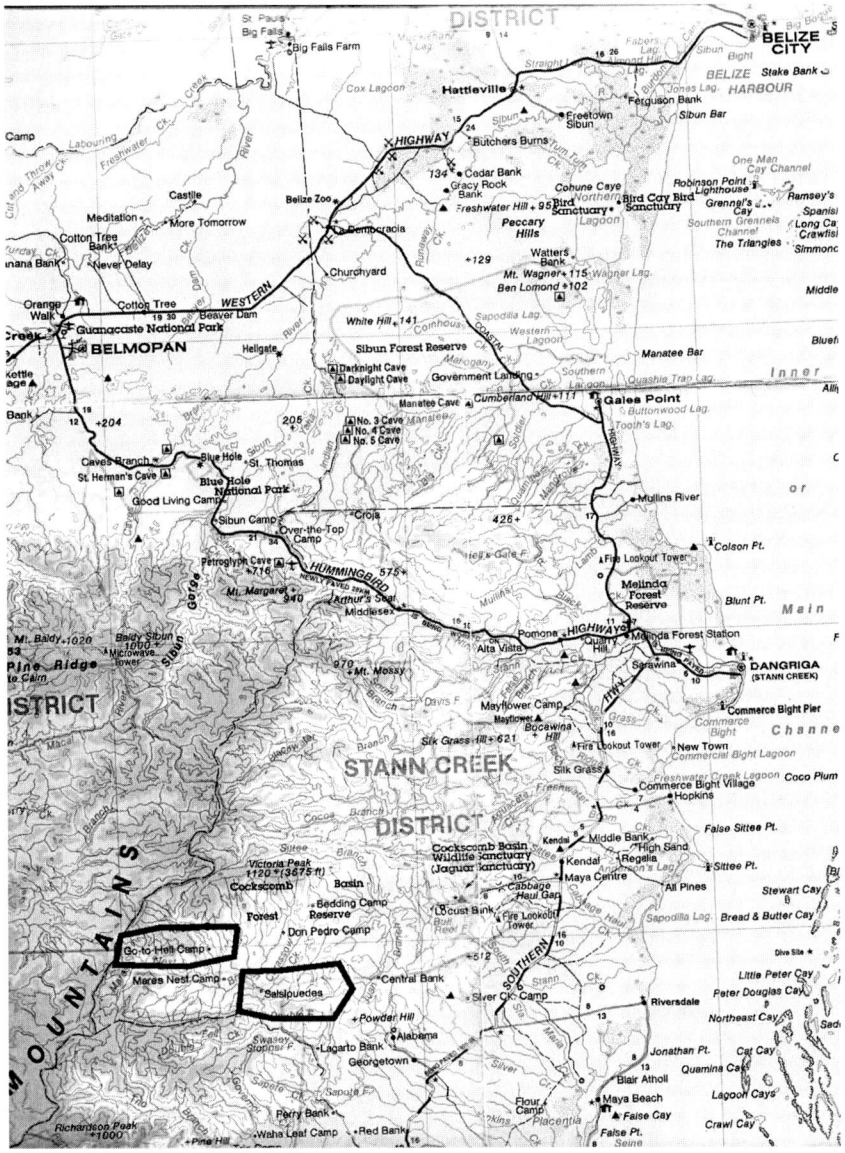

Map 11: Boundary Concessions, 1783/1786

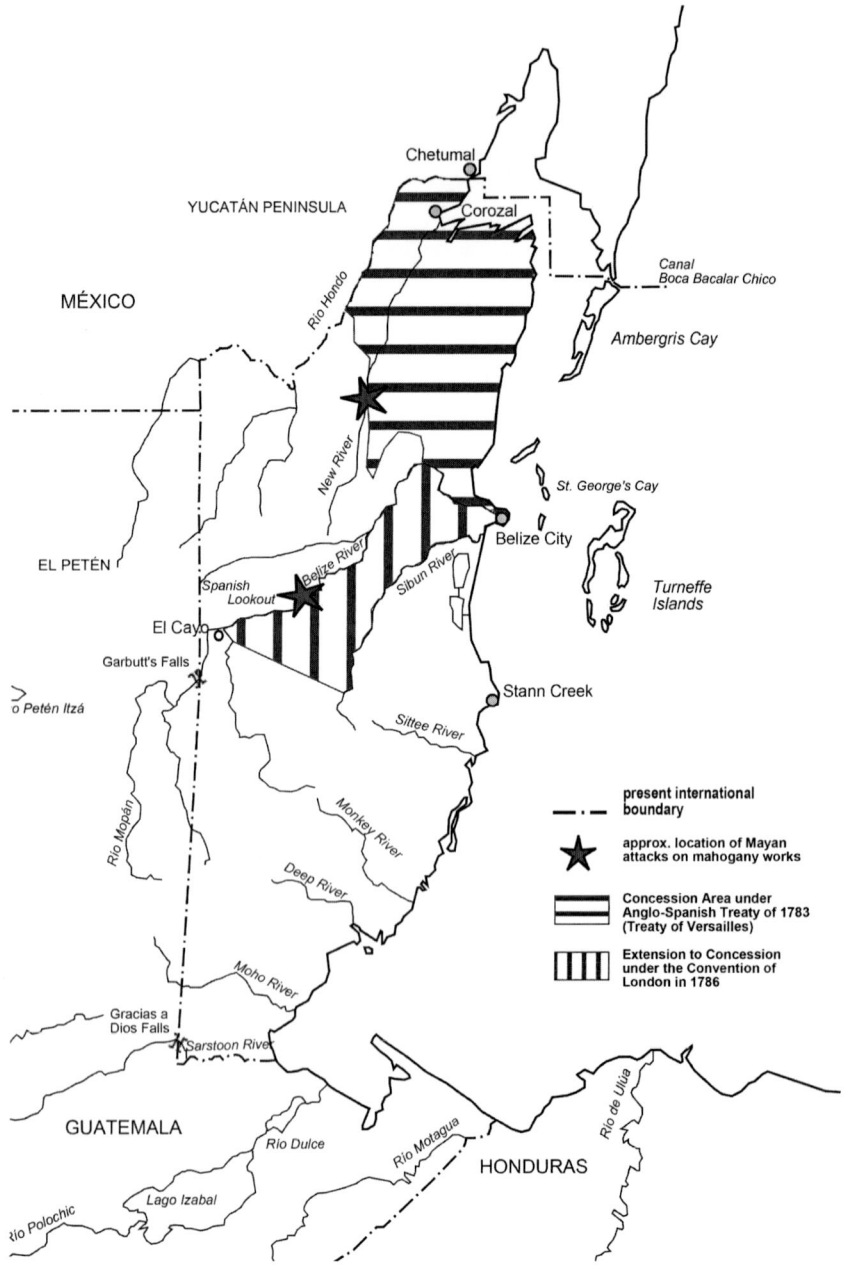

Map 12: The Mosquito Shore and the Bay of Honduras

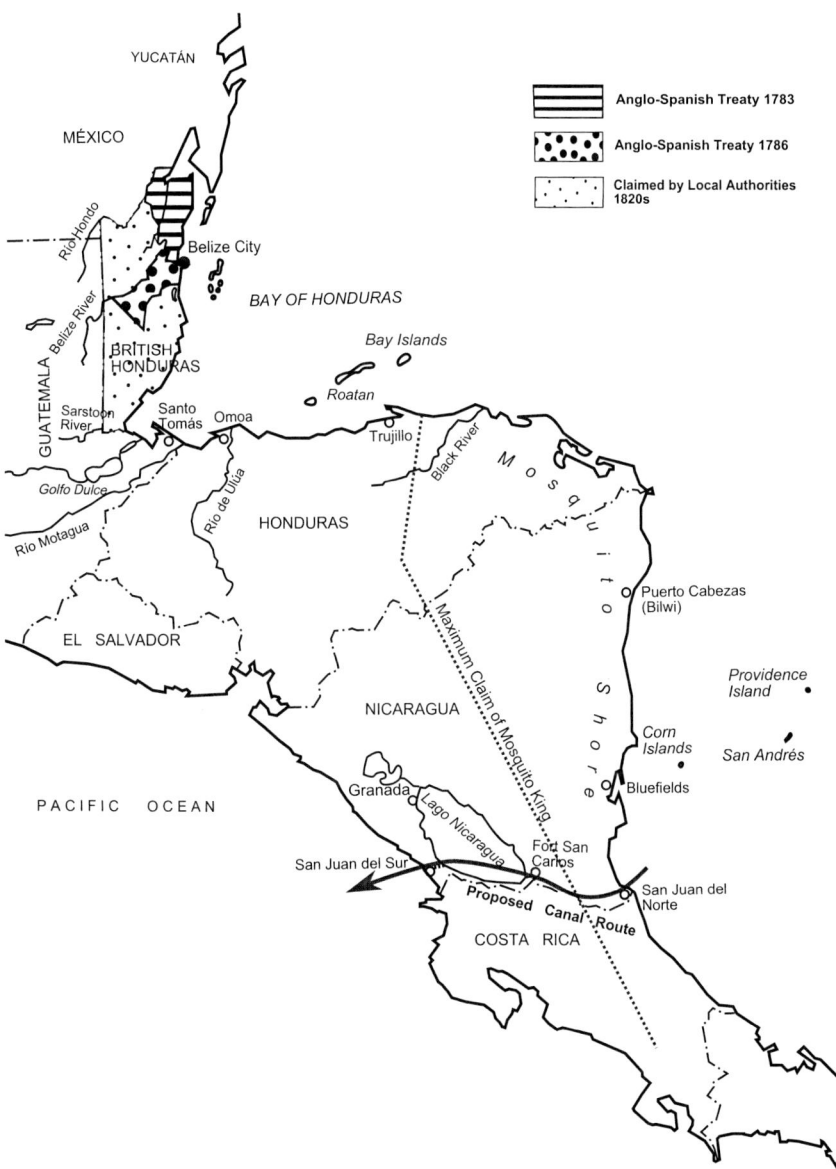

Table 1 – Yearly Exports of Logwood from the Bay Settlement

Year	tons (of logwood)
1717	3,800
1749	8,000
1756	18,000
1787/88	1,786
1798	2,712
1783	7,000
1805	1,270
1846	4,314
1862	7,802
1883	18,082
1889	21,978
1907	6,683
1913	2,812
1927	332
1932	103

Source: Letter from Robert Hodgson, 10 April 1751, PRO CO 123/3 and Grant (1976:39), Dobson (1973:129), Pimm (1934:17), Ashcraft (1973b:52) among others

Table 2 – Value of Yearly Exports of Logwood

Year	Price (£) per ton
prior to	
1660	110–50
(during the Spanish monopoly)	
1670	25–30
1717	16
1728	9
1749	25
1756	11
1768	4
1770	6–5
1772	„... so low as not to pay the freights and expenses incurred in sending it home."
1783	10–8

Source: Mostly from a letter of Robert White, the London agent of the settlers in the Bay, to Thomas Townshend, 10 Feb. 1783, PRO CO, 123/2

Table 3 – Mahogany Exports from the Bay of Honduras

Year	Mahogany (in feet)
1787/88	5,271,275
1799	3,355,000
1802	4,646,000
1805	6,500,000
1846	13,719,000
1858	6,275,374
1913	15,027,520
1927	24,726,313
1932	643,593

Source: Forestry Dept., File No 54/36 and "A Short Sketch of the present situation of the settlement of Honduras ...." by Supt. Barrow, 31 March 1803 quoted in Bolland (1988:17) and Pimm (1934:128) quoted by Grant (1976:39)

Table 4 – Estimated Number of Slave Population in Belize, 1745–1835

	Number of Slaves				Slaves as Percentage of Total Population	Total Population
Year	Male	Female	Children	Total		
1745	--	--	--	120	71	
1779	--	--	--	3000	86	
1790a)	1216	550	411	2177	75	2656
1790b)	1091	515	418	2024	76	2915
1790c)	--	--	--	2500		3959
1803	1700	675	584	2959	75	3945
1816	--	--	--	2742	72	3824
1823	1440	628	400	2468	60	4107
1826	1373	577	460	2410	46	4163
1832	895	435	453	1783	42	3794
1835	686	318	180	1184	47	2543

Sources: Bolland (1977:51), misc. correspondence PRO CO 123 and 137 and censuses of the slave population undertaken in 1790, 1816, 1820, 1826 and 1832, General Registry, Belize City

Table 5 – Approximate Population Figures in the Honduras Settlement

Year	Whites	Free Coloured and Free Blacks	Slaves	Approx. Total Population	Whites as Percentage of Total Population
1735				500	
1742	400		mentioned but no number given		
1745	50		120	170	29,0
1765				1,500	
1779a)	101	40	250	391 for St. George's Cay only; i.e.excl. the inland timber camps	
1779b)	500		3,000	3,500	14,0
1789				cerca de 2,000	
1790a)	261	371	2,024	2,656	9,8
1790b)				2,997	
1803	225	775	2,959	3,959	5,7
1806	222	877	2,527	3626	6,1
1809	?	?	3,000	3,810	
1823	217	1,422	2,468	4,107	5,3
1829	250	2,266	2,127	4,643	5,4
1831	265	1,591 excludes free coloureds	2,027	3,883 excludes free coloureds	

Sources: Archives of British Honduras, Vol. 1:70,73,80,93 and 129; PRO CO 123/9, 15, 17, 35 and 128/10,12 in Dobson-Leon (1958:380, 172:337) and Lucas Gálvez to Antonio Valdéz, 1787, AGI-Mexico 3108, in Calderón Quijano (1944:360) and diary of Llobet 1790, Ibid:361

Chapter
Five

The Bay Settlement
in the 19ᵗʰ Century

In the first decades of the 19ᵗʰ century, the Bay Settlement (or Honduras Settlement) experienced an economic boom. This was the consequence of the establishment of a lucrative entrepôt trade with Central America and a continuing high demand for mahogany on the European market. In the late 1820s the revolutionary change in Atlantic transport[1] led to an expanding of the shipbuilding industry which, in turn, increased the need for quality mahogany as construction material.

1. The Establishment of a Mono-Economy

For more than three quarters of the 19ᵗʰ century, the economic activities in the settlement were focused entirely upon the export of mahogany.[2] Logwood exports came second but in relation to mahogany were minor. Until 1830, the intensity of mahogany trade fluctuated considerably due to the occurrence of alternating cycles of boom and slump, as can be seen on Table 6.

Responsible for the significant boosts in production was an increasing demand for mahogany, by both shipbuilding and railway companies. "Honduran" mahogany was highly esteemed as a panelling wood in railway carriages during the European railway boom and for hulls, panelling and interiors of sailing and steamboats. Apart from additional demands created by the furniture industry, mahogany was a much favoured construction material, for example for docks,

---

1 Nevertheless, several decades of technological advances were still needed until all steam-powered vessels were able to operate regular scheduled crossings and seriously rival sailing ships. It was not until the 1920s that regular all steam crossings were introduced, making the journey across the Atlantic in just 14 days.
2 The most common types mahogany were of the Swietenia, Carapa and Tapirira species.

houses, and church interiors and it was also used for sculptures, pianos and ornaments.

The fluctuations in the export figures were not only due to variations in demand but also to significant variations in quality from one "batch" to another. Although the large quantities of mahogany imported into Great Britain from British Honduras in comparison to other countries (see Table 7) might indicate a superior quality of "Honduran" mahogany, this was not the case and mahogany from Cuba and Haiti was said to be much harder.[3]

It was nearly impossible to precisely determine the quality of the wood, because the methods used (for example drilling holes into trunks) were considered as unreliable and unsatisfactory. Therefore, it becomes difficult to calculate the exact value of mahogany exports from the Bay of Honduras and the figures given in Table 7 should be regarded as estimates only. Since prices varied according to quality, mahogany from British Honduras was traded at a lower price compared to mahogany from Cuba and Haiti. The lower price of "Honduran" mahogany is one reason why British Honduras was the main source of mahogany imports into Great Britain during this period.

Another reason for why the price for mahogany from "Honduras" was lower and such large quantities entered Great Britain, was the occurrence of a far-reaching political event in Europe, indirectly encouraging the importation of mahogany from the Bay Settlement: After the French formed an allegiance with Russia in 1807, the Baltic – until then Britain's traditional and major source of timber – could no longer be reached by British ships. As a consequence, prices for timber suddenly went up and since Britain's prestige was heavily dependent on a strong navy of wooden ships, the only option was to pass an act to enable a duty free import of timber from British colonies.

Although the British Bay Settlement was not an official colony, it had always enjoyed some sort of preferential treatment from the logwood days. And despite the fact that the various Navigation Acts were therefore, strictly speaking, not applicable, the settlement was able to benefit from the sharp increase of duties on foreign timber. Whereas "Honduran" mahogany could now be imported into Great Britain at a lower rate of duty, the indirect application of the Navigation Acts also meant that "Honduran" timber merchants were no longer able to export mahogany to the American market, where transportation costs were less. However, even with the favourable tariff conditions, apart from the period between 1841 and 1850 as shown on Table 7, "Honduran" mahogany made only a small contribution to the total British timber market.

---

3   See also Naylor (1988:100)

After its peak in 1846 the mahogany trade began to fall into a depression and the dangers of a mono-economy became apparent. The decline in the exportation of mahogany was due to a combination of several factors: Over-exploitation, uneconomic management, a fall in demand (which was principally due to the replacement of wood by iron in the shipbuilding industry), and the abolition of the protective tariffs in 1846.

2. The Bay Settlement Becomes an Entrepôt for Central America

The foundations for the development of the Bay Settlement into an important trading post were laid in the 17th century when the Central American Spanish colonies saw contraband trade as the only means of achieving economic independence from Spain. After the British were given the *Asiento de Negros* in 1713, the monopoly for the slave trade in the Americas, the settlement's role as entrepôt became even more important: Its facilities enabled a continuous supply of labour for Central America's indigo industry and it presented a chance for Central America – especially the *Audiencia de Guatemala* – to market its own products (mainly cochineal and indigo for British textile factories), while at the same time gaining access to European commodities.

Since, at that time, the ongoing diplomatic controversy over British territorial rights to the Bay Settlement was still far from being resolved, it is ironic that the Central American merchants found little alternative but to channel their trade through the port of a British settlement. As far as the Spanish colonies in Central American were concerned the facilities offered by the Bay Settlement, together with the establishment of the free trade with Britain, gave the independence movement an impetus to make headway.

From approximately 1800 to 1850 the British settlement in the Bay became the most important trading centre in the Western Caribbean and was rapidly replacing Jamaica as an entrepôt. The very existence of the settlement and its facilities for the development of a trading post enabled Britain to play a predominant role in Central American commerce. And it did not even have to make considerable efforts to achieve this status, for example it was still unwilling to take definite steps towards a proper recognition.

What were the necessary preconditions for the Bay Settlement to develop into such an important entrepôt?

- **First**: From around 1810 onwards, Spanish threats upon the settlement had ceased and the area started to be considered safe. Yucatecan officials were too concerned with their own affairs (i.e. the beginning of the independence movement in Mexico) to plan any more attacks upon the British settlement and as a consequence, trading activities in the Bay began to expand.
- **Secondly**: After the independence of the Spanish colonies in 1821, Britain's chances of trade with the Central American Federation (1823–1840) increased even more. It was seen as an almost natural course of events that Britain should now legally continue what it had been doing in a clandestine way for more than a century. Moreover, during the heydays of the entrepôt trade (from 1821–1851), the Federation, and later the new republics, did not possess a commercial navy capable of crossing the Atlantic and were dependent on British vessels for their exports and imports alike.[4]
- **Thirdly**: Between 1821 and 1849, Britain was able to offer extremely favourable market conditions to Central America, simply because it was able to channel the entire Anglo-Central American trade through a British settlement. The fact that the British market continued to give preference to products originating from British colonies, was advantageous for Central America and the Bay Settlement alike. Central American products could be imported in large quantities into Britain, merely because they were trans-shipped at the mouth of the Belize River and could be declared as having originated from a British (*de facto*) colony. Therefore, the import duties levied in Britain for these "colonial products" were less, and as a consequence, Central American products became more competitive on the European market.
- **Fourthly**: The Bay Settlement was considered a very secure place for the necessary business transactions arising from the trans-shipment of the various cargoes. Because the Central American Federation, and later the new republics, was constantly in a state of civil war, the majority of trade (apart from a small number of individual British traders stationed in Guatemala) was carried out through branches of British merchant and commission houses and/or agents established in the Bay. As a consequence, a number

---

4   However, at that stage, Britain's hegemony in the Central American trade could still have been threatened: if, for example, the ideally situated port of Santo Tomás de Castilla at the mouth of the Río Dulce, or the island of Roatán had been opened up for trade, they would have been able to seriously rival the British Settlement in its role as entrepôt. Both places were within jurisdiction of the Central American Federation (Guatemala and Honduras) and if circumstances had been different, other nations would also have been able to participate in and profit from the trade.

of British merchants, predominantly Scots, started to establish themselves in the settlement and began to act as bankers in a private capacity.

- **Fifthly:** Due to the nature of Central America's topography, both the more developed regions and the centres of production and consumption were situated in the fertile Altiplano regions and in the Pacific lowlands. These areas were separated from the Atlantic by uninhabited and mostly impenetrable mountain and jungle regions. Because of the absence of an all year inter-oceanic canal, long and hazardous journeys, which were only possible during the dry season, had to be undertaken by mule both ways. But despite this major drawback, the Atlantic route via the British Settlement was given preference. Compared to the alternatives of the time[5] it was the only feasible possibility for Central America to engage in trade relations with Europe.

In the 1820s, 80% of all the Anglo-Central American commerce was channelled through the settlement. During the period of 1821–1851 between seventy and one hundred merchant vessels left its harbour for Great Britain, the United States and other European destinations annually and an average amount of twelve boats was constantly present in the port, ready to leave.[6] Making a stop-over at the settlement in 1839, the US emissary to Central America, John Lloyd Stephens, commented that "Balize is a place of large commercial transactions ... four ships, three brigs, sundry schooners, bungoes, canoes and a steamboat were riding at anchor in the harbour ..."[7]

What kinds of products were channelled through the Bay Settlement?

Due to their light weight, little bulk, easy conservation and the high prices achieved, the following articles were ideally suited for export:

Cochineal dye: A scarlet-red dye, derived from carminic acid produced by female cochineal insects living permanently attached to various species of nopal cacti hosts. Europe had a high demand for cochineal and in the 1830s, almost all of Central America's cochineal was sent to Great Britain via the Bay Settlement.[8] From 1827–1836, in most years cochineal came second to ma-

---

5   In the beginning of the 19th century the other alternative, the opening up of a communication route towards the Pacific (to receive the few merchant vessels which ventured to navigate the tortuous Magellan Strait), was considered more complicated and therefore less promising.

6   See Naylor (1988:132–134)

7   Stephens (1969:11,18)

8   The main centre for the cultivation of nopal cacti was Guatemala (in the vicinity of present Guatemala City and Antigua) where the initial small scale production soon came to be a substantial industry. 70.000 live insects (or 1½ kg) were needed to obtain ½ kg of

hogany in the value of goods exported from/via the Bay Settlement and from 1837–1851 cochineal dye constituted the highest value of exports.[9]

Indigo was the second most important export article channelled through the Bay and for a long time had been an article of high demand for Europe's textile industry. Indigo dye produced all shades of blue and prior to the 1830s Central American indigo was said to have been of superior quality. After that time the quality of indigo harvests declined. Despite efforts to duplicate the processing methods from India in order to meet its standards, from 1845 onwards indigo from Central America was no longer competitive.[10]

Among the various forest products changing hands in the Bay Settlement were, **sarsaparilla** (or Blackberry bush), the root of which was used for medicinal purposes, and **balsam of Peru**, a versatile and much sought after ointment made from the resin of a tree native to Central America and Southern Mexico (and, although in much smaller quantities also to northern South America).

Tortoiseshell was another product channelled through and directly exported from the Bay Settlement but due to sporadic demand in Europe exports were infrequent. The shell of the hawksbill turtle was used in luxury furniture and for the manufacture of certain ornaments such as combs. In comparison to the exports of tortoiseshell directly from the Bay Settlement, the exports of tortoiseshell from Central America via the settlement were considerably less, because one of the main shipping areas for hawksbill turtles at that time were the waters off the Mosquito Shore, which were not within Central American jurisdiction.

In terms of imports, the majority of British goods destined for Central America were shipped via the British Settlement in the Bay of Honduras, which from the mid-1800s onwards was increasingly referred to as "British" Honduras as mentioned. In 1831 it was the second largest importer of British manufactured goods after Jamaica. Between 1821 and 1851, three to four million yards of cotton and linen material originating from Liverpool, Manchester and Glasgow

---

cochineal dye. Nowadays, cochineal dye is still in use as an organic colorant in the cosmetic, pharmaceutical and food industry (for example prior to 2006 it gave Campari bitter its characteristic red colour).

9   In 1823 approximately 240,000 kg and in 1825 approximately 130,000 of cochineal dye were shipped from the Bay Settlement while only 15,000 kg reached Great Britain via Chile and Peru. Cf. Naylor (1988: 200–240)

10   Indigo dye was obtained by decomposing the green plant whereby a substance found on the plant was hydrolysed to glucose and indoxyl. 100 kg of the green plant were necessary to obtain approximately 300 grams of dye. The chemical formula for indigo dye was announced in 1883 by Adolf Bayer, and a commercially viable process was in use by 1894.

were sent to British Honduras, from where it was trans-shipped.[11] From the mid-1840s British-made merchandise exported to Central America via the Bay also included **lace, cotton thread, dresses** and other clothing, **woollens, leather articles, crockery** and **china, soap, iron,** and **shot.** Among foreign goods and merchandise from British colonies were **mercury, paper, silk** from India and other European countries and **spices,** such as cinnamon and cloves. Coffee, another major export article from Central America, mostly Costa Rica, was not (or in very insignificant quantities only) channelled via the Bay Settlement.[12]

Once merchandise had reached the mouth of the Belize River it was handed over to Central American merchants whose responsibility was the loading of goods onto smaller ships bound for Lake Izabal. From there the goods were taken on mules to Guatemala (and smuggled into Mexico) or to Omoa in present Honduras by using the Motagua River (see Map 13).

In sum, the facilities provided in the Bay Settlement were indispensable for Central America's economy. Notwithstanding its importance for the region, the commercial entrepôt never came to reach its full potentials.

What were the main obstacles for a further expansion of the trade?

- **First:** Despite the introduction of a regular steam crossing to the Caribbean in 1839, there was no scheduled steam boat service to British Honduras which continued to have to depend on monthly sail boats from Jamaica for the transportation of merchandise to and from the Bay. Only in 1850, approximately the time when the entrepôt trade began to decline, regular steamboat itineraries came to include both Greytown on the Mosquito Shore and the port at the mouth of the Belize River, present Belize City, in British Honduras.

- **Secondly:** After the merchandise had finally reached British Honduras, had been trans-shipped and sent to the port of Río Dulce on Lake Izabal (see Map 13), too much of a hazardous journey followed. In the decades after independence, overland transport was very poor and inadequate, and presented serious seasonal limitations especially since the combination of narrow paths and riverine waterways could only be used in the rainy season. Means were scarce and technical possibilities limited to improve the

---

11   See Naylor (1988: 103)

12   Coffee started to be exported relatively late when the road to the largest Pacific port of Costa Rica, Punta Arenas, had been completed in 1846. Naylor (1988: 200–240) has done extensive research on the role the Bay Settlement played as an entrepôt for Central America and provides detailed commercial statistics, obtained mainly from the Public Record Office in London.

situation, for example by building all-weather roads and/or railway lines. Promising plans in the late 1830s to build a canal on the Río Dulce and to open up the Río Polochic for steam boats never materialised.[13]

- **Thirdly:** Trade was carried out mainly by an interchanging of products based on momentary market values according to methods which resembled the ones used in barter trade. The first British official in Guatemala, Consul O'Reilly, who was murdered after only three years of having been in office, reported in 1825 that

In nineteen cases out of twenty the merchants of this country went to British Honduras with hard dollars, indigo or other produce and bought or bartered with the merchants for British goods.[14]

As a consequence, financial arrangements had a tendency to be difficult and complicated. One reason for this completely inefficient monetary system was the usage of a variety of different currencies. In the early days of the settlement, the preferred form of exchange was by "Bay currency", i.e. by means of logwood. From 1784 onwards, local regulations were altered and business was transacted in Jamaican currency. When the massive trade with Central America brought *pesos* and *reales* into circulation and the growing influence of the United States after the gold rush introduced "gold dollars" to the Bay, financial chaos was programmed. The various measures taken were inadequate and the confused currency situation continued until 1894 when parity of exchange between the British Honduran and the US Dollar was adopted.

Apart from these major drawbacks, a series of other contributing factors existed ultimately leading to the final decline of British Honduras as an entrepôt for Central America, and especially Guatemala.

First and foremost the decline of British Honduras as principal commercial entrepôt for Central America was not so much the result of a decrease in trade volume, but rather because other trading possibilities had become available to the Central American merchants.

---

13   The idea behind the plan to build a canal on the Río Dulce, the narrow stretch between the *Golfete* and Lake Izabal, and to open up the Río Polochic for steamships was to enable the transportation of merchandise to Guatemala City and Cobán via Telemán and Salamá in Baja Verapaz (see Map 13). The building of a railway from the Caribbean port of Santo Tomás de Castilla was not commenced until 80 years later, as late as 1908.

14   Guatemalan Consular Reports 1826, Board of Trade Records 6/47, quoted in Dobson (1973:136)

In the late 1840s the major Guatemalan import-export merchants (and also to a lesser extent those of El Salvador and Costa Rica) began to engage in direct trade with companies based in Liverpool, Manchester, Sheffield and Edinburgh. Only Honduras, the less developed and poorest of the Central American republics, continued to have to content itself with trading via the merchant houses of British Honduras.

From 1849 onwards, with the elimination of the trade restrictions of the Navigation Acts, the Central American merchants were free to ship their produce to Britain and other European destinations by using ships of those nations that offered the most favourable conditions. They were, therefore, no longer dependent on a location with British connections.

The opening of the Panama inter-oceanic railway in 1855 brought about a general development of commerce on the Pacific coast. This railway, together with the possibility of other projected trans-isthmian routes across Nicaragua and Honduras as mentioned in the previous chapter, greatly reduced Central American dependence on British Honduras as a trading post.

The economic development of the United States also accelerated the decline of British Honduras as an entrepôt. The Central American merchants soon showed an increasing tendency to turn to the US as a source of supply rather than to Britain. By 1894, trade with the United States had completely substituted the colony's trade with Central America and regular steamboat routes were being operated between British Honduras and New Orleans.

Finally, Britain's lack of initiative to invest in British Honduras, also contributed significantly to the decline of the settlement as a commercial trading post. If Britain had been prepared to support her future colony at an earlier stage, it would still have been able to consolidate its role in the Central American trade, for example by building roads, warehouses or ports to make the transactions more efficient and facilitate the expansion of commerce.

3. Socio-Economic Consequences of the Economic Boom

The extraction of mahogany depended largely on human labour and during the various cycles of booms the demand for more labourers was constantly growing. Therefore, one by-product of the economic boom was an increase in population. Between 1839 and 1841, for example, population figures rose by 280%, from 2,946 to 8,235.[15]

---

15 Census of 1839: General Registry Belize 1841; Parliamentary Papers 1844, XLVI (591) and Dobson (1973:338).

Because the entire economy was dominated by the exportation of mahogany, the fluctuations in the demand for the wood naturally also led to fluctuations in the profits the British settlers obtained from the trade, which seriously affected the social and economic life in the settlement. As reported by a 19th century observer

> *When London and Liverpool prices showed an advance in the Rates for logwood and mahogany, there were cheerful, smiling faces in the counting houses... when prices fell there was dullness everywhere; lounging woodcutters on the bridge or around the grog-shops ...*[16]

Since mahogany was the only major export crop, the Bay Settlement had become dependent on Great Britain for the import of supplies and other necessities. With the help of the entrepôt trade the settlement was able to, at least temporarily, reduce this colonial dependency: In exchange for letting British ships anchor and trans-ship in its harbour, a kind of tribute in the form of Central American foodstuffs and cattle (needed urgently by the forest industry for transportation) was charged. However, the decline in the settlement's role as entrepôt was imminent and due to the fact that it coincided with the slump in the mahogany trade (from the late 1840s onwards), a general economic depression began to develop and once more intensified the dependency upon the metropolitan market.

For most of the 19th century, mahogany not only dominated the economic and social matters in the settlement but also the political life. As a consequence of the general mahogany boom, the settlement's peculiar form of government, consisting of the Magistrates and the Public Meeting, came to be entirely in the hands of a few wealthy and influential cutters. As mentioned, this "very arbitrary aristocracy"[17] held executive powers, remained in control of legislature and judiciary, monopolized the ownership of land and succeeded in challenging the London appointed superintendents.

With the onset of the entrepôt trade, the arrival of merchants and agents and the opening up of Commission Houses, the dominance of the old families was severely shaken. The Commission Houses, founded by British companies especially for the purpose of facilitating the growing entrepôt trade with Central America, entered into direct competition with the old settlers and internal conflicts were inevitable. This elite, who had engaged in contraband trade for

---

16   Gibbs (1883:114)
17   "A Narrative of Publick Transactions ...", PRO CO 123/10

decades without any outside interference whatsoever[18], was now seriously challenged by the newcomers and the opening up of British branches.

Once the dominance of the old families was broken by the representatives of British merchant houses, the settlers lost control of the administrative and political apparatus and became increasingly controlled by the metropolitan government. This can be seen as one of the reasons why the British Foreign Office expressed a greater willingness towards taking the necessary steps for the recognition of the settlement from the late 1820s onwards. In fact, the territory had been treated as a colony for some time, without ever having been declared as one.

Here it is important to note that when the British government eventually began to seriously consider recognition, it did not happen out of the desire to subjugate the settlement and its conglomerate of inhabitants, consisting of local and expatriate Whites, Creoles, Blacks, Mestizos, native Indians, Garinagu, and other minority groups. Generally speaking, although it was mostly in the local settlers' interest to become an official British colony, the attitude of the settlers

> ... *at one moment they are humbly submitting their neglected situation, at another they scarcely acknowledge that the Authority of the Crown extends over them* ...[19]

was as ambivalent as that of the Colonial Office. Ambivalent or not, as a matter of fact, Britain's freedom of action at that stage was very limited precisely because of the anomalous diplomatic situation with Spain.

The economic boom, the general expansion of trade and the growing population made apparent the need for governmental reforms. For example as far as membership of the Public Meeting was concerned, from 1820 onwards,[20] White British males had to prove one year's residence and £ 500 worth of visible property and coloured men born in the settlement had to possess £ 1,000 in property. As a consequence, legislation and administration came to be in the hands of an even smaller elite. When more and more land became monopolized by a small amount of local-metropolitan partnerships, the problems in connection with the monopolization of landownership were aggravated.

---

18 For example, in the 1820s one of the most powerful residents of the old elite was Marshall Bennett. Apart from being one of the largest landowners, he was a leading mahogany merchant, the biggest slave owner, held the post of Magistrate for 22 years, was senior judge of the Supreme Court, agent for Lloyds of London and a colonel of the settlement's militia.

19 Supt. Arthur to Secretary of State, 1819, PRO CO 123

20 But possibly only until 1827 according to Minutes of Public Meeting, 24 July 1820, in Burdon (1935:II,232).

4. Diplomatic Consequences of the Entrepôt Trade

The increasing importance of the Bay Settlement in the entrepôt trade with Central America had far-reaching diplomatic consequences, triggering a chain reaction which eventually induced the British government to take another tentative step towards the recognition of the settlement. Aware of the commercial potentials of the Bay Settlement and sensing trading opportunities, it finally threw their scruples about Spanish sovereignty over board and passed an act to sanction a formal governmental institution in the settlement.

A Supreme Court was established which, according to John Lloyd Stephens, had become indispensable in "a place of large commercial transactions [where] contracts are daily made and broken, or misunderstood ..."[21] When Stephens was invited to attend a court session, he was both shocked and amused about the peculiarity of this institution. A professional lawyer himself he remarked that the settlement's version of a Supreme Court "stands as an anomaly in the history of English jurisprudence ... all was done in a familiar and colloquial way" and the "gentlemen of the bar" were missing altogether:

> ... Balize [Belize] was the last place made ... there was not a single Lawyer in the place, and never had been; As there is no bar to prepare men for the bench, the judges, of course, are not lawyers. Of the five then sitting, two were merchants, one a mahogany cutter, a mulatto [and] second to none of the others in character and qualifications, a doctor.[22]

For the Central American Federation, the official sanctioning of the Supreme Court by Parliament added fuel to the old controversy of sovereignty and it was immediately questioned whether the British had any rights to sanction any form of permanent government at all.

While initially the blooming entrepôt trade with Central America was profitable for all parties concerned (the British trading companies, the settlers in the Bay, the Central American Federation, and Mexico), the entire Central American economy soon became dependent on the British Settlement. However, this was not to the liking of the Central American merchants: Although the settlement was vital for Central America's economy, the Federation's (and Mexico's) ultimate goal in mind was to make it superfluous as intermediary and develop Central America's own economic potentials.

---

21   Stephens (1969:18)
22   Ibid, p. 17,19

As a consequence, the Central American Federation (and from 1839 onwards Guatemala) and Mexico began to claim to have inherited from Spain territorial rights to British Honduras. The reasons for the Central American Federation and Mexico taking this course were obvious simply because in the early decades of the 19th century, the settlement reaped a rich harvest of import and export duties from the entrepôt trade. The very basis of this claim was that the respective areas, before independence, were included in the former *Capitanía General de Guatemala*.[23] Whereas Mexico signed several treaties (in 1826, 1893 and 1897) with Great Britain settling any territorial disputes once and for all, Guatemala pursued a different policy insisting to have inherited the territorial rights to the areas conceded to the British woodcutters by Spain. However questionable this claim might have been, the issue was to trouble the colony of British Honduras until independence and even continues to flare up on certain occasions in modern Belize and Guatemala alike.

The arguments brought forward by Guatemala, were (and are) hardly justified. To start with, the British Parliament passed the act to sanction the establishment of the Supreme Court in 1820, *before* Central America's independence from Spain. Thus, provided the act is interpreted as another tentative assertion of British sovereignty over the territory, the Central American republics had no legal rights.[24]

Last but not least, the status the British settlement received during the entrepôt trade enabled it to consolidate its influence in the general development of Guatemala in the decades after independence. Only recently have Belizean and Guatemalan scholars given more emphasis to the role the Bay Settlement

---

23 The claim was based on the doctrine of *uti possidetis iure* which, although some Latin American states were in favour of it, has never been adopted as a principle of International Law. The doctrine states that in the case of a colony achieving independence from the colonial power the territorial rights of the former shall be automatically inherited by the new independent nation. The British government in turn supported the counter doctrine to *uti possidetis*, which held that rights could only be inherited if a territory was actually occupied by the respective colony at the time of independence. In 1821 the settlement was clearly occupied by British settlers. In simple terms, it was *never* occupied by Spain and not even by one of the states of Spanish origin and therefore, there can be no legal basis to this claim.

24 This complex issue provides enough material for a paper of its own and it would be beyond the scope of the present study to go into more details here. Nevertheless, the Guatemalan claim shall be discussed again in Chapter Six, in connection with the colony's aims to achieve independence. For the reasons why Spain gave up its rights and the subsequent claim by Guatemala and Mexico see Dobson (1973:186–196), Humphreys (1961:3), Waddell (1961:31–49; 1988:16–28), Clegern (1988:8), Murphy (1987:256–269) and Byrd (1990:17–28) among others.

played in Central America's transition from Spanish to British economic dependence throughout the first half of the 19th century. Some Guatemalan scholars have even gone as far as to investigate to what extent the British settlement actually participated in the Guatemalan independence movement.[25] Most questions asked, however, still remain unanswered and more detailed studies have yet to be made regarding the influence of the British settlement upon Central America and especially upon Guatemala.

The influence the Bay Settlement had on Guatemalan affairs becomes especially evident in the following aspects: From 1830–40 the Guatemalan government, eager to launch programmes of economic and social reforms, such as the development of the north-eastern departments, began to approve foreign colonization schemes. The prominent "Belizean" resident Marshall Bennet was the only entrepreneur to have the connections and potential to help realize such a massive colonization plan, thought to be the key for accomplishing economic improvement. Bennet formed a colonization company with a London-based firm and was granted almost the entire province of Verapaz but the colonization scheme was a complete failure. A Guatemalan "New Liverpool in the province of Verapaz" was never founded and the overly optimistic project of establishing a connection from the Caribbean via the Río Dulce and Río Polochic to Cobán in Alta Verapaz and on to Guatemala City, as mentioned above and shown on Map 13, never materialised.[26]

My point in bringing up the importance of the interactions of the British settlement with Guatemala and Central America is to suggest that it might be worthwhile reviewing the "Belizean" role in the economic development of Central America: Judging by Bennett's commercial activities in Guatemala and Central America, the impact British individuals and British merchant houses based in the future colony of British Honduras had on Central America might have been stronger than hitherto believed.

---

25 See for example Chinchilla Aguilar, "Belice en la Independencia de Centroamérica", *Anales de la Sociedad de Geografía e Historia de Guatemala*, XXXVII (1964), pp.107–110 and the research done on Belize-Guatemala relations by Byrd (1990:17–28).

26 Among Bennett's other efforts to ease the precarious economic situation in Central America was the operating of a silver mine in Honduras. In Guatemala, he was also the owner of the San Gerónimo sugar estate, formerly in possession of Dominican priests. For further details on Bennett's commercial activities in Central America see for example Byrd (1990:20).

5. The Abolition of Slavery and Its Consequences for the Settlement

The beginnings of the anti-slavery movements can be traced back to the last third of the 17th century but it was not until the late 18th century that Wilberforce, a prominent leader of the anti-slavery movement, started a parliamentary campaign in favour of abolishing slave trade. When the news of the slave troubles at Santo Domingo (the present Dominican Republic) reached England, the arguments brought forward by the members of the planter class, started to work against the abolitionists. It took several introductions of the bill and a change of political climate in Britain, until the first act for the abolition of the slave trade was passed in 1807. Nevertheless, slaves continued to be transported from one British colony to another, often under the pretext of being needed as domestic servants.

In this context it bears mentioning that abolition not only became possible merely because the endeavours of Wilberforce and his supporters finally bore fruit or the fact that the government was more open for reform. It has often been argued that economic rather than humanitarian interests were responsible for the abolition of the slave trade: With the growth of industrialization, a free market economy, where labourers would earn their own money and spend it on whatever commodities they needed, obviously was much more profitable for a free enterprise economy than the slave system. In 1811, Parliament adopted another law proclaiming slave trading to be a criminal offence but due to the lack of a fresh supply of labour, this new law signified even more pressure for those slaves already working in the colonies.

It was not until 1833, under the pressure of the public and the Anti-Slavery Society, that the Abolition Act, eventually leading to full emancipation, was passed. The main intention of the Act was to enable emancipation as smoothly as possible and the Treasury was authorized to pay adequate compensation to the planters in compensation for the loss of their slaves. The slaves were to be free immediately but in most colonies they had to undergo a period of apprenticeship[27] for seven years, which was cut by two years in 1838. The example set by Britain was gradually followed by the other European nations and some of the American states but the methods adopted to abolish slavery were different

---

27 To avoid any abrupt social changes and where possible retain labour, the "ex-slaves" were to become "apprentices". In reality, this meant that in most colonies they had to perform the same tasks for the same masters they had been working before emancipation.

from one nation to the other,[28] depending on whether or not they decided to apply the transitional period of apprenticeship.

After several years of uncertainty whether the Act was applicable to British Honduras or not (and, as a consequence, after several years of illegal slave trade via Jamaica), Superintendent Arthur was instructed in 1834 to apply the new laws also to British Honduras. The Act was regarded as being valid for all British subjects, regardless of living in a British colony or in a Foreign Country and through this proclamation, for the first time, some recognition was given to the settlers of "Honduras" by being officially recognized as British subjects.

In British Honduras, one precondition for the payment of compensation and the slaves being "promoted" to apprentices was the registration of all slaves over six years old. Since the slave owners were interested in achieving an as accurate as possible counting, the first slave register compiled in 1834, listing 1,188 male and 725 female slaves, can be regarded as reasonably accurate.[29]

The directions as to how compensation was to be paid out were issued for all British colonies alike. However, since the actual payment required a more elaborate administrative and judicial system, most of the indications could not be applied to the small settlement with its still primitive form of government. The instructions received from London had to be modified accordingly causing much upheaval and internal chaos in the settlement.

The compensation claims for "Honduran" slaves were the highest of the West Indies. As mentioned in the previous chapter, even before abolition, the value of a skilled male slave was higher than elsewhere due to the nature of forestry work, the different treatment given to the slaves, and the extra shipping costs from Jamaica to the settlement. The average prices paid in British Honduras for slaves between 1822 and 1829 and the average amount of compensation

---

28   The Mexican Republic and the Central American Federation (1823–1840) had already completely abolished slavery by 1829. France decreed the immediate emancipation of slaves in 1848 and the Dutch began the emancipation of their slaves in 1863. The government of Buenos Aires enacted that all children born to slaves after January 21, 1813 should be freed and in Colombia, slaves born after July 16, 1821 should be liberated on attaining their eighteenth year. Puerto Rico's slaves were freed in 1873 and Cuba's in 1880. Due to the thriving world market for coffee, Brazil enacted in 1858 that their slaves should be manumitted in 20 years from that date, i.e. as late as 1878.

29   Archives of Belize (AB), Slave Register 1834, in Burdon (1934). According to the register, boys under 19 were mostly employed as waiting boys, the majority of men between thirty and fifty years of age were described as woodcutters and as they became older they began to work as carpenters or "plantation men". Girls under the age of ten worked as housemaids and seamstresses, younger women as house-maids, servants, domestics, chambermaids, cooks, and seamstresses and the more mature women between twenty and fifty were employed as washerwomen and cooks.

awarded in 1834 in comparison to other British colonies of the time can be found in Table 8.

In 1838, the apprenticeship period was terminated in all British overseas possessions and full emancipated was granted, also in the, then *de facto,* colony of British Honduras. Immediately after emancipation the Public Meeting decided that indentured labourers (mostly Africans captured from Spanish slaving ships and at disposal via Cuba) should be recruited. Due to the many difficulties involved, the indenture system in British Honduras did not last long and was abolished in the very same year. Contrary to predictions, the acute shortage in labour never occurred thanks to the availability of a number of free Garinagu and Miskito Indian labourers. But the days of the mahogany boom and consequently the great demand in labour were counted and from the late 1840s onwards, only ten years after the abolition of the apprenticeship system, an economic depression became manifest.

5.1. The Social Conditions of the Former Slaves after Emancipation

The establishment of the apprenticeship system in 1834 did not fundamentally change the status of the Black population in British Honduras in the sense that the transition was not from slavery to freedom, but rather from one system of labour control to another. Theoretically, the ex-slaves were now able to earn wages in whatever occupation they chose, but only after having worked for free for a certain amount of time for their previous masters. As far as the apprentices were concerned the new status was very confusing to them. According to a correspondence of 1834

> *… much dissatisfaction has been evinced on the part of the manumitted Slaves. They do not, nor can they be easily made to, understand the obligations attached to their freedom. Their idea is that the King has made them free & therefore that the making them work for Six Years longer without pay is an act of injustice …*[30]

Prompting some of them to set out to seek real freedom by escaping into the Petén and to Omoa.[31]

After emancipation, the majority of freedmen continued to cut mahogany mainly for two reasons: One, because of the high demand of labour due to the

---

30   Supt. Cockburn to John Lefebre, 13 Aug. 1834, PRO CO 123/45
31   See Supt. Cockburn to Commandant of the Petén, 6 Sept. 1834 and Supt. Mac-Donald to Commandant of Omoa, 28 Sept. 1837, AB R.8

mahogany boom and two, land was simply not available to the Black population and there were no alternatives to seeking employment in the forest. In fact, forestry work was the only viable income alternative: Access to land, which would have been a necessary requisite for becoming an independent subsistence farmer and no longer depend on mahogany cutting, was not possible for the Black population at the time.

Moreover, educational programmes for the former slaves and their children were scarce and not at everyone's disposal. Although the various superintendents encouraged the starting of free schools and the fervent endeavours to promote religious education by several missionaries, mostly Baptists and Wesleyan, attendance of the Public and Sunday Schools was very low.[32]

Since it was in the economic interest of Britain to ensure that the supply of workers should continue, the Colonial Office feared that if the former slaves owned land it would eventually discourage them from working in the forest. When Crown land finally became available for the freedmen in 1838, it was declared that the hitherto gratuitous land grants were no longer free and "… grants of land were only to be made on payment of £ 1 per acre."[33] Crown land lay south of the Sibun River and for the most part was idle mainly because it did not have such an ideal riverine network and the mahogany there was of inferior quality. The imposition of a price on Crown land was, among various other reasons, responsible for why in British Honduras unlike for example Jamaica, Trinidad, and British Guiana, a large peasantry was never able to develop.[34]

The non-availability of Crown land for cultivation acted in favour of the mahogany houses due to a newly devised contract system that would secure labour and bind the labourers to their employers. A fundamental principle of this contract system was the paying of wages in advance, which evolved from the traditional practice of giving provisions to the slaves before disappearing into the bush. The intention of the so called "advance system" was to enable labourers to purchase their supplies and other necessities before leaving home. In British Honduras, due to the seasonal nature of forestry work, this "advance" was paid out shortly after having been recruited, usually around Christmas time. But cash money was mostly spent during the festivities and the labourers

---

32 The Anglican chaplain of the time regarded British Honduras as a stronghold of the Protestant faith, being "the only Protestant settlement between the boundaries of the United States and Cape Horn". The Reverend Matthew Newport to Horton, Jan.12ᵗʰ 1825, PRO CO 123/36

33 MacDonald to Secretary of State, 9 Feb 1839, AB R.14

34 Cf. for example Augier (1960:187) and Bolland (1977:121).

had the need to buy their supplies in the camp, from the employer's own store ("truck system") and at a much higher price than in Belize town.

The "advance system" was combined with the "truck system" forcing the labourers to take a percentage of their wages in actual goods from their employer's store in the bush. Thus, the labourers were continuously kept in debt and a vicious circle was formed.[35] In 1888 the Colonial Secretary criticized that labourers were "… kept in debt by their employers for the purpose of securing a continuance of their labour, as such labourers consider themselves bound to serve until such debt is extinguished."[36] These employment practices became part of the Government Laws of British Honduras and continued to be in use for a considerable length of time.

Even if the status of the Black population in British Honduras fundamentally had not changed much and the former slaves had practically no alternative but to continue to work in the forest, their social situation, according to contemporary records, and in terms of the local standards, must have been reasonably tolerable:

> *I might have fancied myself in the capital of a negro-republic … They [the Blacks] were a fine-looking race … and well dressed, the men in white cotton shirts and trousers, with straw hats, and the women in white frocks with short sleeves and broad red borders, and adorned with large red earrings and necklaces …*[37]

5.2. Remnants of African Cultural Heritage in Belize

With emancipation the former slaves began to be more conscious of their cultural heritage and the practice of African tradition experienced a revival. To what extent African customs actually survived in Belize is difficult to evaluate. Records are few and incomplete mainly because the Black population was mostly illiterate and therefore traditions could only be passed orally. On the other hand, the White observers, such as visiting travellers, colonial supervisors or local settlers often had the tendency to be biased and/or display a lack of understanding.

In general, the policy of the administrative body in the settlement was to suppress the efforts made by the Black population to practise their customs.

---

35 For a detailed description of the "advance and truck system" see Ashcraft (1973: 35–7), Bolland (1977: 122, 1988: 106–8, 160), Evans (1948: 246), Morris (1883), Burdon (1935, 1852) and The Honduras Almanack (1830) among others.

36 Handbook of British Honduras (1888: 215).

37 Stephens (1969: 11–12)

Out of fear of an increased likelihood of rebellions, large gatherings of Blacks were seen as suspicious, as it was, for example, the case with rituals such as the witchcraft practice *obeah* and the extended burial rites of the Garinagu people, *dügü* and *beluria* (from Spanish *velorio,* "wake"). These ceremonies combined elements of witchcraft with religion and magic and were seen as a means of manipulating and controlling life. The chief-shaman (*obeah*-man or *buyei*) often assumed a leading role in the community and was believed to have supernatural powers and knowledge of charms, amulets, fetishes, and symbols used for all purposes including the curing of illnesses. Although *obeah* and similar witchcraft rituals were officially prohibited in 1791, they continued to be held secretly and on special occasions are still practised today.[38]

Death and funeral rites constituted an important element in African culture. African belief held that a deceased's spirit would re-join its ancestors, therefore death was seen as liberation from slavery. These rites are called "wakes" and are a mosaic of African and European cultural elements. Belizean wakes are characterized by a simultaneous presence of mourning and rejoicing, music, and religious rituals of African origin as well as of the Anglican Church: "… wakes present a tolerable resemblance of the Irish wakes …"[39] The holding of an all-night wake is still practised today among the Black population and the Garinagu of modern Belize, accompanied by loud mourning, chanting, drinking, dancing, and the rhythm of drums.

The playing of drums was, and still is, an essential component in all regular gatherings. In the first decades of the 19ᵗʰ century, the use of *gombay* drums was frequently suppressed because, according to the settlers, the nocturnal sessions were intended to cause "… noise and much disturbance in the Neighbourhood, as to deprive the Inhabitants therein from enjoying their natural rest."[40] From 1830 onwards these ceremonies began to be recognized and tolerated as part of African cultural heritage

… there can be nothing more calculated to impress a stranger with surprise than the different formations of their drums and the variety of their dances.[41]

---

38 For example to convey negative spiritual energy, a stuffed cloth doll (a *puchinga*) is sometimes buried under an enemy's doorstep, a procedure which is said to cause illness or even death.

39 The Honduras Almanack (1830: 17–8)

40 Thomas Potts, Andrew Cunningham, Robert Douglas and James Hyde to Supt. Hamilton, 3 May 1806, PRO CO 123/17 quoted in Ibid.

41 The Honduras Almanack (1830: 18)

and the practice of *gombay*, a most impressive rhythmical performance, has survived until the present day.

An important aspect of these ritual gatherings was a renewed tribal identification which temporarily helped maintain, resuscitate and re-arrange certain aspects of African cultural heritage. A historical document of 1830 suggests that the Black people of British Honduras, apart from trying to cling to their tribal identity, were also attempting to recreate some political organization among themselves, at least as far as it was possible within the limits imposed by the settlement's political and administrative body.

> *… to preserve themselves distinct and to uphold their customs, each nation selects one from their body to whom they give the title of king … who exercises a certain species of lordship over their respective subjects; … [they] seem to uphold their original systems, prejudices, superstitions, and amusements, to as great a degree, as can be allowed consistently with the regulations of civilized society …*[42]

In order for the slaves and former slaves to fit into this "civilized society" it became a requisite that they should be baptized to encourage the adoption of Christian practices. In the years from 1812 until 1829 about 1,500 slaves and manumitted slaves were baptized.[43] The effect of these baptisms upon the Black population is difficult to assess. The baptisms most likely may have been a *pro forma* act only and may not have entailed any subsequent involvement in church activities or identification with Christianity at all. The intention behind the baptisms was to inhibit the maintenance of African rituals and customs but, in the long run, it is hard to evaluate if and to what extent these efforts actually bore fruit.

In connection with a discussion about the maintenance of tradition it is worth drawing attention to an interesting phenomenon which – although universal in character – I noticed especially widespread in Belize. Among the Black and Creole population alike, tradition, and with it culture as such, is seen in a much wider sense. There tends to be a considerable element of power attached to its verbal usage and it does not necessarily always have to be ancient or old to receive this powerful status. No matter how long a tradition has existed, the mere *belief* that it is old suffices to give cultural expression its authority.

On many occasions I was also able to observe that newly invented traditions are often passed as old for the mere purpose of cultural survival. As is well known,

---

42 Ibid, p. 6–7
43 "Return of Baptisms …", by Rev. John Armstrong, 16 Dec.1823, PRO CO 123/34, "Return from the Church Register …" by Rev. Mathew Newport, 19 Oct.1829, AB R.2.

values by which members of a community live show a tendency to be revealed and expressed in its respective traditions. When these values are in danger of dying out, the holding on to traditions serves to consolidate cultural identities and/or counter other ethnic groups. I consider it probable that it was precisely this amalgamation of the existing old and newly invented traditions, together with the willingness of the different African tribes to accept the melting pot of a common African cultural heritage, that made possible the survival of certain remnants of African cultural heritage in Belize. The Black population in Belize seems to have succeeded in identifying as African as such by both creating and reshaping new common traditions and customs for the purposes which suited them best.

5.3. The Formation of a Creole Society

The first arrival of African female slaves was the beginning of a steady creolization process as a result of widespread co-habitation between the original White settlers, the Baymen, and their domestic slaves. As can be seen from Table 9, after abolition and emancipation this process was accelerated. Between 1829 and 1881 the percentage of Whites in the total population of the British settlement fell from approximately 5,4% to just 1%. It must be emphasized however, that creolization was not the only factor responsible for the reduction of Whites in the total population. The massive fall in the percentage of Whites between 1848 and 1881 for example, was also due to a large scale immigration of Mestizo refugees from the Maya War (*Guerra de Castas*) in Yucatán.

In the 1830s the population of British Honduras was composed by five different ethnic groups: Those of pure African ancestry, those of mixed African and European blood (the Creoles), a few White families, a small group of Garinagu and some Maya tribes, the latter of which, at that stage, remained hidden in the recesses of the forest. The Creoles mostly resided in Belize Town and, in numbers, soon came to be the most predominant group.

Although in Belize, compared to the sugar islands, the Creoles had always been enjoying preferential treatment

> *The system of intolerance practised in other colonies is not maintained in Honduras, on the contrary … the people of colour in this Colony have ever enjoyed many of those Civil Rights, that have never been allowed in any of the islands … they [the Whites] have always treated the Gentlemen of colour as themselves …*[44]

---

44   The Honduras Almanack (1830–6–7) and letter to the newspaper *Honduras Gazette*, 24 Nov.1827

they were still not given the exact same rights and privileges as the White settlers.

George Hyde, for example, an influential Creole mahogany merchant, who could trace back his ancestry to the old Baymen, was not only dissatisfied with his own status but also with the social situation of the entire coloured population in British Honduras in general. He became a pioneer in the fight for the extension of civil rights to the free coloureds and in 1827 made several petitions to London complaining that a Coloured man

> … *though his exertions might acquire him wealth, he must still remain in a condition of comparative degradation, on the sole ground of his Mother being a woman of colour, he is excluded from sitting as a Juror, serving as a Magistrate … or from filling any Public Office of Trust, or Honour.*[45]

These petitions and subsequent personal visits to London finally made the Public Meeting pass an act to concede equal rights to the free Coloured (but at the same time denying these rights to the Black population). Finally, in 1831, the free Coloureds, "this deserving class of His Majesty's subjects [who] had long been debarred from various privileges and immunities" were to be seen "as good as White" and were entitled to have "the same Rights and Privileges … as British Subjects born of White Parents."[46]

In British Honduras (and to a certain degree also in the Caribbean colonies), by allowing the Coloured population certain social and economic privileges, it was hoped that they would function as allies in the event of slave conspiracies.[47] In comparison to other slave societies, the social difficulties created by emancipation and the law to treat Whites and Coloureds equal, seem to have been less evident in British Honduras. The traveller Stephens, on the whole, presented a rather favourable picture of the interaction between Whites, Creoles and Blacks. This is what he had to tell of an invitation where he was seated between two Creoles

---

45 George Hyde to Lord Bathurst, 3 Feb.1827, PRO CO 123/28

46 Minutes of Legislative Meeting, 4/5 July 1831, PRO CO 123/42, in Ibid: 93–4.

47 For example in the Southern states of the US, where Blacks were a minority, slave revolts were less feared and the incentive towards creating a Coloured "buffer-caste" was almost non-existent. In the US, generally speaking, a person with the least 'taint' of African blood was seen as a Negro, whereas in Brazil and in the West Indies greater social fluidity existed.

> *By chance a place was made for me between the two coloured gentlemen
> ... both were well dressed, well educated, and polite. They talked of their
> mahogany works, of England, hunting, horses, ladies, and wine; and before I
> had been an hour in Balize [Belize] I learned that the great work of practical
> amalgamation, the subject of so much controversy at home, had been going
> on quietly for generations.[48]*

According to the above account it can be deduced that the "Coloured gentlemen", the Creole elite with White ancestry on both sides, had turned into successful merchants and were well integrated in the White circles.

From 1847 onwards, the *Guerra de Castas* in Yucatán between White and
Mestizo Yucatecans and Maya, was to have a strong influence upon the Creole
population. It marked the beginning of a massive immigration of Mestizos into
present Belizean territory, a phenomenon that was to last for almost fifty years.
With the coming of as much as approximately 9,500 Mestizos during a time
span of nine years,[49] the Creole population felt their social position threatened,
although, in reality there was very little contact between the two groups. Nevertheless, to distinguish themselves from the newcomers, the Creoles endeavoured to strengthen the liaison with the White settler families. More than ever,
the Creole elite referred to its Anglo-Saxon connection and developed a tendency to look down on the colony's other ethnic groups (the aforementioned
approximately 9,500 Mestizo immigrants, 3,000 Garinagu, 4,000 indigenous
Q'eqchi' (formerly spelled Kekchi) and Mopan Maya and the Maya from Yucatán) and to regard their respective cultures as foreign and inferior, or even to
ignore altogether that they had a culture of their own.

Gradually, this behaviour was adopted by the majority of Creoles despite
that they themselves were hardly better off than the other ethnic groups they
so looked down upon. Although the above mentioned groups lived in the
northern, southern and western regions of the territory and not in Belize Town,
where the Creole population was concentrated, this attitude had a polarizing
effect on the society as a whole. In 19ᵗʰ century British Honduras (and throughout most of the 20ᵗʰ century and to a certain degree until the present), cultural
and social distinction was/is not perceived primarily in racial and colour terms
of White and Black (as was the case in Jamaica), but in terms of being Brit-
ish-oriented or not. And clearly, the above mentioned minority groups were
not.

---

48   Stephens (1969:12)
49   The Blue Book for 1857, PRO CO 137 estimated a population of 10,000 in the Northern
     District, which was said to also include a number of Maya and Creoles.

When the Mestizo immigrants started to engage in agricultural activities, the Creole population began to propagate a myth that mahogany cutting required more strength, was more masculine and therefore would only be suited to the Creole physique and mentality. As a consequence, they regarded agricultural work as being beneath their dignity.[50] This attitude, which to a certain degree still persists today, was shared by the Black population and was also partly responsible for why agriculture came to be a domain of the Mestizos.[51]

After the settlement had been officially declared a British colony in 1862, another reinforcement of Whites, consisting of more representatives of London merchant houses and approximately four hundred Scottish tradesmen entered the colony. Among the original Baymen as well as the White immigrants of the late 1840s, a Scottish element had always been prominent and in the second half of the 19th century economic hardship in Britain, brought about by the repercussions of urban industrialization, led to an increased emigration of Scots.[52] The colony's shaky enclave economy provided ideal preconditions for attracting various sorts of entrepreneurs and adventurers. Henry Fowler, Colonial Secretary of the time, gave the following picture of this group of expatriates, of which he himself was a member: "The Europeans or Whites (principally Scots) are birds of passage, business or duty calling them there, and but very few entertain the thought of making permanent homes in the Colony."[53]

This new and more recent immigration gave the already well advanced creolization process another boost, as suggested by a report in the *Times of Central America* of 1896, "the constant stream of young Europeans fall to Creole ladies."[54]

---

50 This statement by Gibbs (1883: 175) suggests that the Creoles' preference for forestry work was inherent whereas Bolland and Shoman (1975: 69) argue that this particular attitude developed out of having been forcefully subjected to this kind of work.

51 A small amount of Creoles also established villages at or near a mahogany camp and started to cultivate small plots. These peasants were welcomed by the mahogany firms because they helped reduce the cost of provisions for the mahogany workers.

52 Most Scottish immigrants were sons of Edinburgh lawyers and/or merchants or highland estate owners (lairds). Surnames of the "Scots clique" were McIntyre, Logan, Douglas, Connor, McMurrich, Currie, Brodie, Campbell, Gentle, Harley, Grant, Wilson and Craig among others. Although most of these immigrants had been to University, they preferred to pursue business careers abroad and aspired to reproduce mid-Victorian Edinburgh in British Honduras. For example, around the turn of the 20th century, a St. Andrew's club was founded in Belize town, where the anniversary of St. Andrew, the patron saint of Scotland, was celebrated in true Scottish tradition (see Judd 1992: 91–2 and Ashdown 1987: 150). Of the Scots merchant clique only James Brodie, the owner of a major supermarket in Belize City, seems to have "survived" as a merchant until the present day.

53 Fowler (1879: 50)

54 *Times of Central America*, 10 April 1896, quoted by Ashdown (1981: 33)

Another consequence was that this reinforcement of White Europeans displaced most members of the Creole elite in their role as the leading merchants. In the long run, however, the Creoles were able to permanently retain their social status by taking other well esteemed positions, such as mahogany contractors, managers of smaller estates whose owners had gone back to England (absentee landlords), newspaper proprietors and editors, owners of retail stores or simply as "gentlemen". Around 1900 the Creole elite at last succeeded in sharing influence and power with what was left of the old settler families and the remaining pure White members of the Scots clique, two groups which, by now, were beginning to merge. They all formed a community of interest, and this time the respective colonial administrators appointed by London were also included.

The Creole elite, together with the Scottish merchants and White settler families, formed a powerful lobby that exerted considerable influence on the colony's administration, for example by refusing to introduce neither income nor land tax or by not investing in roads or railway projects. In an article in the *Times of Central America* of 1895 critics complained that "So long as this clique continues to govern the Colony, so long it will remain the same miserable neglected place."[55]

Creole society was characterized by the existence of basically two different classes: A relatively small, but influential Creole elite who belonged to the upper and middle class of the colony's society and a vast majority of Creoles who were given employment by the influential Creoles and the White settler groups.

In reality, for the majority of Creoles despite that, in theory, all coloured persons were given equal rights, there were very few possibilities and the achievements of Creoles were generally limited to the Creole elite and to certain individuals of the rest of the Creole population.[56] Only after 1862, when the settlement became an official colony and with the subsequent demand for government posts, did the chances for the Creoles belonging to the middle class increase.

Nevertheless, the majority of Creoles were still not identified as a separate cultural group. They were simply a working group which included Creoles and Blacks. Although the Creole population varied in colour and physiognomy, depending on the individual's pedigree, most Creoles retained a good bit of their Negroid features. But there also existed, and still exists, a group which could have perfectly passed for White outside the colony. And it was this group which was the most prestigious and had the best chances of working in the above mentioned well esteemed professions. As a consequence, the already ex-

---

55   *Times of Central America,* 1 Feb 1895, cited in Ashdown (1979: 42).
56   Cf. Judd (1992: 265).

isting class hierarchy became even more rigid and pronounced. For example *The Honduras Almanack* mentions that

> *… from the Black to the White by law, there are seven or eight legalised ranks, through which descent must be proved to have passed, before the privileges of an European are open to them [the coloureds].*[57]

And it was precisely this attitude which was responsible for why the European genes, which had always been venerated by Creole women, were now even more cherished. The lighter the colour of an offspring was, the more closely it would be linked to the colony's elite and the better would be its prospects for the future.

Ever since the beginnings of the creolization process this rigid class hierarchy was deeply rooted among Creole and White people alike: For example in school, children who were nearly White were said to be the most intelligent. According to Stephen's travel accounts[58] "… the brightest boys, and those who had improved most, were those who had in them the most White blood". Equally, the mistress of the girls' school (it was not specified whether she was White or Coloured) informed him that "… though she has had many clever Black girls under her charge, her White scholars were always the most quick and capable."

As far as the social interactions between the Creoles and the Black population (African born or born in the colonies) were concerned, and contrary to some of the West Indian plantation societies, we have very little evidence for social tension and contemptuous behaviour on the part of the Creoles. This was despite, and possibly because of, the fact that a large percentage of Creoles still had to rely on mahogany cutting for their income and therefore was working alongside the Blacks in the forest.

The following observation by Superintendent Anderson in 1836, claiming that coloured women had no aversion to marrying Black men gives additional support to the above argumentation:

> *No Antipathy however exists on the part of the Creole Women to the Native African Men everything depending upon the degree of Civilization at which the Africans shall arrive and his competency to support the Woman in Comfort.*[59]

---

57 The Honduras Almanack (1830:8)
58 Stephens (1969:16–17)
59 Supt. Anderson to Secretary of State, 28 April 1836, AB R.6

However, according to historical evidence, inside the home occasional tensions did seem to have existed: Incidents were said to have occurred, when some of the free Coloured concubines of the White contractors and merchants – regarding themselves as having been particularly successful in climbing the social ladder – administered much ill treatment to Black domestic servants.[60]

One important consequence of the massive creolization process is that over time, the Creoles developed a very ambivalent social identity. This was because in their social status, they saw themselves somewhere between the White elite and the Black ex-slaves. To consolidate their own social position, they were therefore in favour of perpetuating the existing colour/class hierarchy. After all it helped to maintain their intermediate status, above the former slaves but clearly below the Whites.

Whatever history, colour or social position a Creole had, there existed an important element which bound all Creoles together: It was the belief that *they* were the true inhabitants of the colony which was justified by their, however remote, descent from the old Baymen and their Anglo-Saxon genes. Regardless of the status a person had within Creole society, in relation to the rest of the population, a Creole always had a preferential status.

This ambivalent social identity can still be observed today among the Creole population of modern Belize. For example, the lines of the national anthem of the independent Belize "Arise! ye sons of the Baymen's clan" ... or "Our fathers, the Baymen, valiant and bold" are a perfect reflection of this attitude: On the one hand the Creoles (at the time of independence in 1981, when the anthem was composed, they accounted for approximately 40% of the total population) are still proud to be the "sons of the Baymen's clan". On the other hand they also realize, some more than others, that they are also the descendants of an African population who was submitted to slavery by the very Baymen and their successors, of whose descent the Creoles are so proud of. The composer of the national anthem, a Creole, seems to have taken for granted that the nation's other inhabitants, the Mestizos, the Maya, the Garinagu and other minority groups, in order to be able to join in the chorus, would also be prepared to temporarily regard themselves as "sons of the Baymen's clan".

---

60   As it was for example the case with the coloured mistress Duncannette Campbell (Scottish surname!), who punished her slave Kitty in an extraordinary cruel and severe manner. Mentioned in a report of Superintendent Arthur to Lord Bathurst, 7 Oct.1820, PRO CO 123/29

6. Maya Resistance in the 19ᵗʰ Century

Maya resistance in the 19ᵗʰ century manifested itself in the form of a major Maya uprising in the south and east of Yucatán which extended into the north-western corner of British Honduras and the simultaneous revival of anti-colonial activities in the western regions, close to the Guatemalan border.

6.1. The Maya War in Yucatán *(Guerra de Castas)*

This war was a revolt of the Maya of Yucatán against the Mestizo population and the White settlers of Spanish origin. It began in 1847 and was one of the most successful and largest Amerindian uprisings.[61] The *Guerra de Castas* was a peasant revolt and a reaction to the changes occurring in the economy of Yucatán after 1821, when the forces of capitalism began to enter rural areas and the state authorities started to take over Maya land. The first one and a half years of the uprising coincided with the war between Mexico and the United States from 1846 to 1848 (at the end of which Mexico lost California to the United States), and the heavy fighting in Yucatán led to a further intensification of Mexico's political and economic problems.

For half a century various different Maya tribes were fighting successfully defending the exclusive right to their lands and on several occasions managed to re-assert their independence. Eventually, the war led to disunity among the rebel groups, especially between the most tenacious group of the rebels, the Cruzoob Maya and the more peacefully orientated Icaiché, the latter of which were much more inclined to enter into peace agreements with Mexico.[62] Finally, two years after a massive military attack on the Cruzoob Maya in the 1890s, the war came to an end and the Mexican Government created the new Yucatecan state of Quintana Roo.

---

61 The term *Guerra de Castas* (Caste War or War of the Races) refers to a kind of caste system that developed in Yucatán, in which the "pure" indigenous Maya found themselves at the very bottom of the socio-economic ladder. For the basic historical outlines see for example Reed (1964), Clegern (1967), Bradley (1973) and Jones (1973: 3–13).

62 The Jesuit scholar, Fr. Richard Buhler (1987: 101–1), convincingly suggests that one of the causes for the disunity between the main two rebel groups was their different usage of the godparent system (*compadrazgo*). According to Jesuit records, the more peaceful tribe, the Icaiche, asked the Jesuits to bring Mestizo godparents to them, which shows their desire to maintain personal relationships with the more dominant Mestizo/Ladino class. The Cruzoob Maya however, picked their *compadres* from their own ethnic group and their own socio-economic class, which strengthened social and ethnic solidarity and laid the foundations for a successful revolt against the more dominant social class with whom there were no contacts.

6.2. Diplomatic and Socio-Economic Consequences of the Maya War for British Honduras

Although the Maya war can primarily be seen as a consequence of the Spanish colonization of the Yucatán Peninsula, we must bear in mind that in geographical terms, the entire modern Belize was also part of Yucatán and consisted of three Maya provinces. The northwest of 19th century (and present) Belize, to which the fighting extended, is considered to have been within the sphere of influence of the ancient Maya province of La Pimienta as can be seen on Map 5 and formed part of the southern colonial frontier.

From the very beginning, the territory of present Belize was directly affected by the war and actual fighting took place in the north-western regions causing permanent socio-economic changes in the Maya population.[63] As a consequence of the *Guerra de Castas* and the subsequent internal struggles among the Maya population, several Maya groups and subgroups began to retreat to the isolated Yalbac Hills region in the western parts of British Honduras (see Map 14), the last Maya stronghold. In the long run, the repercussions of the war were also of significant importance for the development of the future British colony and for the demarcation of the borderline with Northern Mexico.

6.2.1. The Definition of the North-Western Boundary

From the 1770s onwards, the continuous expansion of the British woodcutters towards the west and into regions inhabited by several Maya tribes had caused friction between the mahogany companies and the Maya, as mentioned in the previous chapter. Throughout this conflict, the definition of the boundary areas with Mexico was a critical issue as a consequence of the ongoing controversy of British control over the territory.

Already in the 1790s, according to the terms of the Convention of London of 1786, which re-affirmed Spanish sovereignty over the territories occupied by the British, Mexico had started to claim large portions of land in the north of British Honduras. This encouraged the Icaiché Maya, the tribe who had, by then, made peace with Mexico and had inhabited the very region through which the boundary was to be drawn, to lay claim on these lands themselves. From this moment on, the Icaiché insisted on their right to demand rents from

---

63   The Maya in Southern Belize, the present district of Toledo, mainly Q'eqchi' and Mopan who re-immigrated from the Verapaz and Petén areas of Guatemala, were left relatively undisturbed by both the activities of the timber companies in the central and northern regions and the repercussions of the *Guerra de Castas* in Yucatán.

individuals and companies[64] who had occupied parts of the disputed area be-tween Blue Creek and Río Bravo (see Map 13 and 14) for the purpose of mahog-any extraction.

Alarmed by these actions, the rival rebel group, the Cruzoob Maya, who had not submitted to Mexican authority, decided to come to the defence of the British with whom they formed an alliance in exchange for arms and ammu-nition. A number of merchants in Belize Town began to engage in a profitable arms trade, which lasted until the final days of the *Guerra de Castas* in the late 1880s and to which, at least in the beginning, the British officials turned a blind eye.

From the 1860s onwards, Mexico's position to negotiate border definitions began to weaken due to both the war in Yucatán and the constant civil war in the central parts of Mexico. After Britain recalled her diplomatic representative (in protest over the execution of Maximilian of Austria by Mexican rebels in 1867), the negotiations over the north-western boundaries of British Honduras were postponed.

Meanwhile, the merchants in British Honduras continued the profitable arms trade with the rebel Maya, this time with London consent. The ulterior motives were to avoid a mass immigration of refugees into the colony, which would have been the case if the Cruzoob Maya had lost their strong position. Finally, when the British ceased to supply arms to the Cruzoob, the war ended. After guaranteeing free navigation to merchant vessels between Ambergris Cay and the Mexican port of Chetumal (a wise step in the long run since this turned out to be economically very advantageous for modern Belize), a treaty was signed in 1893 and ratified four years later.

6.2.2. Anti-Colonial Activities in the North-West and West of British Honduras

After the Icaiché Maya, who were indigenous to the extreme north-west corner of the colony and its adjacent territory in Southern Yucatán (see Map 13 and 14), had made peace with Mexico they initiated their retreat further south, into "Belizean" territory. Together with the Maya refugees from Yucatán who had settled there previously, the Icaiché began to establish small settlements in the present Corozal and Orange Walk Districts and in the west of the colony, the present Cayo District, where various other Maya villages already existed (see Map 14). The villages had been founded by a group of Maya who had been forced to leave Yucatán in the early years of the war and the Maya refugees from Spanish colonial Petén. The presence of Maya in this last stronghold may even

---

64 Cf. Dobson (1973: 219) and Cal (1991: 25)

have been continuous since Tipu, the headquarters of Maya resistance in the 16ᵗʰ and 17ᵗʰ centuries, but there is not enough evidence to support this theory.

In the 1850s, following the first serious encounters of the Maya with the woodcutters,[65] the British timber companies succeeded in reaching an agreement with both the "endemic" Maya and the Maya refugees from Yucatán. To ensure their co-operation and facilitate their handling, they were brought under the authority of the colonial administration by introducing a clever policy and appointing their leaders as symbolic commander-in-chief and/or several other persons as *alcaldes*.[66]

On various occasions however, this conglomerate of Maya tribes decided to turn against the British and support the newcomers, the Icaiché Maya, in their fight against the encroachments of the mahogany firms. According to the records, the Icaiché did not recognize British territorial claims in the northwest of the colony and had been attacking mahogany camps since 1856 demanding rent for cutting on "Mexican territory".[67]

Refusing to be controlled by Mexican authorities, the Icaiché were using their friendly relationship with Mexico only as a pretext to act on the authorities' behalf and to harass the mahogany cutters who were definitely cutting outside the limits of the London Convention. After an army of 125 Indians attacked the mahogany camps between the Río Bravo and Booth's River (see Map 14), there was considerable panic in the colony and appeals for troop reinforcements were sent to Jamaica.[68] In one decisive battle the rebels of Western Belize, by now all concentrated in the Yalbac Hill region (see Map 14), were subdued and their villages destroyed.

Nevertheless, the Icaiché continued to attack camps and terrorize the Northern District until 1872, when a serious battle led to the death of the Icaiché leader forcing them to surrender. Ten years later, a meeting finally took place at Government House in Belize Town, between the head of the Icaiché, "General" Santiago Pech, and Governor Harley. In this meeting, and under the threat to impose a trade blockade upon the Maya, the Indian leader agreed to respect the boundaries claimed by the British.[69] Seen in retrospect, it remains

---

65   See for example Rhys to Seymour, 3 Nov.1862, AB, R.78 and McKay to Austin, 24 Dec.1866 in Burdon (1935, Vol.3: 275).

66   The term *alcalde* is a heritage from Spanish colonialism. An *alcalde* was the principal magistrate and administrator of a Mayan village council.

67   See for example Seymour to Gen. E. John Eyre, 12 Nov. 1862, AB, R.81

68   See AB, R. 93 passim and R. 95, Harley to Austin, 9/15 Feb. 1867 and Court of Inquiry, 25 June 1867, Burdon (1835,Vol.3: 290).

69   Memorandum, 13 Oct. 1882, AB R. 93. For a detailed study on Maya-British relations in 19ᵗʰ century Belize see for example Bolland (1988:100–112).

an incontestable fact that the Icaiché Maya, together with their associates, succeeded in delaying further expansions of British colonial invasion for almost thirty years.

After this brief account of the historical details of the anti-colonial activities of the Maya in 19th century colonial British Honduras, we can now summarize the following:

In contrast to the 16th and 17th centuries Spanish intrusions upon the Maya of present Western Belize, the impact of British colonialism was much more serious. Although the early Spanish *entradas* were socially disruptive, the Spaniards only passed through these regions on their way to Tayasal, the capital of the powerful Itzá, they wanted to bring under control. And since any attempts to convert the Tipu Maya of Western Belize were in vain, the Spanish never seriously attempted (or were not able) to permanently settle in this area. As a consequence, the different Maya groups in the vicinity of Tipu succeeded in remaining relatively isolated. In the second half of the 19th century, however, on account of the Icaiché, Cruzoob and other splinter groups having been directly driven into the border conflict between Mexico and Britain, the socio-economic repercussions for the Maya population were much more severe:

Not only was their customary freedom of movement denied to them, but they also no longer had the right to determine their own political units and jurisdictional boundaries. In addition, the Maya were also no longer able to be in control of their land and its resources which had far-reaching consequences. Their land, the *milpa*-fields, not only provided the necessary supply of corn: To the Maya, land was much more than a natural resource; it was seen in philosophical and supernatural terms, a traditional attitude that continues to form part of Maya culture until the present. Hence, losing control of their land had a very disruptive effect on Maya society as such.

As far as the Icaiché Maya were concerned, they had to pay a high price for their success in temporarily blocking the British advance into the north-western regions of the colony. Due to repeated conflicts with the lumber companies, the Icaiché came to lose the rights to their land which eventually led to the destruction of their ethnic identity.[70] The Icaiché no longer exist as an identifiable group, the remaining survivors of the tribe having been assimilated into other Maya groups.

At this point it must be emphasized that, paradoxically, British colonial presence also had a positive influence upon the Maya, or, more precisely, the ones escaping from the *Guerra de Castas* in Yucatán. In a certain sense, the peculiar manner of the colonization of British Honduras acted in favour of the

---

70   Cf. Cal (1983: 25)

indigenous population, at least temporarily. As a result of the ambiguous diplomatic status, large portions of the entire region remained, apart from the growing settlement at the mouth of the Belize River and the inland mahogany camps in the vicinity of the rivers, relatively undeveloped and isolated until well into the 19th century, thus creating ideal preconditions for places to retreat to.

Moreover, British Honduras was considered politically stable and safe, especially in comparison to the "Spanish" republics, where anarchy and chaos reigned. If, I argue, the British had not been occupying "Belizean territory", the area would have developed in the same way as the neighbouring republics and the Maya would not have found shelter and protection from the violence that continued north and west of the boundary limits.

Undoubtedly, British colonial presence had also negative consequences for the indigenous population. From the second half of the 19th century onwards, the Maya's presence was seen as a potential threat to the monopoly the British held over the logging operations. Although the Maya of Western Belize had always concentrated on subsistence farming (*milpa* cultivation) and never even attempted to cut timber, they did, on some occasions, settle on land "owned" by the mahogany companies. Generally speaking, the Maya were welcomed as long as they grew their *milpa* on unoccupied land and moved to the north to work as agricultural wage labourers on the sugar cane farms, operated by the Mestizo immigrants from Yucatán. But on actual and potential mahogany land they were obviously interfering with the interests of the lumber companies and the authorities had to find a way of dealing with the Maya of Western Belize.

To facilitate the integration of the Maya into the colonial administration, their leaders and selected citizens were given symbolic political rights. The Maya in turn agreed to lease tracts to the mahogany firms as long as they would receive payments for allowing exploitation of their land and the authorities would respect their internal political arrangements within their communities.[71] On many occasions, however, the mahogany cutters avoided these payments and the Maya launched attacks on the timber camps forcefully demanding their rights.

Finally, on the subject of interactions between the Maya and the lumber companies during the revolt, one fundamental question arises:

Why did the Maya, particularly the Icaiché tribe, who had gained *de facto* control over vast stretches of land, never attempt to extract logwood or mahogany themselves or turn to large scale agricultural activities? The Icaiché as well as the Cruzoob had high potentials as far as the cultivation of large communal

---

71   Cf. Cal (1992:389)

milpa fields was concerned.[72] For example, at the very height of the *Guerra de Castas,* when they had to provide provisions for their armies of as many as four hundred soldiers, the leaders of both Maya groups were perfectly capable of directing the efforts of the community toward growing *milpa* fields on a larger scale.

So why did they not start cultivating sugar cane and/or extract timber? There would have been a strong market for both sugar and rum, and the precious wood in Southern Yucatán and British Honduras. In addition, the marketing of sugar, rum, and timber would have created substantial revenue for the war against the foreign enemy and the intertribal strife. Why then, were these potentials not developed?

Was it because the Maya peasantry was not motivated enough to cultivate its *milpa* commercially, to engage in other agricultural activities or extract mahogany in order to establish themselves as small-scale entrepreneurs? And if so, how can this be explained?

Provided the Maya actually did have the potentials at one stage, their reluctance to start marketing agricultural produce and/or timber may have been deeply rooted in the past: One plausible explanation might be that due to their ancestors experience with food shortages, famines, and epidemics they may have opted for a more conventional way of cultivating the land by continuing to practise their family based subsistence-economy on smaller units, with the use of the ancient techniques and always in co-operation with the community. For the Maya, the importance of land was/is not restricted to its agricultural value and according to their supernatural beliefs, they might have been convinced that as long as certain rules in connection with their sacred *milpa* were not violated, livelihood, and therefore survival, would be guaranteed.

6.2.3. The Immigration of Mestizos

There can be no doubt that in comparison to the chaotic situation in the neighbouring "Spanish" republics … where all the evils of tyranny and anarchy subsist simultaneously …,[73] one consequence of the colonization of Belize by the British was that the region was politically stable. According to the opinion of Superintendent Seymour in 1857, the region

> *… has in the last few years appeared as if it was intended an experiment to see what can be made of the Spanish Americas …*[74]

---

72   Ibid. (384–6)

73   Report sent to London by Supt. Seymour in 1857. In Clegern (1967:169[15])

74   Ibid.

In the second half of the 19th century, two groups benefited from this safe environment: The several Maya tribes seeking refuge from the revolt in Yucatán and the north-western region of present Belize and the many thousands of Mestizos/ladinos[75] as well as some direct descendants of the Spanish colonists who felt threatened since anyone of European descent was liable to be massacred. These fears were not unfounded; after six years of war, the population of Yucatán was almost halved. Although many refugees returned after the violence finally ceased, thousands opted to stay in British Honduras and by 1850, approximately sixteen villages had been established in the northern part of British Honduras.

Although censuses of the time tend to be far from accurate since their preparation was difficult and very much affected by language problems and the poor communication between the Northern District and Belize Town, undeniably, they show the growing "Spanish" element in the population: By 1856, over one quarter of the total population were Mestizo immigrants from Yucatán. Of a total population of almost 20,000 there were 5,500 residents (mostly Mestizos) living in the Northern District which included the village of San Pedro on Ambergris Cay.[76]

Only three years later, the first of the regular official censuses gave a total population of more than 25,000, of which already 57% were Yucatecan immigrants and residing in Northern Belize. Of the Yucatecan immigrants 57,1% (6,737) were Mestizos, 9,6% (1,129) were White Mexicans of Spanish ancestry and 33% (3,933) were traditional ("pure") Maya.[77] Since most Mestizos were Roman Catholics, the wave of immigrants also brought the Catholic Church into British Honduras and an increasing number of Jesuit priests arrived to cater for the newcomers.[78]

---

75   The term "Mestizo" or "ladino" refers to an ethnic group of Central Americans of European, predominantly Spanish, origin who consider themselves "White". They exclusively use the Spanish language, do not use Mayan traditional dress and show a tendency to deny their Indian genes, even if physically, they might not be distinguishable from the "pure" Indians. The terms "Mestizo" or "ladino" refers to the urban classes, rural labourers and peasantry alike. They usually put more emphasis on cash-crops and participate in a regional market-economy and/or in small scale commerce and many employ Mayan wage labourers. The term "ladino" is not to be confused with either the "ladin-language" (German Ladinisch), a Rhaeto-Romansh language spoken in the South Tyrol/Trentino/Veneto region in Northern Italy nor the "ladino-language", a nearly extinct Sefardic-Spanish language spoken by Sefardic Jews in isolated regions of the Balkans, the Middle East and North Africa.

76   1956 Census, AB R.55

77   1861 Census, AB R.74

78   From then on the Catholic Church established its presence in British Honduras. Initially, the Jesuits came from different European countries, but the responsibility for the British

Most of the Mestizo immigrants were small scale cultivators in Yucatán and had been living off the land in some form of subsistence agriculture by cultivating *milpa*. Agriculture was part of their lives and they were allowed to rent tracts of land from the major landowners in the north who encouraged them to cultivate sugar cane, thus initiating the agricultural development in the colony. The land on which they settled was only of marginal interest to the mahogany companies and there is no evidence that the Yucatecan immigrants were involved in the mahogany industry. Apart from sugar, corn, and tobacco, urgently needed subsistence crops were also cultivated, which helped reduce the dependency on imported produce.

The occupations of the immigrants ranged from landless labourers to *rancheros* and planters and their complexion from dark-skinned to more lightly skinned to White, all of which were (and still are) locally referred to as "Spanish", especially by the Creole population. This massive immigration had a great impact on the other large group, the Creole population which by now, consisted of both a powerful Creole elite and a Creole middle class with a preferential status.

The huge influx of Mestizos was to entail far reaching socio-economic consequences for British Honduras. The immigrants had established themselves in the north and were primarily dedicated to agriculture but their industriousness, interest in commerce and light skin not only paved the way for entering into the business circles in Belize Town but also facilitated the establishing of international (especially US) connections. A new elite of Mestizo families emerged and was gradually entering into competition with the Creoles. Although the local and expatriate Whites still monopolized the higher levels within the civil service and the Creoles were firmly established in the middle and lower ranks, the latter began to see their social status threatened despite the fact that higher posts were hardly available for Mestizos. As a consequence, the Creoles' dependency on the British for their own socio-economic and political advancement was temporarily intensified.

This had a polarizing effect on the colony's society, the repercussions of which, although to a lesser degree, still persist today. One example is education: For over 150 years the Creoles were under the patronage of the British who made them believe in the superiority of British educational institutions. Angli-

---

colony was soon transferred to Missouri in the United States, bringing mainly American Jesuits of German and Irish ancestry into the colony. Jesuit influence was expanded and in 1887 the Catholic St. John's College, which continues to be the most prestigious secondary school in Belize, was founded. By 1921, much to the displeasure of the British administrators and the Anglican Church, more than 60% of the colony's inhabitants were Catholics.

can and Methodist schools strictly operated in conformity with British educational schemes, enabling the best students to go to England for further study. The very fact that the Creoles were eligible for European education helped to temporarily maintain their social status and distinguish themselves from the Mestizo population.

It did not take long however, until a shift towards Catholic dominated education occurred. The Catholic Mestizos were taken under the Jesuits' wing and started to attend the local Catholic schools. For example the Jesuit-run St. John's College in Belize Town offered education for children from the Mestizo middle class as well as for talented students from the lower classes. More important than being a Catholic institution was and is the college's orientation towards North America with possibilities of post-secondary education there.

At present, Britain's former dominant position in Belize has long given way to an increased US influence and as far as education is concerned, young Belizeans now show an increased tendency to consider going to the United States for post and secondary education and no longer to the United Kingdom.[79] Generally speaking, the cultural and economic bond with the former mother country is no longer strong enough to overcome important obstacles (such as the lack of direct flights from Europe to Belize) and compete with the United States or even delay its strong influence on modern Belize.

The coming of the immigrants from Yucatán and the efforts to establish agriculture in the north were of immense value to the colony: At that time a serious general economic depression was beginning to manifest itself which was principally caused by the decline in the exports of mahogany. After the Mestizo *rancheros* had proven the commercial viability of sugar production for export, land *per se* not only became more valuable but also more easily available for farming purposes.

In order to fully comprehend why the agricultural development in the Northern District had become so vital, we must turn back to the late 1840s, when the first signs of this economic depression became evident.

---

79   However, from the many conversations I had with Belizean Creoles it became clear that the traditional access to UK education continues to be a powerful means for the Creole middle class to consider themselves superior to the "Spanish". Cf. also Judd (1992:163 ff).

7. The Beginning of a Permanent Economic Depression

The mahogany trade in the Honduras Settlement had always fluctuated a great deal due to irregularities in the demand but from the late 1840s onwards a persistent depression set in and the days of the economic boom were counted.

What were the reasons for this stagnation?

To begin with, the decision by the British Parliament to gradually reduce duty on foreign timber had negative consequences for British Honduras. Despite heavy protests from the colonies, by 1846 hardly any duty was imposed on imported wood and the "Honduran" timber merchants were left on equal terms with the other timber producing areas. The "Honduran" settler elite and their agents who had become dependent on Empire tariff protection and were involved with the London lobby system, made several petitions to the Colonial Office, but they could not prevent the elimination of the old colonial preferences and the introduction of free trade in most raw materials.

The other reasons for the depression were of internal nature: In 1867 and in the years immediately after that date, the depression could be blamed on "the incursions of the Indians, which cause the withdrawal of the mahogany gangs from the infested districts"[80]. When the fall in exports persisted it became obvious that the Indians could no longer be used as a scapegoat. During the boom in the mahogany trade between 1835 and 1844, the over-intensive exploitation had led to a deforestation of the main river banks. In the years to follow, the continuing high demand and the "get-rich-quick mentality" of the contractors encouraged the woodcutters to penetrate less accessible areas and cut young and immature trees. Moreover, appropriate measures for conservation and reforestation were not taken and since natural regeneration is extremely slow, the exhaustion of large areas of forest was unavoidable.

Another important internal reason why the stagnation persisted was a general rise in production costs which was mainly due to the following two circumstances: A sharp rise in the cost of haulage as a result of the woodcutters moving further into the forest and more away from the rivers in their search for new mahogany stands and the complete lack of an efficient transport system.

Despite several petitions and considerable support from the colonial administrators, the "Honduran" settlers were never successful in persuading the Home Government and/or the mahogany companies to develop the interior and introduce more efficient transport methods to replace the traditional system of hauling the timber by cattle to the river embankment and sending the logs downstream to the coastal warehouses.

---

80   Longden to Grant, 17 May 1869, AB R. 98

There is no denying that the absence of a cohesive railway system and the non-existence of reliable all weather roads did slow down the colony's progress and was a major impediment for its future socio-economic development. In general, the whole issue of investing in the colony's infrastructure became entangled with the diplomatic considerations in relation to the Anglo-Guatemalan border disputes. The main problem was that both parties failed to reach an agreement as to which route an eventual proper railway should follow:

Basically, two options existed: Should the railway route run west along the Belize and Sibun Rivers into the Petén (which would have enabled the lumber companies to get access to the rich forests across the border) or was it wiser to contemplate a more southerly course and on to Cobán in the province of Alta Verapaz, from where an eventually connection to the projected Guatemalan railway line along the Motagua to Guatemala City would have been possible? The fact remains that whatever route the proposed railway would eventually have taken, it would always have raised discontent one way or the other, further troubling the already explosive relationship between Great Britain and Guatemala.

It was not until 1910 that several provisional roads and four minor insignificant short distance railway lines were built. They mainly ran from the centre of logging operations to the nearest river only, as was, for example, the case with the logging railway from Gallon Jug to Hill Bank lumber station on the New River, as can be seen on Map 15. Owing to the nature of the terrain, the operating of these logging lines often involved difficult technical operations and innovative technical devices.[81] The handling of these devices was dangerous and maintenance difficult and costly, and the railways were discontinued after a maximum usage of approximately two to nine years. Three of these four mini logging railway lines were dismantled in the 1930s, and the two more important lines have had roads constructed on top of the former tracks.

Until the second half of the 20th century, when the construction of a more or less cohesive network of permanent all weather roads was initiated, logging operations in British Honduras had suffered from a strong seasonal dependence: Transportation on the waterways was limited to the rainy season and the days after, which meant that for several months in the year production was at a standstill.

In addition to the aforementioned infrastructural problems, one of the main reasons responsible for the persistence of the economic depression was

---

81 For example when logs had to be hauled down a steep slope to the river embankment aerial ropeways and innovative log chutes, including winches and railcars, had to be used.

the fall in demand for mahogany. This can be attributed mainly to the substitution of iron for wood in the construction of ships and the growing competition
from other regions, for example West Africa, where mahogany substitutes were
produced at lower costs. Within twenty years, mahogany exports from British
Honduras were reduced by approximately 78%, from 13,719 superficial feet in
1846 to 5,436 in 1858 to a mere 3,007 in 1868.[82]

In sum, it was a combination of three factors which led to the decline in the
profitability of the mahogany trade: The depletion of forest reserves, a sharp
rise in production costs and a fall in prices resulting from the increasing competition from abroad.[83]

Apart from the decline in the mahogany trade, two more incidents occurred which, in the long run, were to have a negative effect on the colony's
economy. It was the decline of the transit trade with Central America and the
Maya revolt in Yucatán, for (and not counting the profitable arms trade to the
rebel groups) the entire trade with Yucatán was cut off during the war.

7.1. Socio-Economic Consequences of the Chronic Economic Depression

Ever since the beginning of the mahogany trade, the prosperity of the settlement had always been influenced by the status of the mahogany exports and
fluctuations in exports had always seriously affected the social and economic
life in the settlement. But when a permanent decline of the forestry industry
manifested itself, together with the simultaneous general decline of the trade
activities with the colony's neighbours, the depression became chronic. The
crisis escalated and local merchants were increasingly forced into insolvency.
They either had to sell out to competitors, put their mahogany works up for
auction, yield their business to creditors to meet outstanding debts, and enter
partnerships with more capital intensive mahogany firms based in London.[84]
With the arrival of an increasing number of British and Scottish merchants
and more representatives of London firms, the local merchant and landowning
class suffered a further setback.

---

82   Source: 1846: Gibbs (1883: 93, 102); 1858–1868: Longdon to Grant, AB R. 98

83   Although information on mahogany prices is scarce and unreliable, from the sources
     available it can be deduced that prices fluctuated a great deal and fell rapidly. See for ex-
     ample Longdon to Grant, 17 May 1869, AB R.98, in Ibid.

84   Examples of these newly formed types of companies were James Hyde & Company,
     Young Toledo & Company or Carmichael Vidal & Company, some of the names indicat-
     ing that London firms bought mahogany works of many of the old settlers.

From the second half of the 19th century onwards, one of the largest mahogany companies, James Hyde & Company, started to transfer their registered mahogany works to the metropolitan owned British Honduras Company, which emerged as the predominant landowner of the crown colony. As a consequence, the firm was able to expand, often at the expense of other landowners who were forced to sell their land. By 1875, it became the Belize Estate and Produce Company (BEC). This London based company owned approximately one fifth of the country in the Northern District, which at that time also included parts of Western Belize. With their land in other areas of the colony, about 50% of all the freehold land was owned by the Belize Estate & Produce Company.[85]

In short, one of the most direct consequences of the chronic economic depression was a definite trend toward the consolidation of metropolitan land ownership and the creation of latifundia (large scattered landed estates), the latter of which were characterized mostly by absentee landowners.

The prolonged depression also affected the labour market. The demand for labour, which had been very high prior to the onset of the depression, was drastically reduced along with a simultaneous lowering of wages. Although the situation was somewhat eased by the beginning of the plantation agriculture in the 1860s and the southward migration of large number of people to work on a projected railway at Puerto Caballo in present Honduras, the reduction of the demand for labour can be seen as one of the root causes of today's chronic unemployment and poverty.

As we have seen, the mahogany industry came to completely dominate the economic activity in the colony. In compliance with the restrictions imposed by the Spanish, apart from the small subsistence cultivations of mostly plantains, food crops for domestic consumption were not grown.

In this context the following question arises: Why did the local settlers and merchants not ask themselves whether these restrictions, which were purely out of political and not economic reasons, would still be relevant after Central America achieved independence from Spain? The restrictions as such surely would not have been an impediment for the settlers. After all they had been ignoring Spanish rules ever since the beginning of the first settlement in the Bay of Honduras. Why then did the powerful merchant elite of British Honduras not encourage the cultivation of crops for domestic consumption?

---

85 Cf. Handbook of British Honduras (1988/89: 81), London 1988. Although the Belize Estate & Produce Company (BEC) has cast off some of its poorer and less valuable idle land, it continues to be the biggest single landowner. In 1971, the company still was in possession of 42% (close to one million acres) of all the privately owned land. Cf. Bolland and Shoman (1977: 105).

With regards to the decades following Central American independence, this question can be partly answered, as the profitable transit trade provided the settlement with cattle, fruit and other produce for the consumption of the local population. From the late 1840s onwards, when the entrepôt trade began to decline and the exports of mahogany fell drastically, the situation became critical. Due to the complete absence of an alternative cash crop, the existing colonial dependency was further increased. British Honduras was far from being self-sufficient as far as foodstuffs were concerned and basic staples such as maize, beans, and rice as well as canned meat, and canned milk, had to be imported. Although the immigration of small scale cultivators from Yucatán in the second half of the 19th century temporarily eased the situation, generally speaking, the local economy was not able to fall back on a dynamic peasantry, which would eventually have been capable of supporting the economy and reduce the import of basic foods.

In the beginning of the 20th century this dependency on imported foodstuffs was intensified with the only difference that British Honduras became increasingly dependent on the US rather than on the mother-country. The commercial activities with the US re-affirmed, at least temporarily, the strong position of the colony's mercantile elite. As a consequence, by being in a position to set an example for a preference for imported goods, it was the local mercantile elite itself who further contributed to the growing dependency of the colony's economy. Both the White and Creole elite and the relatively small group of middle class (composed of the rest of the White population, White and Creole civil servants, and clerks) were now able to afford and show a preference for imported manufactured and processed goods and it was in the interest of the leading merchants in the colony *not* to develop economic branches outside the timber industry, such as pork-raising for the production of salted pork and a large scale growing of corn, wheat, beans, and rice.

For other groups in the colony, the possibility of starting entrepreneurial activities not in connection with the timber industry was extremely limited. In addition, because the purchasing power of the majority of Creoles and Blacks was very restricted, and the elite and middle class Whites and Creoles preferred imported goods, a local market was virtually non-existent.

The *Guera de Castas* in Yucatán and the subsequent influx of Mestizo was to bring a change. The immigrants were able to rent land from the major private landowner in Northern Belize and began to cultivate sugar cane. Eventually, the agricultural activities in the Northern District contributed to the creating of a local market since more and more Mestizos started to engage in wage labour, which in turn increased their purchasing power.[86] Moreover, a tendency to encourage commercial activities outside the timber industry was beginning to manifest and temporarily helped to ease colonial dependency.

Nevertheless, the prevailing patterns of land tenure continued to limit the opportunities for increasing the supply of locally grown food crops. The rents charged by the contractors of the absentee landowners were a major impediment for the peasants to put more land into cultivation. In addition, most peasants were apprehensive about engaging in wage labour, because they always considered it only as an additional activity to *milpa* farming and were very cautious about relying on money alone. Although the Mestizo farmers were taking part in the local market economy, they preferred to continue concentrating on subsistence farming. As a consequence, the situation was not fundamentally altered and the colony's economic activities remained dependent on the forestry mono-economy.

8. The Need for Economic Diversification

The decline of the transit trade, the beginning of an economic dependence and the rise in population made the need for economic diversification and the growth of a domestic market more apparent than ever.

Although the community was taking for granted that the timber resources were inexhaustible, the various superintendents did realize that the heydays of the mahogany industry were counted. In 1856 suggestions were made to financially support the Northern District and by 1867 it had become clear that agriculture was the only hope of the colony. Also, there was an increased apprehension that a break in the fragile relations with the neighbouring countries would cause serious problems in the food supply. In fact, this was a well-founded fear because as the Yucatecan war went on, all trade was interrupted.

In British Honduras, one of the essential preconditions for agriculture to develop on a wider scale – a large and reliable labour force – did not exist. This was mainly due to the following reasons:

A large percentage of the Black and Creole population had developed, for various reasons, a certain aversion to agricultural activities. The export of timber was still by far more valuable than that of sugar and the labourers of African origin, being accustomed to the hardships of forestry work, were kept at work in the forest. In fact, in most cases the forest workers had little choice but to remain in the woods. Fearing an eventual competition from the nascent ag-

---

86   Cf. Cal (1991: 217)

ricultural industry, the mahogany merchants exercised an effective means of labour control, the "advance and truck system", as mentioned, which made it extremely difficult for the forest labourers to start working in agriculture.

As far as the Maya population was concerned, the image held of them by the settlers and mercantile firms had long changed. Already in 1835, the developers hoped that the native population could be induced to work in the forest and on the plantations. Indeed a large percentage of the formerly independent Mestizo *rancheros* and some of the Maya refugees – who, in fact, had been the pioneers in the planting of sugar cane, corn, and vegetables – began to work as wage labourers on the first sugar cane plantations on the larger estates. However, the expectations to recruit large numbers of Maya and Mestizos as full-time wage labourers were soon thwarted because both the Maya and the Mestizos still being very cautious about relying exclusively on wage labour. Therefore, they continued to regard this new activity only as complementary to their own subsistence *milpa* farming.

In the 1870s, *milpa* farming began to pose a threat to the lumbering interests. After some of the Maya villages had been destroyed in the western regions, the Maya once more were seen as potential plantation labour force

> ... *the indigenous Indian might be made available to some extent could he be induced to quit his scattered village-homes, and this is perhaps the cheapest labour to be procured.*[87]

For the plantations in the south, however, it was never possible to recruit enough labour, although the planters employed local Garinagu and a small number of Blacks and Creoles who at that time did not work in the forest and ventured to leave Belize Town.

Due to the continuing labour shortage in the entire country, the only solution for the establishment of commercial plantation agriculture was to encourage large scale immigration. Contrary to an official statement made locally in 1856

> ... *certainly this is not a likely country to tempt persons to migrate ... when there are so many more tempting fields of adventure in other parts of the world, and in better climates than this ...*[88]

---

87   Gibbs (1883:162,176). This statement is especially interesting since the author of the above was an officer in the very same Field Force which had destroyed the Mayan villages in Western Belize in the first place.

88   AB, Blue Book, Returns for 1856 quoted in Ashcraft (1973:42).

a number of immigration schemes were introduced. Although several incentives were given to prospective immigrants (for example certain measures were taken to abolish the annual tax on foreigners), in the long run, these schemes did not have the desired effect. After British Honduras became an official British colony in 1862, several acts were passed to allow extensive immigration and the importation of Chinese indentured labourers. According to an official report of 1881, and as can be seen on Table 10, the colony's population came from a diversity of countries.

The demand for development-orientated immigrants coincided with the beginning of the American Civil War. In an attempt to stop the cotton trade in the South, the North American Federal Government blocked much of the Southern states' coastline with the result that contraband centres in Mexico began to flourish. After that it was foreseeable and only a matter of time until the merchants of British Honduras – the colony being the nearest British port – would grasp this trading opportunity and supply the Confederates with arms and ammunition. Having established this connection, the majority of the colony's influential citizens viewed the Civil War as an opportunity to increase immigration into British Honduras. It was made clear that Southerners would be welcomed, for example Young Toledo & Company began to engage in extensive advertising and even opened up an immigration agency in New Orleans.[89]

In the beginning, the colony's authorities hoped that, along with White Confederates, emancipated slaves could also be attracted to immigrate but after the Federal Government turned down the proposals for the immigration of the freedmen, immigration policy was concentrated on White settlers only.

Considerable efforts were made on the part of the colony to attract Confederate planters with the ultimate goal to "… change this colony from an unknown wilderness into a garden teeming with all the wealth and beauty of the tropics."[90] Governor Austin even hoped that if enough White Southerners came to the colony, Great Britain would be willing to grant independence in the near future. However, of the just over one hundred Southern families who did come in search of their fortunes, very few actually stayed in the colony for

---

89 This was not the first time that settlers from North America decided to emigrate to the Bay Settlement. During the American War of Independence, several British orientated families left the American colonies and, together with English and Scottish settlers from the island of Roatán, came to the Bay. After the Spaniards had taken a large number of the settlement's original (English and Scottish) inhabitants to the dungeons in Havana, a reinforcement of settlers was urgently needed and most welcome. The American/English families eventually settled on Cay Caulker, where many of Belize's oldest families still reside today.

90 Lt. Governor Austin, 9 July 1867, AB R. 98

a longer period. Deterred by the hardships of pioneer life in the virgin forests and the relatively high prices for Crown land, especially in comparison to other Central and Latin American countries,[91] and after finding out that cotton was an unsuitable crop for the colony, they returned to the United States or left for Guatemala or Honduras.

Eventually, the price on Crown land was lowered, buyers were attracted and Governor Austin also succeeded in persuading one of the largest land-owners in the colony, Young Toledo & Company to offer plots of land for free in the untouched forests in the vicinity of present Punta Gorda in the south "… to every male adult from the Southern States of America or of Anglo-Saxon origin who will settle on those lands …"[92] The Southern families who decided to remain founded the "Toledo Settlement" in the south of British Honduras, acquired large tracts of land and started to plant sugar cane but their impact on the agricultural development of the colony was only marginal.[93]

Other small groups of immigrants included several Italian and German families who were settled on Crown land in the Stann Creek area, but poor organization, antiquated and unsuitable farming techniques and the inefficiency of transport facilities to the market in Belize Town did not enable them to start plantations. In 1871 several landowners succeeded in obtaining East Indian labour, especially after this policy had been successful in Trinidad and British Guiana. Most of the approximately 170 East Indians were employed in the southernmost district, the present Toledo District, where they later turned to the growing of rice. Several hundreds of immigrants from the West Indian islands also came to the colony, mainly working on the short lived banana plantations in the south.

In sum, the colonial schemes for immigration as well as the efforts of the colonial authorities to promote agricultural development did not bear fruit. We may even go as far as to say that the only massive influx of immigrants into the colony, the Mestizo refugees from the *Guerra de Castas* in Yucatán, was not the result of the colonial immigration policies. And curiously, it was the Yucatán immigrants who laid the foundations for agricultural development in British Honduras.

---

91 After the American Civil War most Latin American countries wanted to attract Southern immigrants and Brazil even offered land for free.

92 Austin to Grant, 13 March 1867, AB R. 92

93 The southern settlers were reinforced by a group of White Methodists from Mississippi. Together, they formed a closed community and established twelve sugar estates in the vicinity of Toledo but since they were unwilling to employ coloured labour and their Methodist's beliefs were against the distilling of sugar to alcohol, economic ruin was programmed. Cf. also Dobson (1973: 247–249).

8.1. The Establishment of Sugar Plantations in the North

Compared to the limited success of the sugar cane estates in the south, the pioneering efforts of the Mestizo planters, the *rancheros,* in the north were more successful. By doing so, some of the *rancheros* were able to develop a regional commercial centre in the Northern District. In this economic location, they were not only more protected from the metropolitan merchant interests in Belize Town, but also well placed to profit from the transit trade with Yucatán (after the worst of the *Guerra de Castas* had passed) and Cuba. Some planters were also capable of negotiating and entering into successful business partnerships[94] with firms in London and Belize Town.

After the "small but rather profitable plantations"[95] of the Mestizo and Maya settlers in the north succeeded in satisfying the internal demands, the first exports of rum and sugar took place in 1857. When the planters had proven the economic viability of the exportation of sugar, within a few years, the big landowners, being convinced that the new crop would turn into a substitute cash crop for mahogany, became attracted to the cultivation of sugar. As a consequence, both the Mestizo *rancheros* and Maya were now seen as a potential source of labour for plantation. But the Maya continued to be extremely hesitant to rely exclusively on wage labour and the authorities decided that, as an incentive, the respective *alcaldes* of the Maya villages would be permitted to allocate plots of Crown land for milpa cultivation. Even if the Maya were now able to hold small plots of land, proper land tenure was deliberately made far from secure, to make the Maya more available for wage labour.

Within a decade of the first exports of sugar by the Mestizo farmers, the production and export of sugar was taken over by large companies. The biggest producer was the British Honduras Company, which had established extensive plantations of sugar cane by 1868. In the seven years from 1862 to 1868 sugar exports from British Honduras more than quadrupled. But regardless of this gigantic rise in sugar exports, timber exports were still considerably higher,[96] and in the long run it was not possible to overcome the economic dependency on timber. Notwithstanding the huge increase in the production and exportation of sugar, the industry soon stagnated.

---

94   Cf. Judd (1992:164)

95   Supt. Stevenson to Gov. Barlee, 5 April 1856, AB R.55

96   According to reports, exports of sugar rose from 397.176 lbs. in 1862 to 1,706.880 lbs. in 1868. Lt.Gov. Longdon to Gov. Grant, 19 June 1868, and AB R.98, Blue Book for 1867 in Burden (1935,III: 305–6).

Why was the sugar industry not able to develop any further? Essentially this was because certain changes in the world market towards the end of the 19th century had a negative influence on the industry: For example, the growing competition from beet sugar resulted in a collapse of prices for cane sugar, a phenomenon which had already affected the sugar planting efforts by the Confederate immigrants in the south. As a consequence, a steady decline in the exports of sugar and rum was inevitable. These major changes along with the primitive production methods that prevailed prior to the installation of a modern sugar mill in 1936 can be seen as the most serious impediments for an increased production and exportation of sugar from British Honduras.[97]

One counteractive measure was the distillation of the molasses into rum. By 1856, the big sugar plantations had adopted this necessary step, and began to distil considerable amounts of spirits. In 1867 over 50,000 gallons of rum were produced, of which approximately 5,000 were exported.[98] Rum production also gained in importance during the 1920s, when a number of Mestizo farmers were able to profit from the exportation of rum during the United States Prohibition.[99] Today, Belizean rum with the brand name "Caribbean Rum" is processed at the Cuello Rum Distillery, named after the important pre-Classic Maya centre "Cuello", the remnants of which are still visible on the distillery company's lands.

8.2. Further Attempts at Economic Diversification

After the successful development of the sugar industry in the north, from 1877 onwards, more efforts were made to diversify the economy and make the colony agriculturally self-supporting. Several innovations and a variety of new crops, such as coffee, cocoa, coconuts (copra), and cotton were introduced. While cotton proved to be totally unsuitable, in 1890 the domestic requirements of coffee were already grown in British Honduras, including a small surplus for export. Nonetheless, the major hindrance for development remained the non-existence of an efficient transport system to the coast.

In this context, it is well worth mentioning that the state of agricultural development in British Honduras in the last decades of the 19th century was

---

97   It was not until after 1937 that the interest in sugar production revived but exports were not resumed until 1953 when British Honduras was given an initial quota of 5,000 tons (which was soon raised to 25,000 tons) in the Commonwealth Sugar Agreement (see Dobson 1973: 270).

98   Blue Book for 1867 in Burdon (1935, III: 305–6).

99   Cf. Judd (1992: 161)

very different to that of the majority of Spanish Central American countries: By the end of the 19th century, Guatemala had already succeeded in developing its coffee plantations on a large scale with the result that coffee became a major export crop and by 1908 its railroad to the Caribbean Coast had been completed. El Salvador and Honduras, though on a smaller scale, managed to develop their banana production commercially and Honduras was able to build a railroad, connecting the main banana-production sites with the three banana ports on the Caribbean coast and the largest commercial centre (present San Pedro Sula), sixty kilometres inland. In Costa Rica several privately owned rail-lines were opened, enabling the establishment of the first modern inter-oceanic system of banana-production by the Del Monte Company and attracting investors who eventually formed the United Fruit Company in 1899.

In late 19th century British Honduras, the most promising crops for development were **bananas and plantains** because they could be grown closer to the coast and transport was generally easier. With the arrival of the more re-form-orientated Governor Barlee in 1877, for the first time the possibility of exporting bananas to the United States market was seriously considered. Eager to promote the colony's prosperity during his appointment, the new governor began to take actions for transferring the monthly mail route from Jamaica to a fortnightly service with New Orleans.

The decision to replace the subsidized mail route to and from Jamaica was made despite strong internal objection: The colony's merchants and residents feared that the discontinuation of a regular mail service to Jamaica would not only have a negative influence on the exchange of correspondence between British Honduras and London but would also put an end to the direct commerce with the West Indies – and especially Jamaica – as well as to the military arrangements British Honduras had made with the latter. Another concern was that the opening up of a direct service to New Orleans would eventually come to completely Americanize the British colony. But there was no turning back. If one wanted to open up the possibilities of export to the US, the changing of the mail route was a necessary precondition for the entire Central American trade was directed towards New Orleans.

With the partial solution to the transportation problem and access to the North American market, British Honduras started to invest in banana-production, in fact, the only commercial agricultural undertaking the British settlers ever engaged in. A mild land rush to the southern regions of the colony took place and the industry remained prosperous for some time. In 1906 the building of a short distance railway (only twenty five miles long) was initiated to join the centre of production around the banana station of Middlesex and the port of Stann Creek and the nearby pier at Commerce Bight (see Map 15). After the turn of the century, the industry appeared sufficiently prosperous to make the United Fruit Company (Elder & Fyffe) purchase a large estate in the Stann Creek valley in 1911 and cultivate bananas on a large scale.

The promising banana industry, however, suffered a severe setback when plant disease struck the bananas. As a consequence, the United Fruit Company abandoned the estates and the industry began to sink into a depression, from which it has been able to recover only recently, with the planting of disease resistant varieties. In the late 1980s the figures for the exportation of bananas have shown a significant increase and bananas are listed as the fourth major export article of Belize.[100] The less delicate plantains, or cooking bananas, were never affected by the plant disease and continued to be successfully planted and exported until the present.

Attempts to diversify the economy also extended to the forestry industry. Apart from mahogany and a small amount of logwood the following types of wood were also exported: Secondary hardwood such as the heavy, strong and lasting **Santa Maria** wood (used mostly for planks on bridges or boat masts), the very hard and durable **sapodilla wood, rosewood, cedar** (highly esteemed by the cigar making companies in Cuba and the Southern states of the US) and softwood, mostly **pine.**

Another product, which falls into the category of forestry products and showed an enormous increase in the late 1890s, was **chicle (gum).** Chicle is the white latex-like sap that is "bled" from the sapodilla tree and was much valued by the timber industry and the chicle harvesters alike. In reality, most of the chicle was gathered just across the Guatemalan border in the Petén. It was carried to the "production sites" in "Belizean" territory, where it was boiled until solid blocks could be made which were then shipped on the Belize River to the coast. The chicle-production for export brought a large amount of immigrants from the Petén into the north-western regions of British Honduras.[101]

Apart from the profits gained from the exploitation and preparation of chicle, the colony also benefited indirectly from the chicle boom by charging Guatemala duties for the transportation of chicle on the Belize River and the usage of harbour facilities.[102] After the Second World War chicle was replaced largely by the use of synthetic materials, resulting in a drastic decline in the amount of

---

100 See Abstract of Statistics, Issues 1985,1989, Central Statistical Office, Belmopan.

101 It is highly possible that a considerable percentage of these immigrants were the descendants of escaped "Belizean" slaves who had managed to cross into Guatemala during the 1820s. See also Buhler (1976).

102 The exports of chicle rose from 260,000 lbs. in 1899 to almost 3,500,000 in 1914, the United States' chewing gum manufacturers being the main customer. Caiger (1951:143).

chicle produced and exported. The commercial exploitation of chicle, together with the aforementioned growing of bananas for export, initiated a definite shift of economic orientation towards the US. This is also reflected in the official adoption of parity of exchange between the British Honduras and the United States dollars in 1894.

With regard to any further attempts to diversify the forestry industry, there would have been one more viable option: It would have been the extraction of the valuable dye from logwood, especially that it was still exploited and exported, although compared to the 17th and 18th centuries, in much smaller quantities.

Why did the colony's residents not show any initiative to process logwood? If the technique of how to produce lasting dyes was unknown to them, why did they not show any interest in importing the know-how and look for investors to provide the necessary technical equipment, for example mills? From the 1780s onwards, the Europeans had already mastered the art of achieving long lasting dyes and the Maya too had their, albeit primitive, methods of how to obtain dye from the heart of the logwood tree.

Admittedly, an eventual dye-producing industry would have been rather short-lived, as aniline based dyestuffs began to replace natural dyes in the second half of the 19th century. But so was the extraction and production of chicle and yet, it gave the local economy a temporary boost. If British Honduras had been able to produce its own dyes, its economic dependency would definitely have been reduced. Quite possibly even, investors would have been attracted and as a consequence, further economic possibilities would have been opened.

Among the other miscellaneous export articles that temporarily contributed to a diversification of the economy were **rubber, sponges, shark-skin**, and **crocodile-hides.**

Tortoiseshell and **live turtles** were export commodities that came to play an important role in British Honduras and therefore deserve to be looked at more in detail: From the early buccaneering days, turtling had been an activity practised extensively in the entire Bay of Honduras and all along the Mosquito Shore. Tortoiseshell *(carey)* was obtained from the horny shields of captured hawksbill turtles and was a highly valued material in Victorian England for the manufacture of various articles such as combs, frames for eye-glasses, fans, cigar and cigarette boxes, furniture (veneers and inlays), and for interior decoration. Exact information on the amount of hawksbill turtles captured is scarce, and therefore it is difficult to establish reliable export figures, but according to shipping records a large number of cases containing hawksbill shell (approximately 300–400 lbs. per case) left British Honduras during 1864–1912.[103]

---

103 Cf. Craig (1966: 42) and Parsons (1985: 104–112)

From 1830 onwards, when all steam-powered vessels were able to make the journey across the Atlantic in just 14 days and at the same time increase their cargo, commerce with Great Britain began to be more regular and a considerable number of **live turtles** (or "heads") were exported from the colony's harbour, which functioned as a central depot for the shipment of live green turtles. The animals were transported in special wooden tanks on board large steamers. The regular ship bound for Liverpool, for example, was able to consistently carry thirty three heads of green turtle. According to contemporary newspaper records, the export of live turtles reached its peak in 1869, when 5,520 heads of mature green turtle were shipped from British Honduras.[104] Once in Britain, the turtles were sold at auctions at the dockside, and gourmet restaurants being the ultimate destinations of these animals.

With a steadily growing demand, prices rose and due to the introduction of modern fishing techniques, such as turtle nets, signs of overfishing soon began to manifest. It has often been claimed that it was the colonial turtle industry (and with it the European population as a whole) that was responsible for the occurrence of overfishing and the subsequent decimation of the hawksbill and green turtle population of British Honduras. However, we must bear in mind that the colonial turtle industry was in the hands of a group of individual businessmen on both sides of the Atlantic who created the demand for the translucent tortoiseshell and turtle meat in the first place, reaping a rich benefit from the industry. Besides, at that time, only a small percentage of the European population could afford to buy these luxury articles.

As a consequence of overfishing, the number of turtles in British Honduras and its adjacent coastal waters began to decrease vehemently. In combination with trade restrictions and the rising costs in transport, the business came to a standstill in the 1920s.

Although the colonial turtle industry initially boosted overfishing in British Honduras and its adjacent coastal waters, which ultimately led to the hawksbill and green turtle becoming endangered species, local exploitation too has always played an important role. We must bear in mind that the pressures of local consumption of turtle eggs (obtained mostly through poaching) and the meat of the green turtle, which continues to serve as a supplement to the diet of a large number of the Caribbean population, have always been a threat to the species. In the present day, these pressures continue to be significant. Together with natural predators, an increasing development of deserted beaches and a lack of educational awareness in the local population are the real hazards for the conservation of the species.

---

104 *Honduras Gazette and Colonial Advertiser*, mentioned in Craig (1966: 47)

After elaborating on the various efforts to promote substitute agricultural development and other forestry products besides mahogany and secondary hardwood, as well as the endeavours to encourage trade with a number of miscellaneous articles to gradually reduce the problems of a mono-economy, the following conclusion may be drawn: Due to the lack of definite British support and the prevailing internal hostile attitude towards agriculture by the timber interests, it would have been very difficult for agricultural enterprises to succeed over a long period of time. After a temporary upswing, further attempts to develop commercial plantation agriculture and introduce a wider range of export articles soon faltered and eventually declined. As a result, British Honduras was once more left dependent on its timber resources. Nevertheless, a variety of crops for subsistence and the limited internal market continued to be grown by individual Maya, Mestizo, Garinagu, Black and Creole farmers.

8.3. Impediments for an Alteration of the Basic Economic Structure

One of the main restrictions for a re-orientation of the extractive economy towards commercial agriculture and the development of agriculture on a large scale was the fact that legislature continued to be controlled by the timber merchants. In addition, the news spread in 1898 of the possibility of constructing a railroad to the Sarstoon River (the southern border with Guatemala) to facilitate the extraction of logwood along with the rumours of the gold potentials of the Maya mountains in the south, put a halt to any measures to initiate agricultural development.

Another obstacle for the development of agriculture was the amendment of the existing labour laws in favour of the forestry merchant group. These new laws literally prevented the forest workers from seeking other opportunities of how to earn a living and, by directly inhibiting the growing of a peasantry, were responsible for delaying economic diversification.

Moreover, to reduce the possibility of competition from agriculture, the timber merchants' lobby succeeded in temporarily obstructing a further development of the existing modest internal market: Hardly any public works were undertaken and it was endeavoured to keep public spending at a minimum. In short, too much emphasis was placed on export while the internal market was neglected. Potential entrepreneurs were left with few opportunities outside the forestry industry and there was very little inducement for investing in the colony. There were no roads, the internal riverine transport system was inefficient and only one inadequately equipped port, with no docks or deep-water quay. Also, the availability of land was limited to Crown land in the south, which at that time was still considered only partially suitable for agriculture.

By this stage, the economy of British Honduras became trapped in a vicious circle: Without an infrastructure to offer, it was difficult to attract investment and immigrants, both developers and labourers. And without a certain amount of revenue (which, in turn, only could have been generated by an increased number of population), it was impossible to provide the necessary infrastructure for the colony to prosper. Although, at one stage, agriculture in British Honduras had received a substantial boost, a large peasantry was never able to develop, as it was for example the case in Jamaica, Trinidad and British Guiana.[105]

Apart from the aforementioned main impediments – the existing labour laws to the advantage of the forestry industry, the neglect of the internal market and the lack of infrastructure – what were the other restrictions for the development of agriculture on a larger scale?

To begin with, the uncertainty as to the status of the settlement and its boundaries was a major inhibition for early agricultural development and the growing of a peasantry. Superintendent Cockburn reported in 1835 that "… no outside capital can be expected to come into the country until the questions of sovereignty and boundaries are settled."[106] But the British government still refused to officially sanction the development of agriculture, an attitude which remained unchanged even in the decades following the independence of the Spanish colonies in Central America. Britain was still disinterested in developing plantations in the territory and the few petitions by the Public Meeting for the cultivation of agricultural crops were repeatedly turned down. The Colonial Office in London was apprehensive that a positive decision would entail the starting of negotiations with Spain, a step one was not prepared to take yet.

A significant hurdle for the development of a peasantry was also the prevailing pattern of land tenure: In British Honduras a price was imposed on Crown lands and small farmers had to lease plots from the contractors of the absentee landowners. Since the annual leases were subject to change, this arrangement did not encourage the Mestizo and Maya peasants to put more land into cultivation. As far as the majority of Blacks and Creoles were concerned, generally speaking, throughout the first half of the 19th century, farming was considered as a poor option. Again, this was to the advantage of the timber

---

105 For example in British Guiana, by 1838 almost 5,000 of the approximately 15,000 emancipated slaves possessed and cultivated a total of 7,000 acres of land. Similarly, in Jamaica, emphasis was placed on developing an internal market system and to distribute abandoned sugar estates into small plots, thus creating the necessary preconditions for the freedmen to make a living by enabling them to dedicate their activities to small scale farming. Cf. Augier (1960:18) and Bolland (1977:123–4)

106 Report of Supt. Cockburn, Feb.1835 quoted in Burdon (1935, *1835*).

industry because without land, money and a means of subsistence there was no other realistic alternative for the emancipated slaves and Creoles but to continue to cut wood, particularly because the forestry industry was still in a position to offer higher wages.

In this context we have to ask ourselves the question whether it would not have been possible for the heads of families to make suitable arrangements with the landowners, to enable the workers' families to leave Belize Town and settle on a piece of land, grow their own subsistence and market an eventual surplus. There can be no doubting that this would have been one first step towards satisfying the growing internal market.

In British Honduras this development never occurred which was mainly due to the following: Black and Creole women (unlike the Garinagu and Miskito and to a certain extent also the Maya and Mestizo women) were simply not accustomed to engage in the cultivation of subsistence crops. This may be seen as a consequence of a pattern which evolved during slavery; the existence of domestic slaves. And people who had domestic slaves before emancipation most probably continued to employ them afterwards. By getting paid for their services, the women were able to contribute significantly to the family's subsistence, especially if we consider that – thanks to the system of labour control, "the advance and truck system" -, the men were likely to return from the forests in debt at the end of the season. Compared to farming, the domestic work of the Black and Creole women was a much more efficient way of securing an income.[107]

By now it has become obvious that the "advance and truck system" was a major hindrance for the development of a peasantry: Once the advance was spent the workers were forced to obtain their supplies at a much higher price and on credit from the employer's own store in the camp. Thus, they remained in debt and had to continue to work for the same employer to try and work off the debt. But even if the forest labourers had been able to pay off their debts, it would have been very difficult to lease small plots of land. By the 1850s a large percentage of potentially available good agriculture land was uncleared bush, practically inaccessible and therefore was only attractive to more capital intensive firms, speculators and/or large scale woodcutters. As mentioned above, between 1850 and 1880 most of the old settler families were forced to sell out vast

---

107 In countries where domestic labour is still widespread, this pattern persists to the present day. For example in rural Guatemala, it continues to be very common among Indian women to commute to Guatemala City to work as domestics to secure the financial income in case their men end a month's work in debt. The "advance system" was not an invention of the British and on some of the larger estates in Guatemala, debt peonage still exists.

tracts of land to larger mahogany firms. These firms were continuously in need for more labour to resume the woodcutting operations and the development of a peasantry was not in their interest.

Although most forest labourers were literally bound to their employers by the "advance and truck system", a small amount of Black and Creole workers managed to stay clear of debts and succeeded in obtaining small plots of land, leasing or squatting, mostly in remote, largely wild and unexplored regions, and a long way from the only market in Belize Town. This land tenure, however, was extremely insecure because tenancy rights were not protected by the government. Moreover, the reluctance to invest in an improved transportation system and in the development of the internal marketing system did not make peasant farming a feasible long term alternative. Consequently, the existing peasants became part-time peasants only and continued to be dependent on wage labour.

During the administration of Governor Barlee (1877–1882), this economic structure started to change. The colony at last modified its land tenure and began to take initial steps towards improving the market possibilities, which were highly disapproved by the local landowning elite and forestry merchant group.[108] At last, it seemed that there was some incentive given to the "urban" Black and Creole population. So far they had been reluctant to modify their attitude towards agriculture, due to the lack of prospects. The growing of bananas promised new economic possibilities and potential planters and unemployed Blacks and Creoles were lured to the countryside. A mild moderate migration from Belize Town to the south began, but in general, the expectations were never fulfilled and the potential planters and farmers-to-be ended up as wage labourers.

Seen from a present-day perspective, some of the above mentioned impediments for the development of agriculture on a large scale, in a certain sense, turned out to be also advantageous for modern Belize. If consolidation of land had not taken place and if plots had been easily available, more land would have been cleared and put into cultivation. While on the one hand, this would no doubt have supported the local economy and helped to reduce the colony's dependence on imported foodstuffs, on the other hand, the clearance of vast amounts of forest would have meant the habitat loss for most of the region's wildlife, as it was the case in many of the neighbouring countries. In the Petén region across the Guatemalan border, as well as in Honduras and Mexico, large portions of land are now completely deforested and there is virtually no wild-

---

108 See Archives of Belize, "Memorial urging Barlee's recall", Memorial to Secretary of State, 13 Sept. 1880, AB R.115: 660–69.

life left. Due to the low population density in Belize, and the aforementioned obstacles for increased development, this has not been the case in Belize. Approximately 60% of Belize's land area is still covered with forest, providing an ideal refuge for a variety of flora and fauna.

In the 1980s, Belize began to advertise a new nature-based facet of tourism, ecotourism. Despite constant monetary problems and growing pressure from agricultural and industrial interests, the government succeeded in protecting several large remote and untouched stretches of rainforest, by officially declaring them as nature reserves and wildlife sanctuaries. These areas continue to be inhabited by a diversity of wild animals and attract the interest and funds from a number of international conservation groups as well as a substantial amount of tourists. The growing tourist industry enables an increasing percentage of the local population, especially rural, to earn a living by working as guides, rangers, in hotels etc., or by providing accommodation. If there had been more development in the 19th and most of the 20th centuries, the amount of population would have risen significantly. A higher population density, in turn, would have largely destroyed the region's ecosystem and wildlife, which, as a consequence, could never have become one of modern Belize's most valuable assets.

9. An Official Colony at Last

From the middle of the 19th century onwards, the local White and Creole elite not only ceased to be in complete charge of the political administrative system (the magistracy and the Public Meeting), but was also forced to cede control of the settlement's economy to British companies. In fact, as soon as the dominance of the old elite was broken and an increased interference of British companies became evident, the British government showed a greater willingness to assert its sovereignty over the territory.

In whose interest was an assertion of British sovereignty? First and foremost, it was the local elite who had been making pleas for some time because they were convinced that once the settlement was recognized as an official British colony, preferential tariff treatment would be applied. Secondly, the London partners of the various newly formed timber companies were very interested in speeding up negotiations for a more defined status, particularly since the metropolitan businessmen were greatly concerned about the security of their land investments.

In the late 1840s, with the onset of large scale sugar production which, strictly speaking, was violating the terms of the Anglo-Spanish treaty of 1786, the Convention of London, it was high time for Britain to react one way or another. By now, there were many interests involved and it was too late to stop agricultural activities. Britain at last decided that the time had come to start the preparations for assuming full sovereignty.

In 1850, the Clayton-Bulwer treaty was signed between Great Britain and the United States, at which both governments pledged "not to occupy, fortify or colonize any part of Central America". This vague wording, interpreted by the British to apply only to future occupations and to exclude British Honduras and the neighbouring Bay Islands off the coast of present Honduras, prompted the British government to announce that "Her Majesty does not understand the engagements of that Convention to apply to her Majesty's Settlement of Honduras or its dependencies."[109]

In 1854, Britain decided to ignore Spanish claims and settle the issue of sovereignty once and for all by providing "Honduras" with a formal constitution. A new Legislative Assembly was instituted and without any subsequent comment whatsoever on the part of Spain. In 1861, the inhabitants of British Honduras renewed their pleas for colonial status and sent one more petition to London, "… your Petitioners humbly submit to your Majesty, that the time has now arrived when British Honduras should be in name, what it really is in fact, a Colony …"[110] and this time their request was crowned with success.

In 1862, almost exactly two centuries after the first logwood cutters established themselves at the mouth of the Belize River, "Her Majesty's Settlement in the Bay of Honduras" was formally declared as the official colony of British Honduras. In 1870, the Legislative Assembly (which had evolved out of the traditional Public Meeting) surrendered its privileges of self-government and in 1871 a Crown Colony form of government was introduced. It meant that a new Legislative Council was formed whose members were nominated by the Crown instead of being elected. With British Honduras being a Crown Colony, supervision from Jamaica became unnecessary and from 1884 onwards, British Honduras was no longer subject to the authority of Jamaica.

The establishment of British Honduras as an official British colony in 1862 was strongly interconnected with the complex issue of marking the territorial boundary with Guatemala. In the Dallas-Clarendon Treaty of 1856, Britain publicly declared that it would withdraw from the Mosquito Protectorate and from the Bay Islands provided the southern limit of British Honduras would be acknowledged as the Sarstoon River, the current border with Guatemala. By this agreement, the total area of British Honduras was almost doubled, reach-

---

109 Cf. Bloomfield (1953: 21)
110 Burden (1935: 235–36)

ing its present-day extension of 23,000 km², and was now twice as large as Jamaica, the largest British colony in the West Indies until then.

In 1859, a boundary agreement was signed between Great Britain and Guatemala (the Aycinena-Wyke Treaty), at which the British government agreed to help finance the building of a road from Guatemala to the Atlantic, thereby facilitating the commerce for both countries. The wording of the respective article concerning the road was, once more, extremely vague,[111] clouding the issue ever since. As a result the Anglo-Guatemalan Treaty of 1859 became one of the most thoroughly discussed international treaties.

Fundamental differences between the two governments in interpreting the treaty eventually led to the collapse of the supplementary convention of 1863 whereby Britain would have agreed to pay 50,000 pounds sterling towards the construction of the proposed road. To this very day, the controversial road issue remains unsettled and Article VII of the 1859 treaty was never ratified. In 2008 a special agreement was signed between Guatemala and Belize where both parties committed themselves to undertake the necessary procedures to submit to referendum the decision to bring to the International Court of Justice the final settlement of the territorial dispute. Given that in 2013 Guatemala has unilaterally withdrawn from holding said referendum, this complex topic is likely to keep diplomats and experts in international law occupied for some time to come.

9.1. The Role of Economic Motives in Establishing Colonial Policy

At this stage we have to ask ourselves the following question: Did economic motives play an important role in establishing colonial policy? And if so, to what extent? One of the reasons put forward by the settlers to persuade the Colonial Office to grant colonial status was that they themselves were perfectly aware that the increased agricultural activities might eventually entail repercussions and lead to negative reactions from Spain. On the one hand the, strictly speaking, illegal agricultural activities may have been helpful in increasing the attention of the British government toward the British Settlement in the Bay of Honduras, in the sense that they prompted the British to define the diplomatic

---

111 Article VII of the Aycinena-Wyke Treaty: "They mutually agree conjointly to use their best efforts by taking adequate means for establishing the easiest communication (either by means of a cart-road, or employing the rivers or both united ...) between the fittest place on the Atlantic Coast near the settlement of Belize and the capital of Guatemala ..." The treaty was signed by Guatemalan Foreign Minister Pedro de Aycinena and British charge d'affaires and ambassador to Guatemala Charles Lennox Wyke.

status. On the other hand, however, it is very unlikely that they provided a sufficient economic motive for the British in establishing colonial policy.

Even if we take into account that the decision of the British government to assume full sovereignty cut off the North American market for British Honduras and the local timber merchants were forced to export exclusively to the mother country, there still remains the question if and to what extent this was economically advantageous for Britain. In other words, what benefits did Britain actually gain from declaring the settlement as part of the Empire?

The fact that the entire contingent of the colony's mahogany was now exported to Great Britain was, if at all, only of a short-lived economic advantage for the mother country. What is more, one has to consider that the time span, during which British Honduras was indeed the major source for Britain's mahogany, was relatively short, only four years (from 1847–1851) to be precise. In the second half of the 19th century, the demand for mahogany in Europe had started to decrease, mahogany alternatives gained in importance, and Britain increasingly purchased timber from Canada and re-established its former connections with the Baltic, much to the displeasure of the timber merchants in British Honduras, as discussed in the previous chapter.

In addition to the above argumentation, it is important to remember that the British government assumed full sovereignty at a time when a prolonged period of economic decline was beginning to manifest itself. This made the colony of British Honduras a true colonial dead end. The British government even had additional expenses: During the many years, the local Legislative Assembly had attempted to convert the colony into a Crown Colony, the mother country had already been providing a helping hand against eventual attacks, as was, for example, the case with the Maya attacks on the mahogany camps. But from 1871 onwards, when Britain granted Crown Colony status, it did have to bear the full burden of the colony's defence.

Having examined the possibility that economic motives most likely played a minimal role, a possible conclusion would be that the British government was prepared to take this step only because, sooner or later, it would have had to make a decision, one way or another. If we decide to support this theory and if we decide to *neglect* the inhabitants' claim that Britain held the title to the territory by right of conquest (the siege over the Spanish fleet in the Battle of St. George's Cay in 1798), and knowing that the area was not acquired in any spirit of imperialistic expansion, there is no escaping the conclusion that, in reality, British Honduras became a colony by diplomatic victory only or even by happenstance.

At the diplomatic level, the reasons for granting colonial status seem to be more obvious, although in some cases economic and political motives might in reality have been behind apparent purely diplomatic moves. For example at the establishment of the official colony of British Honduras was beginning to take shape, the United States was too much distracted with its own Civil War to be overly concerned about a small place in Central America. A re-examination of the ambiguous Clayton-Bulwer Treaty of 1850, where the validity of British occupation of the territory was once more questioned was simply not on the agenda.

It is also interesting to speculate how much the projected inter-oceanic canal across the isthmus, which was to run across part of the British Protectorate of the Mosquito Coast on land in possession of the Miskito Indians, influenced the decision to finally grant colonial status to the British Settlement in the Bay of Honduras. Although the canal, once completed, would not have belonged to any individual state, was to be under joint British/United States control and was to provide a right of way for all shipping, as far as the British were concerned, the territory of British Honduras (as well as the Mosquito Coast and the Bay Islands) suddenly gained in importance: It would have provided an ideal strategic base for the British Navy in times of trouble and especially when it might have become necessary to block the entrance of the canal. Therefore, Britain was very eager to maintain and consolidate its long established presence in the area and one way of accomplishing this goal was to convert British Honduras into an official British colony.

This was not the first time the projected inter-oceanic canal was connected with establishing colonial rule. The interest of the British in a route across the isthmus manifested itself in 1852, when they, clearly in pursuit of long-term economic and diplomatic interests, boldly proclaimed the "British Colony of the Bay Islands", at that time considered to be a dependency of British Honduras, the British colony-to-be. While Britain never intended to seriously colonize the Bay Islands it did not want the islands to come under the control of the United States, because it would have endangered the British foothold in Central America.

The Bay Islands, however, were a short-lived colony. After only four years of existence, in the Dallas-Clarendon Treaty of 1856, Britain agreed that they were to be part of the Republic of Honduras. Three years later, in the treaty between Great Britain and various Central American states, the Bay Islands were finally handed over to the Republic of Honduras, despite the wishes of the islands' inhabitants, which were mostly British or of British descent. In the end, the small Bay Islands proved to be of significant importance because they served as a pawn of no little value to demand a larger territory concession in British Honduras.

From today's viewpoint it is not easy to assess to what extent the decision by the British government to assume full sovereignty for and grant colonial status to British Honduras might have been influenced by economic motives. But there still remains one fundamental question: Did Britain actually do anything with the colony? The answer is: For the next 75 years, very little.

In this respect, British Honduras was in no sense unique: Until the post 1918 period, the general British imperial policy was that colonies would have to pay their way. Only after a Colonial Development and Welfare Act was passed in the late 1930s, did the British government begin to adopt policies of promoting economic development and social welfare in her colonies. Before that time, the British government hardly ever initiated economic development and only the most essential investments in permanent infrastructure were made. Economic development was to be the sole concern for the private sector.

In the case of British Honduras, the surge of private investment (for example in steam mills for sugar and rum production) was only transitory and the discussions and subsequent endeavours to build a coherent railway system turned out to be unavailing. There was hardly any incentive for private enterprise and not enough revenue could be raised to provide the necessary infrastructure to attract immigrants and investment. In 1931, after a major hurricane struck the region, British Honduras, by then already suffering from the Great Depression, was finally granted a small development fund. Despite the opposition of the timber interests, this financial aid was also used to promote the development of agriculture and to start the building of a road network.

Map 13: British Honduras in the 19th Century

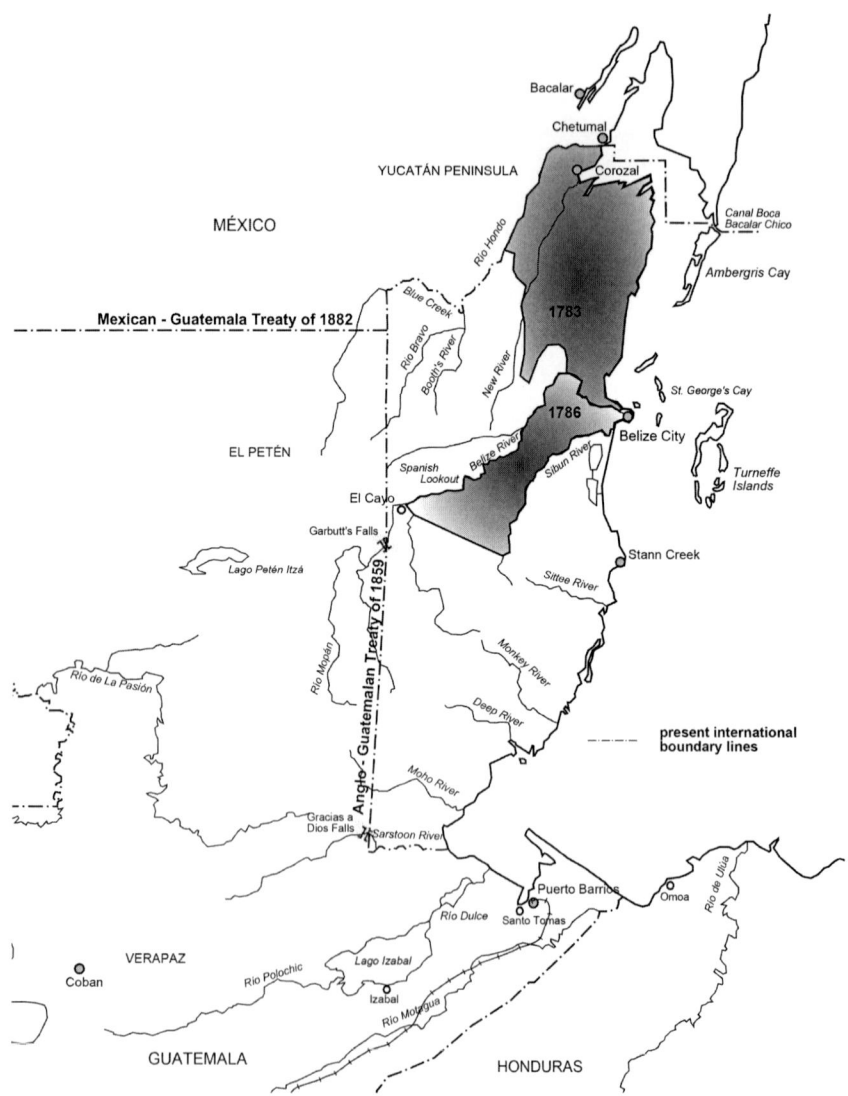

Map 14: Maya Resistance Centres and Settlements in the 19ᵗʰ Century

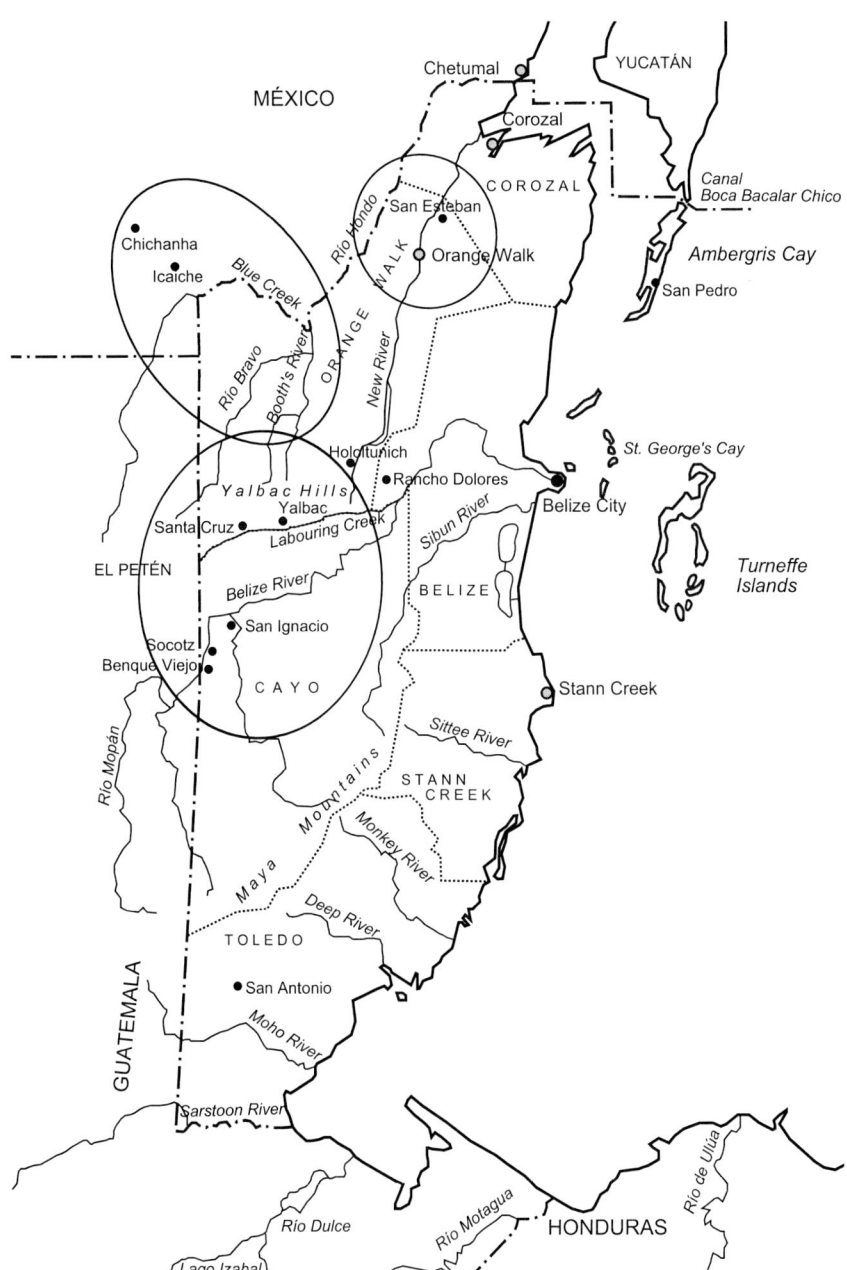

Map 15: British Honduras – Communication Routes

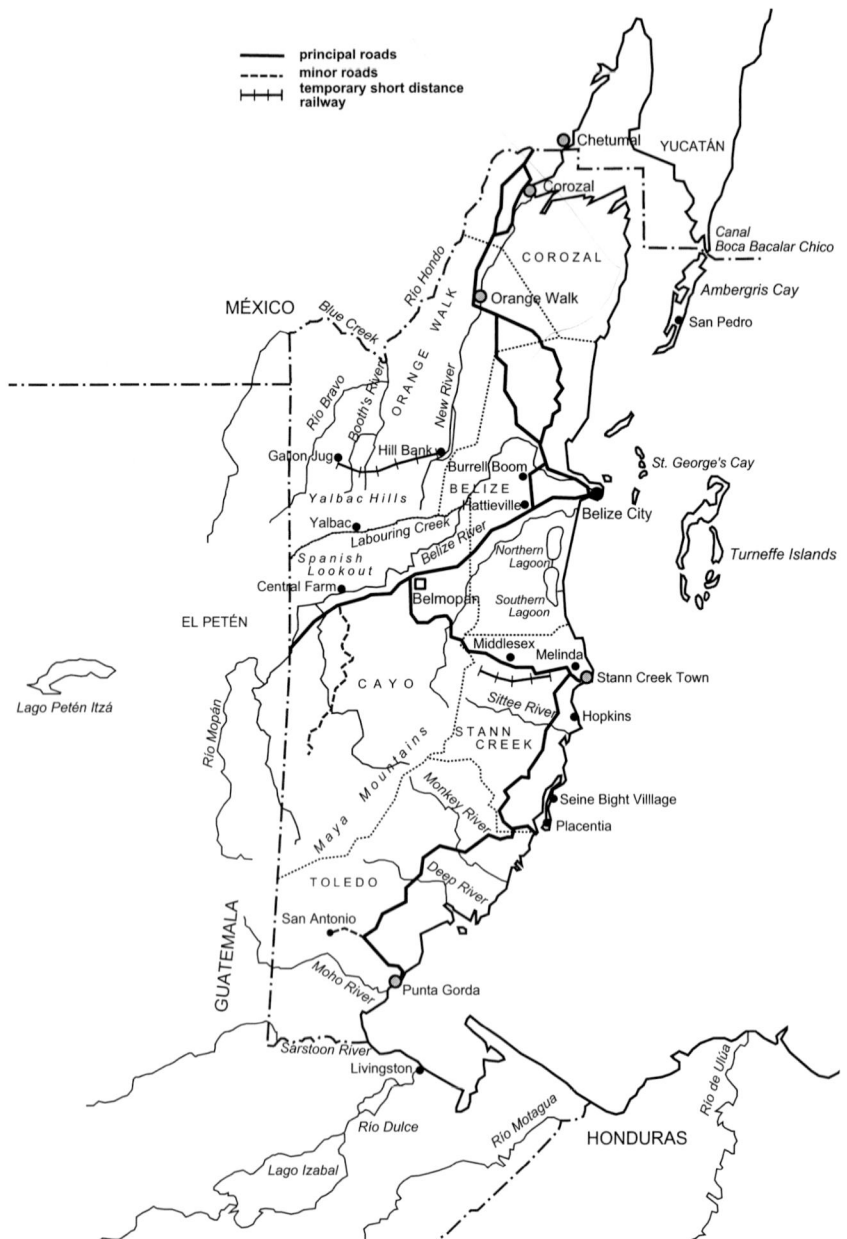

Table 6 – Mahogany Exports from Belize, 1798–1846

Year	Mahogany in 1,000 feet
1798	1,347
1802	4,646
1805	2,434
1819	6,142
1821	4,234
1827	6,905
1830	4,557
1837	8,500
1845	9,320
1846	13,719

Sources: 1798–1804 Col.Office Rec., 123/15; 1805 Col.Office Rec., 123/17; 1819–20. Quarterly Returns of Exports from Belize, in Col. Off.Rec.,123/15,16,28–31 and 34–42 and Bolland (1977:159); 1837–1846 Gibbs (1883:93,102,106 and passim)

Table 7 – Mahogany Imports into Great Britain

Year	Place of Origin	Quantity in tons	Official Value in £
1841	British Honduras	14,976	134,832
	Haiti	3,075	28,437
	Central America	608	4,866
	Cuba	381	5,361
	(via) Nueva Scotia	149	1,196
	Jamaica	118	944
	Bahamas	80	1,025
	and even smaller quantities from Guatemala (Santo Tomás), Colombia and via the United States (New Brunswick)		

Year	Place of Origin	Quantity	Official Value in £
1846	British Honduras	20,696	189,453
	Cuba	9,577	76,617
	Haiti	7,054	64,463
	British poss. of the Gambia	270	2,161
	followed by Central America, Mexico and the Bahamas		
1850	British Honduras	18,765	172,216
	Haiti	7,742	73,521
	Cuba	3,832	30,618
	followed by Central America, USA and The Gambia		

Sources: Public Record Office, London, Customs 5, Vols. 30–42 (1841–1850) quoted by Naylor (1988:239–40)

Table 8 – Prices Paid for Slaves and Compensation Received

Colony	Average of Prices Paid for Slaves 1822–9	Rate of Compensation for Slaves
Honduras	£ 120. 4. 7½	£ 53. 6.9½
British Guiana	£ 114.11. 5 ¾	£ 51.17.1½
Trinidad	£ 105. 4. 5½	£ 50. 1.1¼
Barbados	£ 47. 1. 3½	£ 20.13.8¼
Jamaica	£ 44.15. 2¼	£ 19. 5.4¾
Bermuda	£ 27. 4.11¾	£ 12.10.5½

Source: Account of average of sales in colonies affected by abolition of slavery. Parliamentary Papers 1837–8 (64), XLVIII 329 printed in Dobson (1973:175)

Table 9 – Percentage of Whites in the Total Population of Belize

Date	Percentage of Whites in Total Population	Total Population
1829	5,4%	3,883
1845	4,0%	9,809
1881	1,0%	27,452
1946	4,0%	59,220
1991	0,8%	189,392

Sources: 1829: table (5); 1845: Squier (1858:588) and Bolland (1977:188); 1881: Gibbs (1883:158); 1946: Belize Census 1946 in Waddell (1961:64); 1991: Abstract of Statistics (1994:14), Central Statistical Office, Belmopan

Table 10 – Place of Birth of the Population of British Honduras in 1881

British Honduras	18,811
Yucatán	4,088
Central America	1,975
United Kingdom	186
Jamaica	834
Barbados	204
Other British Colonies	267
East Indies	175
United States of America	125
Africa	394
China	68
Germany	46
followed by Spain, Italy and France	

Source: British Guiana and British Honduras Settlement Commission's Report, (Evans 1948)

CHAPTER

SIX

FROM CROWN COLONY TO INDEPENDENCE TO

MODERN BELIZE

1. Towards Independence – A Long Process of Decolonization

In the first decades of the 20th century, British Honduras only counted a population of approximately 40,000 and life in the colony was characterized by economic difficulties, unemployment, and social discontent. The situation got worse after 1919 when thousands of Creole and Black soldiers returned from their service in the British Army. Together with the workers who had come back from the Panama Canal Zone, they found themselves without employment upon their arrival and began to launch heavy protests. The problems of unemployment intensified with the mechanization of the timber industry since the usage of tractors continuously reduced the amount of labour force needed.

The riot of 1919 with strong racial components is commonly known as the "ex-Servicemen Riot". Although initiated by men in uniform approximately three thousand enraged Belize City residents also took part. This violent riot triggered a long chain of events. One of the direct consequences of these unrests was an increased public interest in the ideas of Marcus Garvey, a Jamaican-born powerful mass leader and founder of the Universal Negro Improvement Association (UNIA).[1] Garvey's visit to Belize City in 1921 to render support to the Belize City branch of said organization set fire to the slowly emerging Black confidence. In the longer term, another far-reaching consequence of these protests was the emergence of nationalist politics.

---

1   All over the US, the Caribbean and Central America various organizations within the UNIA, such as the Black Cross Nurses and other institutions to boost Black self-confidence and businesses began to spring up.

Several reform projects were started, the "Black Cross Nurses" being one of the most important. The main undertaking of this organization was to survey, report and improve the poor sanitary conditions in Belize Town and elsewhere in the country. Until the late 1920s women were exclusively in charge of these social welfare programmes. Many of these women were, in fact, social and political pioneer activists working in the streets at a time when the members of the British-derived Creole middle class men were dedicated to closed social clubs and benevolent societies.[2] In 1931, a devastating hurricane and the beginning of the World Depression made the socio-economic hardships even worse.

In 1934, Antonio Soberanis Gómez, an ardent public speaker founded the Labour and Unemployment Association. Due to the influx of immigrant workers from Central America and México in the 1930s competition for employment was increased especially that in Belize labour laws were inexistant at that time. This situation led to massive demonstrations demanding laws for minimum wages for labourers and a eight hours working day.

Again, women were actively involved in these protests and were holding their own political meetings. It is remarkable that these courageous women even addressed and confronted colonial governors demanding general women suffrage, equal opportunities with men and the same rights for all ethnic groups in the country.[3]

This was also the time when the first organized labour unions and several social action groups under the patronage of the Jesuits and closely associated with the Alumni Association of the Jesuit-run St. John's College in Belize City evolved. It did not take long until the workers' movements started to challenge the colonial system. For example in 1934, demonstrators organized a boycott of a number of leading merchant houses and a general sawmill strike at the biggest mahogany company, the British Estate & Produce Company (BEC). Parallel to these actions, and as a result of the aforementioned Jesuit-sustained organizations, political activities sprang up in earnest and a growing nationalism was beginning to manifest itself.

In 1949 the People's Committee (PC), the forerunner of the People's United Party (PUP) was formed under the leadership of John Smith, Leigh Richardson, George Price and Philip Goldson (all St. John's College graduates) among others. Many working women signed up as well and among the pioneer women of that period were nurse Vivian Seay, Emma Boiton and Gilda Lewis.[4] Along

---

2   Cf. Judd (1992) and Macpherson (1992, 2003 and 2007)

3   See Macpherson op.cit.

4   For details see Macpherson (2007) who in her goundbreaking study provides detailed information on the role these female activists played in Belize's national movement and

with the above mentioned prominent men, these women were at the forefront and key figures in Belize's nationalist movement playing a crucial role in the process of nation-building.

At the same time Belizean leaders became aware of developments elsewhere. In Jamaica self-government was already well under way and neighbouring Guatemala saw a rise of the middle class societies under Juan José Arévalo and Jacobo Arbenz.

From the end of World War II British Honduras began to make strong efforts towards regaining self-government. In 1871, in order to be given Crown Colony status, the local Legislative Assembly had to dissolve itself and many privileges were no longer valid. This had long been regretted and the forming a government – with the ultimate goal to free British Honduras from imperial control – became of paramount importance.

From 1947 onwards – inspired by India which had become self-governing in the same year – anti-colonial speeches were increasingly to be heard in the "Battlefield", the site of today's Central Park and the first open public forum of Belize City, officially named a "city" three years previously.

The general unrest prevailing in the colony was soon taken advantage of by the Guatemalan government: It argued that due to the fact that no agreement could be reached between Britain and Guatemala with regards to the controversial Article VII (to jointly establish the "easiest communication" between Guatemala City and the Atlantic Coast), the treaty had lapsed and it was entitled to lay claim to the territory of British Honduras. In March 1945 the Guatemalan government adopted a new constitution which declared that the entire territory of British Honduras formed part of the national territory of the Republic of Guatemala.

Retrospectively seen, one might well be tempted to not take Guatemala's position too seriously and shrug it off merely as a means of camouflaging her own expansionistic ambitions in the area. On the other hand however, the post war left-leaning Arévalo and Arbenz governments may indeed have been guided by a genuine anti-imperialistic ideology. And, considering the rhetoric still used by left wing groups in Guatemala when approaching the subject (*... Belice, otra cuña británica en Centro América*, "... Belize, another British wedge in Central America") it seems very plausible that at the time when Guatemala was repeatedly pressing the Belize issue, it might actually have been fully convinced of its mission to liberate Central America from the last traces of British imperial power. Whatever may have been the case, the border was

---

the struggle for independence to come.

ritain considered as the illegal occupant of Guatemala's putative
nt, Belice.

Britain was outraged, it suggested settling the controversy by sub-
mitting the case to the International Court of Justice. But the Guatemalan government refused the offer and the case never came before the court. Instead,
Guatemala actually threatened to invade British Honduras in 1948, which
prompted Britain to dispatch warships to keep guard of the colony's waters and
to deploy infantry troops to patrol the Guatemalan border. At the first signs
of Guatemala's intentions to invade and occupy British Honduras (and with
the aid of El Salvador in return for the permission to settle a large number of
peasants over a ten year period), Britain dispatched a Royal Air Force aircraft
carrier, a flight of fighter aircraft and Harrier jets as well as a reinforcement of
troops to British Honduras.

Apart from being in charge of the colony's defence, the presence of the British military also contributed directly to the economy, since the upkeep of the
garrison (provisions and equipment for its personnel, maintenance of and fuel
for cars, aircrafts etc.) generated a substantial annual income and helped to
create jobs. The contingents succeeded in repelling several Guatemalan forays
across the border, but the fear of a military takeover by Guatemala remained
present, even after independence.

In British Honduras, the nationalistic movement re-emerged more vigor-
ously during the 1950s as a result of several burning issues, such as the question
of a West Indian Federation to which British Honduras was strongly opposed
because it was apprehensive about a possible mass immigration of some of the
surplus population of the West Indies. At present, fears and resentments against
visiting or already established West Indians in Belize still linger on and may be
seen as a consequence of this reluctance to form a West Indian Federation.

Another event causing much public discontent and accelerating political
development was the devaluation of the pound sterling in relation to the US
dollar, a highly unpopular decision as far as the colony's citizens were concerned. The devaluation led to a rise in the costs of all imports from the US. As
a consequence the cost of living rose sharply while the purchasing power of the
population continued to decrease. In return, and as a small consolation, the devaluation of the British Honduras dollar made possible the continued export of
the colony's products to Great Britain. Nevertheless, this measure was not sufficient enough to ease the crisis brought about by the precarious economic situation and the problems of unemployment and insecure seasonal employment.

Massive emigration to the US and Great Britain followed reaching its peak
in the years after the disastrous hurricane Hattie in 1961. Today, as much as
38% of Belize's total population live in the US with the largest concentration of

expatriates being in Los Angeles, Chicago and New York.[5] The implicati.
this large scale emigration on modern Belize will be discussed in the followin₂
section.

Afraid of serious social disorders, the local government dispatched the following cable to London

> *Grave situation exists British Honduras – following devaluation of local dollar which will worsen if immediate steps not taken – government efforts provide work for large number unemployed ineffectual because of lack of purchasing power – stop – ... conditions of unrest – fruitful ripe for communist and other subversive influence – stop ...[6]*

with the aim to request immediate help from the British government in the form of development funds and immediate expenditures on the building of an all-weather road to provide at least temporary employment.

The widespread agitation was a good opportunity for a group of enthusiastic young, middle class Creoles (all closely affiliated to the newly formed General Workers Union), to form the first political party, the Peoples United Party (PUP), which won a majority position on the Belize City Council. The party leaders showed strong anti-colonial feelings with a clear goal in mind: Taking definite steps towards initiating the decolonization movement. Some scholars[7] have ascribed this attitude to the party leaders' strong Jesuit connection. All PUP leaders had attended St. John's College, whose North American Jesuit priests, many with Irish names and backgrounds, were said to have had a considerable influence in fostering anti-British feeling within the colony. This theory, however, although not to be rejected at first glance and worth looking into in detail, is far beyond the scope of this book.

From the beginning the PUP leaders were clearly pro-US, opposed to joining the short-lived West Indian Federation (dissolved with the independence of Jamaica in 1962 after only four years of existence), and exhibited more positive feelings towards Central America. In 1950 the party leader declared that "People do not consider themselves part and parcel of the British West Indies, but

---

5   Although it is impossible to give exact figures because of the significant number of undocumented Belizeans in the US, a reasonable estimate is that there are between 110,000 and 120,000 Belizeans residing in the US. The number of Belizeans in the greater Los Angeles area is estimated to range from 50,000 to 55,000.

6   Cable to Greenidge, Papers relating to the British Empire, Rhodes House Library, Oxford, Box.20, File 2, ff 3–9, cited in Dobson (1973: 332).

7   See, for example, Setzekorn (1975: 217)

parcel of Central America, with whom we have long had ex-
~~~nd commercial ties."[8] This position was heavily criticized by
~~~l minority party, the National Party. It was composed mostly
~~~ts and political opponents to the PUP and was clearly defeated
~~~first general elections under adult suffrage in 1954, where the
PUP won eight of the nine seats.[9]

In 1961 hurricane Hattie completely devastated Belize City and other coastal settlements causing severe economic damage. Subsequent aid projects made possible the PUP's long dream to start the construction of a new, and hurricane safe, capital inland – present Belmopan – in order to break the monopoly of power of Belize City and to better incorporate all districts into national politics. The PUP leaders also hoped that, in the long run, most of Belize City residents could be re-located to the more salubrious new capital. The long-term objective was to encourage the establishment of an agro-industry in that area which would have provided employment on a large scale. But neither of these plans materialized. The remaining residents of Belize City could never be induced to leave their home and settle in Belmopan, despite having to face the most adverse conditions such as periodical tropical storms, overcrowding narrow streets, open sewers, poor health conditions, inadequate water supply, continual subjection to insects, rats, pests, invasions of land crabs, extreme heat, and high humidity.

The evolution from a local internal political structure to a democratic party system was an important criterion for granting more autonomy to the colony with the result that a new constitution came into force.

Soon after this first move full internal, elected self-government (Home Rule) was obtained in 1964. It consisted of a bi-cameral legislative system and was substantially modelled on the Westminster parliamentary system. This change meant that British Honduras became also fully responsible for its internal affairs and economic development. The power of the Governor was reduced and the leader of the PUP, George Price (a Creole and ex-St.John's pupil with a North American post-secondary education who claims to have Maya blood) was made Premier of the first PUP government. Britain remained in charge of foreign relations, defence and internal security. Until 1993 it maintained a contingent of British soldiers in the country to seal its border with Guatemala, a decision which prompted the latter to break off diplomatic relations with London and to once more close the border with Belize.

---

8   In *The Belize Billboard,* 5 Feb. 1950
9   Ibid, 30 Nov. 1951

For several years the relationship with Guatemala remained tense and in 1968 proposals in the form of a draft treaty were submitted by the US mediator Webster suggesting a stronger affiliation with Guatemala. In fact, this would have equalled a quasi-annexation and would have meant a close co-operation of Guatemala with British Honduras in the areas of defence, commerce and economic development.[10] The "Webster Proposals" were fiercely rejected by Premier Price and the general public alike and, as a consequence, the Anglo-Guatemalan problem continued to remain unresolved.

At the political level the 1960s and 1970s saw both Black Power and feminist challenges to the party system.[11] After Belizean students had returned from the US, Jamaica and the UK, several Black Power groups emerged. Together with a number of other parties they began to form the new opposition.[12]

Meanwhile, the boom in the sugar industry beginning in the 1950s was capable of easing the economic hardships caused by unemployment. Like a magnet, the north attracted large numbers of people in search of wage labour.[13] Immigration in connection with the expanding sugar industry was mainly to two towns (Orange Walk and Corozal) and to the surrounding countryside.

In the 1960s and 1970s the sugar cane industry played an important role in the economy of Belize, as shall be discussed more in detail in section 6 (Economic Development in the 20th and 21st century) at the end of Chapter Six. The boom in the sugar industry lasted from 1955 to 1985 and raised the standard of living of both the Maya and Mestizos, allowing the latter to actively take place in national politics. During the 1980s this mono-crop system, being highly dependent on fluctuating world sugar prices, started to become very vulnerable and in 1985 the Corozal sugar factory was forced to close down for good.[14]

In 1971 the government offices were transferred to Belmopan, which to the present practically consists only of a large administrative centre, modelled on

---

10   The Guatemalan president at that time, Miguel Ydigoras Fuentes, a puppet of the CIA and the US government, allegedly allowed his country to be used as a staging ground by US equipped Cuban mercenaries prior to the Bay of Pigs invasion. Today, public opinion in Belize still holds that one of the concessions made by the US was that it would assist Guatemala in its claims against Belize. Here, the question arises whether or not the Webster Proposals of 1968, calling for a closer co-operation with Guatemala, may have been part of this scheme.

11   Cf. Macpherson (1992, 2003 and 2007)

12   For an extensive overview of the different political factions of that time see Shoman (1987,1994).

13   As a result, the southern regions were largely depopulated, which was, apart from internal migration, also due to emigration to the US.

14   Ibid.

Maya architecture. The eye-catching buildings resemble a Maya plaza structure and were intended to be an acknowledgement of the country's indigenous population. Even the new capital's name, "Belmopan" ("Bel Mopan", after the indigenous Mopan Maya), underlines the Maya theme. Ironically, the new capital seems to have become almost a "contemporary ceremonial centre" and no substantial industries have been established around Belmopan. Contrary to the Ministry of Overseas Development Report of 1974, in which Belize City was regarded as a "dying city on which no more maintenance should be done",[15] Belize City has not lost its importance as a trading and mercantile centre, despite minimal "maintenance" being done.

In 1973 the country's name was legally changed from British Honduras to Belize. In the same year a resolution to join the Caribbean trading block, the Caribbean Community and Common Market (CARICOM), was passed. From Guatemala's point of view this was taken as an act of provocation. It immediately renewed its claim, this time with the intention to win public support among the Guatemalan people. For example public buses carried colourful posters with slogans such as *"Belice es nuestro"* (Belize is ours) and on official Guatemalan maps of the 1990s, only a *"límite departamental"* (District boundary line) marked the international border between Guatemala and Belize, which, along with the other 22 departments, was officially denominated *"Departamento de Belice"*. In reality, for the Guatemalan government Belize was a useful trump card played whenever there was the need to distract the Guatemalan public from the socio-economic difficulties within the country itself, especially during elections times.

Strongly connected with Guatemala's claim over Belize was the development of Guatemala's El Petén, which had become a turbulent and more densely populated new frontier area due to the activities of local logging companies and the increased interest of foreign entrepreneurs to exploit the region's valuable oil resources.[16] The expected economic boom led to massive land speculation and several military campaigns were undertaken throughout the 1980s to wipe out the area's native population by force. Although the great oil boom never materialized, clearly, the anticipated feasibility of exporting oil from the Petén reserves via pipelines running through Belizean territory strongly influenced Guatemala's adamant position.

---

15   In *Belmopan: An Ex-Post Evaluation*, London, Ministry of Overseas Development (1774: 36) cited by Everitt (1986: 30)

16   For more detailed discussion on the role the Petén played in the border dispute between Guatemala and Belize see for example Byrd (1987: 25–40, 1990: 22, 1991: 15–6) and Waddell (1961a: 468–469).

The ever-present possibility of a Guatemalan invasion continu
of the principal impediments for Britain to grant independence a
to be willing to assume all the responsibilities of a full independ
mala actually threatened invasion two more times, in 1975 and 1978, prompting
Britain to keep a battalion of troops, and a flight of fighter and ground attack
aircraft in Belize after 1975. Needless to say, under such circumstances, Great
Britain was not prepared to guarantee Belize's territorial integrity after independence. From 1975 onwards, the Government of Belize successfully adopted
a policy that has now become known as the "policy of internationalization of
the Belize question", which eventually helped to change Britain's mind.

One of the consequences of this diplomatic initiative on part of Belize was
that the rest of the world became fully aware of Belize (not counting the Maya
boom in the 1930s when the region was a prime destination for British and
international archaeological expeditions) and its cause. What was even more
important for the country was that this initiative won the support of the United
Nations, a number of Caribbean nations and the Non-Aligned Movement. Belize established an "Office of the Belize Government Representative" at the
UN Headquarters in New York and in all respects conducted its lobbying as
if it were an independent nation, which was, strictly speaking, violating the
constitution. The British government decided to turn a blind eye to this fundamental question and, the British mission was even issuing UN credentials
for the representatives from Belize. By "internationalizing" the Belize cause, it
was achieved that the negotiations for independence were continued separately
from the Guatemalan issue, despite the failure of discussions with Guatemala.

In 1981, Belize was granted independence and Britain was finally willing
to continue to provide military protection. Backed by the United Nations and
with all its territory intact, Belize at last became independent, exactly twenty
years after Britain had basically agreed that her colony could become fully
self-governing at any time. In the same year, the new nation joined the Commonwealth, the UN and the Non-Aligned Movement. Taking into consideration that British Guiana and the British colonies in the West Indies (with the
exception of St. Kitts and Nevis) were all given their independence in the mid-
1970s and mid-1980s[17], it inevitably leads us to the question of what the main
reasons responsible for this delay were:

- **First**, the persistent Guatemalan threats to take what was considered as
  their territory, by force if necessary, made the Belizean government, not

---

17   Jamaica and Trinidad & Tobago in 1962, British Guiana as Guyana in 1966, Grenada in
     1967, The Bahamas in 1973, St. Lucia, Saint Vincent and the Grenadines in 1979.

confident enough to assume the responsibilities of a full independence, solicit the maintaining of a British military garrison after independence. Since Great Britain generally preferred to grant independence without having to assume any defence responsibility and was not willing to grant this request. Eventually, internal demand (which had its roots in the opposition party) grew loud that there should be no independence until a suitable defence guarantee had been agreed upon. Guatemala's territorial pursuit triggered a chain reaction: It led to a dependence on an external military protection rather than making the effort to call on the determination of the country's own people to provide for their defence. This dependence, also called "Harrier mentality", came to affect all aspects of political life and provided a significant obstacle for the on-going decolonization process.

- **Secondly,** for a long time the lack of economic viability was also responsible for the delay in granting full internal self-government. A country that had lost its economic raison d'etre would have been especially vulnerable to infiltration from outside, if it had been left completely on its own too soon.
- **Thirdly,** the country's multi-ethnic society was considered as a destabilizing factor, especially because British Honduras did not have an adequately trained civil service to provide enough assurance for the protection of its minority groups. As expressed in a 1951 report

... there is far less risk in giving more power to and placing greater responsibility in the hands of the people in a homogenous society than in a society of a cosmopolitan character ...[18]

In 1985, after almost thirty years of George Price's PUP government, the UDP (the United Democratic Party), which had been formed out of several opposition parties approximately ten years before, won elections with Manuel Esquivel becoming Prime Minister.

In 1991, Guatemala's second civilian government headed by President Jorge Serrano recognized the independent state of Belize by officially respecting the right of Belizeans to self-determination. This decision was driven by increased socio-economic concerns within Guatemala, indisputably a contributing factor to making Guatemala comprehend the increasing necessity for mutual co-operation with Belize. Nevertheless, the issue of the Guatemalan claim never

---

18 Report of the Constitutional Commission, Belize Government Printer, 1951, paragraph 40, quoted in Shoman (1987: 208–9).

ceases to flare up and Belizeans, consciously or unconsciously, still consider it as a threat to the country's sovereignty.[19]

In 1993, to the dismay of some Belizeans, the British announced the withdrawal of their defence troops and Belize definitely lost the status of a "quasi British Protectorate". Although the British forces remained in Belize in a new role (the British government decided to establish a training facility, which was greatly welcomed by the Belizean government), Belize now had to stand on its own feet and for many Belizeans the question they asked themselves more than ten years ago came up again and began to grow in importance: Would independence and the final withdrawal of the British defence force merge into a new and different colonialism? After all newly independent nations are always vulnerable and there is never a lack of potential recolonizers.

As we have seen in Belize, the decolonization process was an extensive one in every way and one would assume that the country had all the necessary time it needed to adjust. Even so, for a long time, the feelings of Belizeans were characterized by general fear and some sort of sluggishness to take full responsibility for their life, institutions, economic development and defence. In addition, Belizeans are a multi-ethnic mix and have not long ago started to become fully secure in their cultural identity. As a consequence, Belizeans, as any other people in similar circumstances, have the tendency to adopt particular types of attitudes and outlooks from countries beyond their borders. In the case of Belize, the life styles, tastes, ideologies, economic, foreign and domestic policies from abroad have been copied slavishly, as will be discussed in the following section.

In Belize, remnants of a dependence on the former colonial power are still noticeable, which may be the most enduring legacy of the colonial era. Only that in Belize, in a certain sense the mother country is increasingly being replaced by the United States. Because of this very dependence, the potential dangers of "re-colonization" are present at any time, maybe not so much in the political and economic, but rather in a psychological sense.

---

19 For example in 1994, to once more distract from the heavy domestic disorders within Guatemala itself, the Guatemalan government decided to revive the Belize issue. When the UN was to recognize the sea charts Belize had prepared to mark its maritime areas, Guatemala's Foreign Minister confirmed in a letter to the UN that his country still held a claim to certain land areas of Belize and to maritime spaces in the Caribbean Sea. It was also stated that until these territorial disputes would remain unresolved, Guatemala would and could not accept the Belizean sea charts (cf. Shoman 1994: 273–4).

2. The Gradual Extension of US Influence on Belize

Throughout the second half of the 20th century, the presence of the British military was crucial in providing adequate protection from the possibility of an invasion by Guatemala.

Notwithstanding the importance of British military to provide an adequate amount of security, a gradual alienation with Great Britain, in favour of US presence, had long begun to take place. In order to fully comprehend the growth of US influence on Belize, which is of economic, political, social, cultural, and educational nature, it is first necessary to briefly touch on the history of the expansion of US involvement throughout Central America.

Approximately fifty years after North America won its independence, the newly formed United States of America began to emerge as a dominant power in the Americas, the Monroe Doctrine providing full justification for this assertion of authority. With the US military support of Cuban Independence in 1898 and with the construction of the Panama Canal, Britain definitely ceased to play a dominant role in Central America and the Caribbean. In the first decades of the 20th century the US began to invest heavily in the neighbouring countries of British Honduras, and to safeguard US interests, marines were landed in many Central American (and Latin American) countries to assist the various dictatorships.

Because Great Britain continued to claim full sovereignty over British Honduras, in a certain sense, British colonialism was able to shield this particular region from the various strong and direct military, political and economic US interventions which took place in the neighbouring Central American republics. However, in the long run, Britain was entirely helpless in putting a halt to the growing US orientation of her colony and the spreading of US ideologies.

Direct trade relations between British Honduras and the US began in 1877 when the mail route was changed from Jamaica to New Orleans. This was a necessary measure to boost the colony's banana industry, to open up the North American market, to increase its export capacity and to be able to compete with the other Central American banana-exporting countries. No longer having Jamaica as intermediary, the exchange of correspondence from London to British Honduras and vice-versa lasted even longer, which had an adverse effect on the trade relations between Great Britain, while at the same time intensifying the commercial activities with the United States. For example from the 1900s onwards, in addition to lumber, chicle was becoming an important export commodity destined for the North American market. Moreover, during the Prohibition era in United States in the 1920s the British colony served as a convenient entrepôt for liquor from Canada en route to Mexico, from where it was smuggled into the US. Until the Prohibition law was repealed in 1933, the export duties from the illegal liquor trade were an important source of revenue for British Honduras.

By the 1930s, United States trade with British Honduras rivalled that with Great Britain and as a consequence, US investment, which had been minimal so far, experienced an increase. The US was beginning to play a major role in the economy of the British colony and British financial interests, especially those of the British-owned mahogany company and biggest single landowner, the Belize Estate and Produce Company (BEC), were forced to face major competition from US companies. So as not to lose control over the forestry industry, the British government authorized a loan to start a sawmill but in the long run this measure could not put a halt to the growing of US influence in the economy of the colony (even though the BEC succeeded in remaining British-owned until 1980, when it was bought out by a North American company). In 1935, Governor Sir Alan Burns, wrote that

> *The whole colony is, however, largely influenced by the comparative proximity of the US and the people as a whole are more Americans than British in their outlook. This may be due to a limited extent to the cinema, but is more directly attributable to the influence of trade and education.*[20]

Although the devaluation of the Belize dollar in 1949 temporarily improved the competitiveness of British products, in the same year 70% of all imports into British Honduras originated from the US. When a sugar quota was granted to Belize in 1961, the US became the colony's most important trading partner and exports to the US almost tripled. In 1981, the US bought 60% of Belize's exports, supplying 35,4% of its imports. Although after that date, both exports and imports started to decrease, the US still remains Belize's main trading partner. According to the statistical figures of 2009, the US contributed with 30,7% to the total of Belize's export volume, the UK with 29,7% and Nigeria, Cote d'Ivoire, Finland, Italy and Spain with 4 to 5%. The import partners were the US (33,65%), followed by Mexico (14,7%), Cuba (8,5), Guatemala (6,75%), Spain (6,7%) and China (4,12%).[21] Imports from the UK were too insignificant even to appear in the statistics.

As was already the case in the 1960s, during the early 1980s the territory of Belize and its adjacent shoreline in Guatemala once more came to be of strategic interest to the United States. Concerned about its own interests in Central

---

20   Burns (1949)
21   CIA, the World Factbook Online, Belize 2009

America, the US was eager to safeguard a vulnerable Belize from revolutionary activities. Especially after Belize had become independent, the US government was worried that the activities and ideologies of leftist rebel groups stationed in neighbouring northeast Guatemala might filter through and would make Belize an entrepôt for the Guatemalan rebel and Cuban arms trade alike and therefore ripe for communist infiltration.

The intense economic contacts with the US have become indispensable for providing much-needed sources of foreign exchange. This includes the investments made by individual North American nationals residing permanently and semi-permanently in Belize, the remittances from Belizean expatriates, and marijuana-cultivation and trafficking.

During the 1980s the US expanded its diplomatic presence: Twenty nine diplomats were stationed, compared to only nine from the UK and today one of the largest buildings in Belize City houses an enormous US Embassy and Consular Section.

Especially over the last three decades Belize has become attractive for a considerable number of US nationals who seem to enjoy the advantages of settling in a relatively unspoilt environment, on cays surrounded by turquoise waters, and intact marine life, in a pleasant climate and in a politically and financially stable, relatively safe (in comparison to neighbouring Guatemala and certain regions in Mexico) and, last but not least, English-speaking country.

The economically strong and steadily increasing groups of US citizens soon began to engage in all kinds of businesses, mostly land investment and speculation. Many acquired Belize citizenship after a short while and were thus able to get directly involved in the local economy, for example by opening up tour-operating agencies or conducting their own estate agencies. In 1981, when Belize became independent, 80% of all privately owned land (which makes up about one half of all Belizean territory, the other half being government lands) in Belize was owned by US nationals. As mentioned above, the dangers of re-colonization, seen in a psychological sense, are present at any time which inevitably leads to the question whether the increased presence of US expatriates can be seen as a substitute for the old, White British settlers just like in colonial times. And, taking the argument further, may the increased US involvement in the domestic economy of Belize already be interpreted as signs of a new dependency or quasi re-colonization?

After a change of government in 1985, a new development strategy was introduced, aiming to attract foreign, principally North American investment. Foreign ownership of land was even more facilitated and with inviting announcements in the international press, such as

We welcome the serious investor who is willing to enter into a partnership of development in a stable, English-speaking country … I [Prime Minister Esquivel] invite investors to share with us our vast potential for development, our untapped natural resources. Take advantage of … Belize opens her arms to you in welcome …[22]

the UDP sought to demonstrate its openness to foreign investment by creating a favourable investment climate. Foreign investment was now viewed as the very engine of growth in Belize. At the same time prognoses were made for a significant trickle-down effect on both the domestic economy and the local social community.

Notwithstanding the attractive conditions it did not bring in the anticipated investment. Many investors used the incentives and the possibility for foreign land ownership (prior to 1973 there was no limit to the amount of land non-Belizeans could own) not to start production, but for their own benefit, such as land speculation or tax evasion in their country of origin. Although a flood of investors (mostly North Americans) has been exploring investment possibilities ever since, most private US investments have been relatively small operations, with a high concentration in the tourism industry.

While for US nationals, settling or retiring in Belize has become more and more attractive, for Belizeans emigration to the US in search of better employment possibilities, better housing, and better health care facilities, continues to be a viable option. Just as the coming of US citizens undoubtedly has left its marks on Belizean society, the constant flow of emigration of Belizeans to the US, has equally contributed to the process of Americanization in Belize.

After 1945, as a result of a general policy to assist former colonies – and what may be seen as the remnants of certain commitments on part of the former mother country – large numbers of Belizeans, along with a number of West Indians, migrated to Great Britain in search of better opportunities or on scholarships. Regardless of the fact that Belizeans were welcomed in Great Britain, a far greater percentage preferred to migrate to the US mostly to work on farms in the Southern states. Already during the Second World War over 2.000 Belizeans moved to the Panama Canal Zone to contract employment with North American companies. After the disastrous hurricane in 1961, when Belize was plagued by economic hardship and chronic unemployment, many opted for emigration to the US.

---

22 Excerpt of an advertisement in a supplement of the *Financial Times* (London), 16 Oct.1985, quoted by Kyle (1990: 40).

Despite the massive emigrations of Belizeans to the United States, more recently, the employment difficulties within Belize do not seem to be the catalyst any longer pushing Belizeans, the majority being young men, into this permanent migration track. Not counting the poor employment opportunities for secondary school and college graduates, and professionals and post graduates returning from abroad, several jobs have been made available by several new infrastructural projects and a promising tourism, sugar and citrus industry.

But in very many cases the desire for emigration seems to be guided by other motives: The first one is because the flood of Mestizo immigrants increasingly causes dissatisfaction among the Creole population, a crucial issue we shall take up in the following two sections, and the second is based on certain attitudes rather than immediate necessity. In Belize, immigrating to the US (often planned only for a limited amount of time) continues to be very much in vogue because it is bound to raise social prestige for the emigrants and their families left behind.

What were (and are) the consequences of this massive out-migration? A positive thing is that the money sent home to thousands of Belizeans depending on remittances constitutes an important source of foreign exchange and is estimated to be about 15% of the GDP. One of several negative consequences is the massive emigration of Belizeans, a large number of which tended (and tend) to be the more highly skilled, which represents a considerable loss to the domestic economy. The truth is that each person emigrating has been educated at a substantial cost to the Belizean tax-payer and the loss of every single migrant means a zero return on society's investment in that particular individual. For a small country such as Belize with a shortage of skilled people (with or without secondary or post-secondary education) in the first place, such a substantial brain drain is difficult to bear.

Another far-reaching socio-economic consequence of this massive out-migration is the fact that the emigrants clearly contribute to the increase and spread of US culture and life-styles within Belize: In many instances the expatriates are responsible for the livelihood of their entire family in Belize. Not only do they remit cash but also send other commodities such as food, household goods, clothes, toys, televisions, electronic equipment etc., thereby creating greater preferences for US consumer goods.

On the one hand, the socio-economic impact Belizean expatriates have had (and continue to have) was positive for the country in many ways. In 2005 Belizeans abroad sent home remittances at the value of 160 million Belizean dollars. The recent building boom in Belize City is only one example: Where dilapidated houses once stood on overgrown lots, new or renovated houses can now be found. With the money they have earned abroad some Belizeans eventually return to invest in the country and start businesses. Socio-culturally, expatriates also have had an impact on music, sports, and the spread of techno-logical advances in Belize.

The other side of the coin is that the steady flow of cash from abroad has be-gun to create an alarming inertia and passivity among those who are supported by expatriates. For example, Belizean households, being often extended house-holds – out of necessity – and increasingly characterized by the absence of men (in Belize, women are currently heads of approximately 30% of all households), have come to rely overly on cash remittances from abroad. It has also been noted, that there has already been a decline in the use of local resources, as is especially the case with land for small farming. One observer commented[23] that no matter how much the women, young children and elderly may be will-ing to farm, the men who were responsible for clearing the bush in the past have left and, as a consequence, the remaining family may be much more in-clined to contemplate selling their plots in order to satisfy their needs.

Other examples of direct US influence on Belize include education and cul-ture. A considerable degree of influence was created by US missionaries work-ing in Belize City, several other small towns and in rural areas, and the estab-lishment of schools mostly run by North American Jesuit priests. In 1986, the North-American orientated UDP government replaced the Belize College of Arts, Science and Technology, an all Belizean institution, with the University College of Belize which, in fact, is a branch of a small college of Michigan. In addition, educational institutions in the US generously offer scholarships for post-secondary education, readily taken advantage of from the Belizean youth.

With regard to Belizean culture, and in the opinion of many local citizens, it has long become one which "copies America too slavishly". From the mid-1990s onwards, a very powerful medium of cultural formation has been sat-ellite television. It came to affect the life-styles, dress codes, buying patterns, eating and sleeping habits of Belizeans and was (is) a contributing factor in cre-ating more relaxed moral standards, at the same time strongly influencing cul-tural and social patterns. Direct TV broadcasts, and more recently the internet, have removed the time lag which used to exist between the metropolis and the colony. Due to this very time lag the metropolis, in a certain way, was practi-cally unreachable, at least for the masses. Nowadays, for 24 hours all year round, a large number of Belizeans, as any other society in the same circumstances, are able to watch live broadcasts or video posted on websites. And what is more access is not only given to developments in the "the metropolis" or, as a matter of fact, its substitute but worldwide. In pre-satellite and pre-internet times, the

---

23   See Palacio (1993: 3–13)

flow of events were far away, filtered by the local elite as it was done in colonial times, and perceived only with a substantial delay, dimly and indirectly.

In Belize, satellite television and, more recently, the internet may also have triggered an interesting phenomenon: There is a strong indication that certain US products and fashions seem to have lost at least some of their spell, their magic. After all, things that can be seen on a screen at any time of the day are no longer so special when they can, theoretically, be acquired by everyone. As a consequence, Belizean products ("proud product of Belize"), for example garments, food, handicrafts, all sponsored by campaigns such as "buy Belizean", are experiencing an increasing popularity. No doubt, this has a positive effect for Belize and may help to form a strong national cultural identity.

From the above we have seen that the impact the US has on Belize is massive and has evidently left its mark on its society. In addition to the reasons given above, the general process of Americanization is also directly related to the role of US Aid (USAID): More precisely to the influence this organization has on government programmes and policies and to the various projects it launched in order to "rescue" Belize (as well as the other Central American countries) from the general and economic crisis, thus posing a threat to North American interests in the area. The Belizean government has also contributed its share to the propagation of US ideologies, by agreeing to have a powerful Voice of America transmitter stationed and by accepting that a gigantic "army" of Peace Corps workers operate countrywide, with the result that in the 1980s, Belize had the highest per capita Peace Corps ratio in the world.

Socio-economically and socio-culturally, US influence on Belize is continuing to grow and it is too early to tell if it is for the better or for the worse. Given the fact that the overall penetration of the "American way of life" into all aspects of Belizean society has become a reality, Belizeans will have to seriously face the threat of being "re-colonized" by a foreign culture. For Belizeans, the big challenge for the future will be not to mimic an US life style but to endeavour to nurture their own national identity by finding ways of how to evaluate their multi-ethnic cultural backgrounds. At the same time it is indispensable that they learn to deal critically with the culture and way of life that is imposing itself, because otherwise they may not be able to resist such a powerful invasion in the long run. Only then will Belizeans be able to succeed in not being absorbed by the ideologies of a foreign cultural power.

3. Belize: Haven for Immigrants – Consequence of British Colonization?

If we take into consideration that the only indigenous people in the present territory of Belize were different groups of Maya, then, strictly speaking, most of Belizeans today are descendants from a non-native background and would have to be categorized as "immigrants". Whereas this might apply to Mestizos, Garinagu and other minority immigrant groups, Afro-Belizeans clearly do not classify as immigrants, since they have not come to Belize on account of socio-economic reasons in their country of origin.

The reason for the region becoming a haven for immigrants may, in my opinion, be seen as a direct consequence of the many peculiarities of the British "colonization" of Belize. Belize had and still has high potentials for immigration, an unusual pattern which is not shared by the other Central American states and CARICOM members. Basically, three very powerful incentives for outsiders to move into the country exist: One is the high rate of out-emigration of native Belizeans; the second is the country's peaceful political climate, especially in comparison to the neighbouring Central American countries. But maybe the most important reason for why Belize is so popular with immigrants is its low population density: In 2009, after more than three decades of massive immigration, it was still as low as approximately thirteen inhabitants per square kilometre.[24]

Not taking into consideration the various geographical and climatic reasons, this low population density is a direct result of the official British disinterest in colonizing and assuming sovereignty over the territory and, as a consequence, the lack of support for the settlers by the British government. The neutral position of the British government, the insecure nature of logwood and mahogany cutting, the belated attempts to diversify the economy in an eternally disputed territory with a more than ambiguous status, surely, were not ideal preconditions for settlement on a large scale.

However strong the tendencies to condemn colonial rule as such may be, in my reasoning, and in the case of Belize, credit should also be given to it. After all, some of the consequences of the peculiar colonization of Belize are positive: Indisputably, if, from the very start, the Bay Settlement had not had a rudimentary social organization based on democratic principles, various stages of ele-

---

24 For example, in El Salvador, the population density is approximately 235 per square kilometre. In Belize, approximately 315,000 inhabitants live on 23,000 km², whereas in El Salvador, five Millions populate 21,200 km².

mentary forms of government, and a formal government based upon the law of Great Britain and finally, if the area what is now Belize had not become a British administered colony, the political and social history of Belize would have developed quite differently. This is provided the region would ever have become a separate nation at all. Taking the argument even further, Belize would never have evolved into a relatively stable region in an unstable neighbourhood and would never have become safe and orderly enough to be able to function as a host the gigantic floods of immigrants to come.

Admittedly, the rhetoric chosen in 1859 by Superintendent Seymour

> *Though no very great value is probably attached to this Settlement its occupation by us has been of incalculable benefit to the neighbouring republics, and indeed to humanity …*[25]

seems to have been a convenient way of justifying the civilizing deeds in the name of British imperialism, retrospectively seen, the facts speak for themselves: Despite persistent socio-economic hardships and political tensions, Belize has suffered least dramatically from the repercussions of economic exploitation, ethnic social discrimination, political violence, and the negative consequences of excessive foreign intervention which the Central American states (and many other decolonizing societies) have had to face in recent times.

In the first half of the 19th century, labour shortages and a major re-organization of the colony's work force after emancipation for the first time led colonial officers to consider immigration from the neighbouring Spanish speaking countries. Almost thirty years later, encouragement for immigration was no longer needed: In 1860s, the Yucatecan War (*Guerra de Castas*) was at its peak and the first wave of Yucatecans had already fled south, entering British Honduras. The arrival of Central Americans on a large scale (from Guatemala, El Salvador, Honduras, and Nicaragua in declining numerical order) began in the late 1930s, with the coming of immigrant workers for whom there was still a great demand. Beginning in the mid-1970s, as the colony began seriously moving towards independence, Belize once more was able to absorb large numbers of refugees and displaced persons (mostly Mestizos with a small amount of Maya and Garinagu) who fled from civil war in their own countries.

---

25 Supt. Seymour to Darling (Governor of Jamaica), Report on the Blue Book, 1858; 22 June 1859, AB, R. 65.

3.1. Mestizo Immigrants

During a massive Mestizo immigration wave lasting from the late 1970s to the late 1980s an estimated number of 40,000 – 70,000 Mestizos have settled in Belize, a figure which also includes a relatively small number of Garinagu and Maya.[26] According to the official census of 2000, 11% of the total population of approximately 240,000 were Central American immigrants. The three main sending countries were Guatemala (56%), El Salvador (17,6%) and Honduras (15,5%) and accounted for 98,6% of all immigrants. This rate is similar to the corresponding figures for 1991 and 1980.[27]

However, it is important to emphasize that the above counts only reflect those who stayed in the country legally. Although the immigrants were given official immigrant status in the 1984 amnesty, the number of undocumented Mestizo immigrants continued to be significant throughout the late 1980s and 1990s. After the amnesty, several estimates have been compiled to record the illegal presence of Mestizo immigrants in Belize. According to these estimates, the number of undocumented immigrants ranges between 50,000 to 60,000.[28] Assuming these estimates to be correct, it means that by 1991, when the peak of immigration was beginning to subside, more than 28% of the total population was born outside the country.

The inward migration of Central American refugees had a major impact on the demographic balance between the two largest ethnic groups, with the result that Mestizos by far came to outnumber Creoles. Whereas in the 1980 census, 30% of the population were Mestizos and 40% Creoles, the estimates for 2010 predict 49% Mestizos and 25% Creoles. The Maya (Mopan, Q'eqchi' and Yucatec Maya) account for 11%, and the Afro-Amerindian (Garinagu) for 6% of the population. The remaining approximately 9% are a mix of Mennonite farmers of German and Dutch origin (3,6%), East Indians (2,8%), Whites from Europe (of whom approximately 1,758 are British), the US and Canada (0,8%), Asian settlers from mainland China, Hong Kong and South Korea (1%) and a group (1%) from the Middle East (Lebanese, Syrians and Palestinians).

Initially, the Belizean authorities were not overly concerned with this gigantic wave of immigrants. First, it was believed that the immigration was just another harmless episode in the long tradition of migration between Central American countries and Belize and vice-versa. Secondly, Belize's sparse population density seemed to perfectly justify such a lenient approach towards im-

---

26   Cf. for example Palacio (1990), Stone (1990a: 102; 1994: 186) and Solís (1994)
27   Belize Central Statistical Office, Population and Housing Census, 2000
28   Cf. Palacio (1988), Stone (1990a: 102) and Kroshus-Medina (1992: 148)

migration. Indeed, at first sight, and especially in rural Belize, it appears that there is still sufficient land available capable of absorbing a large number of immigrants. But the low population density is a deceptive figure since the government still retains control of one half of the available land in Belize (the former Crown land) of which a large portion is only of marginal agricultural value. The other half of arable land in Belize is held by private owners, a high percentage of them being foreign speculators who sell plots at prices far beyond the reach of most Belizeans and immigrants.[29]

The real motive behind this ostensibly casual attitude seemed to be something else, and far more intricate: At present, immigration is still being controlled to a minimal degree because there appears to exist a silent consensus among policy makers in the government to continue maintaining what are practically "open borders" due to the fact that immigration is considered one of several factors of how to lower the cost of labour in the nation's economy. The availability of immigrants serves as a pool of cheap labour and is an important prerequisite for a country wanting to attract investment which is still viewed as the very engine of development and economic growth.

Why did such large numbers of Central Americans have to leave their countries in the first place? One of the main factors responsible for the massive deterritorilization in Central America was the consequences of the heightened political and socio-economic crisis in the sending countries, especially Guatemala and El Salvador. This crisis culminated in open civil war between the government forces, backed by the army, the landowning class, the wealthy merchants, the working classes and their sympathizers, and peasants. The history of how this dilemma evolved has been widely covered elsewhere and there is no need to dwell on it here.

In discussing the coming of Mestizo immigrants into Belize, a diversion becomes necessary: Given the fact that by 1984, a large amount of immigrants were Mestizos refugees (including some Maya), the majority of them being native to the department of El Petén but also to Alta Verapaz and Izabal (see Map 16), three regions heavily plagued by civil strife, there might exist yet another reason for the increased immigration into Belize. This leads us back to the Anglo-Guatemalan dispute over Belize. In retrospect, and if seen from a different perspective, we may even go so far as to interpret the massive influx of Mestizos as an indirect consequence of the peculiar British colonization of Belize.

According to Guatemala's point of view it was the British occupation of Belize that deprived the Petén of its possibility of economic development. Throughout the diplomatic conflict between Guatemala and Belize, among the

---

29   See Bolland & Shoman (1977:124:126)

key issues put forward by Guatemala were the granting of an internal navigable channel in Southern Belize, free port facilities in Belize City and Punta Gorda, unimpeded transport of goods and people, and the construction of pipelines in order to export Guatemalan oil through Belizean territory.[30] Guatemala argued that if the development of El Petén would have been carried out on an east to west line, thereby taking advantage of the region's natural outlets to the sea, i.e. the Belizean shoreline in the east, instead of the long line running from north to south and then west to Guatemala City, as it was actually the case, "… most likely a more dynamic and efficient development of that region would have occurred."[31]

Whether or not we decide to lend credence to the above argument, inevitably, the following questions arise:

- **First:** If sufficient development had taken place in the Petén region from the Atlantic/Caribbean (that is the Belizean) side, either as a theoretical consequence of the British having ceded parts of Southern Belize or having granted certain concessions conducive to El Petén's development, would the civil war in Guatemala have taken a different course? Would it have affected the region differently?
- **Secondly:** If the Petén had seen more development, would there have been fewer displacements and would it have been possible to stop the massive and continuous flow of people seeking asylum in Belize?[32]
- **Thirdly:** As a consequence of the civil war, the Petén-Belize (Cayo District) border has become notoriously famous for clandestine activities of all sorts. Regardless of whether or not Guatemala was granted the use of the waterways towards the Belizean coast, the illegal flow of goods and people

---

30 The oil euphoria occurred as a result of the discovery of a large oil strike in El Petén and after the government had made plans to exploit the region's oil reserves. However, the great oil boom never materialized, one reason being the destruction of oil installations by the guerrilla.

31 Cf. The Belize Question, Guatemala, Ministry of Foreign Affairs, August 1981: 18, quoted by Byrd (1991: 16) and Waddell (1961a: 468–469).

32 Throughout the 1970s and 1980s the Petén was a base for the *Fuerzas Armadas Rebeldes* (FAR) with guerrilla activities being concentrated on paralyzing the area's oil-extraction by trying to damage pipelines and oil-rigs, immobilizing military installations and check-points, and interfering with road-construction, upon which the military declared open war on the FAR and their sympathizers in El Petén. The war peaked between 1982 and 1984, thousands of settlers lost their lives and those living within relatively easy access to the Belizean border (especially in the heavily affected municipalities of La Libertad and Sayaxché, areas, which at the same time, were the core areas for oil-exploration) fled into Belize.

from the Petén into Belize was unavoidable. In addition, various factions of narco-traffickers have established their base in the Petén during the recent years. This also had a negative impact for Belize and leads us to an interesting issue: If the Petén had been developed and had become more stable and, as a consequence, would not have been affected by civil war to the same degree, would this particular border in the northwest of Belize now be equally a centre for kidnapping, drug-trafficking and the flow of illegal weapons into Belize and vice-versa?

Although these questions most likely will remain unanswered, the above theory should be subjected to closer scrutiny: At all events, a more balanced view of the circumstances leading to the on-going Belizean-Guatemalan debate would not only be beneficial for future discussions in trying to settle the eternal conflict between the two countries, but also because of the pressing need to generally reinforce the bilateral relationship to enable a closer cooperation between the security forces of both countries.

Most Central American Mestizo and Maya immigrants – apart from a small amount of merchants – were and are unskilled peasants coming from rural or semi-rural areas. The Mestizos (mostly Salvadoreans) who did not squat on private and/or government lands became registered and were settled within special UN funded refugee settlements, in the vicinity of Belmo**pan**, hence derisively dubbed "Salva**pan**" by Belizeans. Being used to farm work, the immigrants would have provided an indispensable additional labour force for the realization of the government's plans to foster agro-industrial development on a large scale, such as export-orientated cacao production. But, in fact, only small farming communities of newly arrived Salvadorean and Honduran Mestizo immigrant families and Belizean-born Central American Mestizos have developed.

The immigrants who were not settled in the above communities went south to work as wage labourers in the banana industry, whose work force consists over 90% of Central American Mestizo and Maya immigrants. As far as the Guatemalan refugees are concerned, in 2000 they accounted for the majority of Central American refugees and have mostly settled in the western and southern border district (Cayo and Toledo Districts). Since then they have maintained this position and increased their share of the immigrant population of Belize. The impact, the presence of Central American immigrants in Belize has had on the national economy and social life in general is substantial and will be discussed presently.

3.2. Mopan and Q'eqchi' Maya

Mopan and Q'eqchi' (formerly spelled "Kekchi") Maya immigrants came from the Guatemalan lowland and/or highland areas and settled in the present Toledo District close to the Guatemalan border (see Map 16).[33] Maya immigration into Southern Belize has taken place stepwise. From the late 1880s onwards the Toledo District of Belize has been an area of shelter for thousands of Guatemalan Maya whose land had been seized by the government and who were fleeing heavy taxation, forced labour and forced military conscription and in the 1970s and 1980s, the political and economic harassment of civil war.

The Mopan and Q'eqchi' Maya were attracted to Southern Toledo because of its geographical proximity to their homeland, its isolation, the availability of arable land and the peaceful conditions in the British colony. The British colonial government did not subject these Maya immigrants to labour and the institution of military conscription was non-existent. Furthermore, due to the lack of roads, the area stayed relatively free of government interference for a considerable length of time. Rent on land (mostly crown land) was not collected regularly; the Maya were left undisturbed and were able to dedicate themselves freely to *milpa* farming. Even in the mid-1930s the majority of Maya immigrant settlements were still concentrated in inaccessible areas close to the disputed borderline (see Map 16), and British colonial control via the authorities based in the district capital was very little.

The reasons for the colonial government pursuing a policy of minimal interference and being willing to tolerate a certain degree of *de facto* Maya autonomy were many and not all of them altruistic in nature: First, the Maya occupied parts of the District where they were not at any time a burden to the government. Secondly, the areas of Maya settlement were of marginal economic interest and the amount of exploitable resources was reduced and thirdly, because the Mopan and Q'eqchi' Maya were ideally suited to populate remote Toledo, an area extremely vulnerable for Guatemalan incursions.

The immigration history of the Mopan and the Q'eqchi' is not the same and their language different and mutually unintelligible.

The Mopan are a lowland group which originally inhabited parts of modern Central Belize and the adjacent Petén in Guatemala. By the late 17th century, a large number of Mopan from the present Petén area were successfully "pacified" and rounded up, especially in the larger *reducciones* such as San Luis and

---

33 The various groups of Yucatán Maya who entered Northern Belize during and after the uprising in Yucatán throughout the second half of the 19th century were dealt with in Chapter Five and are not considered here.

Poptún (see Map 16). The Mopan in the territory of present Belize were able to retreat for several decades into the recesses of the forest, but in the 18th century and around the middle of 19th century (the peak of mahogany extraction in Belize), they began to become a threat to British lumber interest and were forced to leave their homeland and join their fellow Mopan in the Petén.

There, it only took approximately three decades until logging interests once more interfered with the interests of the Mopan, marking the beginning of an organized large scale exodus or re-immigration respectively, into the jungles of present Belize. Some Mopan went to the Cayo District in Western Belize where they mixed with the Yucatán Maya who had settled there previously. But most moved into the Toledo District where, together with the Q'eqchi', they began to create a legitimate Maya enclave. However, although the remote areas of Toledo, and especially the area around San Antonio, was a preferred settlement site for both Maya groups, it would be incorrect to consider Southern Toledo as an exclusive Maya reserve. In the southern regions of Belize a considerable degree of ethnic diversity can be found, with Mestizo (principally from Honduras) and a small amount of Creole, Garinagu and East Indians, living among the Mopan and Q'eqchi'. Today, Belize is the primary location of Mopan speakers, with an estimated total population of between 7,000 and 9,000.

The Q'eqchi' have a completely different history due to the fact that they had a much more troublesome colonial past: Unlike the Mopan, the Q'eqchi' were never "pacified" and conquered by Spanish colonial forces. In the 16th century the Q'eqchi' accepted an arrangement with the Dominican friars under Bartolomé de Las Casas allowing them to preach in Q'eqchi' territory, which soon changed its name from *Tezulutian* ("Land of War") to *Verapaz* ("True Peace"), as the present Guatemalan department is still known. When the Dominicans eventually began to take charge of the political and economic affairs of the Q'eqchi' at the end of the 17th century, a considerable amount of Q'eqchi' succeeded in migrating towards the northeast into present Belizean territory, thereby escaping the dangers of being rounded up (*reducción, congregación*) by Dominican missionaries.[34]

With Guatemala's independence the paternalistic protection by the Dominicans came to an end, but new developments were to harass the Q'eqchi' even more. During the late 1860s the Alta Verapaz region was designated as an area for coffee plantations. Coffee was to become a prime export commodity and

---

34 As mentioned in Chapter Two, this migration was one consequence of the Spanish incursions into Eastern Guatemala. During the process of migration, the Q'eqchi' became more dominant in relation to other tribes in the region, colonizing certain parts of Southern Belize and the former territory of the Manche Chol absorbing what was left of the latter.

the government offered land and tax exemptions to mostly German and English coffee-planters, some of them were based in British Honduras. A new law was enacted allowing the confiscation of most Q'eqchi' lands. In 1890 a few German owned most of the land and by 1914, on the eve of World War I, the production of coffee was mostly in the hands of a few German firms.[35] They used the remaining Q'eqchi' as a source of labour by means of the "advance system", the principles of which were already discussed in connection with African slave labour in Chapter Four.

Prior to 1914, as well as during and after World War I, the Q'eqchi' again had a reason to escape Alta Verapaz, many fleeing the coffee plantations in the highlands for the lowland jungle regions of Belize (but also to the neighbouring Izabal department of Guatemala) where they partly encroached upon Mopan territory (see Map 16). Like the Mopan, the Q'eqchi' were experts in slash and burn subsistence farming, but after the war they also began to engage in various forms of cash-crop production, such as pig-raising and the selling of provisions to the timber crews.

In the 1930s, when the Guatemalan government under Ubico began to enter a phase of extensive state control, the Q'eqchi' once more found the lowlands in the south of Belize attractive for immigration. From the 1950s onwards, with the tentative development of the region by the British Colonial Government, the Q'eqchi' have shown a strong tendency to move to more accessible areas in the vicinity of roads where they started to grow rice and other cash crops. Today, the Q'eqchi' are the most populous Maya in Belize with an estimated 10,000 to 12,500 living in the Toledo District.[36]

Another ethnic minority which figured in the social formation of Belize were

3.3. The Garinagu

The presence of Garinagu (plural of Garifuna) in Belize was first noticed in 1802 in the southern part of the country, then disputed territory. The Garinagu are an ethnic mixture of Caribs, Amerindians and escaped African slaves. Together with the Miskito Indians, the Garinagu (or Black Caribs, as they were referred

---

35   Today, in the Alta and Baja Verapaz region remnants of this period may still be noticed by observant visitors. On many occasions I have been able to notice that some miscegenation has taken place between German planters and Q'eqchi' women and folk etymology holds that the Q'eqchi' language still contains several terms derived from German root words.

36   In Guatemala, according to the 2002 census, the Q'eqchi' population amounts to 852,002 and the Mopan to 2,891. *XI Censo Nacional de Población y VI de Habitación.(Censo 2002), Instituto Nacional de Estadística, 2002.*

to in scholarly literature until approximately the 1980s) had moved along the Caribbean coast of Honduras in search for work with the British woodcutters. There was high demand for labour in British Honduras for only a few years before, in the 1790s, the British had started to extend their woodcutting operations as far south as Deep River, situated already approximately half way in the present Toledo District (see Map 16).

By 1823, when the survivors of the unfortunate Poyais would-be settlers, the victims of the fraudulent "Poyaisian Land Scheme" mentioned at the end of Chapter Four, were rescued from the Black River area on the Mosquito Coast and brought to Stann Creek, a group of Garinagu had already settled there and were hired to clear land for the newcomers. In 1832, more Garinagu came to the British colony to be. They fled from present Honduras after having been charged with treason for supporting the Spanish royalists' failed insurrection against the Central American Federation.

Beginning in 1923, the Garinagu started to arrive in large numbers, after they had to leave the Republic of Honduras where they allegedly participated in a coup to overthrow the republican government. The new group of Garinagu immigrants settled in Stann Creek Town, where they joined the already existing Garifuna community.

But the history of the Garifuna people begins much earlier and takes us to the islands of St. Vincent and Dominica in the Lesser Antilles in the Eastern Caribbean. In the second half of the 17th century, when the first Africans started to come to St. Vincent, the island was populated by Island Caribs. They resulted from a fusion of Caribs from the mainland, who arrived in the Lesser Antilles around 1300 and the Inyeri Arawaks, the latter of which had begun to establish themselves in the Southern Antilles a thousand years before. And as the mainland Caribs were making their migratory journey north and across the Antilles they had partly been subjugating the more peaceful Inyeri Arawaks. Both tribes originated from the region of the Orinoco Delta and the present Guianas.

The members of this new group of Amerindians, who up until the 1980s was mostly referred to as Island Caribs as opposed to those from the South American mainland, retained the Arawakan culture and language and called themselves Callipona or Kalipuna. With time various versions of this term evolved ultimately leading to "Garifuna" (singular) and "Garinagu" (plural).[37]

---

37 Kalipona/Kaliphona or Karipuna/Kariphuna (singular) and Callinago, Kalinago or Kalinagu (plural). According to the dictionary of the French Dominican missionary and linguist Fray Raymond Breton, (1665[1892]), the women of the tribe were mainly of Arawakan stock and called themselves Callipunam (the Arawakan term), whereas the Carib men used the Carib name, Callinagu. Today, historians and anthropologists mostly

The new group settled throughout the Antilles but by the 1630s they were confined to St. Vincent and Dominica.

On St. Vincent they began to merge with African slaves from approximately 150 onwards. In what concerns the arrival of the first Africans on St. Vincent, several theories exist. The most commonly read version is that they reached the island around 1635 having escaped from a wrecked Spanish or Dutch slave ship, carrying slaves believed to be from the region of present Nigeria. However, the fact that the island of St. Vincent did not lie in the path of the normal slaving route, contradicts this supposition. Whether they fled from a slave ship, escaped from neighbouring islands or were forcibly taken by the Caribs, one can safely assume that by the mid-1700s, Africans had made it to St. Vincent where they lived among the Island Caribs and had begun to amalgamate with the latter.

Over the course of a few generations, another ethnic group developed as a consequence of the Africans completely assimilating the Arawakan culture and language of the native Island Caribs. The Africans and Island Caribs emerged as one culturally and linguistically unified group but with different phenotypic features.

The new ethnic group came to be known as Black Caribs, as opposed to the remaining "pure" Island Caribs (the Red or Yellow Caribs) living on St. Vincent and on the other islands of the Lesser Antilles. This new consisted of the offspring of direct Island and Black Carib interbreeding and the Africans who escaped from slavery on the islands nearby, especially from Barbados, Trinidad and Tobago. In short, the Black Caribs are the result of the hybridization of three groups: The original mainland Caribs (or Galibi), the Inyeri Arawaks (out of which the Island Caribs evolved) and Africans.

St. Vincent was one of the last islands of the Lesser Antilles to be settled by Europeans. The Spanish made no attempt to take possession of and settle on St. Vincent and the neighbouring islands, leaving them to the English and French to fight over. Instead the Spanish focused on the more promising regions of South and Central America and Mexico. Although the English were the first to lay claim to St. Vincent in 1627, the French initiated European settlement on the island establishing their colony shortly before 1700.

By that time the Black Caribs had grown into a strong group on St. Vincent. When rivalries started to occur between the Red Caribs and the Black Caribs, the two groups were separated and the east of the island was assigned to the Black Caribs, the ancestors of the modern Garinagu.

As time passed, the Black Caribs began to have more contact with the French living on St. Vincent obtained French surnames and became bilingual.

---

favour the term Kali'na, especially for the various Carib tribes of the Amazon Delta. The term Galibi is applied when referring to the Carib language.

As a result, an infusion of French stems into the Garifuna language occurred. The Black Caribs also adopted the French currency as a means for commercial trading. Soon the British and French started to fight fiercely for territorial control over St. Vincent. Although in 1762 France officially ceded the island to the British, the fight continued over the next three decades, and the Black Caribs were repeatedly drawn into the Anglo-French conflict. On many occasions the Black Caribs sided with the French with whom they had developed a trading relationship. By 1770 the Black Caribs had become so powerful that they forced the Island Caribs to relinquish a portion of land to them. St. Vincent changed hands several times but in 1795 the French had to surrender to the British. The Black Caribs, supported by the French, kept up the fight for another year until they were finally defeated and restricted to a small area of St. Vincent. The early period of European colonization on St. Vincent is reflected in Garifuna language through the presence of some Spanish and English loan words as well as a few hundred French stems, as shall be discussed more in detail in the section dealing with Garifuna language.

As the British began to establish sugar plantations, both Black and Island Caribs refused to give up the island for sugar cultivation. Following a rebellion fomented by French radicals from Martinique, the British feared that the free Black Caribs would instigate slave revolts. Consequently the more African looking ones were classified as menacing and were separated from the more light-skinned and American looking ones. By that time only a few pure Island Caribs were left and the vast majority of Black Caribs, approximately 5,000, were deported from St. Vincent to the present island of Roatán (Rattan or Ruatan as it was spelled on 18th century charts and maps) in the Bay Islands off present Honduras.[38] Of the 5,000 deportees, only about 2,500 survived the voyage to Roatán. Since Roatán was too small and infertile to support such a large number of people, the Spanish allowed the exiles to settle on the mainland.

On the Honduran mainland the Garinagu joined the already existing Africans. At that time the African population on the Caribbean coast of Honduras was mostly composed of the descendants of the early slave population from

---

38   From 1742 onwards the British, in an attempt to gain possession of most of the Caribbean Coast of Central America, had established permanent settlements on the Bay Islands, then considered to be a dependency of British Honduras. Although the British had to evacuate all of their settlements in the Bay Islands in 1788, they had not completely abandoned the idea of extending their foothold on the Caribbean Coast of Central America and Roatán seemed an apt place to deport the Black Caribs. For details on the history of the Bay Islands see, for example, Parsons (1954), Sandtner (1985), Floyd (1967), Sauer (1966), Valladares (1939) and Conzemius (1932). Cf. also the notes of the US emissary to Central America, E.G. Squier (1855).

Guatemala and Honduras and a group of Africans who had arrived from Haiti only one year previously and who spoke French, which the Garinagu/Black Caribs from St. Vincent were able to understand.

In the early 1900s, the Garinagu, along with the aforementioned African population, were used as labour force on the plantations and at the loading stations of the large banana and citrus fruit companies which soon extended their commercial export trading to Livingston and Puerto Barrios in Guatemala and finally Belize City.

As a consequence, the Garinagu began to spread from the Honduran coast along the Caribbean shoreline further north to the Golfo Dulce region of Guatemala and the south of then British Honduras, where they were a much needed labour force for the woodcutting industry. They also migrated south to the Mosquito Coast in present Nicaragua, although to a much lesser degree.

In 1804, the Garinagu founded the settlement of Labuga, Garifuna name for present Livingston at the mouth of the Río Dulce, in Guatemala. The Garinagu soon came to be valued as mercenaries by the Spanish who hired them to serve on the Honduran coast and to protect the fort of San Felipe at the entrance of Lake Izabal in present Guatemala, a most sensitive spot in Anglo-Spanish relations.

For the Garinagu the settlement of Labuga close by functioned as a convenient starting point to get access to wage-work in British Honduras, just a short distance up the coast. Due to the high costs of maintaining slaves and the increasing desertions of slaves to Spanish territory, they were readily hired by the mahogany cutters. Because of the labour shortage and re-structuring of the labour force after abolition and in the 1830s after emancipation, the number of Garinagu in British Honduras steadily increased. Those who were not employed in the forest dedicated themselves to fishing and catching hawksbill turtles, and the cultivation of maize, plantains and poultry. In Belize, the Garinagu established several coastal enclaves such as Stann Creek[39], Punta Gorda, Hopkins, Seine Beight and Barranco.

By no means was Garifuna settlement confined to the southern coast of Belize. In their function as mercenaries and because they possessed considerable multilingual talents, they were capable not only of being very mobile but also of responding to changing situations in the Anglo-Spanish struggles in Central America throughout the first half of the 19th century. According to contemporary accounts, in 1849 almost every estuary of the Central American Caribbean coast, from Southern Belize to Honduras, to Bluefields in Nicara-

---

39   In the 1970s, Stann Creek Town or "Carib Town", as it was also called by settlers in the 19th century, was given the Garifuna name of Dangriga ("standing water").

gua as well as a small part of the island of Roatán, was inhabited by Garifuna people "… the whole coast from Belize to the Mosquito Shore is studded with Carib dwellings …"[40]

This mobility was a deep concern for the forestry industry in British Honduras.

> … it is generally known that the Caribs are of a very erratic and nomadic disposition and for the slightest reason they will immediately emigrate to another part of the coast …[41]

For example in 1859 it was debated whether or not to give the Garinagu the right to apply for leases for town lots in Stann Creek, with the ultimate goal of binding them to their land and secure the Garinagu as a labour force. By 1858, about 2,200 Garinagu, or one tenth of the entire population of British Honduras, were living in the settlement.[42]

In the 1940s, with the decline of the mahogany industry in British Honduras and the banana industry in Guatemala and Honduras, a large number of Garinagu were left without employment. As a consequence they were not spared by the strong trend towards emigration in Central America, which has prevailed throughout the 20th century. Many got involved in the seafaring business which allowed them to emigrate and go to other parts of Central America, the United States and Canada.

After having elaborated on the history of the Garinagu we can now summarize the following: The modern Garinagu emerged in the mid-1700s as a new hybrid ethnic group on St. Vincent in the Eastern Caribbean. They resulted from a biological and cultural mixture between the descendants of the mainland Caribs (Galibis) and Arawaks (who, in turn, came to be known as Kalipuna, Island Caribs, Red or Yellow Caribs) and people of African origin.

Since the Garinagu's first arrival on the Honduran mainland, a mingling with the existing African population occurred and many African cultural expressions, such as religious rituals, food and music were incorporated into the already existing, West Indian, ones. Despite their African origins and distinct phenotypic features, they have traditionally identified more with their Amerindian than African ancestry.

---

40   J.H. Faber (Crown Surveyor) to Supt. F. Seymour, Oct. 21st 1857, AB, R. 58, in Burdon (1935:198).

41   Ibid.

42   Supt. Seymour to Darling (Governor of Jamaica), March 1858, AB, R. 58

Although most Garinagu were converted to Catholicism (in Belize they were converted to Protestantism by Protestant Wesleyan missionaries first), they succeeded in maintaining a separate ethnic group which is united in the struggle to maintain their own cultural traditions and language. In present Belize the Garinagu form about 7% of the total population. In Belize, the National Garifuna Council was founded in 1981. Its aim is to consciously intervene in order to safeguard, promote and preserve Garifuna culture and language. At the same time the council is taking specific measures to improve the general socio-economic development of the Garifuna population, who have to face high illiteracy, unemployment, and crime rates and are still subject to poor housing and inadequate sanitary conditions.

Along with the efforts to revitalize the Garifuna language, emphasis is put on preserving the mastery of dance and music, being also important elements of Garifuna cultural heritage. With the birth and subsequent development of a typical Garifuna music[43] in the 1980s and 1990s, *punta* and its derivate *punta rock,* incorporating traditional elements with more urban styles of music, modern Garinagu have found a powerful musical outlet for the expression and affirmation of their ethnic identity and to create a heightened awareness for Garifuna culture, a rare amalgam of Amerindian and African elements.

A "modern" Belizean, Guatemalan or Honduras Garifuna individual may or may not have native West Indian blood and may not be able to trace back their ancestry directly to the original group from St. Vincent. Rather, they consider themselves to be the descendants of the early African population who had established themselves on the Caribbean Coast of Central America before the arrival of the approximately 2,500 deportees from St. Vincent. However, since at some stage intermingling with the original group from St. Vincent is bound to have taken place, as the years went on, they have come to be recognized and accepted as the descendants of the "genuine" Garinagu, the Black Caribs exiled from St. Vincent, in one way or another.[44]

---

[43] The musician Andy Palacio, who died in 2008, spearheaded a revival of Central America's Garifuna culture.

[44] With regards to the present total Garifuna population, widely divergent estimates exist, ranging between 200,000 to 300,000, the more daring estimates being as high as 500,000. In Central America, the Garinagu are scattered mostly along the Caribbean coast, with the largest concentration in Honduras (around 130,000). The number of Garinagu living in Belize and Guatemala is similar (approximately 17,000 for each country) and around 1,500 are estimated to live in Nicaragua. On the island of St. Vincent and the Grenadines in the Eastern Caribbean, the Garifuna population is believed to be around 2,000 and a small number of Garinagu also live in Canada and the United Kingdom. The US share of the Garifuna population (with the largest concentration in

3.4. Mennonites, Europeans and North Americans, East Indians, Lebanese/Syrians and Chinese

The Mennonites can trace their history back to 1531, when followers of the Dutch priest Menno Simons founded the Mennonite faith during Reformation. Most Mennonite immigration into Belize took place between 1958 and 1962, after almost four hundred years of migratory existence. The first Mennonites originally came from Swiss, Austrian, and German roots and were concentrated mainly in the area around Zurich and Southern Germany. To escape from the imminent religious prosecution (for their non-conformity to the reforms of Zwingli and Luther) and military conscription in Europe they left Western Europe for Eastern Europe (present Ukraine and Russia). When they were forced out of these regions in the last decades of the 19th century and beginning of the 20th century, a large number of Mennonites arrived in Canada and the United States. Smaller splinter groups continued their journey and went to Paraguay and Mexico, from where they finally arrived in Belize. There they were offered land at a reasonable price and settled on the river banks of Spanish Lookout (see Map 16). They were guaranteed complete freedom to practise their special form of Protestantism and to continue their simple agricultural life-style undisturbed and within closed communities according to their own social rules.

In Belize, the Mennonite colonies have succeeded as agricultural pioneers. Thanks to their knowledge of how to tame the jungle, transform nutrient deficient land into fertile land and introduce dairy farming, they have become the most productive farmers in the country. This has had positive effects on the national economy: Apart from producing grains and vegetables the farming efforts of the Mennonites have made Belize self-sufficient in poultry and fresh, quality dairy products.

Over the years, the Mennonites in Belize have undergone significant changes. At present, the Mennonite community is divided into two groups: A conservative group, which strictly adheres to its ancient life-style and clothing and, apart from English, speaks a form of archaic Low German (Plautdietsch) dialect, and several more progressive groups, which have abandoned their original life-styles, clothing and farming techniques for pick-up trucks, modern western clothing and farmhouses equipped with all the necessary comforts including electricity and satellite television. All Mennonites operate their own schools, businesses, banks and churches and are exempt from military service

---

New York and Los Angeles), is between 50,00 and 100,000, but more precise figures are difficult to obtain since a fair number of Garinagu stay in the US undocumented.

and certain taxes. Today, close to 10,000 Mennonites, about 3% of the t[...] population, are estimated to live in Belize.

With regards to other European immigrants, apart from the predominantly English and Scottish immigrants in the second half of the 19th century, comparatively few Europeans have permanently moved to Belize. In the 1880s a few French and German families (for example the Hofius, Hildebrandt, Oswald, Winzerling, Hoffmann and Demel) have made their home in the British colony. Most of these families engaged in trading activities in Belize Town and intermarried with the Scottish merchant elite. Some Germans established an agricultural colony in the south. Others had to leave Belize on account of World War I and those who stayed have assimilated. Today, there is little which reminds of the German presence in Belize, except for the name of a hardware store, Hofius Hardware, in Belize City.

British expatriates in Belize are not as numerous as one might expect, but some British have been appointed as representatives of international development and conservationist agencies. As far as North Americans are concerned, a few families from the Southern states were attracted to British Honduras in the late 19th century. Over the past few decades the presence of North American expatriates has been steadily increasing; they have the tendency to settle on the cays or in the Cayo District and engage in tourism and investment. European and North Americans are listed as "White" in the censuses, and amount to approximately a mere 1% of the total population.

Other immigrants to Belize include a small number of East Indians, pejoratively known as "coolies". They came to Belize to work mostly as indentured workers on the sugar plantations. After completion of their indenture, many moved to Belize City, and after the 1930s, they began to intermarry with Creoles. Today, 3% of the total population are listed as East Indians who set themselves apart merely by their physical characteristics, their tradition in food and their Hindi-influenced phonology.

In the 1890s itinerant Lebanese and Syrian salesmen, pejoratively known as "Turks", arrived in the Western Caribbean and settled in the Honduran towns of Puerto Cortés and around San Pedro Sula, and in Belize's Cayo District, near the Guatemalan border. Initially, they dedicated themselves solely to the chicle trade but soon began to take over the small retail trade throughout the country, and account for 0,1 % of today's population. Immigration of relatives from their respective home country has been steady but small. Although many are becoming hispanicised and creolized to a certain degree, on the whole, they tend to retain a strong self-identity.

The first Chinese were transported to British Honduras in the 1800s. Most of the approximately four hundred initiated work on the sugar plantations but

out for both sides. Some died and some fled to neighbouring
aining Chinese seem to have assimilated, mostly to Mestizo
century has seen two waves of Chinese immigration, one
̣os and 1930s, when most Chinese arrived via the Central American states, and a second which began in the mid-1980s and continued throughout the 1990s. Before and after 1997, the year the British lease of Hong Kong
expired, the strong trend of Hong Kong Chinese immigration increased even
more. More recently, Belize has also become very attractive for Taiwanese investors. They were attracted by several Economic Citizenship Programmes, de-
signed by the Belizean Government to induce large amounts of foreign investment and stimulate entrepreneurial activities while at the same time obtaining
revenues. Today, about 0,5% of the total population are Chinese.

4. The Difficulties in Belize's Multi-Ethnic Society

In the previous section I have supported the view that the peculiar form of
colonization of Belize enabled the colony to develop into a stable region in an
unstable neighbourhood which was an essential precondition for being capable
of receiving such a large influx of different groups of immigrants.

Here, I would like to take this argument a little further and the question
needs to be asked if and to what extent the colonial policy was also responsible for
fostering the development of the present difficulties (tensions, prejudices, stereotyping) in the interactions between the different ethnic groups in present Belize.

It was clearly a tendency of colonial policy to segregate each ethnic community in order to prevent the forming of any alliance between them. One
way of separating the different groups from one another was to encourage economic specialization according to alleged "racial" aptitudes. For example, the
Creoles and those of pure African descent were thought to be particularly suitable for the difficult nature of forest work – and less so for agriculture –, which
is thought to be the much disputed background to the Creoles' aversion to
agricultural activities. Similarly, teachers were often Garifuna, on account of
their multi-lingual talents, and the Mestizo and Maya were believed to be best
suited for agricultural work.

After British Honduras obtained self-government in 1964, this pattern of
specialization lost some of its importance but remnants of it are still present in
Belize's social structure today, and may partly be held responsible for certain
ethnic frictions. The multi-ethnic character of the colony's society was high-
lighted by a strong tendency for distribution and local concentration of ethnic
groups, a pattern which persisted, with only little changes, until after World

War II and continues to be evident in modern Belize: Creoles and Afro-Belizeans tend to reside in Belize City and those who live in rural areas mostly remain within the Belize District. The Garinagu have settled in the south of the colony while the Northern District is a region dominated by Mestizos. Only the Maya are present in more than one district, but in rural areas only, with the majority of them living in the south.

By this division, interaction with the different groups was minimized with the consequence that feelings of insecurity, envy, suspicion, distrust, and the building of tensions were encouraged. Over time, the different ethnic groups were burdened with racial, ethnic and cultural stereotypes, which intensified actual and imagined ethnic differences. The ultimate aim was to achieve that the different communities would all look up to the elite (white and Creole) who was in control of the administration and the economy.

In addition, the great disparity in the distribution of the population between towns and countryside intensified the above conflicts. In 1946, more than 20,000 people (or over a third of the total population) lived in Belize City, while the smaller towns contained about one-fifth and the rural areas two-fifths of the total population of approximately 60,000.[45] Belize City was the centre of all activity and it was not before the 1970s that measures were taken to facilitate communication with the districts. The government approved several projects to ameliorate the condition of the existing, mostly primitive roads and for the building of new all-weather roads to improve infrastructure in order to lessen the various tensions which formed because of certain feelings of inferiority in the rural population.

While the theory that the colonial policy of segregation was responsible for fostering the development of conflicts among the various groups is worth consideration, there exists at least one counter-argument: It might be argued that the residential and occupational separation of ethnic groups did not only have negative consequences. It might have been precisely because of the separation of the different communities that few occasions for confrontation, and therefore little opportunity for conflict, was created. As a consequence, although certain feelings of prejudice and tensions have unavoidably evolved (and continue to evolve due to the recent influx of Central American immigrants, as will be discussed presently), they have not reached the levels of severe ethnic conflicts, as was the case in many other, racially and culturally heterogeneous, decolonizing societies.

---

45   See Census of British Honduras, 9 April 1946, Government Printer 1948, Table B/C on page VII and XV respectively, and Report of British Guiana and British Honduras Settlement Commission (Evans 1948).

Another positive by-product of this policy of separation was that the residential isolation of each group came to be a basis for the development of strong feelings of communalism leading to a growing of self-confidence and self-identity of each group. This, in turn were most essential prerequisites for: One, accepting racial and cultural pluralism since in Belize no group is likely to ever establish a hegemonic position and two, the emerging of a nationalist movement needed to initiate the process of decolonization and the building of a multi-ethnic nation.

In an attempt to examine the socio-economic problems in Belize's plural society in detail, two main areas of difficulties may be isolated: Friction between the different ethnic groups and competition between native Belizeans and foreign-born workers, the so-called "Refugee Problem".

4.1. Friction Between the Different Ethnic Groups in Belize

In Belize, ethnic friction occurs between Afro-Belizean themselves (i.e. the Creoles and the Belizeans of pure African descent) on the one side and in their interactions with "Spanish" Belizeans (or *panias,* a derogatory Belize Kriol term for Mestizo and designating anyone of "Spanish" descent), the Garinagu, Maya-Belizeans and the few Whites (or *bakras* (for "back raw"), the name given in Kriol for the white man who is foolish enough to not use a shirt to protect him from sunburn) on the other. Until the 1950s each of these groups tended to live in geographically isolated enclaves, even if they worked at the same plantation or at the same production site in the forest.

4.1.1. Tensions Between Creoles Themselves and Antagonistic Feelings Towards the Garinagu

As far as the tensions between Creoles[46] themselves are concerned, the subject of Creole identity has to be examined more in detail: Until a few decades ago,

---

46   Contrary to common belief, the sole use of the term to denote a person of mixed blood is erroneous for the word "creole" has no connotative meaning of colour or race.

In the English language, the word "creole" emerged in the mid-18th century via Spanish *criollo* and French *créole,* "person native to a locality" possibly a corruption of the Spanish *criadillo,* diminutive of *criado* meaning "one bred or reared in one's household" but formerly also "child". Another possible etymology is that it derived from Portuguese *crioulo,* diminutive of *cria* "person, especially a servant, raised in one's household". Whether it has a Spanish or Portuguese root, both forms derive from the verb *criar* "to bring up" from Latin *creāre* "to produce, create".

Historically the term has had different meanings depending on the geographic location: In the Spanish and French colonies the term originally was used to describe any person born in the New World and of European descent, as opposed to somebody coming directly from the metropolis. In Brazil, with the exception of the southernmost

most Creoles were proud to think themselves of being the descendants of the very "Baymen's clan". Today, we have to differentiate because, in reality, two groups of Creoles have evolved, even among the elite. Depending on which group refers to the Baymen, different types of heritage are evoked, intentionally or unintentionally. For example, while some Creoles continue to regard themselves as proud descendants of the original inhabitants, the old established families and the Baymen, whom they hail as founding fathers of the settlement, others agree with contemporary descriptions of the Baymen: "a crew of ungovernable wretches" or *"un conjunto de vagos"* (a crowd of vagabonds).[47]

This dichotomy among the Creoles was responsible for

- an ambivalent attitude towards the mother country and colonialism as such, especially before and shortly after independence and
- the emergence of antagonistic feelings between Creoles themselves as well as the immensely complex relationship with the country's other ethnic groups, principally the Mestizos.

As explained in Chapter Five, in colonial British Honduras, the members of the Creole elite had fought hard until they were finally granted a more favoured position, were seen almost equal to Whites and eventually began to share power with the colonial elite, even though this ascendancy was only granted to certain individuals and not to the entire Creole group as such.

During the 1950s and 1960s, at a time when elsewhere in the Anglophone Caribbean the British link was long being rejected politically, institutionally and culturally, in Belize, most of the Creole elite still showed a strong tendency to remain "conservative", for example by favouring the Protestant religion instead of adopting Catholicism, and maintaining if not glorifying the British connection. For a long time, especially in comparison with other Caribbean

---

state, *crioulo* designated both Black slaves born in the Americas and people of Black and European descent. In the Anglophone countries, where the colonization pattern was different and there was much less need to differentiate between someone who came from the metropolis or was born in the colonies, "creole" designated a person of mixed Black and European ancestry.

Today, the term *criollo* is also used as a synonym for "local, national" and to highlight native cultural expressions and qualities, to specify native foods, plants, breeds of animals and literary traditions (*criollismo*), and to reinforce Latin American/Central American cultural identity and express devotion to the respective "American" country. It is used to describe local cultural and literary expression and depending on the geographical location, a "Creole" or "criollo" may be a person of African, mixed African and European and "pure" European descent – or even a horse, in the case of the *criollo* horse breed.

47   Cf. Uring (1726: 354–58) and Calderón (1944: 65)

British colonies, Belizean Creoles maintained and idolized their pride in the values of British culture. Obviously, as long as British army contingents were responsible for guaranteeing Belize's territorial integrity, it was difficult to deny the importance of the British connection.

When the first movements of resistance to the colonial system emerged, the representatives of the Creole elite once again were divided into two groups, a smaller group whose mostly Catholics members participated openly in the resistance and a larger one which only practised limited resistance. The general attitude of the second group was one of accommodation. Along with the identification with the colonial establishment came certain privileges which they were most eager to keep. For a long time, the prevailing attitude among most Belizean Creoles was that one should try to get something out of the colonial authorities rather than attempt to challenge the system.

Earnest tensions emerged when conceptions of Creole identity began to change gradually: From a stigmatization of African descent to a more confident expression of being a native Belizean, while at the same time identifying with British cultural values and social aspirations. For example the Creoles spoke the closest approximation to Standard English, as will be discussed in the pertinent subchapter.

It did not take long until the culturally assimilated Creoles started to look down upon those who preferred to conserve their African identity. Likewise, other groups, especially the Garinagu, were regarded as inferior whose culture was branded as half-savage. This attitude, undoubtedly, resulted from fear on account of the Black Carib/Garinagu's resistance against the French and the British colonizers on the island of St. Vincent in the West Indies way back in 1780s and 1790s. In 1811, according to an entry in Governor Burdon's collection of documents, the Garinagu were considered by the Magistrates of the settlement as a "Most Dangerous People [who] would subject themselves to imprisonment by remaining in the settlement for more than forty eight hours."[48]

The Protestant missionaries and the Catholic Church were also partly to be blamed for the growing prejudice of the Creoles towards the Garinagu. For instance, Methodist missionaries visited Garifuna enclaves in the 1830s, criticizing their cultural heritage (what the missionaries called "devil dancing"), and their "Catholic" beliefs allowing polygamous unions, and encouraging the Creole population to join in the criticism. In a similar manner, the Catholic Church influenced the Creoles to adjust their opinion of the Garinagu. The weekly Jesuit newspaper "The Angelus", which existed from 1886 to 1895, openly described the Garinagu as "savage and pagan" and called for them to be pun-

---

48   Archives of British Honduras, Burdon (1935,Vol:146)

ished for performing the *dügü*, a complex trance healing ceremony combining witchcraft, magic and religion.

In 1838, after emancipation and the termination of the apprenticeship period, every attempt was made by the colonial elite to eliminate any vestiges of a previous existence of slavery. Anglo-cultural norms were to be adopted while at the same time attempting to suppress any arising feelings of a common African ancestry of Creoles, those of pure African descent and the Garinagu. For example the Creole working class was persuaded to see Garifuna traditions as inferior and supposed signs of underdevelopment, which, in fact, was only a pretext for the anti-Garifuna prejudices that flared up throughout the 19th and 20th centuries.

The colonial socio-economic and political structure aggravated the growing alienation between Creoles and Garinagu. Until about 1950, all affairs of the colony were directed from Belize City, where both the Creole elite and Creole working class were concentrated, thus making it much easier for the latter to adopt the values and attitudes of the Creole elite, with whom the colonial government shared power.

For the reasons explained above and despite the existence of ambiguous feelings among the Creoles with regard to colonialism, paradoxically, they all saw themselves as inheritors of "British civilization" and responsible for maintaining British cultural norms. This was an attitude found especially among the Creole colonial servants, a profession that came to be typical for the middle class Creoles of Belize City. The other ethnic groups, according to the Creoles' opinion had yet to demonstrate their "patriotic" identification with the country, something they found was especially true for the Mestizo community.

In discussing the ambiguous identity of Creoles and their antagonistic feelings towards those of pure African descent and the Garinagu it is important to emphasize that as time passed, a unique phenomenon developed in Belize. Unlike in the English speaking Caribbean islands, the term "Creole" has come to include also the Afro-Belizeans of pure African descent.

4.1.2. The Hostility Between Creoles and "Spanish"

The hostility between Creoles and "Spanish" (the Belizean equivalent of "Mestizo" or "Ladino") is equally rooted in history: It began in the second half of the 19th century after the large influx of approximately 8,000 Mestizos, more than doubling the colony's population. This massive immigration of "Spanish" reinforced the exclusivist nature of Creole identity and caused the forming of putative fundamental cultural and ideological distinction. Not only had this attitude a considerable destabilizing influence on the colony's social life in the past, it also continues to be present in today's popular consciousness, especially in connection with the waves of immigrants from Central America, as will be discussed presently. Generally speaking, the main reason for the propagation of certain myths about alleged "Spanish" vices was because the Creoles, who regarded themselves to be "the only true Belizeans", saw their privileged position endangered.

What were these alleged "Spanish" vices that continue to influence people's minds in present Belize? It is, for example, the long-existing notion that the "Spanish" have a certain propensity to start violent machete fights, as described in the 1840s in the accounts of Thomas Young, an English traveller along the Caribbean coast of Honduras and the Mosquito Coast

> ... they [the Spaniards] must be kept in small gangs, or they will Most likely quarrel, and fight with that dangerous weapon the long spear-pointed knife [machete], which they wear in a sheath fastened to a belt around the waist.[49]

Dishonesty was thought to be another weakness of the "Spanish character". Around the same time, For example, the Scottish traveller Robert G. Dunlop, who resided in Central America for three years in the early 1840s, already commented that he had

> ... never found any native of Central America, who would admit that there could be any vice in lying; and when one has succeeded in cheating another, however gross and infamous the fraud may be, the natives will remark "Qué hombre vivo" (what a clever fellow) ...[50]

In modern Belize, these supposedly Central American and Latin American cultural idiosyncrasies, together with a number of other typical Latin characteristics listed by Harrison, the author of several evaluations of Latin American socio-economic performance,[51] still seem to influence the minds of most Creo-

---

49   Young (1842:115)

50   Dunlop (1847:336)

51   Lawrence E. Harrison (2000[1985]:132–50), for many years the director of USAID in several Central American and Caribbean countries, propounds the theory that some of the by-products of Spanish colonization, especially certain world views and authoritarian social structures inherited from Spain, continue to influence much of the cultural environment in the former Spanish colonies. He argues that these Latin idiosyncrasies have a negative impact on socio-economic development and are directly responsible for the present political and socio-economic difficulties in Latin and Central America. In addition, he compares the development in the Latin and Central American former Spanish colonies to those countries which have been exposed to British rule and where these

les and, although to a much lesser degree, of assimilated Mestizos. After all, it cannot be denied that these traits clearly coincide with the negative stereotyping and prejudices against the Central American immigrants.

In this context, the question for Belize is in how far the demographic impact of the 1980s and 1990s will entail fundamental changes for the country. And here, the question needs to be asked whether certain specific cultural traits may favour or inhibit the realization of socio-economic development, and if, how they should be taken into consideration, if at all possible. Although this issue must be approached with caution I am, nevertheless, very much inclined to support the theory that the many Latin American idiosyncrasies mentioned in the footnote above have been and are, indeed, development-negative.

Another reason for the growing antagonism between Creoles and "Spanish" was religion. Although the Protestant Creoles were (and are) in a clear minority, they had strong colonial attachments and began to foster resentments against Catholicism, the "Spanish" religion. Catholicism was numerically much stronger, distributed throughout the colony, much more culturally and ethnically varied and at the same time more representative of the lower class. As it turned out, from the Protestant Creoles' point of view their fears were not completely unfounded, since the first political leaders in earnest were Catholic Creoles, who had the Jesuits as their mentors.

4.1.3. The Creoles' Resentments Against Whites

In present Belize, the economic success of the Mestizos, the expatriate Whites and, to a limited degree, also the Chinese has led to an internal shift of power. Therefore, the resentments of Creoles against Whites have turned out to be less dramatic. Due to the fact that both Creoles and Whites are no longer dominant to the same degree and hardly any animosity exists between the two groups.

On the other hand, the attitude of the remaining all-White elite towards the Creoles seems to be a very ambiguous one. While some of the Whites have shown a strong tendency to identify, or quasi-identify, both as White *and* Cre-

---

peculiarities are thought to be absent (Australia, New Zealand, Canada, and Barbados among others).

According to Harrison, some of these development-negative idiosyncrasies are: 1) Family is considered to be the only focus for loyalty, paranoia exists beyond. 2) Focus on the present or past rather than the future. 3) An overreliance on luck and the supernatural. 4) Avoidance of group action without clear personal gain in view. 5) Exaggerated concern over dignity and manliness. 6) Sensitivity about shame, but little sense of guilt. 7) Reliance on status over achievement, 8) Male parents arbitrary and inconsistent upbringing; therefore widespread suspicion and little sense in child of self-control in later life.

ole and are not at all opposed to the creolization of their families, others keep a greater distance, intentionally or unintentionally. This may, among other reasons, be a result of the coming of new communication media to Belize. The White elite has been deprived of the once held privilege of transmitting, and filtering, "metropolitan" values to the masses. Via satellite television and with modern communication channels, the masses now have direct and simultaneous access to "the outside" and the White elite is no longer able to both find and affirm their privileged status locally. As a consequence, a shift has occurred and the very few members of the remaining all-White elite are becoming more and more internationalized. They commute between their homes on the Belizean cays and Miami, Houston, New York, London etc., and tend to intermarry with wealthy Americans and/or Europeans they have met abroad, their friends increasingly being foreign investors and a mixture of multinational businessmen. Thus, their identification with Belize tends to be much less.

4.2. Competition and Tensions Between Native Belizeans and Foreign-Born (Mostly Central American) Workers

Despite the country's long history of immigrant inflows, the unexpected arrival of tens of thousands of Central Americans into Belize during the 1980s has outweighed any migration experience in the past. The causes of this immigration were discussed in the previous section but what are the consequences of this migration?

With the massive immigration of Central American refugees and displaced persons, the friction of ethnic groups in Belize reached new dimensions. The Creoles' attitude towards the country's other ethnic groups was intensified when the term "Creole" began to undergo one more semantic change. At present "Creole" not only includes those of pure African descent, it has also come to connote "native" in contrast with "alien", which has become the standard term for the "Spanish", Maya Indians, Garinagu, West Indians, (especially Jamaicans) and other minority groups.

A discussion of this complex issue has to focus on the impacts the recent major demographic change has had on the host society and on Belize as a nation on the one side, and on the socio-economic integration problems of the immigrants on the other.

4.2.1. Impacts of Central American Immigration on the Host Society and on Belize as a Nation

Massive population inflows cause an especially heavy impact on small nations. In Belize, the ratio of refugees to natives for 1989 was one in 39, which ranked the country tenth in the world in this category.[52]

While social relations between Creoles have shown much improvement over the last decade, and only very attentive observers may be able to perceive any lingering resentments, any visitor who stays in Belize for longer cannot fail to notice a national hostility (especially in Belize City) against Central American immigrants and their descendants. In addition, the mass media adds fuel to the fire: By giving extensive coverage to the issue, it propagates the prevailing anti-Central American immigrant ideology which, as a consequence, has come to assume the characteristics of a widely accepted fact.

Although triggered more recently by the long-running tensions on account of Guatemala still not wanting to relinquish its claim to large portions of Belize's territory in the south-west, the hostility against the new arrivals is merely a continuation of the ever-present prejudice against the "Spanish". This behaviour, most likely, is a residual attitude derived from British colonial antagonism towards the "Spanish" republics, especially Guatemala. In many cases, the reaction of "Belizeans" (and, paradoxically, this also includes the meanwhile acculturated descendants of the 19th century Mestizo immigrants) against the immigrant inflow is expressed in terms of stereotyped ethnic, cultural and national dissimilarities.

While the colonial attitude towards the "Spanish" republics continues to play a role in the mystification of alleged endemic fundamental differences between people of Latin and those of British (as well as other European) and/or North American background, the influence modern political forces have on public consciousness must also be considered. Colonialism has become a convenient scape-goat for the present persisting immigration problem in the sense that recently, opportunistic local politicians have shown a tendency to stir up any dormant feelings of resentments against British colonialism, and anything connected to it. This approach, unquestionably, has fed popular reaction against "Spanish" immigration.

One of the factors responsible for these difficulties was, and continues to be, the increasing competition between native Belizeans and the newcomers, which is due to the following reasons: Belizean Creoles, "Spanish" Belizeans, Garinagu, and Maya (especially those who have not been able to assume own-

---

52   United States Committee for Refugees (USCR), 1990 World Refugee Survey: 1989 Review, quoted in Stone (1994:186)

ership of plots of land), were put in direct competition with incoming refugees as far as land and rural employment was concerned. Desperate for cash, particularly in rural areas, immigrants were not only prepared to have more tolerance towards exploitive conditions but also accept much lower wages, i.e. in comparison with the wages a Belizean worker would get for the same type of work. In the citrus groves in the south, for example, where 56% of the workers are "Spanish" (either "Spanish"-Belizeans or recent Central American immigrants), Belizean workers have complained that jobs are being taken by non-Belizeans from neighbouring Spanish speaking-countries.

According to a survey done on the state-run banana farms in the south, by 1993, of the nearly 1.400 field workers employed on twenty two of the country's twenty three commercial banana farms, only 7% were Belizeans, approximately divided equally between Creoles, Garinagu, Mopan and Q'eqchi'. 34% of the workers came from Guatemala, 32% from Honduras and 25% from El Salvador.[53]

As far as the Belizean government is concerned it is interested in keeping a certain amount of labour willing to work for the lowest wages, and tailors its immigration policy accordingly. Apart from the fact that the extension of citizenship also means additional votes, in conformity with the country's current development priorities, cheap labour is an essential requisite for generating growth in the citrus and banana industries as well as for attracting investment.

The impact the large scale arrival of Central Americans has had on the host society and on Belize as a nation is both profound and widespread. The competition between native Belizeans and Central American immigrants, who in Belize are pejoratively referred to as "aliens" or *paisas* (from *paisano,* in this case "foreigner"), and have come to be interchangeable synonyms for "refugees", has emerged as one of the most pressing policy issues involving a variety or related factors.

Although it has become an accepted fact that there is an on-going need for cheap labour (for example in the expanding agro-export, the tourist sector, construction, the growing Mennonite farming enterprises and private households), it cannot be denied that the availability of cheap and easily controlled labour has actually led to the displacement of unionized Belizean workers. This has caused a mass exodus of Creoles and Garinagu to the US, which has major cultural and social consequences for Belize's society.

Moreover, the strains on the social infrastructure (by providing adequate housing, health care issues, additional resources for the prevention and treatment of diseases), caused by the presence of a large number of undocumented

---

53   Cf. Moberg (1994:5)

persons, were considerable. The making available of additional resources needed to extend Belize's meagre social services in order to accommodate such as large number of immigrants presented and presents a major challenge.

Another consequence of the large scale arrival of Central Americans was that many Belizean men and women of working age saw their jobs in danger and have emigrated, or are considering emigration. This, in turn, creates a heavy burden for the tax payer which is mainly for two reasons: One, the departing Belizeans are generally more educated than those who do not consider emigration and two, the country receives largely unschooled persons in return who eventually have to be educated at least to the average level of native Belizeans. Costs for the tax-payer arise twice, the first time for the education of those who later leave (the substantial brain drain as mentioned) and then for the basic education of the incomers, who, besides, tend to have larger families than the departees.

But one of the most drastic impacts of the massive immigration of Central Americans for Belize as a nation is the following: Although Belize has successfully thwarted Spanish invasion since 1798, in an almost ironic twist of fate the country is experiencing a gradual – or, as a matter of fact, not so gradual if we look at the immigration statistics – transformation from an English-speaking country to a country where almost half of the population speaks Spanish. The massive Hispanic immigration combined with the large scale emigration of Creoles and Garinagu to the US has, among some Belizeans, led to growing fears that Belize is undergoing a process of "latinization".

Over the past decades, these fears have been nurtured by the increased hispanization of both Lebanese/Syrians and Chinese. According to the 2000 census, 56% claim to be fluent in Spanish and 46% consider Spanish to be their primary language. Threatened by these data and frustrated with the "open-door" immigration and refugee policy, both the Creole elite and Creole middle class are concerned about a potential loss of the cultural and political dominance they have enjoyed for so long, while the Creole working class claims that refugees receive better treatment than native Belizeans. In sum, they all express the common concern that continuing unchecked immigration could, in the long run, seriously endanger the ethnic balance of the population.

From the 1990s onwards, "maintaining the ethnic balance" has become not only a political issue but also an euphemism for a controversial and complex topic and has been much discussed ever since: One, preserving at least the ideological remnants of the assumed privileged position of Creoles in Belizean society and two, putting a halt to the continued emigration of dissatisfied Creoles. For the latter, these two arguments are convincing enough to justify informal discrimination and antagonism against the Spanish-speaking "aliens".

In this context then, one question arises: Is it possible that these fears of latinization could be one of the reasons for an increased orientation of the Creoles towards the US and if so, will these ties with the US, as well as the presence of North American/European expatriates and West Indians and to a certain degree also their creolization, mitigate the on-going latinization process, both cultural and language-wise?

In general terms, the image most Belizeans (again, this came to include the descendants of the 19th century Mestizo immigrants) have, or would like to have of themselves, is that culturally, they have a closer affiliation with the people of the Anglophone Caribbean islands. Since the beginning of the first wave of immigrants from Yucatán in the late 1840s, there has been a tendency to ignore the fact that there have been greater biological and cultural additions to the Belizean population from the neighbouring Central American countries than from elsewhere.[54]

This attitude continues to be present and may be seen as a direct consequence of British colonial rule in so far as it implanted upon Belizeans the idea that they should ignore their migration history and look away from their immediate environment while favouring an orientation towards the mother country. In more recent times, however, local political forces seem to have succeeded in persuading Belizeans to replace their orientation towards the former mother country by an approximation to those who have experienced the same or similar form of colonialism.

Finally, another serious difficulty in connection with the Central American immigrants has become visible. Mestizo newcomers were able to blend in easily with Belize's plural society since they hardly distinguish themselves from the Belizean-born Mestizos, who are a mixture of different origins. Therefore, most Creoles find it hard to differentiate between the "alien Spanish" from the "Spanish" republics, the Belizean "Spanish", and the acculturated Maya. This can be noted especially in the Northern districts where the line between the more acculturated Maya and the "Spanish" is becoming increasingly blurred.

Naturally, this is a contributory factor to the existing tensions between Creoles and the above two groups and greatly offends "Spanish" and Maya-Belizeans, who see the Creoles' failure to differentiate as an attempt to symbolically deny them their rights as Belizeans. As a consequence, and in order to

---

54   From 1861 to 1940 the number of immigrants from Central America was four times as high as that from the English speaking Caribbean. In 1980 and 1991 immigration from the English speaking Caribbean accounted for only 4,5% and 3,3,% respectively of all foreign born in comparison to a total of 73% and 88,7% respectively born in Central America and Mexico. Cf. Dobson (1973: 251) and Palacio (1993: 3–12)

prevent this to happen, there is, as I was able to witness several times for myself, a growing tendency among some of the Belizean "Spanish" to not speak Spanish to outsiders. They prefer to communicate in English first and only after sufficient confidence has set in, they switch back to their mother tongue, a phenomenon which will be briefly touched on in the following section.

After having considered the impacts of the Central American immigration on the host society, the implications for the nation as such, and the reaction of Belizeans to Mestizo immigrants, we shall now examine some of the difficulties the immigrants themselves are experiencing in Belize.

4.3. Socio-Economic Integration Difficulties of Central Americans, Garinagu and Maya

To assure an as smooth as possible assimilation of the Central American immigrants, various integration plans, such as facilities for settlement on plots of land especially dedicated to them, specific education programmes and other innovative strategies, were implemented. These policies and the fact that in Belize, the public sectors are dominated by Creoles are two of several factors which may be partly held responsible for the prevailing anti-Central American ideology, one of the main causes for integration difficulties.

The multi-ethnic society in Belize is very different from the almost homogeneous population in the countries of the immigrants' origin where Blacks, Mestizos, and Zambos (offspring of Blacks and Amerindians) are in a minority and mostly at the bottom of the social ladder. For the reasons mentioned above, upon their arrival in Belize, Central Americans are being inserted into the lower socio-economic strata. A detailed assessment of the socio-economic integration problems of the recent Central American immigrants[55] would be beyond the scope of this book, but some examples will be given below:

In Belize, radical socio-economic improvement has yet to take place and the Belizean way of trying to cope with this fact is a strong tendency to blame the recent large scale immigration for the present situation in Belize. For example, popular opinion holds that Central American refugees are competitors for jobs, education, health care and other limited social resources. Besides, in rural areas the incomers are seen as combative squatters on government lands and are treated accordingly. Especially until the 1990s public consciousness almost blindly associated the various incidents of petty crime, public disorder, burglary, assaults etc. with the presence of the "Spanish". Especially in rural

---

55   For details on the integration problems of Central American immigrants see for example Palacio (1993: 3–12)

areas, this attitude contributed to the on-going dichotomy between the Creoles and the "Spanish" and making reasonably peaceful inter-personal relationships extremely difficult. Not only did the "Spanish" constitute a convenient target for aggression, but also for individual exploitation, especially on the citrus and banana plantations.

The immigrants, a number of which are still believed to stay in the country undocumented, are legally and economically vulnerable and tell of manifold incidents of escalating discrimination, harassment and exploitation. According to personal communication many "Spanish" immigrants arrivals were afraid of Creoles/Blacks *("los negritos, les tenemos mucho miedo")*, and generally preferred to avoid their company. As far as leisure activities are concerned social interaction between Central American immigrants (and their descendants) and Creoles is still limited.

At present, although the friction between Belizean Creoles, Belizean "Spanish" and Central American immigrants is continuously improving, it remains a most critical issue which has yet to be solved. However, socio-economic integration difficulties are by no means restricted to the immigrants from Central America and we must also consider the assimilation problems of the Garinagu and Maya.

As far as the integration of Belize's Garinagu and Maya population in the Toledo District is concerned, the demographic changes have had certain effects. During the first decades of the 20th century, both groups were given small government reservations[56] in a kind of community rental system with no security, where they were allowed to grow food for their own subsistence. Since reservation boundaries were largely ignored the government refused to grant proper private land ownership. As disenfranchised minority groups the Garinagu and Maya are now put in direct competition with incoming refugees for land as well as rural employment. But even if this massive immigration of Central Americans had not occurred (or not occurred to such an extent), from a historical point of view, the integration process of the Garinagu and Maya would not have been without difficulties.

In 1874 the Garinagu were allotted a "Carib Reserve" at Stann Creek (present Dangriga) from where they gradually spread south into the Toledo District and established several coastal enclaves. To the British they were an un-

---

56　These reservations are very different from those in the United States and must be understood in its historical context. In Belize, the government reserves mostly consist of land which was formerly owned by large mahogany companies. At the turn of the century, after the latter went bankrupt, these lands reverted to the Crown and remained government property after independence. For the history of the government reserves in Southern Toledo, see Wilk and Chapin (1990: 32).

usual group of people of colour whom they had never been able to enslave or subordinate. Because of the Garinagu's rebellious past in the West Indies and in the Republic of Honduras, they were seen as a potentially bad example for the slave population and were treated with distrust and general disparagement. Although the colony's elite valued the agricultural produce (plantains, maize, poultry) the Garinagu farmers brought to Belize Town, they had to get a permit to stay in town for longer than forty eight hours otherwise they "would subject themselves to imprisonment".[57]

Even though the Garinagu are increasingly becoming more assimilated, the strong cultural renaissance in the last decades has, at the same time, contributed to retaining cultural and linguistic singularity. Today, the social prejudice Garinagu have encountered for many years seems to be gradually disappearing. Owing to their facility to acquire languages, ambitious Garinagu have long been successful in professions such as teachers (they provide the bulk of Belize's rural teachers) and lawyers. Although a considerable number of Belize's intellectuals, trade unionists, politicians etc. are members of the Garifuna community, the majority of Garinagu earn their living as fishermen, turtlers, and small scale farmers. More recently, some Garinagu have begun to work as tourist guides and participate in a number of nature conservation projects.

The Garinagu's talents in languages have also been very helpful in establishing a link with the Mopan and Q'eqchi' Maya, who populate relatively isolated inland regions of the Toledo District and to whom the following pages will be dedicated. These Maya entered (re-entered, respectively) Southern Toledo in different waves of immigration and under different circumstances mostly between the 1880s and 1930s and still retain their language and culture.

Whereas the Maya of Northern and Western Belize have already initiated a process of acculturation and assimilation by adopting a "Spanish" identity and a relatively undifferentiated "Spanish" culture (which is not without Creole influence however), the situation of the Maya in Southern Belize is very different. In the south, we are still able to distinguish clearly between the Mopan and the Q'eqchi' who, despite sharing the same cultural heritage, exhibit several cultural differences and speak different Mayan languages.

But the Mopan and Q'eqchi' also have a great deal in common. For example, both had and continue to have comparable subsistence economies, by growing corn, beans, and root crops, and raising pigs and chickens. They also have similar local community organizations and are allowed to govern their villages by themselves by bringing decisions before a Public Meeting. It is headed by the *alcalde* who, since 1980, also has limited judiciary authority. The Mopan and

---

57   Archives of British Honduras, Burdon (1935:II:146)

Q'eqchi' have had a completely different immigration history as mentioned but they have had similar experiences in their relations with people from outside their communities. Except for the interactions with Garifuna school teachers, contacts with the larger society have been occasional and only a few times did interactions with the colony's other ethnic groups take place, as was the case with Creole mahogany loggers, Creole colonial government administrative personnel, a small community of East Indians and individual "Spanish" chicle collectors. The British hardly interfered with the Maya. Their settlement was confined to remote Toledo and colonial authorities had little or no contact with them throughout the 19th and the first half of the 20th centuries.

With regard to the impact Spanish colonization had upon Maya populations throughout Central America, there has always been a strong tendency in scholarly literature to highlight the negative consequences. As we know, in present Belize, the Maya were not affected to the same degree as in the neighbouring regions. Nonetheless, in Belize, the "Maya issue" has occasionally sprung up, especially in the years prior to and immediately after independence in 1981.

In discussing the influence British colonial presence had upon the Belizean Maya, first of all it is necessary to differentiate between the Maya in the west and north-west and the ones in the south: The mostly Yucatec Maya communities of the western and north-western regions were clearly affected by the violent encounters with the logging crews. But first, we must remember that these fights took place in the vicinity of the mahogany camps set up in Maya territory and secondly, these camps were owned by individual London-based companies, which saw in the interference of the Maya a threat to their immediate interests. As a consequence, the mahogany companies began to manipulate the local elite and colonial authorities, safely living in Belize Town and far away from the camps in the jungle, to act to their advantage. Therefore, strictly speaking, colonial rule as such cannot directly be made responsible for the violence committed on part of the mahogany companies.

The violent encounters between the mahogany companies and the Maya did not affect the Mopan and Q'eqchi' in the very south of the colony, in the present Toledo District. Without wanting to be a colonial apologist, I have come to support the position that for the Toledo Maya, for several reasons, British colonial presence even had positive effects:

- **First:** If the present Toledo District (which was unofficially claimed by local authorities in the 1820s, more than 40 years before the settlement was officially declared a British colony) had not been part of British Honduras, it would have been virtually impossible for the Mopan and Q'eqchi' to leave

Guatemala in the first place. They would never have been able to migrate to a safer region where neither forced labour nor military conscription existed and where they were protected from Guatemalan harassment. In British Honduras they were welcomed, because – from the British point of view – it was advantageous to populate the area. Officials were convinced that several pockets of Maya in the vicinity of the border (according to Guatemala, a disputed border) would deter the Guatemalans from encroaching into British territory.

- **Secondly**: The fact that the colonial government left the Toledo Maya mostly to themselves indirectly helped to preserve Maya identity. One reason why the colonial authorities in Belize Town were not overly concerned with their assimilation (the task of assimilating the Maya was taken over by English and North American Jesuit missionaries) was because the inexistence of an all-weather road prevented colonial administrative personnel from being present on a regular basis. The swampy terrain in rural Toledo posed a major obstacle for the realization of any road projects and it was not until 1940 that the first road between a Maya village and the coast was opened.

In the Toledo District, so far, there has been no neighbouring group whose ethnic identity could be adopted by those Maya families who actually wanted to "modernize". This is completely different to the north, where the Maya live in close proximity to a hispanicized Mestizo-community, are relegated into a low-status position in relation to that community and hence have begun to adopt this new identity. In comparison to the Yucatec Maya groups in the north, both the Mopan and Q'eqchi' have succeeded in retaining their identities. From the late 1970s onwards, however, they have gone separate ways as far as their integration and assimilation is concerned.

At present, of these two subgroups the Mopan are the more acculturated despite retaining strong continuity with their past and a clear cultural identity rooted in their rituals, family ties, folklore, dances (such as the ancient "Deer Dance" and modified versions of the "Dance of the Conquistadores"), traditional music played on marimba, harp, violin and drum. Nevertheless, they have been very receptive to "modernization" and have adopted many innovations and economic changes which they have integrated into their lives. Due to the fact that the Mopan have occupied less swampy terrain in upland areas or drier spots in the lowlands, they have been able to farm on good land and therefore have a relatively long history as cash crop producers. By the 1930s, the Mopan had become significant exporters of corn, rice, and beans to the rest of Belize and even to Jamaica. Contrary to the Q'eqchi', the Mopan identify with

Belize and being Belizeans although, from the late 1960s onwards, they have begun to consider themselves primarily as Maya. They take much pride in being Maya, claiming common cause and kinship with their Q'eqchi' neighbours and with the Maya in Guatemala, with whom, they do not maintain significant ties.

The Q'eqchi', who originally lived in the highlands of the Alta Verapaz District of Guatemala, are less acculturated and are the most self-reliant and at the same time the poorest, and most neglected, ethnic minority in Belize. Fleeing the oppression and forced labour by German coffee planters between the 1880s and 1914, the highland Q'eqchi' settled in the dense jungle regions of Southern Belize. There, they lived completely isolated at first but, as the Mopan, eventually became involved in various forms of cash crop productions, mainly selling provisions to logging crews. In the mid-1930s, when the British Government appointed a Liaison Officer to encourage the Q'eqchi' to move northwards, some settled in more accessible areas in close proximity of roads where they began to concentrate on the growing of rice and other cash crops for the local market.

Q'eqchi' culture is considerably distinct from that of the Mopan. For example many traditional beliefs about the world and human relations as well as the supernatural have been incorporated into Catholicism, notwithstanding the fact that Protestant missionaries began to convert the Q'eqchi' in the 1970s. But the veneer of Roman Catholicism under which the ancient Maya rites are still practised is fairly thin. The Q'eqchi's knowledge of Classic Maya folk tales and myths, a mixture of their ancient religious beliefs and Catholicism, is widespread, which is not, or much less, the case with the Mopan. Traditional skills, such as pottery making (although pottery has been largely replaced by plastic articles), and building houses have survived and the lore about herbal medicine is passed on from generation to generation and increasingly also to the outside world. There has been renewed interest in the traditional fiestas and the art of embroidery. Although women still wear their beautifully embroidered blouses, the *huipiles*, as a means to demonstrate their Maya identity, more recently, a growing number of women have opted to use other garments, for climatic reasons, as they say.

With the building of the Southern Highway and roads to San Antonio and other Maya villages, Southern Toledo has become more accessible and the Q'eqchi' have come in contact with other people and cultures: Mestizo merchants, Creole government officials, Garifuna teachers and, until 1993, a contingent of the British military who was stationed there to patrol the Q'eqchi' villages along the Guatemalan border. In addition, interaction with agents of international organizations who have concentrated on improving their way of life in the "name of progress" has become inevitable.

Very few of the above groups of people with whom the Q'eqchi' interact, willingly or unwillingly, have sufficient insights about Q'eqchi' culture and language with the result that a good deal of stereotyping, mistrust and misunderstanding on both sides occurs. For example, since it is not uncommon among outsiders to fail to differentiate between the two indigenous subgroups, the Q'eqchi' are sometimes taken for Mopan or simply classified as "Indians". As a consequence, many Q'eqchi' complain that they have to face several forms of discrimination and are looked down upon, in some instances even by the Mopan.

Unlike the Mopan, Belizean Q'eqchi' retain social, religious and commercial contact with their place of origin and are informed of events there by the *"cobaneros"*, visiting traders from Cobán, the capital of Guatemala's department of Alta Verapaz. With the acquisition of transistor radios, the Belizean Q'eqchi' were able to catch several Guatemalan broadcasts from Cobán in the Q'eqchi' language. Consequently, the contact with Guatemalan Q'eqchi' has intensified, at the same time leading to a growing awareness among them that they were being ignored by the Belizean government. As a counteractive measure, the government was prompted to broadcast in the Q'eqchi' language putting on air programmes of general interest and basic issues of health care.

To facilitate integration, considerable efforts have been undertaken to extend the road system in rural Toledo, increasing the frequency of interactions with people from outside the Maya community even further. This has had negative socio-economic consequences, especially for the Q'eqchi'. During this initial phase of "modernization", their conduct was often characterized by fear, confusion, embarrassment and a lack of self-esteem.

Throughout the past years, several programmes have been introduced reflecting the particular linguistic, social and cultural needs of the Toledo Maya with the aim to promote and assist with their integration into society whilst maintaining their heritage. As a result, from the late 1970s onwards, the "modernization" process has been accompanied by an increased sense of pride in the Maya identity. Population among the Toledo Maya is on the increase thanks to improved health services and because of immigration from Guatemala's departments of El Petén and Alta Verapaz. There is every reason to believe that in the years to come both the Mopan and Q'eqchi' will play a considerable role in the economic development of the presently habitable inland regions of Southern Toledo.

4.4. Positive Consequences of Ethnic and Cultural Pluralism

So far, I have concentrated only on the difficulties in Belize's multi-ethnic and multi-cultural society and on examples of negative repercussions of the convergence of peoples and cultures, some of which may indeed be seen as relics of the country's colonial past. Although a great deal of Belize's current social problems can be ascribed to its society being divided by national antagonism, the ethnic and cultural pluralism of Belize also has many positive aspects:

As far as the massive influx of Central American immigrants is concerned, from an economic point of view and in order to make the country more economically viable, it was an absolute necessity to increase its population. Without foreign labour Belize's agro-industries, the main source of the country's foreign exchange would practically be non-existent. As a consequence, an increased founding of rural settlements took place. From 1970 to 1994, the percentage of the rural population has increased by 6,5%. In 1994 it accounted for 52,5% of the country's total population but according to the estimates for 2010 the percentage has gone down to 48%.[58]

Another positive and important after-effect of the large scale immigration from Central America, despite the many hostilities and difficulties, was that it enhanced the feeling for national culture among Belizeans themselves, in the sense that they have begun to fully appreciate their own "Belizeaness". For example, the more acculturated Mestizo-Belizeans, who might hitherto have considered themselves to have come from a completely different cultural background than the Creoles, are now becoming aware that they have much more in common with their fellow Belizeans than with the recent Guatemalan, Salvadorean or Honduran immigrants. This is vividly demonstrated by the, sometimes not frictionless, interactions between Belizean "Spanish" and Central American "Spanish" immigrants. On the other hand, the new attitude has a positive effect upon the recognition of the values of cultural pluralism. In the long run, this recent awareness will be very beneficial for Belizean society and the nation as such. It proves that in Belize a form of national culture, which goes beyond the obvious physical differences, has emerged.

Belize does not only have strong ethnic diversity but also strong cultural pluralism. This is vividly demonstrated by the existence of many languages, folklore, handicrafts, different traditions of preparing special foods for festivities, artisanal skills (as dory manufacturing and the making of musical instruments), popular dances and the usage of traditional musical instruments etc.).

---

58   Source: Abstract of Statistics for 1994, 1991 and, 1980 and 1970, Central Statistical Office, Belmopan

This is especially true for the Maya and the Garinagu, who continue to practise their traditions.

In a wider sense, this cultural and, as a matter of fact also and ethnic, pluralism may be seen as a remnant of colonialism. Why?

In colonial times it was aimed to keep apart the different ethnic groups with the purpose of inhibiting the natural interaction of cultures co-existing within one community. The various cultures not only remained largely isolated from one another but also mutually suspicious. Moreover, the location of the two major agricultural export crops in completely separate regions – sugar in the north and citrus in the south – and at a fair distance from one another, offered little opportunity for cultural integration. However, despite reinforcing existing differences and fomenting antagonistic feelings between the different groups, the policy of segregation and separation, indirectly, may also have had positive consequences.

Taking this, admittedly a little adventurous, chain of thought further, we may even go as far as to give British colonialism credit, albeit unintentionally, for retaining ethnic and cultural pluralism. To the present day plural cultural heritage has remained alive and has made good use of the divisions of colonialism. As is the case with the Maya and Garinagu, their culture, in fact, has recently seen a revival precisely because of this long cultural isolation.

In sum, and retrospectively seen, by maintaining socio-cultural singularity, the policy of segregation and separation enabled plural cultural heritage to survive and ultimately helped to preserve culture in Belize.

Having taken a closer look at the various difficulties in Belize's multi-ethnic society, we may be able to reach the following conclusion:

The process of decolonization and the building of a nation seldom runs smoothly and completely free of conflicts between different racial and ethnic groups. In present Belize, although the tensions and frictions may not have reached a very high level, the problems of a multi-ethnic society are still unresolved and the issue remains an ever-present concern for politicians and the public alike. The goal for Belize will be to fully complete the decolonization process by achieving a peaceful co-existence of cultural and racial groups in the context of a new "Belizeaness" and by creating a sense of national identity that respects the fact of continuing racial and cultural pluralism.

The plural cultural heritage of Belize was a most essential prerequisite for the building of a national culture. One effective means of accelerating this mechanism is to ease the integration difficulties of the country's ethnic groups. In this respect Belize has achieved much progress over the last decades and the following factors have helped to set this motion in progress:

- **First:** With the development of an all-weather road network and a reliable communication system, contact between the country's ethnic groups began to take place on a steadier basis, paving the way for the establishment of social relations, although different in intensity and nature, among the various groups.
- **Secondly:** Within the process of nation building, more emphasis has consciously been given to increase awareness of the various cultures existing within Belize, as expressed in the slogan "Many Cultures, one Nation", which can be heard frequently on the radio as well as during political propaganda speeches. This has created a new self-awareness among the different groups, especially among the Garinagu and Maya. It also had a positive effect on social interactions as such, facilitating cultural integration. In an additional effort to pay respect to the country's different cultures, two new "ethnic holidays" have been declared.[59]
- **Thirdly:** Although Belizean society continues to be characterized by a strong polarization, the increased rate of inter-ethnic mixtures (i.e. especially between Mestizo and Maya, and Creole and Garinagu) has, among other reasons, led to a fundamental structural change of Belize's society. Ethnicity no longer seems to be the sole criterion for social differentiation but rather colour and class.

It remains to be seen whether Belizeans will be able to develop and nurture their own plural cultural heritage. Because only by consolidating Belize's national culture, can an increased national identity be fostered. And, in the long run, only a solid and confident national identity may reduce the ever-present danger of being "re-colonized" by a more dominant foreign culture.

5. Belize, a Multi-Lingual Nation

In most multi-ethnic and multi-cultural nations, one language in common is seen as a unifying factor and a way of establishing a national identity. But in Belize, recent developments seem to indicate that this is not the case. To the different ethnic groups of Belize, the rediscovering and reasserting of their re-

---

59   The "Pan American Day" (or "Columbus Day") pays tribute to the culture of Belize's Mestizo population. The "Garifuna Settlement Day", which remembers November 19th of 1832, the day a large group of Garinagu from the Bay Islands in Honduras joined about two hundred others, who had settled at the mouth of Stann Creek some twenty years previously. Among the various other "ethnic" festivals and fairs are the Mestizo Carnival celebrations and the "Deer Dance Festival" of the Toledo Maya.

spective separate ethnic and socio-cultural identities remains a major concern, and in order to accomplish this, language is one of the most important tools.

Counting Belize Creole (known as "Belize Kriol English" by its speakers), a Creole language spoken by 37% of Creoles and more or less also understood by a number of Belizean-born Mestizos, Belize is a tri-lingual country with Standard English being the language of socio-economic necessity. Apart from English, Belize Creole and Spanish, the Garifuna language and three Mayan languages are also spoken.

5.1. The English Language in Belize

In Belize, the English language continues to be the key to social mobility, whether it is for office jobs at home or scholarships abroad. English is the official language of the country and the general medium of instruction and examination at schools. It is the first language of Belizean Creoles (or second language respectively, because Belize Creole is considered to be a separate language and not just a vernacular), who will get noticeably "vexed", when a well-meaning visitor to Belize happens to congratulate them on their fluency in the language. Although only 5,6% claim to speak the English language as main language at home, proficiency in Standard English is 56%.

5.2. Belize Creole (Belize Kriol English)

Belize Creole[60] or Belize Kriol English (a term coined by Belizean Creoles in the 1990s) is the primary language of a vast majority of English speakers (with the exception of North American and English expatriates) and is spoken in most homes in Belize City and in the Belize District. Anyone not familiar with

---

60 The development of Creole languages was a general feature of colonization. A "Creole language" is not to be confused with a "Pidgin language". A "Pidgin" is one which develops as a *lingua franca,* a simplified trade language between speakers of different languages when meeting under certain socio-economic, socio-political and socio-cultural conditions. The newly formed Pidgin words are usually pronounced according to the phonemic and morphemic patterns of the speakers' own language with syntactical constructions also being carried over from the original language. Pidgin only serves for contact purposes; the speakers' own language is always retained and continues to be spoken at home.

Only when Pidgin has become more useful than any of the original native languages and when the children born into these newly formed communities start using Pidgin instead of their parents' language, i.e. when Pidgin acquires native speaker standard, does the development of a Creole language, which is the second phase in the development of a contact language, begin.

Belize Kriol may find it rather difficult to follow, although a considerable part of its vocabulary and syntax is from the English language.

The substrate languages of Belize Kriol are the Miskito Coast Creole and several West African languages such as Wolof, Fula, Twi, Ibo, Mandingo and Ashanti. Its lexical borrowings, apart from Standard English, come from a variety of sources:

Among the many words borrowed from the Miskito Coast Creole I have been able to identify are the terms for different types of boats (*pitpan, dori* from Miskito *duri* and adopted by Standard English as "dory"), the names of animals (*gibnat,* for the Belizean rodent "gibnut" from Miskito *ibinha),* trees (*supa,* a certain species of palm tree), plants, fishes, insects, reptiles, birds etc. The term *waika* refers to a clearly identifiable ethnic group in Belize, of Miskito ancestry and lighter-skinned than most Creoles, and *waawa* means shy, childish, and incompetent. Some linguists even go as far as to maintain that Belize Creole is "… an offshoot of Mosquito Coast Creole."[61] However, most of these words are hardly recognizable as Miskito words since they have undergone a process of folk-spelling and were consequently folk-etymologized.

African loan words usually refer to food, African culture and tradition, medicinal and other plants. For example *nyam* (to eat greedily from Wolof *nam* or Twi *enyam*), *obeah* (from Twi and meaning "witchcraft"), *okro* (edible pods from a tropical plant named "okra" in English, from Ibo *okuru*) to name but a few.

Lexical borrowings from Spanish cover a wider range of references and include the following: Terms for medicinal herbs, kinship (for example *compadre/ comadre,* which initially described the relationship between the godfather/godmother of a child and its parents but, at present, its usage has, in Spanish as well as in Belize Kriol, been extended to mean "close friend"), and administration (*alcalde,* a mayor or representative of a village council), *braata* (from *barato,* meaning "inexpensive") and *manzana* (Spanish land measure) as well as *fiesta* (public celebration, festival), *okestra* (from o*rquesta* for the English "orchestra"), *maracas* (this Spanish term has an Amerindian/Carib etymology and is used for a hand held percussion instrument made out of an empty calabash filled with seeds), and *potrero* (from *potrillo,* "a young male horse"). Spanish loan words also include the names of a number of popular Spanish and Amerindian food items and drinks such as *tamales, enchiladas, tacos, garnaches, chimole* (from *chirmol,* a sauce with chilli, tomatoes and onions), *reyeeno* (from *relleno,* "filling" or "stuffing"), *mole* (a black sauce made of chili pepper and chocolate),

---

61   Cf. Holm (1986:13). For a more detailed list of plausible lexical borrowings see for example Holm (1977:1–17, 1978) and Young (1989:5–8)

salsa and *panades* (from *empanadas,* meaning "pasties" or "pies"), *caldo (soup),* and *fresco* (a refreshing drink) and *orchata* (from *horchata*, a traditional Spanish/Central American beverage made out of rice).

Loan words from the Garifuna language are very rare, most likely as a result of the troubled history of social relations between the Creoles and Garinagu. One of the very few identified lexical borrowings from the Garifuna language is *grupa,* for the fish spelt "grouper" in English.

As far as Maya loan words are concerned, there are not many in Belize Kriol, which is basically due to the lack of contact between the Creoles and the various groups of Maya, since both native and immigrant Maya lived a largely self-sufficient life. Among Maya loan-words, apart from the meanwhile hispanicized names of the Maya dishes mentioned above, are the widely used *milpa* ("small farm" or "maize field"), or *metate* (the stone to grind maize before cooking). Although few Maya words have actually been borrowed into Belize Kriol, it bears emphasizing that a number of Maya words entered Belize Kriol via Standard English. The following words are some examples of Maya borrowings into Standard English: "Cigar" (from Maya *sik'ar,* "to smoke", from *sik'* meaning "tobacco"). The term for Belize's "Cays" – even if the etymology is thought to be from Spanish *cayos* (islands, reefs) – may have been originally derived from Yucatec Maya *kay,* meaning "fish". Likewise, the English "shark" may have a Maya etymology (from *xok,* meaning "shark"). The English "hurricane" could also be derived from the Maya *hurukán,* although etymological dictionaries generally seem to give preference to Carib or Arawak origins.

From the early 1980s to the 1990s, extensive discussion was taking place whether or not to adopt Belize Kriol as the official national language of Belize. Among other reasons, this was mainly born out of the idea to give Belize a new and stronger identity, which, especially in view of the recurrent flare-ups of a possible invasion from Guatemala, has gained in importance. Eventually, arguments against adopting Belize Kriol as the official national language were found to outweigh those in favour.

Until the 1980s, Creoles constituted approximately 60% of the total population of Belize but today, the percentage has gone down to 25%. Responsible for this demographic shift was the huge influx of Central American immigrants on one side and the emigration of approximately 85,000 Belizean Creoles to the US on the other.

Returning to the subject of Belize Kriol, this language has become an important symbol of national identity. It serves as a tool to express and reinforce Creole identity, not so much in terms of ethnicity but rather in a cultural sense. By speaking Kriol, speakers first of all seek to signal that one is "Belizean" and one's affiliation to the Creole culture.

Today, Kriol is spoken as a primary language by 37% of the population. In addition, the more acculturated among the Belizean-Mestizos and the first generation of the Central American immigrants more or less understand Kriol and claim to have a moderate to fair command of the language. If we decide to lend credence to less conservative estimates, then, about 75% of the total population speak Kriol, in one form or another.

However, although Belize Kriol is spoken in every Creole household, is used in more intimate and casual functions within Creole society and in the interaction with more acculturated individuals of other ethnic groups, we must bear in mind that Belize Kriol is *not* the language the entire nation depends on for complete inter-personal communication.

Despite Belize Kriol playing a fundamental role in fomenting national identity, in my opinion, the importance of the first languages of the country's other ethnic groups is extremely unlikely to diminish. In Belize, language definitely does not serve as a pretext for providing a sound basis for national identity. In a wider sense, this would imply that, in Belize, a national language might not even be necessary.

5.3. The Spanish Language in Belize

Since the victory over the Spanish fleet in 1798 (the Battle of St. George's Cay), Belize has successfully thwarted Spanish claims. But if we base ourselves on the country's immigration history and the demographic trends of the 1980 and 1990s, at first sight, it seems that the country is quietly experiencing a subtle transformation into a Spanish speaking-country. After 1984, when the Government of Belize granted amnesty to all illegal aliens, the official number of Spanish-speakers increased by approximately one third. According to the official census of 2000, of the almost 50% of Belizean Mestizos, 46% claimed to be fluent in Spanish and use it as a first language.

Although the language of instruction at school is English (up to about the age of eight, classes are taught in both English and Spanish and in the upper classes, English replaces Spanish) and although Mestizo students become bilingual, the language spoken in the majority of Mestizo homes remains Spanish. Whereas most Belizean-born Mestizos and some of the immigrants from Central America are bilingual, and with the descendants of the latter slowly becoming bilingual, only very occasionally does one come across Creoles who speak Spanish as an additional language. The Garinagu, on the contrary, who have retained their own language, are not only fluent in Belize Kriol but also use Spanish as an auxiliary language. This, no doubt, puts them at a certain advantage in comparison to the Creoles, for example when dealing with the exclusively Spanish-speaking immigrant work force on the banana farms and citrus groves in the south.

Among Belizean Mestizos, being bilingual (or trilingual in case they also speak Kriol), has had significant social consequences in the sense that they have become wary of which language to choose in social interactions.

For example, a foreign visitor (i.e. provided he or she is fluent in both English and Spanish) has to be well informed on the Mestizos' present socio-economic situation, in order to be sensitive enough to know which Mestizos actually prefer to be addressed in Spanish and which do not. Although Mestizo features can be clearly distinguished, it is quite difficult to differentiate between the generations of Belizean-born Mestizos and the more recent Mestizo immigrants. The Belizean-born Mestizos, who fully identify with Belize and for status purposes and depending on the social situation, locality and context of the conversation, may prefer to be addressed in English, but the more recent immigrants and their children, for the same reasons of identity or because they simply are not confident enough in English, prefer to be spoken to in Spanish.

Addressing the Creoles is more straightforward. Most Creoles do not understand Spanish at all and are clearly offended when accidentally spoken to in Spanish. In some cases, when Creoles do speak a small amount of Spanish, they pretend not to understand Spanish at all.

In short, when addressing Mestizos or Creoles in Belize, the entire "success" of a conversation might depend on whether or not one has sufficient inside knowledge and finds just the right amount of tact.

On the other hand, the Garinagu who, in most cases, can hardly be distinguished from the Creoles and are generally more or less fluent in Spanish, by no means mind to use Spanish. This may largely be due to their amalgamated identity, as mentioned. When the Garinagu started to enter British Honduras in large numbers in the first decades of the 20th century, they brought along their own variety of Spanish while, at the same time, retaining the Garifuna language. Having lived on the Caribbean coast of Central America since their first arrival in 1797, they had become hispanicized, to the extent that they all spoke fluent Spanish and most of them had Spanish surnames.

Since the first massive influx of Spanish-speakers in the second half of the 19th century, the Spanish language of Belize has remained relatively isolated. Until after 1950, an all-weather road system did not exist in Belize and no railway has ever been built. The only method of travelling was by using the country's navigable waterway system. It was not until the mid-1960s that radio broadcasts could be heard in Belize and it is only since the introduction of Spanish language programmes on the radio and the coming of satellite television to Belize that Belizean Spanish-speakers have access broadcasts in Spanish.

Some programmes, especially radio programmes, are made in Belize but the majority of Spanish television broadcasts are received from Mexico and the United States.

Generally speaking, although Spanish is taught as a secondary language (and at some schools only), not enough emphasis is placed on correcting certain linguistic vices, which might have developed due to the aforementioned communicative isolation of Belizean Spanish-speakers from other Spanish-speaking countries. This relative communicative isolation has facilitated linguistic change and the development of at least two regional varieties[62] with several phonological and lexical differences.

From the 1980s onwards, with the onset of the massive waves of Spanish-speaking immigrants from the neighbouring Central American states, Belizean Spanish-speakers no longer experience the same degree of communicative isolation. This has had significant influence on the Spanish language spoken in Belize. The influx of Spanish-speaking immigrants has created a new awareness among Belizean Spanish-speakers, who are increasingly becoming conscious of their linguistic idiosyncrasies, such as phonological differences, archaic forms etc.

At the same time many English and Kriol speaking Belizeans expressed fears that the Spanish language might eventually replace English and emerge as the primary language of Belize; fears which were not completely unfounded. As it turned out, however, the coming of satellite television, the ongoing boom in the tourism industry and the presence of several North American expatriates, who in a certain sense may be seen as representing "a new class of White and English-speaking settlers", have given a boost to the English language in Belize.

Apart from a Belizean variety of Standard English, Belize Kriol, and Spanish, the two other main languages spoken in Belize are the Garifuna language and three different Maya languages.

5.4. The Garifuna Language

In spite of the structure of the Garifuna language being similar to Yoruba, a West African tongue, it is essentially an Amerindian language, and more precisely, a Carib/Arawak hybrid. Garifuna is a unique language because although

---

62   For example in the west of Belize, the Cayo District, one can perceive the frequent use of *voseo*, which is due to the linguistic influence from Guatemala where the *voseo* is in widespread use. In the north of Belize, the Corozal and Orange Walk District, this particular language characteristic is not present at all.

it is of South American and West Indian origin, today, it is only spoken in Central America and by a Black population.[63]

Depending on where the Garinagu eventually settled, the Garifuna language would have been influenced in different ways. In Belize, by the English language through contact with English speaking woodcutters and English and Creole speaking Creoles and Black slaves. In Guatemala, Honduras, and Nicaragua the Garifuna language would be influenced mostly by Spanish. In Belize, Garifuna is spoken by approximately 16,000 but only in one village, Hopkins, is it officially taught.

In its morphology and syntax Garifuna is clearly an Arawakan language but it also has many affixes from the Carib language. For example, one distinctive feature of Garifuna is that it has different words for the same term. This does not affect the entire vocabulary but when it does, the terms used by men generally derive from Carib and those used by women from Arawak.[64]

Today, the Garifuna vocabulary is considered to have borrowings from five different languages: Arawak (70%), Carib (5%), French (15%), and Spanish and English (10%). Many basic words cannot deny a strong French influence, for example days of the week and the counting system from four onwards, which goes back to the original Black Caribs of St. Vincent adopting the French currency for trading purposes. Some examples of French to Garifuna derivations are *mudu* (*mouton,* "sheep"), *amarieda* (*marier,* "to marry"), *simisi* (*chemise,* "shirt"), *veru (verre,* "glass"). A selection of Spanish to Garifuna derivations include *bino* (from *vino,* "wine"), *jabadu* (from *zapato,* "shoe"), *gabaido* (from *caballo,* "horse"), *garada* (from *carta,* "letter", "book/paper"). More recently, new borrowings from Spanish and English have entered the language in order to describe technical terms. Although in its phonology Garifuna is strongly influenced by African languages (mostly Yoruba), not more than a handful of African loan words exist.

---

63 The Garifuna language is now in peril, it is losing ground to Spanish, English and Creole. There are still an estimated 90,000 Garifuna speakers, most of which live in Garifuna communities on the Caribbean Coast of Honduras. Due to the relative isolation of Garifuna villages it is believed that the Honduran variety of Garifuna has retained more archaic expressions than the varieties spoken elsewhere. In Guatemala, the Garifuna community lives in Livingston (Labuga) on the Caribbean Coast and there are an estimated 17,000 speakers. With the increased emigration of the Garinagu to the United States, a fifth variety evolved, American Garifuna. In Nicaragua and in the Lesser Antilles the Garifuna language has become extinct.

64 For further information on the Garifuna language refer to for example Taylor (1967,1977) and Cayetano (1996).

The Garifuna language plays an important role as a means of expressing and affirming the cultural identity of the Garifuna people and many efforts are made to minimize the risk of its disappearing. Even so a growing number of Garifuna speakers have preferred to use English, Kriol, or Spanish as their first language losing proficiency in Garifuna.

5.5. The Three Mayan Languages – Yucatec, Mopan and Q'eqchi'

Each of the three groups of Maya living in Belize also speak different Mayan languages: Yucatec is mainly spoken in the north and northwest, Mopan and Q'eqchi' in the south.

These Mayan languages of Belize (as the other of the approximately twenty-four living Mayan languages still spoken by nearly three and a half million speakers in the southern and south-eastern provinces of Mexico including Yucatán, Guatemala and one region in Honduras) are linguistically closely related in phonology and grammar, but they are, for the most part, not mutually intelligible.

With regards to the Maya acquiring a second language, a regional difference exists in Belize: The Maya in Northern Belize, having become assimilated to Mestizo culture, have adopted Spanish as their second language. In the south of the Toledo District, the Maya, some of which had as their second language a sort of pidgin-Spanish up until the 1940s, are increasingly becoming bilingual with English and/or Kriol as their second language. Many of the "Toledo Maya" are even trilingual; they are fluent in Q'eqchi', Mopan and English and/or Kriol and among the older generation some also speak Spanish.

After having analysed the different languages in Belize, a concluding remark must be added: Throughout Belize, in inter-ethnic communication or when two or more speakers differ in status, background or individual code competence, multiple code use occurs frequently. As a consequence, code-switching, being highly motivated by social and cultural constraints, is in widespread use. Code-switching can be noted between Belize Kriol and English among the Creoles on the one side, and between Spanish and English among the Mestizos on the other. The Garinagu are the most "flexible". They use whatever code a situation may require and apply their own language as an additional vernacular. Among the Maya, code-switching between the respective Maya language and Spanish and/or English and Kriol has not been noted so far, or at least to a much lesser extent.

Coming to the end of the chapter on the different languages of Belize I would like once more to draw attention to an interesting detail: In Belize, the various cultural groups have always distinguished themselves on the basis of ethnic identity, and language was one very effective means of expressing a person's individuality. Therefore the importance given to the different languages was always very strong, especially after the first immigration waves in the second half of the 19th century.

More recently, however, a tendency has become evident for colour and class – and with it the respective language – to supersede ethnicity as a main criterion for ethnic differentiation. As a matter of fact, the term "Creole" has been extended, in many cases simply referring to the "mixture" between an individual of Afro-European descent with any other ethnic group, whether Mestizo, Garifuna, and even Maya. As a consequence of this trend, the lighter skinned and straighter haired Creole, the more acculturated among the Mestizo, and increasingly also some Maya, begin to see themselves as forming one group whereas the darker skinned and curlier haired Creole/Afro-Belizean and Garifuna consider themselves part of the other.

6. Economic Developments in the 20th and 21st Century

In the late 19th century a vehement decline of the forestry industry began to manifest itself, mainly as a result of the depletion of many mature commercial species of wood because of over-harvesting and unwise forest management. In the early 20th century North American demand for mahogany and chicle (gathered seasonally from the sapodilla tree, *Achras zapota)* led to a temporary revival of the industry, but with the falling of prices during the world wide depression in the 1930s and the development of a chemical substitute for chicle, forestry declined once more and has not recovered ever since. Most of all, the industry suffered from uneconomical production methods (even after the first sawmill was started in 1933), the old dependence on river transport during the rainy season (until well after 1950 a coherent road system was inexistent) and bad management.

Moreover, due to the fact that virtually no concern was given to reforestation, areas within easy reach had been depleted by then and soon it became too costly to penetrate further inland to extract the logs. In 1935, mahogany, cedar and chicle were still the major export commodities, making up 82% of total exports. But while production costs continued to rise, demand went down and prices started to drop. The days when the forestry industry provided the sole base for the colony's economy were definitely gone.

In order to overcome the economic crisis, which was intensified by a devastating hurricane in 1931, the colony, more than ever, began to undertake strong efforts to diversify its moribund economy by initiating several programmes to promote agriculture. Regardless of all these efforts, a severe internal crisis characterized by unemployment and food shortages developed. It had become apparent that as a consequence of British colonial rule, the following pattern had developed: Production of primary goods for external markets and a reliance on imported raw materials, consumer goods and technology had developed. Among the top priorities of the mid-1990s, apart from achieving self-government, was to gain greater economic independence and to become self-sufficient in food production. Out of this crisis, organized labour and with it the first nationalist movement evolved.

The 1960s and 1970s were a time of economic expansion with sugar being a primary export commodity, followed by citrus products, bananas and marine products. Rice, beans, and honey were also exported, earning much-needed foreign exchange while at the same time helping to make Belize more self-sufficient in food.

Belize's **sugar industry** began to expand very rapidly after the World War II and has been the single most important foreign exchange earner ever since. The sugar industry, as well as the citrus industry, developed with a strong impetus from colonial government policy. In 1964, the first sugar mill in Corozal in Northern Belize was taken over by a British transnational company, Tate and Lyle (now known as Belize Sugar Industries), who, by 1985, had withdrawn totally from the production side of the industry, only maintaining an interest in marketing.

Until 2000 Belize sold approximately 50% of its sugar production to preferential markets under a negotiated price above the market price (Lomé Convention, United States Sugar Quota) which protected the industry from price fluctuations on the world market. When the reform of the EU Sugar Regime came into effect in 2000, raw sugar prices were gradually reduced going up to a full 36% cut in 2010. The price cuts in raw sugar affected Belize's sugar export earnings heavily and had major socio-economic consequences for sugarcane farmers and workers in the Corozal and Orange Walk Districts. However, in the new Sugar Protocol under the Cotonou Partnership Agreement replacing the Lomé Convention, Belize was again given a fixed quota of sugar exports to the EU market on a preferential basis.

As to the **citrus industry**, although there has been a rapid expansion since 1945 with the activities of the Colonial Development Corporation in establishing new citrus groves, the industry is still suffering from production inefficiencies mainly because cultivation practices do not conform to current agricultural technology. As a consequence, the Belizean citrus industry remains fragile since citrus exports are, at times, severely affected by adverse weather conditions and by price fluctuations on the world market. **Orange and grape-**

fruit concentrates account for the major part of citrus products exported but orange and grapefruit oils, fresh fruit and fruit juices are also exported. From 1980 to 1992 the total production of citrus concentrate has more than tripled which can be traced to citrus concentrate from Belize having been granted duty free access into the United States in 1981.

The sugar and citrus industries have come to dominate agricultural production, both through production and manufacturing and the activities of the sugar factories and the citrus processors.[65]

Banana is the third major agricultural export crop. In 1985 the private sector took over the farms and made several investments to put an increased acreage under production and to improve productivity. In addition, improvement of local infrastructure and an increased usage of fertilizers by the private growers led to an additional planting and higher yields. In the two years after privatization took place, the exportation of bananas was more than doubled. Recovery from a disease in 1991 was quick and since then export volumes have been on the increase.

The marketing of bananas in Belize was completely taken over by the Fyffe's Group (an Irish subsidiary of the United Fruit Company, present Chiquita Brands International) with whom Belize has a long term contract. Up until 1992 the entire banana production was shipped to destinations in the UK. In Belize the commercial production of bananas is carried out at a higher cost than in competing Honduras and Costa Rica (Del Monte and Standard Fruit Company, now Dole Fruit Company). If it had not been for the preferential tariffs Belizean bananas enjoyed in the EU until 2000, Belizean bananas (and the same principle applies for citrus products and sugar) would have been placed at a competitive disadvantage because of higher production costs. After changes in the quota system were introduced in 2000, Belizean banana exports (just like Belizean sugar and citrus fruits exports) are now able to once more benefit from alternative preferential market arrangements.

The export of **marine products** has also become an important branch of Belize's economy. From 1980 to 1992 the value of exports nearly tripled and from then on fisheries production has been growing consistently. The necessary transactions for the exportation of marine products are carried out through several Belizean fishing co-operatives, which will be discussed more in detail in the following section. Prior to 1993, a large portion of foreign earnings from marine products came from the sale of frozen lobster tails but since

---

65 The two main citrus processors in Belize are the Citrus Company of Belize, whose major shareholder is the Cooperative Citrus Growers Association of Trinidad and Tobago and Belize Food Producers, a wholly owned subsidiary of Nestlé.

then, farmed shrimps have surpassed lobster tails as a foreign exchange earner, which reflects the increased production of several shrimp farms within Belize.

Apart from frozen farmed lobsters, lobster-tails and shrimps, frozen conch, whole cooked lobster, frozen whole fish (mostly red snapper), fish fillet, crab and also aquarium fish are exported. The potential for expansion of the fishing industry is high but whether or not enough concern will be given to wise management and to the protection of the environment remains to be seen. Overfishing in general, and especially pressures on lobster stocks, will continue to cause significant stress on the industry.

As far as **primary forestry products** are concerned, although more concern has been given to improve the management of existing stands, the extraction and exportation of primary forestry products played a decidedly minor role in the 20th century Belizean economy and continue to do so at present. Efforts to substitute the export of mahogany with secondary hardwoods (Santa Maria, *nargusta* and *ziricote)*, and to initiate the production of by-products (plywood and resin) have not been very successful. Nevertheless, exports, and with it pressure on the already much depleted forest reserves, are most likely to continue especially that, the Belizean government leased several new logging concessions on government land to foreign investors, for example a Malaysian logging company. Recently, there has been a resurgence in the export of forestry products. Reforestation and natural regeneration of existing pine stands and artificial regeneration of fast-growing hardwood species is in progress.

Up until the 1960s, tortoise-shell or *carey* (for the manufacture of a wide variety of items and inlays in furniture, musical instrument, spectacle frames etc.), alligator skins (for handbags and shoes) and shark-skin leather were included in the list of forest products exported.

Other traditional export commodities are (in order of the total value of exports) **molasses, papayas, cocoa beans, chicle, honey, pepper sauce, mangoes** and **mango concentrate** and **veneer sheets.** Papayas, mangoes and mango concentrate and homemade Sharp's pepper sauce are *new* exports of which there have been large increases due to the considerable emphasis that has recently been placed on the diversification of the agro-industries. Also a relatively new agricultural effort is the more intensive growing of cacao beans. Although the crop is native to Belize and was already grown by the Maya, commercial production of cacao is a relatively complicated and high cost venture. This is partly because there is a four year waiting period before crops bear fruit for the first time and that production in Belize is still a *milpa*-type operation. In short, in Belize, commercial production of cacao is not achieving its peak potential as yet. Cacao is cultivated in Southern Toledo mostly by Maya (Mopan and Q'eqchi') farmers.

Although agricultural production and other export sectors, such as the fishing industry and the introduction of a variety of new crops, have come to replace forestry as the base of Belize's economy, other sectors too have been successfully developed over the last decades.

Successful activities in the **industry sector** include several food processing industries, for example a sugar refinery in the north, citrus processing plants in the south, a number of fish-freezing and canning factories, as well as several export-orientated garment factories. The production of industrial goods for domestic consumption has also become relatively well established and will be discussed in connection with the development of a domestic market in the following section.

Another sector with great potential is the **service sector.** From 1986 to 1990, growth was very strong in the areas of telecommunication services, partly reflecting the expansion of domestic and offshore financial services, and the significant rise in incoming tourism. Tourism statistics for Belize indicate sustained increase of visitors. From 2001 to 2008 overnight stays have increased by 21% to 26%.[66] Tourism also led to a strong growth in "trade, restaurants and hotels", which has brought certain benefits to the population.

A relatively new facet of tourism is cruise tourism. It began in 2000 when the first cruise lines started to include Belize as a permanent port of call in their itineraries. Since Belize Harbour itself is too shallow for cruise ships to dock at the Belize City pier, ships have to drop anchor farther out, near English Cay about twelve nautical miles off Belize City or in the port of Dangriga, 58 km to the south. Although cruise arrivals began to decrease in 2004 (which was, among other reasons, due to adverse weather conditions in the hurricane season lasting from June until the end of October), cruise tourism today is considered to be an important and permanent part of Belize's tourism landscape.

In Belize, tourism is a valuable source for generating much-needed revenue and foreign exchange. Over the past years, the economy has shifted its focus towards tourism and eco-tourism as a potent sector to help boost national growth, despite the fact that income from tourism is not stable and will remain vulnerable and dependant on global economies. At present, the tourism and eco-tourism industry is thriving and has come to contribute more foreign exchange than trade.

Belize's economy took a new turn with the **discovery of oil**. Since the days when Belize was still a British colony numerous geology reports have indicated Belize's high potentials for oil. However, despite major oil companies having explored Southern and Central Belize for fifty years, diggings remained un-

---

66   Belize Tourism Board (BTB), Travel and Tourism Statistics 2008

successful until the Belize Natural Energy Company (BNE) announced an oil discovery in commercial quantities at the end of 2006.

Belize Natural Energy is a small pioneer company formed in 2002 by two Irish-born women and a Belizean engineer. After a new report had linked Belize's complex geology to the one of Mexico down through Guatemala and into Belize, oil was finally struck in the Yalbac Hill formation at the Mennonite community of Spanish Lookout (see Map 16) and in the Hill Bank formation further to the northeast.[67] In late 2010 production at ten Spanish Lookout wells was an average of 4,000 of high quality crude oil per day.

Although a large portion of Belize's territory and much of its offshore regions have been allocated out in petroleum concessions to eighteen different companies with a wide range of foreign shareholders, BNE remains Belize's only company producing and exporting oil. Crude oil is mainly shipped to Costa Rica, Panama and Texas but some is also transported overland to El Salvador. As far as drilling offshore is concerned, a movement has started questioning the government's offshore drilling concessions in the vicinity of the sensitive Barrier Reef.

As to the possible existence of ore deposits in Belize, for more than six decades geologists have insisted on the high **gold potentials** of the Maya Mountains in the south. In 2002 moderate quantities of gold were recovered. Since then several companies have been given gold exploration licences and from 2006 onwards three to four kilos of gold (fine course alluvial gold and small nuggets) were actually mined per month.[68] Large portions of the Maya Mountains, however, remain unexplored or under-explored. Among the major obstacles are: Limited road access, the difficult nature of the terrain, adverse seasonal climatic conditions and the high risk involved in investment to overcome these obstacles. In the 1970 and 1980s several mining companies also explored the Maya Mountains in the Cayo District for possible other precious metals. Based on optimistic and promising studies exploration licences have now been awarded to investigate the existence of silver, lead, tin and zinc deposits, none of which have been declared commercially viable as to date.

---

67 The Yalbac Hill formation is seen as an extension of the eastern margin of the Chiapas-Petén Basin, and the Hill Bank Formation may be the equivalent to the lowermost Cobán Formation and the San Ricardo in Guatemala.

68 See article in *Amandala* 10/5/2010
   The areas of the highest interest for gold as well as silver, lead, tin and zinc lies in an area of the Cayo District forming part of the region to which Guatemala has been staking claims. In this areas, for example in the Chiquibul Forest Reserve, incursions from Guatemalan farmers (*xatéros,* who illegally cut *xáte* palms) and the looting of archaeological artefacts have been a constant problem since the 1980s.

Having given an overview of the more recent economic development in Belize we may be able to summarize the following: Within six decades, the Belizean economy has been transformed from one entirely dependent upon the forestry industry (in 1950 forest products accounted for 85% of the value of total domestic exports and in 1994 for 3,5%, decreasing constantly ever since) to a reasonably diversified and continuously expanding agricultural economy. However, agriculture has not yet reached its full potential and additional agricultural development will be possible with more efficient production methods (i.e. more up to date technology) and by introducing new and revised policies concerning the agricultural utilization of larger tracts of arable land.

In what concerns the expansion of Belize's industry, the relative lack of infrastructure continues to be a major impediment for further industrial development. With an additional improvement of Belize's infrastructure and provided the government takes sufficient care in devising and implementing wise foreign investment schemes, further industrial expansion is likely to occur in the near future.

The economic growth of the 1960s through to the beginning of the 1980s was mostly achieved by increased exports of Belize's three main agricultural crops, sugar, citrus concentrates and bananas – which account for 80% of overall export earnings. After 1987, the Belizean export economy expanded sharply, as a result of a further increase in the citrus and banana industries, as well as a growth in the manufacturing sector of the economy, especially the textile and garment industry, and the construction industry. Belizean export markets are still protected by a number of preferential tariffs, which guarantee prices that are significantly higher than the normal market prices.

From the late 1980s onwards, the rise in incoming tourism accelerated economic growth. Both the boom in the tourism and eco-tourism industry and increased export activities have led to a growth in other service sectors, such as finance (banking, insurance) and telecommunications.

Efforts to diversify agriculture have been very successful thanks to the recovery in the production of traditional crops (citrus and bananas) and the introduction of new crops (papayas).

The exports of crude oil bolstered economic growth. In 2008 crude oil exports accounted for almost 60% of Belize's export earnings, but in 2009 export earnings from crude oil went down by one third again.[69] It remains to be seen whether the oil production rate remains consistent or can be increased and whether this would entail significant economic expansion in the long run. Fact is that oil findings have begun to transform the economy of Belize and there

---

69   Statistical Institute of Belize (SIB), Domestic Exports for 2008 and 2009

are still considerable recoverable oil reserves in the country. Despite these very promising trends, the economy of Belize is far from stable, remains vulnerable and is very sensitive to external developments.

6.1. Economic Development – Consequences for the Local Population

In Belize, the time of economic expansion began in the 1960s and lasted through to the 1980s. Responsible for this expansion was a sharp increase in agricultural exports and that it occurred at a time when the country was fully absorbed in the decolonization process. For the first time, Belize had to assume direct control over its public affairs and deal with a number of tasks in connection with the socio-economic development of the country.

In order to be able to assess the actual benefits of economic growth for the local population it is first necessary to touch on the initiatives the government took for development within Belize.

Apart from central government planning and an increased effort at integrating all parts of the country (for example by establishing six districts) to eliminate regional enclaves, among the state's top priorities were physical infrastructure, economic activities and social services.

Physical Infrastructure

The improvement of infrastructural conditions was one of the most important prerequisites for consolidating the country's economic base in order to help increase employment possibilities and ameliorate the socio-economic condition of the local population. The highest emphasis was given to the building of all-weather roads to those parts of the country which had been accessible previously only via waterways, i.e. the southern and the western regions of Belize. Plans to upgrade existing or to build new bridges and to improve and develop port and airport facilities have been realized. Efforts have also been undertaken to provide Belize with a more reliable power supply system, but, despite great achievements, this issue will remain a top priority for some time to come.

Economic Activities

Throughout the above mentioned period, the main objective was to increase yields for the export of sugar, citrus products and bananas as well as to revive the forestry industry. As a consequence, strategies were focused on the building of a base for the private sector. Since 1985, priority has been given to encouraging **foreign investment** and inviting multinational companies to invest in plantation lands and/or factories.

As already mentioned, the land use pattern in Belize was and is different to the other Central American countries. The availability of so much arable land without being cultivated, together with several fiscal advantages offered to private investors, represented (and still represents) a major incentive for investment in Belize. In addition, the government encouraged the formation of an industrial park (by providing factory shells) near the airport and granted logging concessions on leased government land. Rather than to continue promoting development through increasing the consumption capacity and living standards of its population, Belize has sought to lure investment with some of the lowest average wages in the Caribbean Community (CARICOM), which was possible because of the availability of cheap immigrant labour.

However, these attractive conditions did not bring in the anticipated investment. Many investors used the incentives and the possibility for foreign land ownership (prior to 1973 there was no limit to the amount of land non-Belizeans could own) not to start production, but for their own benefits, such as land speculation or tax evasion in their country of origin. After the time span of the fiscal incentives had lapsed, investors left the country abandoning the projects they had started. Such practices were not conducive to economic growth, leaving behind laid-off workers and environmental damage, caused by a lack of concern for reforestation as is the case with foreign logging companies. In some cases, the government itself was to be blamed for such investment failures.

Despite the attractions, only a relative small number of long standing developers have taken advantage of the aforementioned opportunities. Of the foreign investment that did take place, many were only on a short term basis. According to the investors, failures are due to the lack of infrastructure and the undeniable presence of corruption but also, most likely, to an over-optimistic approach. Generally speaking, the trickle-down effect of foreign investment has been relatively marginal, which is one of the reasons why it is so important for the government to commit itself to a responsible and careful handling of future foreign investment.

A far more successful government initiative evolved around the **development of a domestic market.** One of the most essential preconditions for the development of a domestic market was an increased purchasing power. This was mainly achieved through employment created in connection with an expansion of the export-orientated agro-industries. Several measures on the part of the government have facilitated the establishing of a domestic market, both for locally grown agricultural crops and locally produced industrial goods. These measures included repeated attempts at import-substitution by imposing high duties on imported goods and infrastructural improvements to increase internal marketing possibilities.

In the past, the production of crops for local consumption was highly neglected and far more attention was given to developing agriculture for export. As mentioned previously, only 15% of land suitable for agriculture (i.e. about 40% of a total of 23,000 sq. kilometres or 5,7 million acres) is currently under cultivation, but since the mid-1980s, the government has been more open to review its policy with regard to leasing land for agricultural purposes. An important fact here is that during the 1980s, three quarters of these 15% were cultivated by mechanized commercial farmers, whose crops were mostly directed for export. Only *one quarter* of these 15% was used for *milpa* and diversified farming for local consumption. Despite this very small proportion, its impact on the production of staples was considerable, since most agricultural products for national consumption were grown on this quarter alone.

With regard to the marketing of locally produced crops, several major drawbacks existed, although the Belize Marketing Board, a parastatal agency intended to facilitate the marketing for local consumption, was established as early as 1948. But in the end the emphasis given on improving the country's infrastructure, especially the building of reliable roads in remoter regions, has made a significant contribution to easing marketing difficulties. Especially for local farmers who have to rely on public transport, it became much easier to take their produce to market, either in provincial towns or Belize City, since better road conditions enabled buses to keep a daily and more reliable schedule throughout the year.

Belize has attained domestic self-sufficiency in the production of a limited number of the most important agricultural staples including corn, rice (although yields depend highly on the fluctuating quality of harvests), dry beans and plantains. All these staple crops are produced both by several small *milpa* farmers and on a large scale, by multinational companies and/or efficient Mennonite communities. Thanks to the farming enterprises of the Mennonites, Belize has also become self-sufficient in the production of poultry, eggs, fresh milk and cheese. For other agricultural produce, such as most vegetables (they are only available seasonally, on a "feast or famine" basis), the Belizean production methods are still inadequate.

The high quality of local produce, especially the aforementioned dairy products, at last has caused Belizeans to eliminate their prejudice against locally produced food, a prejudice the local merchant-elite had encouraged for more than two hundred years.

The development of a domestic market for locally produced industrial goods would hardly have taken place without the government's import substitution policies and the increased purchasing power of the population. Despite the productive capacity in the country itself still being relatively poor (making it necessary to continue to rely heavily on imports, especially crude materials, fuels, machinery and transport equipment) several local industrial plants have been very successful.

A boost for creating a stronger domestic market was the "Buy Belizean" campaign which, once an increased purchasing power had manifested itself, evolved out of the desire to form a stronger national identity, as mentioned. Several locally produced goods ("proud products of Belize") have been successfully marketed. For example, fertilizer and animal feed plants have been opened and numerous sawmills, a wire and nail plant, and a roofing-material plant have become indispensable and provide the construction and manufacturing industries with much-needed materials. Clothing, beer, rum and soft drinks are also produced for local consumption.

Social and Community Development

From the late 1950s onwards, colonial officers began to take decisive measures to improve social and community development. The major features were the starting of credit unions and co-operatives, the promotion of voluntary organizations (local staff with foreign volunteer help and non-government personnel) with an economic base for income generating. Since the late 1970s, the Belizean government has given further support to the above institutions.

When the government began to show more commitment to the promotion of health services, the rate of physicians and nurses increased. The degree to which health services have improved in Belize can also be seen in an increased number of reported cases of notifiable diseases. For example when reports now show unusually high increments of malaria, this is not because of an actual rise of malaria cases. Rather it clearly demonstrates that health services, especially in rural areas, have become more widespread and that more health personnel has been active to report cases to an increased number of health clinics, where treatment could be administered. Over the past decades, there has been a notable decrease in the rate of infant mortality (from over 5% per 1,000 in 1960, to 2,5 in 1980 to 2,2% in 2011, according to estimates).

Similarly, there has been a substantial increase in educational services available nationally, from the level of infant pre-school to that of the post-secondary. In 1991 national literacy rate was as high as 93% and equally distributed between men and women, a figure which was higher than the rest of Central

America (85% for male and 88% for female). In Belize, functional literacy rate changes from year to year, it is variously estimated at 77% to 94%, the lowest being in the Toledo District. The surge in demand for educational services required an increased number of teachers of which there is still a shortage.

Here, it is worth emphasizing that in Belize, only 13,5% of primary schools are run by the government. Within the past thirty years, the previous monopoly of the Roman Catholic Church has been undermined by the coming of a vast number of Protestant sects, which are especially active in rural areas. A large percentage of primary schools, although government-aided, are under the management of the Roman Catholic Church (approximately 55%) and the Anglican Church (approximately 10%). The rest is run by Adventist, Methodists and other Protestant groups (approximately 21%). With regard to secondary education, the government is much stronger represented. Of the country's 643 secondary schools, nearly one third is run by the government, another third by the Roman Catholic Church, 31 by Adventists, 26 by Anglicans and as many as 214 by other Protestant sects.

Strong attention has also been given to promote adult education. Several government-employed home economics officers have also offered classes in nutrition, sewing, food preservation and craft work, but they have only been successful to a limited degree.

After having mentioned the principal strategies of the government to initiate development within Belize, we shall now continue to take a closer look as to how exactly the local population was able to benefit from economic growth. In Belize, there is a remarkable concentration of the different ethnic groups in distinct parts of the country, a pattern which partly reflects the colonial policy to segregate each community by encouraging economic specialization according to alleged "racial aptitudes", as explained. Today, the Creoles tend to live in the Belize District, the Maya and East Indians in the Toledo District and the Mestizo in the Cayo, Corozal and Orange Walk Districts. Therefore, in each geographical region, the impact of economic growth on the population was different.

As far as the distribution of Belize's work force by occupation is concerned a strong shift has occurred towards the service sector. Whereas in 1994 and 1995 of a total work force of approximately 55,000 only 17,2% were employed in the service sector, estimates for 2011 state 71,7%.[70] The percentage of people

---

70 Here it has to be taken into consideration that in the censuses of the 1990s an "Other" sector still existed and it is not always clear which sectors are defined as "Other". Discrepancies in percentages are, most likely, also due to differences in defining that sector of the economy and the Service Sector.

working in the Agricultural Sector has gone down, from approximately 30% in 1992 to an estimated 10,2% in 2011. So has the percentage of the Industrial and Commercial Sector, from approximately 24% to 18%.

We shall now proceed by taking a closer look at the different sectors.

The Agricultural Sector

Over the past fifty years, the most successful agricultural crop has been **sugar**, grown exclusively in the northern part of Belize, in the Orange Walk and Corozal Districts. It is in this region that economic development has had a most notable trickle-down effect, leading to significant social changes.

From its very beginnings, the sugar industry was able to provide employment for a number of different people, from the farmer to the unskilled/semi-skilled worker and more skilled personnel. This was mainly due to the complexity of the sugar industry, which involves several steps i.e. production, processing and marketing. In response to the opportunities created by the development of the industry, from 1960 to the beginning of the 1990s the population in the Northern Districts has nearly tripled.[71]

At this point, it is worth emphasizing that with regard to industrial development, Belize differs from a number of other developing countries. In Belize, industrial development (more precisely the development of the sugar industry, which to this very day continues to be *the* most important industry in Belize) took place among residents of several small villages and two medium-sized towns and was not confined to large urban communities and their respective plantations nearby. Two major factors are responsible for this development: One, the small population of the country and two, the special requirements of the sugar industry, namely the fact that for logistical reasons, sugar factories should be located in rural areas, close to plantations, villages/towns and transportation systems.

What effects did the boom in the sugar industry, which lasted approximately from 1955 to 1985, have on the population residing in the Northern Districts?

First of all, the boom led to a more equal distribution of public participation in the sugar industry. During the 1960s and 1970s, as the rapid expansion of the sugar industry demanded more land, the government started to buy unused land from large land owners and leased it to small farmers. Between 1971 and 1982, the government had acquired approximately 212,500 hectares (525,000 acres) of land, most of which was leased to Mestizo and Maya

---

71   Abstract of Statistics (1994: 10), Central Statistical Office, Belmopan

cañeros (sugar cane farmers). In addition, the BSI (British Sugar Industries, a multinational corporation evolving out of the British firm Tate & Lyle, the first company to produce sugar on a large scale in 1963), who by that time had experienced heavy losses, divested 2,550 hectares (6,317 acres) of land under mechanized cultivation to *cañeros* and company workers.

Apart from the aforementioned interventions, the government established several funds to protect the cane farmers and provided additional services, for example research support services (chemicals etc.), granting credits at the beginning of each season and loans for houses. Since most of the lands leased to *cañeros* and company workers were the remoter tracts, the government built roads to provide access and provided bulldozers and tractors on a rental basis to clear the land.

When a second factory started operations in 1967, the entire northern part of the country was brought under the influence of the sugar industry and more opportunities were opened for the second group actively involved in the industry, the one employed in processing. The rise of the sugar industry led to fundamental changes in the socio-economic structure of the inhabitants in the north. As we shall see, these changes were not only notable within the region but also in the interactions of the inhabitants with the rest of the Belizean population. The effects of the sugar industry soon began to spread to Belize City.

The necessity to transport sugar and molasses to Belize City harbour created employment in transport, storage and handling, and marine services. Moreover, certain "farmers", especially the ones residing in Corozal and Orange Walk towns, began to realize their potential strength in national politics frequently sending delegations from the north to Belize City. This encouraged local politicians from the north to become actively involved in Belizean politics, eventually increasing their presence at the national level of the House of Representatives.

Now that land was made available to cultivate, the inhabitants of communities which previously relied on *milpa* subsistence agriculture, part time wage labour in the timber industry, or in the bleeding of chicle became cane farmers with steady annual income. Until today, sugar remains a small holder crop: By the mid-1990s, only approximately 5,000 independent cane farmers existed. They sell the largest part of their crop to the Belize Sugar Industries for processing into molasses and crystallized sugar, both for export. The remaining crop is utilized for molasses, which is delivered to Cuello's distillery nearby for the production of good quality rum, mostly for local consumption.

There is no doubt that the early years of sugar cultivation brought economic benefits to the entire population in the Northern Districts. However, for the Maya, especially for those in more remote villages, the repercussions of the introduction of cash into the community had complex and far reaching socio-economic consequences. One effect of the coming of the cash economy to rural villages was that inevitably, it accelerated the change from *milpa* subsistence economy to commercial sugar cane production. This deprived the Maya and Mestizo of several cultural elements associated with *milpa* farming which, in turn, endangered the communities' self-sufficiency associated with food. Another effect was that the introduction of cash began to tear apart ancient structures. For example, rank and social status no longer depended solely on wisdom and leadership qualities through advanced age, knowledge of Maya rituals, customs or traditional medicines. Instead, wealth (and the accompanying purchasing power) began to function as another, albeit dubious, index of rank.

On the other hand, for those "Spanish" (Mestizo) farmers who moved to Corozal and Orange Walk towns, greater possibilities existed because they were more flexible to adapt to the various requirements of the industry. Rather than work their fields themselves, they employed workers to tend their fields outside town and started to engage in the marketing side of the sugar industry. Soon they had enough influence to succeed in obtaining an increase in the amount of sugar (quota) they were allowed to deliver per season. They quickly accumulated moderate fortunes, making it more difficult for smaller farmers to increase their participation in the industry. The Mestizos' interest in business, in general, facilitated their entry into commerce. They began to dedicate themselves exclusively to trade and gradually, the Northern Districts developed into an important commercial centre, especially Corozal Town which is a border town. There the ex-*cañeros,* and now traders were very well positioned to engage in import-export trade on a more professional basis and to profit from entrepôt trade with Mexico. This occurred at a time when the metropolitan merchants and the local merchant elite in Belize City was still in complete control of the entire, and almost exclusively import-orientated, trade.

The growing of the two other agricultural export crops, **banana** and **citrus** has not had such a profound economic impact on the population. First, there was less demand for banana and citrus growers and workers were fewer in numbers. Secondly, they did not start at such a low economic level as the cane farmers. The workers who were engaged in the handling of bananas for export and in the processing of citrus fruits into concentrates and canning were able to carry out their work in or near urban areas (Belize City) where there was always a surplus of labour supply. This resulted in lower wages, especially in comparison to those received by the workers employed in the sugar industry. In addition, the fact that adverse climatic conditions in the south – heavy rains, storms, droughts etc. – make banana and citrus harvests more susceptible to fluctuations, has also influenced the composition of the work force. Workers are only employed according to demand and not on a regular basis.

Thirdly, there is one more important reason why the reasonably successful development of the banana and citrus industries has brought less direct economic benefits to the Belizean population. The exceedingly high proportion of Central American immigrants among the workers has led to increased competition and, as a consequence, tension between native Belizean workers and immigrant workers, as discussed previously. According to a survey done in 1993,[72] of the nearly 1,400 field workers employed on twenty two of the country's twenty three commercial banana farms, 93% were "Spanish", either meanwhile naturalized Belizeans, mostly undocumented immigrants, or workers who only crossed the border for the season. The living conditions of the immigrant workers who mostly lived in closely-cramped and inadequately ventilated huts in midst the banana plantations were generally poor. Their wages varied according to nationality.[73] On the citrus groves, the percentage of Central American workers was not as high (56%). Working and living conditions were less repressive, but otherwise the situation was and still is somewhat similar.

The changing structure of the work force in the banana and citrus industries has had far reaching socio-economic consequences for Belizean workers. Eager to secure inexpensive and more easily controlled labour, the owners and managers of the banana and citrus plantations have shown a strong tendency to lay off unionized Belizean workers and consciously used immigrants to displace native Belizeans and undermine their unions. This was a heavy blow to the achievements of the United General Workers' Union for the availability of cheap and easily controlled labour has led to the displacement of unionized Belizean workers. As a result, unemployment among Belizean workers and out-emigration of dissatisfied Belizeans (Creoles and Garinagu) has risen considerably since the mid-1980s.

Having examined the situation of the country's agricultural work force, the following conclusions may be drawn: In the Northern Districts, the government has actively sponsored the sugar industry by granting several incentives to BSI (Tate & Lyle respectively) and by supporting the independent sugar cane farmers and/or their workers. In the south the potential of the banana and citrus industry was never as great to start with and the government was far less

---

72   Cf. Moberg (1994)

73   While Salvadoreans, who, due to the fact that they were the ones least willing to return home on a voluntary basis, were given the lowest paying jobs, earning approximately BZ$ 250 (US$ 125) per month, Guatemalans earned BZ$ 300, and Hondurans BZ$ 320. In contrast, native Belizean fieldworkers earned an average of BZ$ 370 per month.

supportive. In addition, from the 1980s onwards, an extremely liberal immigration policy led to a significant change in the composition of the work force in the banana and citrus industries, which was much to the disadvantage of native Belizean workers in the field and in the factories.

In sum and as the above clearly demonstrates, the government has not supported the workers in the banana and the citrus industry (including factory workers in and around Belize City engaged in the processing of citrus fruits into concentrates) to the same degree as the cane farmers in the north. As we have seen, in the long run, this strategy led to a primacy of rural over urban areas, ultimately culminating in the economic dominance of one region – the north – over the rest of the country.

The Industrial and Commercial Sector

In this sector, it is the **fishing industry**, or more exactly, certain developments within this industry that have had the most long-lasting effect on the country's population. Commercial fishing for export started in the 1920s, when a Canadian businessman started canning lobster for export. Prior to this date, fishing (with the exception of the colonial turtle industry from the 18th until the beginning of the 20th centuries) was done mostly for subsistence or for sale within the local economy. Similar to the other extractive industry, forestry (which dominated the economy of Belize until the 1950s), commercial fishing, from the first exportation of live turtles onwards, grew in importance on the basis of demands created by Europe and North America.

By the 1950s, a number of foreign buyers had begun to operate processing factories in Belize City, much to the disadvantage of the local fishermen who received only a small percentage of the profits. Out of this situation, the co-operative system, which the colonial government and a Catholic mission helped to establish, began to evolve. In the 1960s, by no longer giving export quotas to individuals and only to co-operatives, the government limited the exploitive practices of individual foreigners, in the long term an effective means of by-passing the foreign middle man.

In many communities, fishing is still done as a main form of livelihood and in some coastal areas and on the cays, it is the back bone of the economy. To this very day, commercial fishing remains essentially a type of group activity in both urban and rural areas. With the exception of Ambergris Cay, it is mostly undertaken by Creoles and Garinagu. Despite co-operatives being in charge of the production process, and thereby also being in control of the group's welfare, the role of the small fisherman continues to be very important. And it is the small fisherman who – via the co-operative system – actually benefits from an increase in the export of frozen fish, lobster, conch and shrimps.

Today several major co-operatives and also a number of smaller and fragmented groups of fishermen exist, the members of which are mostly subsistence fishermen. Among the services rendered to the fishermen and workers are the granting of credits, the supply of boats, outboard motors and other equipment, mostly on a rental basis. Fishing co-operatives have become very successful, especially because they also assist with marketing (filleting, conservation, deep-freezing, packaging, labelling). By supporting the fishing co-operatives, the government has participated a great deal to guarantee that the benefits gained from commercial fishing should remain within the hands of Belizean fishermen.

Over the past decades, constraints on the fishing industry have begun to manifest. In order to reduce these constraints, it would be high time to implement more effective measures to regulate commercial fishing and to ensure the enforcement of laws introduced to enable an adequate protection of maritime resources (for example laws to observe the seasons for lobster fishing), and to encourage a wise handling of the recreational use of the sea. More recently, several actions taken on the part of the government, especially the introduction of new policies on the issue of shrimp and lobster farming, have caused significant upheaval and have given rise to much discontent among commercial fishermen. Interested in financial input, the government has, for example, agreed to allow Taiwanese investors to farm small lobsters by changing the size limit on lobsters. In addition, the farms were also allowed to have lobsters during the closed season, a concession clearly to the disadvantage of local fishermen. The full impact these developments may have on local fishing co-operatives remains yet to be seen.

Other branches of the Belizean industry, such as several small textile and garment industrial plants around Belize City, and the boom in the construction industry strongly interrelated with the expanding tourism industry, have also been successful in creating employment. Especially the construction industry has opened new opportunities for skilled and semi-skilled craftsmen, a profession especially found among Mestizo Belizeans, the "Spanish".

The garment industry, i.e. factories which are usually tied to multi-national corporations has also seen a recent upswing. This branch of the industry provides employment for a large number of women who sew clothes for the export market. For example by 1993, the approximately eleven garment companies in Belize employed close to 1,500 people, of which almost 93% were women.[74]

74　Abstract of Statistics, Belize – External Trade 1980–1992, p.20, Central Statistical Office, Belmopan

Given that the garment industry employs an exceptionally high number of women, I would like to briefly touch upon the role women play in the work force of Belize. A large percentage is, in fact, not classified as working, with many women engaging in informal food vending and petty trading. Together with other unrecorded economic activities of women, craft production and the provision of services such as child-minding, laundry and cooking, it becomes clear that women comprise most of the informal sector of the economy. Apart from manual workers in the export-orientated industries, other female-dominated occupations are nurses, teachers, social workers, clerical workers, secretaries, bookkeepers, domestics in private homes, shop assistants, waitresses in restaurants, personnel in hotels, workers in tourism-related activities etc. Especially for the latter three, the rising tourism industry is continuously creating more demand.

The commercial sector has equally experienced considerable expansion. At present, four major supermarkets exist in Belize City. Over the past two or three decades, Chinese, East Indians and Lebanese have successfully entered in economic niches by opening small retail and souvenir shops not only in Belize City, but also increasingly in rural areas throughout the country.

The Service Sector

From the mid-1980s onwards, a significant increase in the service sector has taken place. Economic growth and development within Belize, the boom in the tourism and eco-tourism industry, and the increased presence of North American expatriates led to an expansion of the banking sector (domestic and offshore financial services, insurances), which, in turn, caused a growth in the area of telecommunication and transport services. This rise of the service sector constituted a significant contribution to increasing domestic employment and national income.

The tourist sector is the most labour-intensive service sector (hotel and restaurant staff, independent tourist guides, tour operators and their personnel) and therefore capable of providing several additional opportunities for both the unemployed or underemployed. Owing to the fact that tourism is characterized by strong backward (or supply) linkages, it is connected with other labour-intensive sectors of the economy. For example, this is very notable in the rise of construction trades (carpenters, plumbers etc.), the souvenir and handicrafts trade, the increased possibilities for skilled or semi-skilled manual workers (craftsmen, people who thatch tourist *cabañas*, gardeners). Other backward linkages of tourism are fisheries (fishermen increasingly deliver directly to hotels) and agriculture although, with locally produced food it is at times very difficult to meet quality standards tourists expect.

Within this context it must be mentioned that a further expansion of the tourism industry, or even maintaining the standards of present tourist services, will require additional infrastructural improvements, which, in turn, will create more employment opportunities. Apart from making more jobs available, several indirect benefits accrue through an improvement of domestic infrastructure. For example upgraded roads will have a positive effect on the domestic economy by enabling the transportation of containers and heavy machinery from port facilities in Belize City and Chetumal in Mexico, the nearest deep sea port. Better road conditions will also be for the benefit of the average Belizean, since they make it easier for public transport buses to keep a more reliable schedule throughout the year. This will also be of advantage to the local farmers to take their produce to market. Even so, criticism has been voiced as to the actual direct spill-over effect of the required, tourism-related, infrastructural improvements on the local economy and the local population.

The government is another sector providing employment. The aforementioned strategies on the part of the government to initiate development within Belize, created several new government jobs within the state apparatus (judiciary staff, police force, administrative personnel, managers and rangers for the various conservation areas, teachers, advisory personnel). Moreover, additional funds allocated to improve medical services led to an increased presence of health personnel throughout the country.

Until the 1990s a large percentage of government jobs (or those related to the government) in Belize City and Belmopan were held by Creoles. Since then, the presence of Mestizos has been constantly rising which is mainly for the reason that government jobs usually are the only possibility for Mestizo graduates, who have, so far, shown less tendency to consider out-migration as a viable option. A large number of Mestizos who work in Belize City (either in government institutions or elsewhere), in fact do not live in Belize City, still the home for a vast majority of Creoles. Many Mestizos prefer to commute daily to the Orange Walk District, where there is reportedly less crime and where they can enjoy a more comfortable standard of living. In the north housing characteristics are generally high and many have succeeded in building their own houses on family plots. In Belize City, in contrast, not only is the crime rate very high, but it would also be very difficult for them to encounter adequate housing. In Belize City and its immediate surroundings, land for construction has become extremely scarce and plots on land reclaimed from mangrove swamps (this business has become very lucrative and is mostly in the hands of foreigners) are usually beyond the reach of the average Belizean.

Finally, in order to examine how other geographical regions were affected by economic development within Belize, we shall take a brief look at the more isolated communities along the coastal plain and inland, in rural Toledo.

The coastal plain, i.e. the coast south of Belize City including the towns of Dangriga and Punta Gorda, is a thin strip extending inland for a maximum distance of approximately three kilometres, fragmented by the estuaries of several rivers and covered mostly by mangroves. Historically seen, these areas served as the site for the cutting of logwood and later as points for river traffic for mahogany logs and other hardwood. From the late 1950s onwards, when economic development shifted further inland toward agro-industries and with the building of roads to provide access to inland regions, the coastal plain began to lose much of its former economic importance. Until the 1920s, the southernmost villages of Belize were close to economic self-sufficiency. The mostly Garifuna inhabitants of Barranco near the Guatemalan border, for example, produced their own staples and sold their surplus to Belize City and across the border. Several attempts at commercial agriculture (banana in the 1930s and rice in the 1950s) proved to be a failure, mostly because of the inability of the government (the Marketing Board) to provide the necessary support.

But these modest attempts at commercial agriculture had already introduced the lure of cash-cropping into southern communities. As villages began to lose their economic base, people (especially young men) began to leave the villages and Punta Gorda Town. They either left the country or moved northwards to Orange Walk and Corozal Districts, where the rapidly developing and government-subsidized sugar industry had a high demand of labour. Others took up teaching and equally left the villages.

Contrary to the developments in the north, the Southern Districts have shown negligible growth in population between 1960 and 1980. In short, the socio-economy of coastal villages, and to a certain degree also of the district town of Punta Gorda, was largely dependent on migration, remittances from abroad and initiatives from the state. Compared to the abundance of support given to the cane farmers in the north from the 1960s onwards, the government gave much less attention to the isolated coastal communities in the south. More recently emphasis has been given to both, integrating all parts of the country and central planning, with newly established credit unions and village councils channelling subsidies.

Today, at first sight, it would seem that subsistence economy (fishing) would be dominant in the smaller villages along the coast, but this is not so. As is for example the case with Barranco, it relies almost exclusively on cash economy. To a large degree, cash is generated from villagers themselves and enters the village economy through several mixed sources, such as the selling of fish, petty trading of homemade food and cassava bread, handicrafts and the performing of odd jobs. Cash from outside comes mostly through periodic wage labour and cash remittances from abroad.

In the Toledo District, inland regions are mostly populated by Mopan and Q'eqchi' Maya. As mentioned, these isolated Maya communities were and are more inwardly orientated, in the sense that migration has hardly taken place and that they have never relied on cash remittances from abroad or other parts of Belize. However, over the past thirty years, an increasing number of Maya have left their villages to work as teachers or have migrated as a whole family to towns or villages closer to roads.

In these isolated villages, the Maya's centuries-old tradition constitutes the supporting pillar of their socio-economy. Especially among the Q'eqchi' Maya, *milpa* or slash-and-burn agriculture is still the method of food production and cash cropping. The main cash crops sold to the Marketing Board in Belize City are rice and beans and it is thanks to these agricultural activities of the (mostly) Maya population that Belize has become almost self-sufficient in these two crops.

In addition, several items are sold in the local markets: Plantains, cassava, root crops, and squash, all planted on plots suitable for intercropping, as well as citrus and other fruits. The slash-and-burn system of land use is very extensive and has always been prone to criticism. Theoretically, in the Toledo District there are still large tracts of land (the former Crown land) available to the population, mainly because the reserve system the government established for the Maya, contrary to other parts of the country, has prevented speculation on land. Since the system was first introduced in 1924, the government has allocated land adjoining each village for *milpa* cultivation. The head of each household pays a minimal fee per year to the government for usufructuary use of the plot. Despite recent expansions, the reserve system has become inadequate, especially that over the last thirty years, the population in rural Toledo has been on the increase. As villagers begin to use land reserved for neighbouring villages, inter-communal conflicts are unavoidable.[75]

---

75 More recently, another factor has contributed to increasing tension among villages themselves and also between different villages. Within the past forty years, a vast number of Protestant sects have taken advantage of this regional enclave neglected by the government and have completely undermined the previous monopoly of the Catholic Church in the Toledo District. By the 1980s, these sects were so firmly established that they were competing among themselves for peoples' attention. Although they provide some basic material benefits to their followers and offer classes for several professions (craftsmen, artisans etc.), they tend to perpetuate sectarianism which increases tension among villages.

Government initiatives on developments in rural Toledo (and rural Belize on the whole) evolved mainly around improving services of the Marketing Board. Most of the corn, rice, and beans produced are sold via this state agency, indirectly managed by the government to buy grain from the farmers and re-distribute it throughout the country. From the perspective of the Maya, the Marketing Board does not provide them with enough services. Apart from the fact that the price paid for grains is government-controlled and underpaid, on several occasions the Marketing Board has had difficulties to meet payments for grain already received. In rural Toledo only a few successful marketing companies (co-operatives) and credit unions have been established.

The building of roads to remote parts of the Toledo District, while indi-rectly threatening the cultural survival of the Maya, has, on the other hand ex-tended economic possibilities. As soon as the road system reaches a village, the process of socio-economic transformation starts. Rice and beans are planted for cash sale, trips to Punta Gorda (the nearest coastal town) to sell these prod-ucts as well as pigs, increase, a truck is acquired, adequately stocked shops are opened in the villages, western-style houses appear etc.

Nevertheless, the standard of living in these remote Maya (mostly Q'eqchi') villages remains relatively low. Despite the fact that several projects having been undertaken by a variety of funding sources to promote additional au-tonomous economic activities (honey-production, pig-raising and marketing, craft-production, cacao-farming),[76] general health care and sanitation, there is yet much room for improvement. In the longer term, these projects have not been as successful as expected, due to the existence of several obstacles. For example, the paternalistic relationship between the government and the Maya, has led many to believe that the government owes them assistance, an attitude which may have negative consequences for the Maya in the years to come.

According to several studies undertaken in rural Toledo, when the outside impetus is taken away, the activities in connection with the aforementioned pro-jects from outside usually slow down and eventually come to a standstill, a phe-nomenon not uncommon among other communities in similar circumstances.

Last but not least, for Belize's Maya populations, several benefits may ac-crue through the successful development of the tourism industry, and in par-ticular, efforts to further develop another niche of tourism, archaeo-tourism.

---

76 For example, in the late 1980s, some Q'eqchi' farmers started to plant cacao beans under organic conditions. The output of these plantations is bought on long term contracts at a fair price by an English chocolate manufacturing company, whose production range includes chocolate with the brand name of "Maya Gold" (the name refers to cacao beans having one been currency for the Maya).

These new strategies, the *"Mundo Maya Project"* for example may, together with a certain scientific revival in Maya topics as such, have a positive effect on the Maya populations of Belize. Not only may a wise and successful pursuing of these new strategies be helpful to the Maya's search for a new identity, but also boost economic activities within communities, such as handicraft production, the setting up and managing of heritage centres, the making and selling of typical Maya food, the preparation and marketing of traditional medicine etc.

After having carefully examined the impact, economic growth and development in Belize had on the population, we may now be able to summarize the following:

The expansion of export-orientated agro-industries from the 1960s onwards, helped to create employment which, in turn, incremented national income. Once an increased purchasing power of the population was achieved, several government initiatives, such as repeated attempts at import substitution and infrastructural improvements to facilitate marketing, led to the successful development of a domestic market, both for locally grown agricultural crops and locally produced industrial goods.

In the industrial sector, the establishment of fishing co-operatives has been very successful. Via the co-operative system, it was possible to by-pass the foreign middle man and it is now the average Belizean fisherman, who is able to reap the benefits from the recent increase in the export of frozen marine products.

Several industrial plants have also been set up locally, creating additional employment possibilities. However, although the government took several measures to offer attractive investment conditions, foreign investment in Belize has entailed only modest economic growth with the spill-over effect on the local population being moderate.

The development of the country's most important industry, the sugar industry, took place among residents of several small villages and two medium-sized towns. In Belize, industrial development was not confined to large urban communities since factories, which for logistical reasons had to be close to plantations, required their personnel to reside nearby. The sugar industry created its own communities which do not fit accurately into the rural/urban dichotomy.

Generally speaking, the government has centred its support on the successfully expanding sugar industry in the country's north, and it is there, that economic growth has had the most obvious and long-lasting effect on the population. The abundance of government support in the Northern Districts, especially in comparison to other areas and Belize's other agro-industries, in the long run, resulted in the dominance of one region – the north – over the rest of the country.

Together with tourism, agriculture continues to be an important sector in Belize's economy. Therefore, a key issue for Belize remains the expansion of the diversification efforts of its agricultural production, along with the consolidation and development of the service sector, especially by committing itself to a responsible promotion of sensible and, at the same time, environmentally-minded tourism.

6.2. The Role of Tourism in Belize

From the post-World War II era onwards, the importance of tourism as an element of international trade has been continuously on the rise worldwide and in many countries, the demand for travel is growing much faster than that for the export of merchandize. Especially in developing countries which have come to regard international tourism as a panacea for chronic trade deficits, the growth of tourism has led to a strong stimulation of the development of the tourist industry. Many of these countries are able to "export" natural beauties more effectively than manufactured foods and other products, even agricultural produce.

In Belize, in the three years after independence (from 1981 to 1984), the then ruling PUP party was inclined to neglect the development of tourism by showing more concern for creating a sense of national identity and the fostering and the implementation of import substitution policies with the ultimate goal to reduce imports. In 1984, a change of government occurred and the UDP, being sufficiently content with the degree of national identity meanwhile established, began to redirect its efforts to the promotion of both the export and the tourism sector. To boost economic growth in general, the UDP designated tourism as its second-highest development priority after agriculture (prior to 1984, tourism was number seven in the list of priorities). Since then, tourism has become the fastest growing branch of the Belizean economy and its potential role for the country's current and long term economic development strategies is significant.

The development of the tourism industry in Belize not only seems to be a fast and effective remedy for chronic trade deficits and a relatively easy way of generating foreign exchange and economic growth (by indirectly providing additional opportunity for the diversification of agriculture), but it also helps increase domestic employment and national income. Nevertheless, the potential dangers of tourism are very much present in Belize and have become clearly visible by now.

Since the early 1970s, considerable criticism has been voiced as to whether tourism-led development would indeed be the most effective measure for stimulating economic growth. The unavoidable importance of the tourist industry for Belize's development has made local and foreign economists become aware of the dangers of the growing dependency on the tourism "mono-crop".

In this context, much concern has become loud, not just in Belize, but in any other country in the same situation. Some critics fervently support the position that tourism may, in fact, set in motion a mechanism for reinforcing and/or perpetuating the patterns created during colonial rule: Exploitation, dependence and international inequity. Others ask themselves to what extent tourism *really* contributes to the national economies and call into question the net economic benefits of tourism-led development, i.e. especially in terms of additional costs in comparison to actual returns. The latter believe that in many countries, economic costs associated with the development of tourism outweigh the actual benefits of tourism being given development priority. They argue that large amounts of capital have to be redirected and invested to up-grade basic facilities and services, and not enough emphasis is given to prepar-ing specific cost-benefit analyses.

Although the direct spill-over effect of the required infrastructural improve-ments on the local economy does not always live up to the expectations of econ-omists and politicians, the above criticism generally tends to ignore the indirect benefits accruing to the population. In the case of Belize, an improvement of domestic infrastructure, including basic infrastructural changes (reliable all-weather roads, better airport facilities, an advanced telecommunications system), is not only essential for maintaining the existing standard of tourist services and a further expansion of the industry, but it also serves to consolidate the country's very own economic base. In Belize, policy makers and a large percentage of the public seem to be quite happy accepting that "dependence on tourism is an una-voidable fact of life" and Belize must "either fall in line or fade out."[77]

However, it cannot be denied that the rapid tourist development has re-sulted in severe environmental strain: It is inevitable that tourist-development projects interfere with Belize's environment and in some cases additional tour-ist accommodations in unspoilt areas have had negative effects on the nation's wildlife.[78]

On the other hand, the fact that most areas designated for further tourist development lack the necessary infrastructure may, for the time being, also act

---

77   Cf. Poon (1993)

78   For example one of the many species suffering from newly built hotels and lodges on re-mote beaches are turtles: During the nesting season, turtles show a strong tendency to return to the same beaches at night to lay their eggs. The strong illumination of tourist accommodations on previously deserted beaches greatly disturbs these endangered an-imals. As a consequence, they become very prone to losing their sense of direction and are no longer able to find their way back to the sea.

in favour of the environment. For example high-tech installations needed to ensure sufficient fresh water supply and provide an adequate sewage system would have to be made and maintained to fulfil the required standards, which would be far too cost-intensive. several projects had to be postponed indefinitely and some of the already existing hotels on remote and unspoilt beaches even had to close down.

While Belize's profile as an (as yet) unspoiled tourist destination is elevated in North America and Europe, Belize's major tourist centre, Ambergris Cay is undergoing an impressively rapid tourist development. The heavy concentration of hotels and tourist activities in San Pedro and its surroundings, a small and ecologically fragile area has caused significant environmental and social strain.

With San Pedro serving as an example, policy makers have become aware of the potential dangers of concentrated tourist development in small areas of the country. During the late 1980s, a re-definition and re-structuring of tourism began to take place. Since then, there has been a definite shift in emphasis towards eco-tourism and archaeo-tourism (the latter through Belizean participation in *"El Mundo Maya"*, a plan to link the major Maya sites of Yucatán, Guatemala, Western Honduras and Belize in a multi-country tourist circuit). Until the early 1980s, the Belizean tourism industry was focused on marine-based activities (diving, snorkelling, deep-sea fishing) along the barrier reef, resulting in a lack of suitable hotel accommodations in the interior. In order to succeed in the effort to re-structure tourism in Belize, more attention was given to the interior, in terms of marketing and investing in National Parks and Maya archaeological sites and an expansion of acceptable and more geographically dispersed tourist accommodations and tourist centres.

From 2000 onwards the cruise sector in Belize has come to play an important role for the Belizean tourism industry. The cruise sector contributes to total tourism expenditure and has a domino effect on the entire economy.

Although cruise arrivals have decreased from 2004 onwards, with more and larger ships being built, Belize may have to take a very cautious approach to the welcoming of cruise ships. Several studies have been made to assess the terrestrial impacts – economic, social and environmental – of cruise tourism. Among the many complaints are: The controversial off-loading practices of waste from cruise liners, the little revenue generated from passenger's expenditure, the relative little spill-over effect for locals (limited supplies of goods and services from local Belize suppliers) and the fact that cruise tourism is competing with, and in many instances even colliding with, conventional tourism, especially eco-tourism.

Belize has to be very wary that its tourism motto "Nature's best kept Secret" and its strategy of promoting responsible tourism ensuring socio-cultural and environmental sustainability may not be seriously challenged by an increased number of cruise ship calls. In fact, with too many cruise passengers, Belize would be "killing the golden goose of eco-tourism"[79], especially when eco-tourists have recently began to voice complaints that the infrastructure and quality of their eco-tourism experience is suffering. Critics have also pointed out that an average stay-over visitor spends more than twice as much per day as the average cruise passenger whose spending is concentrated in the vicinity of the port and Belize City. By contrast, stay-over tourism is spread throughout the country generating a far greater trickle-down effect for the local population. Moreover, although promotional coupons are given to cruise passengers offering discounts for future visits to Belize, only a small number return to Belize as a stay over tourist.

In sum, stay-over visitors are believed to have less negative environmental and social impact on Belize. Despite the positive contributions of cruise tourism, it may be advisable to take adequate measures to mitigate the negative impacts from the cruise industry in order to protect Belize's important stay over market. After all, the benefits of cruise tourism might only be temporary, whereas those of conventional tourism are bound to be of a more permanent nature. One solution would be to "protect" Belize's most valued and valuable eco-systems on the Barrier Reef and the interior by literally "separating" cruise and stay over tourists, offering a limited number of excursions to certain areas of interest, providing access to a limited – and realistic – number of cruise passengers only. Belize has earned an international reputation for its pristine and "unspoilt" tourist attractions – its coral reef, national parks, and archaeological sites – and it would be unwise taking the risk of losing its potent conventional tourist and eco-tourist clientele, which, no doubt, would happen if permanent damage to national tourism assets was to occur.

Therefore, it is imperative to find appropriate, economically, environmentally and socially sustainable, strategies and implement policies that may, in the long run, result in an optimal blend of cruise tourism and stay over tourism guaranteeing only minimal interference.

In Belize, in order to mitigate the negative social and environmental impacts of concentrated tourist development in small areas (as around San Pedro on Ambergris Cay or in Cancún further up the coast in Yucatán), policy makers have tried to redefine tourism as an economic strategy that may be able to preserve, rather than destroy, the country's environmental assets. However, it will prove to be very difficult to completely isolate alternative forms of tourism from the tourism industry as such. An expansion of the tourism industry (be

---

79   Dickerson, M. "The Curse of Daytrippers", *Los Angeles Times* (2006, April 1st)

it alternative or conventional forms of tourism) always requires additional imported goods and foods to keep up quality standards that tourists expect.

Let us leave aside for a moment the urgent need to minimize the negative impacts the rapidly growing tourist industry may cause on the environment and turn to a very hot and pending topic: Over the past couple of years it has become alarmingly apparent that strains of a very different nature are exerting an enormous amount of pressure. Only that, this time, it is not on the environment but on the country as a whole; namely the dramatically rising crime.

High crime rates in Belize constitute an ever growing and continuing problem for the Belizean public, tourists, and Belize security and law enforcement. From 2011 to 2012 alone the murder rate went up by more than 10%. Gang violence is widespread, especially on the south side of Belize City but also in the Northern and Western Districts.

It is a sad fact that tourist destinations are no longer spared from acts of crime. Credit card fraud rings are reported to be active and there have also been complaints of tourists being seduced to purchase drugs and then "set-up" for arrest and the payment of large sums of money. Unfortunately, the ability of the authorities to respond to and prevent crime is restricted.

Apart from organized gang activity, the drug trade is also a significant criminal problem. Belize's geographical position makes it an ideal transit country for organized drug crime. Due to the fact that drug traffic rings (*los narcos*) have long set up their operational base in the neighbouring Petén region of Guatemala, it will be very difficult for Belize, especially taking into consideration its limited resources, not to be drawn into these criminal activities one way or another.

Needless to say, these disquieting developments are anything but conducive to perpetuating the image of Belize being an unspoilt and safe tourist destiny. In any case, this recent issue might pose a serious enough threat to throw the thriving and prosperous tourist industry off balance.

Instead of getting entangled in such gloomy thoughts we had better return to our critical assessment of tourism in Belize. Along with the shift in emphasis towards eco-tourism went the development of another niche, ranging from archaeo-tourism to anthrop-tourism, which was mainly due to the following reason: In the past three decades, Belize has been the locus of a number of internationally-funded archaeological research projects, focusing on pre-historic Maya economies. This had led both to a scientific revival in Maya topics as such, and a boom in archaeo-tourism, which, in the long run, may have a positive effect on the Maya populations of Belize.

It seems that in Belize, policy makers are convinced that the eco-tourism and archaeo-tourism niche is a wise alternative for maximizing the net expected benefits of tourism to the domestic economy. Despite constant and growing pressure from agricultural and industrial interests, the government has succeeded in setting aside large tracts of public lands for environmental purposes. By the mid-1990s, several new nature reserves were established and one existing reserve extended, which is a significant contribution to the protection of some of the least disturbed tropical and subtropical habitat in all the Americas. In addition, to combat the increased pressure on Belize's barrier reef, caused by the rapidly growing tourist industry on offshore cays and on the coast, three marine reserves were created, and seven sites on the barrier reef have been declared World Heritage sites. These reserves and protected sites require a great deal of management, especially when it comes to enforce protective laws. Although the government seems to be sufficiently interested in protecting the country's natural beauties, it remains to be seen whether it will succeed in providing the management required to achieve this objective.

In Belize, eco-tourism is not a new economic strategy and has been in vogue for some time. Mass tourism as well as conventional tourism have simply been demassified by repackaging, relabeling and renaming the product. Just like any other new economic strategy, eco-tourism too has its own dangers and its pros and cons.

One criticism has been that eco-tourism, originally intended to be very different from conventional tourism and not like any other business, has become too much of a commodity. In many cases it is not difficult to perceive that the word "eco-tourism" is nothing but a flowery paraphrasing of "eco-business", i.e. the opening and developing of new markets. Another criticism is that, generally speaking – and with the exception of a recently developed small scale "community-based type of tourism" where villagers themselves provide basic accommodation and food, thus directly gaining modest profits – the potential benefits average Belizeans are able to reap from eco-tourism are relatively small.

During the period when Belize began to establish itself as an eco-tourism destination, eco-tourism has also become a disguise for fostering additional private investment in the name of "sustainable development". Due to the government encouraging foreign private ownership of land (especially on the larger cays), the amount of private US investment in Belize has risen enormously over the past twenty five years, with Belize becoming a popular locus for US developers committed to "sustainable development".[80]

---

80 For example in 1990, the Government of Belize bought much of the formerly foreign owned and largely unspoilt northern two-thirds of Ambergris Cay (Pinkerton Estate), with the promise that it would be the Belizean people who would get back control of land by a meaningful participation. Instead, new "laws" were devised and a development

The fact remains, that in Belize, a large percentage of the entire eco-tourism businesses are being managed by North American expatriates, who have become a very resolute lobby-group for introducing new laws to protect against further tourist development. Some act out of genuine concern for the environment and some because they are eager to protect their own interests. After all eco-lodge owners depend on being able to advertise undeveloped patches of paradise, ideally, within easy reach of their own eco-lodges.

Judging from advertisements in fancy tourist-brochures, nature-travel guide books, and well-presented television documentations on Belize, it may seem that the best that could ever have happened to Belize was to take advantage of the recent enthusiasm about ecology and the protection of the environment, give the development of eco-tourism top priority and team up with the well-meaning international community (governments as well as multi-national environmental NGO's). However, in reality, this might be a dangerous and deceptive strategy in the long run, as it may represent (and possibly even more so than conventional tourism), a form of neo-colonization, characterized by a new dependency and a lack of self-determination.

In Belize, the re-structuring and re-definition of tourism has caused a good deal of enthusiasm and excitement and a visitor to Belize is often a witness to ardent disputes on this subject. Over the last years, discussing eco-tourism, which receives much coverage on local television and local newspapers, has emerged as a favourite national past-time. Eco-tourism has become a catchword and we may even go so far as to say that is has reached an almost "spiritual" dimension, among local Belizeans and expatriates alike. A visitor to Belize cannot fail to notice the presence of large numbers of zealous "eco-missionaries" throughout the country. The vast quantity of foreign aid agencies and conservation groups stationed in Belize (an area of only 23,000 square kilometres!) is also very "impressive". At times, it becomes very difficult not to get thoroughly confused about the role and genuine interest of these multi-national agencies and it is not unusual that they declare open war on one another, just as the foreign powers did in former colonial times.

---

proposal was advanced for the area. In fact, this proposal was nothing but a "sustainable development" contract. It involved huge sums of US$, which would have included the transfer of 7,500 acres (approximately 3,000 hectares) of land to North American developers, who would have been given the task of realizing "an integrated and ecologically sound resort development". In one way or another, the all-inclusive hotels, golf courses, eco-lodges, apartments, villas and luxury homes for North American ex-patriates would have attracted large numbers of tourists committed to "eco-tourism", "pseudo-eco-tourism", respectively. Fortunately though, the contract fell through with the result that, at least for the time being, these dangers are banned.

For the modern eco-traveller (the supposedly intellectual, environmentally minded middle class traveller who strictly claims exemption from the "ordinary tourist" and sees the mere word "tourist" in a pejorative sense), eco-tourism has emerged as a new ideology, to which a great deal of social status is attached. After dedicated "eco-pioneers" come back from a strenuous week of eco-lifestyle in the former remote colonial outpost of British Honduras, preferably as "volunteers rendering their services" to one of the many eco-travel societies, they are bound to impress or raise their social prestige once back within their own community at home, especially because it is widely known that eco-tourists are willing to pay much more for their holiday compared to the average tourist.

One of the many criticism of eco-tourism revolves around the fact that it distorts nature by presenting an unrealistic picture of nature. This puts significant pressure on agencies and guides. They are expected to show as much idyllic wildlife within the shortest time possible because, since this is the very reason why the majority of eco-tourist come to Belize. For example, if a specific location along and inside the Barrier Reef is known for a regular appearance of animals (as is the case with manatees), it does not take long until internal disputes among local guides begin, as to who is allowed to take how many tourists and how often to that particular site to observe, and to take photographs of, the animals. This practice definitely does not serve to minimize the pressures of encroachment by humans on wildlife habitat, which was, initially, one of the main intentions of eco-tourism.

Eco-tourism can never be as "authentic" as advertisements frequently announce. Although nature as a commodity is neatly wrapped up and sold as real and "authentic", it is never consumed as such. One must bear in mind that the average North American and European "eco-traveller" would not be able to tolerate "authentic" conditions (the lack of air-condition or fans, unaccustomed sanitary conditions, insect plague, extreme humidity and high temperatures etc.) in the first place. It is no secret that, the majority of eco-tourists, are shuffled to reasonably presentable and "interesting" sites immediately after their arrival, such as a safe zoo or appealing nature reserves, Maya ruins etc. If possible, a detour is deliberately taken around the real "authentic" places until finally arriving in a comfortable, preferably expatriate-owned, eco-lodge.

On official pamphlets issued by the Belize Tourism Board one cannot fail to notice that a neo-colonial image is deliberately given to eco-tourism. It is hoped that a certain colonial atmosphere will increase the marketing possibilities for the product, i.e. the Belizean nature, wildlife, landscape, culture. For example, black and white photographs in one of the official tourist brochures showing people dressed in turn-of-the-century outfits on horseback, in a canoe, or studying archaeological sites are given a brownish tone during processing to imitate photographic processes from around the beginning of the 20th century. The marketing strategy behind this is obvious; the photographs are meant to convey precisely the adventurous and pioneering spirit of colonial times.

Having given a more in-depth analysis of the role tourism plays in Belize by exposing some of the critical aspects of the form of eco-tourism currently practised, we may be able to summarize as follows:

The importance of the tourist industry to Belize's development strategy cannot be denied. On the one hand, the priority status which has been given to tourism and eco-tourism has led to a growing tourism dependency, which many critics compare to the old colonial dependency of the periphery on the metropolis. On the other hand, nature-based tourism may be Belize's last chance to find the right formula for achieving more economic stability. The formula will only prove to be right, if policy makers succeed in effectively marketing Belize's natural beauties, while at the same time showing sufficient concern for a wise handling of the country's most important economic assets, thereby preserving them for posterity.

At the same time, and in order to avoid a new dependence on the "tourist mono-crop", it would be wise to encourage attempts to further diversify the agricultural sector. And given the fact that more forested areas will have to be converted into potential areas of agricultural productivity, it will be a very difficult task to find the right balance here.

7. We Have Come Full Circle

A discussion about tourism and eco-tourism in Belize sooner or later is bound to lead to the question if credit can be given to British colonialism for creating the necessary prerequisites for eco-tourism to develop. This question gains even more in importance if we take into consideration that in neighbouring Guatemala and Mexico, and also Honduras, forest stands are largely depleted. In these countries, large portions of rain forest are completely deforested by now, with the little that is left – and with it its remaining wildlife habitat – being constantly harassed by timber interests, plantations, and increased slash-and-burn farming, which is mostly due to recent population movements into remoter areas, as is the case in Guatemala's Petén region.

Despite running the risk of being branded as a colonial apologist, I have a strong tendency to believe that in Belize, British colonial presence has indeed created, albeit unintentionally, the necessary preconditions for the country to be able to develop into a prime destination for eco-tourism. Why?

If the Spanish forces had been successful in the first stage of their ambitious colonization plan for Yucatán, Campeche and parts of present Central America, an overland connection would have been established between the important commercial centres in Northern Yucatán and Campeche and Tayasal (modern Flores) in present Guatemala's Central Petén. This overland connection would have led through the area that is now Belize, which would have been colonized by the Spanish there and then. As a consequence, for several reasons extensively discussed in Chapter Two, most likely, a partition of the present territory of Belize would have taken place. Sooner or later, two very large territorial units would have evolved, the northern regions of present Belize would have been incorporated into Yucatán and the southern regions would have become part of the *Audiencia* of Guatemala.

There is every reason to believe that under Spanish administration, the territory of present Belize would have developed more or less exactly in the same way as the present neighbouring Central American nations. The Spanish would have founded settlements and the region would subsequently have gone through the same patterns of *encomienda/repartimiento*, its failure, an economic crisis, eventual economic and political separation from Spain, Federation, a separate nation, civil wars, massive foreign economic involvement etc.

However, history took a different course and due to the Spanish failure to found permanent settlements on the Belizean coast, a few English and Scottish ex-buccaneers were given the opportunity to engage in the cutting and exporting of logwood. These first economic activities on the part of a few individuals and their attempts to settle and persuade England to recognize *their* "Bay Settlement", laid the very foundation for an extremely peculiar form of colonization, quasi-colonization, respectively. Although the English were ultimately given the right to extract wood, the Spanish continued to hold sovereignty over the territory and prohibited the institution of a government and, more important for our present argumentation, the establishment of agriculture.

In sum, several factors in connection with the British colonization of Belize also were, retrospectively seen, responsible for the conservation of large portions of the region's wildlife habitat:

- **First:** *If* the territory had been under Spanish administration, settlement on a larger scale would eventually have occurred and, as a consequence, large portions of Belize's land/forests would have been cleared and subjected to agricultural use. Compared to how the region would, most likely, have developed under Spanish control, as far as the conservation of the environment is concerned, a quasi-colonization by the British and the extraction of logwood and mahogany, although extensive, was probably the lesser of the two "evils".

- **Secondly:** As explained above, from the British point of view, the agricultural restrictions and the insecure and abnormal diplomatic status of "Her Majesty's Settlement in the Bay" were, in no way, ideal preconditions for a British settlement on a large scale. Moreover, large tracts of land had been in the hands of individual London-owned timber companies (even before the region was officially declared a British colony) which limited the free usage of land. Although these factors were clearly impediments for the alteration of the basic economic structure of the colony, in the sense that it retarded the establishment of agriculture and with it the growing of a domestic market (especially for agricultural purposes!), they had a protective effect for Belize's wildlife habitat.
- **Thirdly:** *If* Belize had developed in the same way as the neighbouring Central American countries, such an abnormal diplomatic situation would never have existed in the first place. Most likely, railway tracks would have been cut across dense jungle regions and roads would have been built at a much earlier stage. Although a railway and a road system would have made timber extraction more economic, it would, at the same time, have destroyed forest resources, and, as a consequence, wildlife habitat.
- **Fourthly:** When the British finally assumed full sovereignty over the area, most idle land was declared Crown land. Although this restricted a further distribution of land for farming purposes, it was beneficial for the country's environment.

In no way do I want to imply that the British Government or the British colonial officers stationed in British Honduras, made conscious efforts towards the protection of the colony's wildlife. On the contrary, as late as the 1960s, the jungle and savannah regions of British Honduras were renowned and advertised for superb game shooting.[81] Nevertheless, generally speaking, British colonial presence – whether it may have been out of happenstance or not – had an unintended positive side effect for the protection of the region's wildlife.

But the facts speak for themselves: Whereas in Guatemala's Petén region, just across the border, wildlife has suffered severely from economic exploitation and population movements, in Belize, wildlife has been left relatively undisturbed. Today, about 70% of Belize's tropical forest is still intact and represents a major economic asset.

---

81 Among the prey were animals such as jaguar, tapir, peccaries (wild pigs), gibnut, armadillo and pumas, ocelots, crocodiles, but also deer, quail, pigeons, partridge etc. Cf. Caiger (1951:183)

Over the last two decades, Belize has become a primary destination for tourist and eco-tourists. In addition, the relatively peaceful political climate, before and after independence (which, in my opinion, is another by-product of British colonial presence in Belize), and English being the country's official language has encouraged many private and public US and international conservation groups to release funds and to be active in Belize. These groups also assist in the co-ordination of environmental projects and in the supervising of enforcing wildlife protection laws.

Within the geographic boundaries of Belize, a large variety of endangered species, including non-tropical wild animals, can still be found. For example, there are five different species of jungle cats, such as jaguar (known locally as "tiger" or *el tigre)*, pumas (the local "lion" or *leon de monte)*, and ocelots *(tigrillo)*, agouti, coatimundi (a member of the racoon family), racoon, peccary (wild pig), deer, several types of monkeys, tapir (Belize's national animal, which is closely related to the horse and also kin to the rhinoceros and is known locally as "mountain cow"), crocodiles, parrots, as well as a large variety of birds and plants. Turtles, manatees, dolphins, rays, sharks and innumerable tropical fishes form part of Belize's rich aquatic fauna.

Whether it was a wise decision to designate tourism second in the priority for development and whether the shift to eco-tourism will live up to the expectations of policy makers remains to be seen. Likewise, it is uncertain whether, in the long run, the spill-over effect of the tourism industry will be sufficient enough to actually, and significantly, improve the socio-economic status of the local population.

But what *is* certain, is that the observation Aldous Huxley's made in 1933 when travelling in Central America "… if the world had any ends, British Honduras would certainly be one of them … it is not on the way from anywhere to anywhere else …"[82] has long ceased to bear any significance.

If Huxley was to visit Belize today, he would be impressed as to what has become of "… this strange little fragment of the Empire"[83] and would be forced to reconsider his rather off-hand remark. In an ironical twist of fate which Huxley would surely have relished, it was precisely Belize's centuries of isolation that have led to the conservation of one of its prime assets: A largely intact nature. Belize, the once remote colonial outpost, has become a prospering multicultural and multilingual nation with a population of between 330,000 and 350,000.

---

82 Huxley (1949:35)
83 Ibid.

Map 16: Mopan and Q'eqchi' Maya Migration

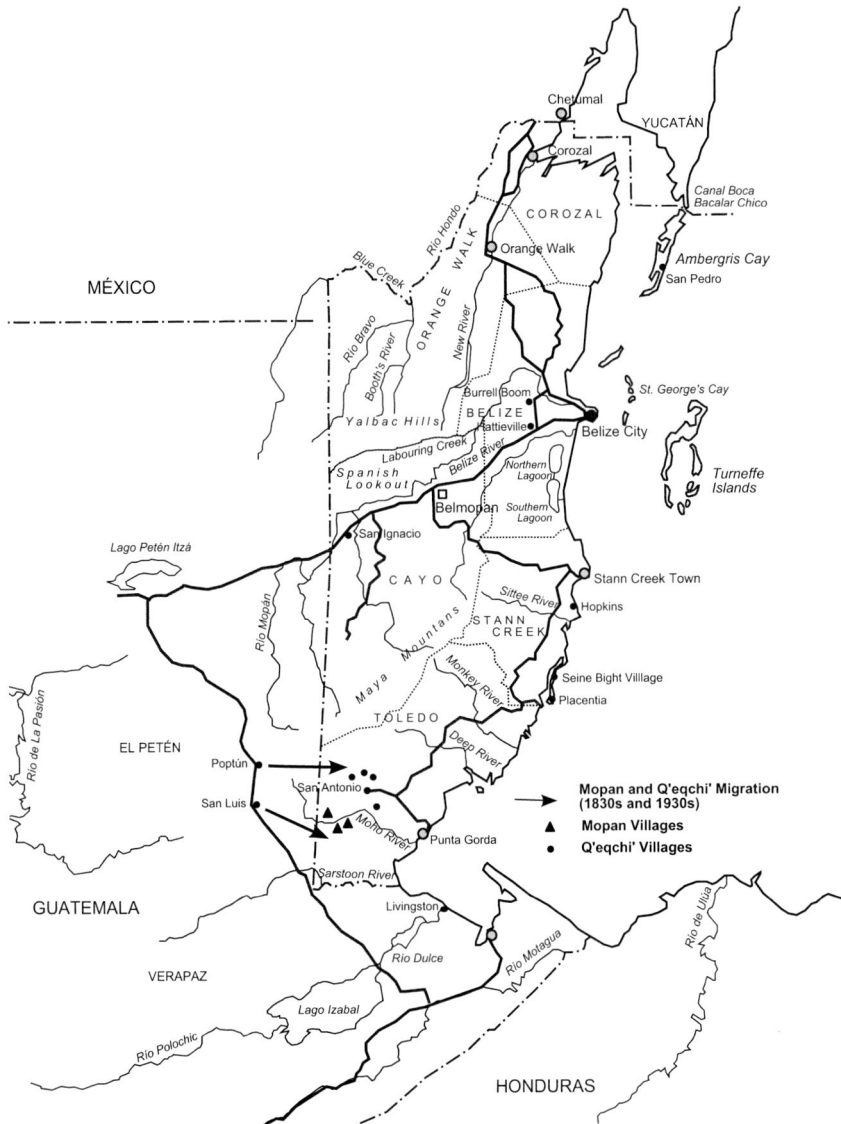

Mopan and Q'eqchi' Migration
(1830s and 1930s)
▲ Mopan Villages
● Q'eqchi' Villages

Bibliography

Albertini, Rudolf von (1976). *Europäische Kolonialherrschaft. 1880–1940.* Zürich: Atlantis.

Andrews, Kenneth R. (1959). *English Privateering Voyages to the West Indies, 1588–1595.* Hakluyt Society, Series 2, Vol. CXI, Cambridge: Cambridge Univ.Press.

Andrews, Kenneth R. (1964). *Elizabethan Privateering. English Privateering during the Spanish War, 1585–1603.* Cambridge: Cambridge University Press.

Andrews, Kenneth R. (1978). *The Spanish Caribbean: Trade and Plunder, 1530–1630.* New Haven: Yale University Press.

Anomymous (1838). *Proposed Colony in the District of Black River on the northern coast of Central America, commonly called Poyais.* Historical Collection from the British Library, London: Effingham Wilson.

Arends, Tulio (1991). *Sir Gregor MacGregor: Un escocés tras la aventura de América.* Caracas: Monte Ávila Editores.

Ashcraft, Norman (1973). *Colonialism and Underdevelopment: Processes of Political Economic Change in British Honduras.* New York, Columbia University: Teachers' College Press.

Ashcraft, Norman (1973a). The Early British Settlement in the Bay of Honduras. *Journal of Belizean Affairs, 2* (September).

Ashdown, Peter D. (1978). The Perversion of History: A Critique of Stephen L. Caiger's British Honduras Past and Present. *Journal of Belizean Affairs, 6* (January).

Ashdown, Peter D. (1979). *Race, Class and the Unofficial Majority in British Honduras, 1890–1949.* Unpublished Ph.D. thesis, University of Sussex.

Ashdown, Peter D. (1981). The Belize Elite and its Power Base: Land Labour and Commerce circa 1890. *Belizean Studies, 9 (5/6):* 30–39.

Ashdown, Peter D. (1981). The Colonial Administrator as Historian: Burdon, Burns and The Battle of St. George's Cay. *Belizean Studies, 15 (1),* 3–11.

Ashdown, Peter D. (1987). The Problem of Creole Historiography. *Readings in Belizean History,* 2nd ed. Lita Hunter Krohn ed., Belize City: St. John's College, 142–152.

Ashdown, Peter D. (1990). Garveyism in Belize. SPEAReports 5, Belize City: SPEAR.

Atkins, John (1735). *A Voyage to Guinea, Brazil and the West Indies*. London: C.Ward and R. Chandler.

Augier, F.R. et al (1960). *The Making of the West Indies*. London: Longmans, Green & Co. Bancroft, Hubert H. (1883–87). History of Central America. 3 vols. San Francisco: History Company.

Barnett, Carla (1992). Looking Beyond the Year 2000: The Implications of Development in Belize's Economy in the 1980s and 1990s. *Belizean Studies, 22,* 3–14.

Barrow, Dean O. (1991). Post-War Guatemalan Foreign Policy and the Independence of Belize. *Belizean Studies, 19 (2/3),* 2–12.

Beck, Thomas and A. Menninger and T. Schleich, eds. (1992). *Kolumbus Erben. Europäische Expansion und Überseeische Ethnien im Ersten Kolonialzeitalter, 1415–1815.* Darmstadt: Wissenschaftliche Buch-Gesellschaft.

Bloomfield, L.M. (1953). *The British Honduras – Guatemala Dispute.* Toronto: Carswell Company Ltd.

Bolland, Nigel O. (1974). Maya Settlement in the Upper Belize River Valley and Yalbac Hills: An Ethnohistorical View. *Journal of Belizean Affairs, 3,* 3–23.

Bolland, Nigel O. (1977). *The Formation of a Colonial Society: Belize, from Conquest to Crown Colony.* Baltimore and London: John Hopkins Univ. Press.

Bolland, Nigel O. (1987). Race, Ethnicity and National Integration in Belize. *First Annual Studies on Belize Conference,* Belize City: Society for the Promotion of Education and Research (SPEAR).

Bolland, Nigel O. (1988). *Colonialism and Resistance in Belize.* Belize: Cubola Productions.

Bolland, Nigel O. (1997). Struggles for Freedom: Essays on Slavery, Colonialism and Culture in the Caribbean and Central America. Belize City: Angelus Press.

Bolland, Nigel O. (2004) The Birth of Caribbean Civilization: A Century of Ideas about Culture and Identity, Nation and Society. Kingston: Ian Randle.

Bolland, Nigel O. and Assad Shoman (1977). *Land in Belize, 1765–1871.* Mona: Institute of Social and Economic Research, University of the West Indies/Jamaica.

Booth, John A., C.J. Wade and T.W. Walker (2006). Understanding Central America: Global Forces, Rebellion, and Change. Boulder: Westview Press.

Borah, Wodrow and Sherburne F. Cook (1963). The Aboriginal Population of Central America on the Eve of the Spanish Conquest. *Ibero-Americana, 45.*

Bradley, Leo (1973). The Last Fight. *National Studies, 1* (1), 14–19, Belize: Belize Institute of Social Research and Action (BISRA).

Brathwaite, Edward (1971). *The Development of Creole Society in Jamaica, 1770–1820.* Oxford: Clarendon Press.

Braun, Bertram (1993). The Enterprise for the America's Initiative: Where Belize Fits In. *SPEAReports, 9.* Belize City: SPEAR.

Bridenbaugh, C and R. (1972). *No Peace Beyond the Line: The British in the Caribbean, 1624–1690.* New York: Oxford University Press.

Brown, Matthew (2006). *Adventuring through Spanish Colonies: Simón Bolívar, Foreign Mercenaries and the Birth of New Nations.* Liverpool: University Press.

Brown, Vera L. (1922). Anglo-Spanish Relations in America in the Closing Years of the Colonial Era. *Hispanic American Historical Review, 5,* 327–483.

Brown, Vera L. (1928). Contraband Trade: A Factor in the Decline of Spain's Empire in America". In *Hispanic American Historical Review, 8,* 178–185.

Bryden, John (1993). *Tourism and Development: A Case Study of the Commonwealth Caribbean.* Cambridge: University Press.

Buesa, Oliver Tomás (1967). Americanismos in *Enciclopedia Lingüística Hispánica, II,* (ed. M. Alvar et al.)

Buhler, Richard S.J. Fray (1976). *A History of the Catholic Church in Belize.* Belize: Institute for Social Research and Action (BISRA), 4.

Buhler, Richard S.J. Fray (1987) The Icaiche of Belize. *Readings in Belizean History.* 2nd edition. Belize: Belizean Studies, St. John's College.

Bulmer-Thomas, Victor (1987). *The Political Economy of Central America since 1920.* Cambridge: University Press.

Bulmer-Thomas, Victor (1995). *The Economic History of Latin America since Independence.* New York and Cambridge: Cambridge University Press.

Bulmer-Thomas, Barbara and Victor Bulmer-Thomas (2012). *The Economic History of Belize: from 17th Century to Post-Independence.* Belize: Cubola Productions.

Burdon, John Sir (1931). *Archives of British Honduras, 1.* London: Sifton Praed.

Burdon, John Sir (1934). *Archives of British Honduras, 2.* London: Sifton Praed.

Burdon, John Sir (1935). *Archives of British Honduras, 3.* London: Sifton Praed.

Burns, Alan (1949). *Colonial Civil Servant.* London: Allen & Unwin.

Byrd, Herman (1990). Belize – Guatemala Relations: Some New Concerns. *SPEAReports 6,* 17–28, Belize City/Mexico: Cubola Productions.

Byrd, Herman (1994). Developments in Guatemala, 1981–1991. *Belizean Studies, 19* (2/3), 3–12.

Byrd, Herman (1987). Oil in Guatemala: An Economic Factor in the Heads of Agreement. *Belizean Studies, 15* (2), 25–40.

Cal, Angel (1983). Anglo-Maya Contact in Northern Belize: A Study of British Policy towards the Maya during the Caste War of Yucatán, 1847–1872. MA Thesis, University of Calgary, Alberta.

Cal, Angel (1991). *Rural Society and Economic Development: British Mercantile Capital in Nineteenth Century Belize.* Unpubl. Dissertation. The University of Arizona.

Cal, Angel (2004). The Belize Maya and the English to 1847. *Readings in Belizean History.* Belize: National Institute of Culture and History (NICH).

Caiger, Stephen (1951). *British Honduras, Past and Present.* London: George Allen & Unwin.

Calderón Quijano, José Antonio (1944). *Belice, 1663(?) – 1821, historia de los establecimientos británicos del Río Valis hasta la independencia hispanoamericana.* Sevilla: Victoria Gráficas.

Campbell, Lyle (1977). *Quichean Linguistic Prehistory.* Berkeley: University of California Press.

Casas, Bartolomé de las (1875/1951). *Historia de las Indias.* 3 volúmenes, Mexico City: Fondo de Cultura Económica.

Casaús Arzú, Marta Elena (1992). *Guatemala, linaje y racismo.* San José, Costa Rica: Facultad Latinoamericana de Ciencias Sociales (FLACSO).

Catzim, Adele (1922). Sewing the Threads of Dependency: Women in the Garment Industry Ten Years after Independence. *SPEAReport 8.* Fifth Annual Studies on Belize Conference. Mexico: SPEAR, 101–119.

Cayetano, Sebastian R. (1996). *Garifuna History, Language and Culture of Belize, Central America and the Caribbean.* Belize: The Author.

Chamberlain, Robert S. (1948). *The Conquest and Colonization of Yucatán, 1517–1550.* Washington D.C.: Carnegie Institution of Washington, 583.

Charlevoix, Pierre François Xavier De (1730). *Histoire de L'Isle Espagnole ou de Saint-Domingue,* Paris.

Chase, Diana Z. (1981). The Maya Postclassic at Santa Rita Corozal. *Archaeology, 43,* (1), 25–33.

Chase, Arlen and Diana Chase (2007). Ancient Maya Urban Development, *Belizean Studies,* 29 (2): 60–71.

Chase, Arlen and Diana Chase (2008). What the Hieroglyphs Don't Tell You: Archaeology and History at Caracol, Belize. *Mayab,* 20: 103–108.

Chinchilla Aguilar, Ernesto (1964). Belize en la independencia de Centroamérica, *Anales de la Sociedad de Geografía e Historia de Guatemala,* XXXVII, 107–110.

Clegern, Wayne M. (1967). *British Honduras: Colonial Dead End, 1859–1900.* Baton Rouge: Louisiana State University Press.

Clegern, Wayne M. (1988). Central America, Belize and the Third World. *Belizean Studies, 16, (2),* 4–15.

Coe, Michael D. (1987). *The Maya.* London: Thames and Hudson.

Coe, Sophie D. and Michael D. Coe (1966). *The True History of Chocolate.* London: Thames and Hudson.

Conzemius, Eduardo (1932). Ethnological Survey of the Miskito and Sumu Indians of Honduras and Nicaragua. *Bureau of American Ethnology Bulletin, 106,* 45, 87. Smithsonian Institute.

Cook, Sherburne F. (1974). *Essays in Population History: Mexico and the Caribbean.* Berkeley and Los Angeles: University of California Press.

Corominas, Joan (1980). *Diccionario Crítico Etimológico Castellano e Hispánico.* Madrid: Editorial Gredos.

Cortés, Hernán (1941). Durch Urwälder und Sümpfe Mittelamerikas. Der Fünfte Bericht des Hernán Cortés an Kaiser Karl V. Ed. und Übersetzer Franz Termer. *Ibero-Amerikanische Studien. 15,* Hamburg: Verlag Conrad Behre.

Cortés, Hernán (1971). *Letters from Mexico.* Translated and edited by A.R. Pagden. New York: Grossmann Publishers.

Craig, Alan K. (1966). Geography of Fishing in British Honduras and Adjacent Coastal Waters. *Coastal Studies, 14.* Baton Rouge: Louisiana State Univ. Press.

Craig, Alan K. (1969). Logwood as a Factor in the Settlement of British Honduras. *Caribbean Studies, IX,* 53–62.

Crowe, Frederick (1850). *The Gospel in Central America, containing ... a History of the Baptist Mission in British Honduras.* London: Charles Gilpin.

Culbert, Patrick (1973). *The Classic Maya Collapse.* Albuquerque: Univ. of New Mexico Press.

Culbert, Patrick (1977). The Origins of Civilization in the Lowlands. *Origins of Maya Civilization,* 3–24. R.E.W. Adams ed. Albuquerque: Univ. of New Mexico Press.

Dampier, William (1700/1906). *Dampier's Voyages. Consisting of a New Voyage round the World, ... Two Voyages to Campeachy, ...* Edited by John Masefield. London: E.Grant Richards.

Davidson, William V. (1979). *Historical Geography of the Bay Islands, Honduras.* Birmingham, Alabama: Southern University Press.

Dávila, Alonso (1533/1864–84). Relación de lo sucedido a Alonso Dávila (1533) ... *Colección de documentos inéditos relativos al descubrimento, conquista y colonización de las antiguas posesiones españolas en América y Oceanía ... 14,* Madrid.

Dávila Garibi, José Ignacio (1939). *Nuevo y más amplio estudio etimológico del vocablo cholocate y de otros que con él se relacionan.* México: Emilio Pardo e Hijos.

Defence of the Settlers of Honduras against the Unjust and Unfounded Representations of Colonel George Arthur. (1824). Jamaica.

Díaz del Castillo, Bernal (1958). *The Discovery and Conquest of Mexico.* Ed. Genaro García, translated A.P. Maudsley. New York: Grove Press.

Dobson, Narda (1973). *A History of Belize.* London: Longman Caribbean.

Dunlop, Robert G. (1847). *Travels in Central America.* London: Longman, Brown, Green & Longmans.

Dunn, F.L. (1965). *On the Antiquity of Malaria in the Western Hemisphere.* Human Biology. 37, pp. 386–93.

Ehrenberg, Richard (1990). *Das Zeitalter der Fugger: Geldkapital und Kreditverkehr im 16.Jhdt.* Hildesheim: Olms.

Evans, Geoffrey (1941). *Report of the British Guiana and British Honduras Settlement Commission.* London, Colonial Office: HMSO.

Everitt, John C. (1986). The Growth and Development of Belize City. *Belizean Studies,* 14 (1), 30.

Exquemelin, Alexander O. (1678/1993). *The Buccaneers of America. Classics of Naval Literature.* Annapolis, Maryland: Naval Institute Press.

Feldman, L.H. (1983). Belize and Its Neighbours: A Preliminary Report on Colonial Records of the Audiencia of Guatemala. *Belizean Studies,* Vol.11 (6), pp.9–20.

Floyd, Troy (1967). *The Anglo-Spanish Struggle for Mosquitia.* Albuquerque: University of New Mexico Press.

Fowler, Henry (1879). *A Journey Across the Unknown Portions of British Honduras.* Belize: Government Press.

Fuentes y Guzman, Francisco Antonio de (1690/1932). *Historia de Guatemala: Recordación Florida, Discurso historial y demonstración natural, material, militar y política del Reyno de Guatemala.* Guatemala, Biblioteca "Goathemala" de la Sociedad de Geografía e Historia: Tipografía Nacional.

Gage, Thomas (1648/1946). *The English American: A New Survey of the West Indies.* Ed. A.P. Newton. Guatemala: El Patio.

Gámez, José Dolores (1939). *Historia de la Costa de Mosquitos (hasta 1890).* Managua: Talleres Nacionales.

Gibbs, Archibald Robertson (1883). *British Honduras. An Historical and Descriptive Account of the Colony ...,* London.

Gibson, Charles (1964). *The Aztecs under Spanish Rule.* Stanford, Calif: Stanford Univ. Press.

Gibson, Charles (1971). *The Black Legend. Anti-Spanish Attitudes of the Old World and the New*. New York: Alfred Knopf Inc.

Gregory, James (1984). The Mopan: Culture and ethnicity in a changing Belizean community. *University of Missouri Monographs in Anthropology 7*, Colombia, 7.

Gómez de Silva, Guido (1995). *Breve Diccionario Etimológico de la Lengua Española*. México: Fondo de Cultura Económica.

Guzmán-Böckler Carlos and Herbert Jean-Lup (1995). *Guatemala: Una interpretación histórico-social*. Guatemala: Editorial Cholsamaj.

Hampshire, Cyril (1972). *The British in the Caribbean*. London: Weidenfeld & Nicholson.

Handbook of British Honduras for 1888–1889. (1888). Comprising Historical, Statistical and General Information Concerning the Colony. Ed. Bristowe, Lindsay and Wright. London: William Blackwood and Sons.

Handbook of British Honduras for 1890–1891. (1890). Comprising Historical, … London: William Blackwood and Sons.

Handbook of British Honduras for 1925. (1925). Comprising Historical, … London: West India Committee.

Haring, Clarence H. (1910). *The Buccaneers in the West Indies in the 17th Century*. London: Methuen & Company Ltd.

Haring, Clarence H. (1963). *The Spanish Empire in America*. New York: Harbinger Books.

Haring, Clarence H. (1964). Trade and Navigation between Spain and the Indies in the Time of the Habsburgs. *Harvard Economic Series, 19*, Gloucester, Mass.: Peter Smith.

Harrison, Lawrence E. (1985/2000). *Underdevelopment is a State of Mind: The Latin America Case*. Lanham, MD, Center for International Affairs: Harward University Press and University Press of America.

Henderson, G. Captain (1809). *An Account of the British Settlement of Honduras*. London: C&A Baldwin.

Henderson, John S. (1981). *The World of the Ancient Maya*, Ithaca: Cornell University Press.

Hernández, David (1984). The Name Belize: An Example of Afro-Caribbean Convergence. *SPEAReports 3*. Belize City: Cubola Productions, 33–43.

Herre, Franz (1985). *Die Fugger in ihrer Zeit*. Augsburg: Presse- Druck- und Verlagshaus.

Holm, John (1977). Miskito Words in Belizean Creole. *Belizean Studies, 5* (6), 1–19.

Holm, John (1978). The Carib in Central America. *Belizean Studies, 6* (6), 23–32.

Holm, John (1978a). *The Creole English of Nicaragua's Miskito Coast* ... Ph.D. thesis, University of London: Ann Arbour, University Microfilms.

Holm, John (1986). The Spread of English in the Caribbean Area. *Focus on the Caribbean*. Eds. Manfred Görlach and John Holm. Amsterdam: John Benjamins.

Holm, John (1989). *Pidgins and Creoles*. Cambridge: Cambridge University Press.

Humphreys, R.A. (1961). *A Diplomatic History of British Honduras, 1638-1901.* London: Oxford University Press.

Humphreys, Francis (1987). The Battle of St.George's Cay. *Readings in Belizean History*. 2nd ed., Lita Krohn ed., Belize City: St.John's College, pp. 85-99.

Humphreys, Francis (1992). Afro-Belizean Cultural Heritage: Its Role in Combatting Recolonization. *Belizean Studies*. Vol.20 (3), pp. 11-15.

Huxley, Aldous L. (1949). *Beyond the Mexique Bay. A Traveller's Journal.* London: Chattoo & Windus.

Jones, Grant D. (1971). *The Politics of Agricultural Development in Northern British Honduras.* Winston-Salem: Wake Forestry Overseas Research Center.

Jones, Grant D. (1973). Maya Intergroup Relations in Nineteenth Century Belize and Southern Yucatán. *Journal of Belizean Affairs,1* (June).

Jones, Grant D. (1983). *The Last Maya Frontiers of Colonial Yucatán. Spaniards and Indians in South-Eastern Mesoamerica: Essays on the History of Ethnic Relations,* Ed. Murdo, J. MacLeod and Robert Wasserstrom. Lincoln: University of Nebraska Press, 64-91.

Jones, Grant D. (1984). Maya-Spanish Relations in Sixteenth Century Belize, *Belcast Journal of Belizean Affairs, 1* (1), 28-40.

Jones, Grant D. (1990). *Maya Resistance to Spanish Rule: Time and History on a Colonial Frontier.* Albuquerque: University of New Mexico Press.

Jones, Grant D. (October 1994). *The Roots of People's Resistance in Colonial Belize, 1544-1744.* Paper presented at SPEAR's 8th Annual Studies on Belize Conference, Belize City.

Joseph, Gilbert M. (1974). British Loggers and Spanish Governors: The Logging Trade and Its Settlements in the Yucatán Peninsula. *Caribbean Studies, 14* (2).

Joseph, Gilbert M. (1987). The Logwood Trade and its Settlements. Part I and II. *Readings in Belizean History,* 32-47, 2nd ed., Lita Hunter-Krohn ed., Belize City: St.John's College.

Joseph, Gilbert M. (1989). John Coxen and the Role of Buccaneering in the Settlement of the Yucatecan Colonial Frontier. *Belizean Studies, 17* (3), 2-21.

Judd, Karen (1992). *Elite Reproduction and Ethnic Identity in Belize.* Unpublished PhD Dissertation, City University of New York.

Klein, Herbert S. (1986). *African Slavery in Latin America and the Caribbean.* New York: Oxford University Press.

Kupperman, Karen (1993). *Providence Island: The Other Puritan Colony,* New York: Cambridge University Press.

Kroshus-Medina, Laurie (1992). Immigration, Labour and Government Policy: Class, Conflict and Alternative Pathways towards Development. *SPEAReports 8,* Fifth Annual Studies on Belize Conference, Belize City: SPEAR, 144–158.

Landa, Fray Diego de (1978). *Yucatán, before and after the Conquest.* Transl. William Gates. New York: Dover Publications.

Landa, Fray Diego de (1598/1996). *Relación de las Cosas de Yucatán.* México: Editorial Porrúa.

Leon, Narda (1958). "Social and Administrative Development in British Honduras, 1798–1843". Unpubl. thesis.

López de Cogolludo, Diego (1688/1971). *Historia de Yucatán, Los tres siglos de la dominación Española en Yucatán.* Tomo I y II. Graz (Austria): Akademische Druck- und Verlagsanstalt.

M.W. (1732). *The Mosquito Indian and Golden River; Being a familiar description of the Mosqueto Kingdom in America, A Collection of Voyages and Travels.* Vol. 6, Ed. A. Churchill, London: J.Walthoe.

MacAnany, Patricia A. ed. (1989). *Prehistoric Maya Economies of Belize.* Greenwich, Conn.: Jai Press.

MacLeod, Murdo J. (1973). *Spanish Central America. A Socio-Economic History, 1520–1720.* Los Angeles: University of California Press.

MacLeod, Murdo J. (1982). *Historia Socioeconómica de la América Central Española, 1520–1720.* Guatemala: Editorial Piedra Santa.

Macpherson, Anne (1992). *Women's activism in the nationalistic movement and the gendered creation of State hegemony in Belize, 1950–1960.* Master's Thesis, University of Wisconsin-Madison.

Macpherson, Anne (2003). Colonial matriarchs: Garveyism, maternalism and Belize's Black Cross nurses, 1920–1952. *Gender and History, 15 (3),* November, 507–27.

Martínez Peláez, Severo (1973). *La Patria del Criollo: Ensayo de interpretación de la realidad colonial guatemalteca.* 2a ed., San José, Costa Rica: Editorial Universitaria Centroamericana (Educa).

Mediz Bolio, Antonio. transl. (1973). *Libro de Chilam Balam de Chumayel.* México: Universidad Nacional Autónoma de Mexico.

Moberg, Mark (October 1993). *Out of Work in the Fields of Gold: Belizean Labour and the Banana Industry.* Paper presented at SPEAR's Seventh Annual Studies on Belize Conference, *Belize City.*

Moberg, Mark (October 1994). *Domination and Everyday Forms of Resistance among Immigrant Workers in the Belizean Banana Industry.* Paper presented at SPEAR's Seventh Annual Studies on Belize Conference, Belize City.

Molina Solís, Juan Francisco (1913). *La Historia de Yucatán durante la dominación española.* Mérida: Impresora de la Lotería del Estado.

Morris, Daniel Sir (1883). *The Colony of British Honduras, its Resources and Prospects; with part reference to its Plants and Economic Production.* London: E.Stanford.

Murphy, James (1987). Belize at Two: Keeping its Appointments with History. *Readings in Belizean History,* Lita Hunter-Krohn ed., Belize: St.John's College, 256–280.

Naylor, Robert R. (1988). *Influencia británica en el comercio centroamericano durante las primeras décadas de la Independencia (1821–1851).* Antigua, Guatemala: Centro de Investigaciones Regionales de Mesoamérica, Serie Monográfica, 3.

Naylor, Robert R. (1989). *Penny Ante Imperialism: The Mosquito Shore and the Bay of Honduras, 1600–1914. A Case Study in British Informal Empire.* Cranbury, N.Y.: Fairleigh Dickinson Univ. Press; London and Toronto: Associated University Presses.

Newton, Arthur Percival (1914). *The Colonizing Activities of the English Puritans.* New Haven.

Newton, Arthur Percival (1933). *The European Nations in the West Indies, 1493–1688.* London: A&C Black.

Olien, Michael D. (1983). The Miskito Kings and the Line of Succession, *Journal of Anthropological Research, 39.2,* Albuquerque, 277–318.

Olien, Michael D. (1988). Were the Miskito Indians Black? *New West Indian Guide,* 62, No. 1,2. Leiden, 27–50.

Oviedo y Valdés, Gonzalo (1851–55/1959). *Historia General y Natural de las Indias.* Vol.3, Madrid: Atlas.

Palacio, Joseph O. (1987). Black Carib History up to 1795. *Readings in Belizean History.* 2nd ed., Lita Krohn ed., Belize City: St.John's College, 110–119.

Palacio, Joseph O. (1988). Illegal Aliens in Belize: Findings From the 1984 Amnesty. In Patricia Pessar (ed.) *When Borders Don't Divide: Labour Migration and Refugee Movements in the Americas.* New York: Center for Migration Studies, 156–177.

Palacio, Joseph O. (1990). Socio-Economic Integration of Central American Immigrants in Belize. *SPEAReports 2.* Mexico: Cubola Productions, 5–25.

Palacio, Joseph O. (1993). Social and Cultural Implications of Recent Demographic Changes in Belize. *Belizean Studies,* 21 (1), 3–12.

Parsons, James Jerome (1954). English-Speaking Settlements of the Western Caribbean. *Yearbook, Association of Pacific Coast Geographers,16,* Cheney: Wahs, 3–16.

Parsons, James Jerome (1985). *San Andrés y Providencia.* Una geografía histórica de las islas colombianas del Caribe. Bogotá: El Ancora Editores.

Peralta, Manuel Maria de (1898). *Costa Rica, Costa de Mosquitos. Documentos para la historia de la jurisdicción territorial de Costa Rica y Colombia.* Paris: Imprenta General de Lahure.

Pompa, Gerónimo (1976). *Medicamentos Indígenas.* Panama: Editorial América SA.

Poon, Aurelia (1993). *Tourism, Technology and Competitive Strategies.* Oxford: CAB, Wallingford.

Randall, Laura (1977). *A Comparative Economic History of Latin America 1500–1914. 1,* Mexico. Institute of Latin American Studies, Columbia University, Michigan: Ann Arbor.

Recinos, Adrian and Delia Goetz. Transl. (1953). *The Annals of the Cakchiquels.* Norman, Oklahoma: University of Oklahoma Press.

Recinos, Adrian. Transl. (1974). *Popol Vuh, las antiguas historias del Quiché.* Mexico: Fondo de Cultura Económica.

Reed, Nelson (1964). *The Caste War of Yucatan.* Palo Alto: Stanford University Press.

Roberts, Orlando (1827/1965). *Narrative of Voyages and Excursions on the East Coast and the Interior of Central America.* Gainesville: University of Florida Press. Rouse. Irving.

Santamaría, Francisco J. (1959). *Diccionario de Mejicanismos.* México: Porrúa.

Sandner, Gerhard (1985). *Zentralamerika und der ferne Karibische Westen: Konjunkturen, Krisen und Konflikte, 1503–1984.* Wiesbaden: Steiner.

Sauer, Carl O. (1966). *The Early Spanish Main.* Berkeley: University of California Press.

Sherry, Frank (1986). *Raiders and Rebels, The Golden Age of Piracy.* New York: Quill William Morrow.

Shoman, Assad (1987). The Birth of a Nationalist Movement. *Readings of Belizean History.* 2nd ed., Ed. Lita Krohn. Belize City: St. John's College, 195–238.

Shoman, Assad (1994). *Chapters of a History of Belize.* Belize City: The Angelus Press.

Simpson, Leslie B. (1950). *The Encomienda in New Spain.* Berkeley: Univ. of California Press.

Sinclair, David (2004). *The Land that Never Was: Sir Gregor MacGregor and the Most Audacious Fraud in History.* Cambridge: Da Capo Press, 2004.

Sloane, Hans (1707). *A Voyage to the islands Madera, Barbados, Neives, S. Christopher and Jamaica*. London: Printed by B.M. for the Author, Vol. 1, pp. ixxvi–ixxvii.

Solis, Marina Laetitia (1994). *This Tranquil Haven ...: A Case Study of the Valley of Peace. Refugee Settlement in Belize*. Mona, Faculty of Social Science: The University of the West Indies.

Stephens, John L. (1841/1969). *Incidents of Travel in Central America, Chiapas and Yucatan*. Vol.I. New York: Dover Publications.

Stone, Michael Cutler (1990). The Afro-Caribbean Presence in Central America. *Belizean Studies*. 18 (2/3), 6–42.

Stone, Michael Cutler (1990a). Backabush: Settlement on the Belmopan Periphery and the Challenge to Rural Development. *SPEA Reports 6*. Third Annual Studies on Belize Conference. Belize: Society for the Promotion of Education and Research (SPEAR), 82–134.

Stone, Michael Cutler (1994). Caribbean Nation, Central American State: Ethnicity, Race and National For*mation in Belize, 1798–1990*. Unpubl. Dissertation. The University of Texas, Austin.

Strangeways, Thomas (1822). *Knight of the Green Cross, Sketch of the Mosquito Shore*. Edinburgh: W. Reid.

Taylor, Douglas MacRae (1967). *The Black Caribs of British Honduras*. New York: Wenner-Gren Foundation for Anthropological Research. Viking Fund Publications in Anthropology, 17.

Taylor, Douglas MacRae (1977). *Languages of the West Indies*. Baltimore and London: John Hopkins University Press.

The [Honduras] Almanack for the Year of Our Lord, 1826. (1826). In Rhodes House Library, Rhodes Trust, Oxford. Belize, Authority of the Legislative Assembly: James Cruickshank.

The [Honduras] Almanack for 1828, 1829 and 1830. (1828, 1829, 1830). The Royal Commonwealth Society, London. Belize, Authority of the Legislative Assembly: Government Press.

Thompson, Eric J. (1938). Sixteenth and Seventeenth Century Reports on the Chol Mayas, *American Anthropologist, 40* (4), 592–603.

Thompson, Eric J. (1956). *The Rise and Fall of Maya Civilization*. Norman, Oklahoma: University of Oklahoma Press.

Thompson, Eric J. (1972). *The Maya of Belize: Historical Chapters Since Columbus*. Belize City: The Benex Press.

Thompson, Eric J. (1984). *Grandeza y Decadencia de los Mayas*. Trad. Lauro J. Závala. México: Edit. Fondo de Cultura Económica.

Thompson, Eric J. (1990). *Mayan History and Religion*. Norman: University of Oklahoma Press.

Torres-Rivas, Edelberto coord. (1973). *Historia General de América Central,* coord./ *Historia Inmediata,* Tomo VI, Madrid: Facultad Latinoamericana de Ciencias Sociales, Comunidades Europeas, Comisión Estatal V Centenario.

Uring, Nathaniel (1726). *A History of the Voyages and Travels of Captain Nathaniel Uring.* London: W. Wilkins.

Valladares, Abel Arturo (1939). *Monografía del Departamiento de las Islas de la Bahía.* Tegucicalpa: Talleres Tipográficos Nacionales.

Vernon, Dylan (1992). Ten Years of Independence in Belize: An Analysis of the Socio-Economic Crisis. *SPEAReports 8,* Fifth Annual Studies on Belize Conference, Belize City: SPEAR, 38–55.

Villagutierre Soto-Mayor, Juan de (1701/1983). *History of the Conquest of the Itzá.* Frank E. Comparato, ed., Culver City: Labyrinthos.

Waddell, David Alan G. (1961). *British Honduras: A Historical and Contemporary Survey.* London: Oxford University Press.

Waddell, David Alan G. (1961a). "Developments in the Belize Question: 1946–1960." *American Journal of International Law,* 55, 468–469.

Waddell, David Alan G. (1988). Britain, British Honduras and Belize". *Belizean Studies,16* (2), 16–28.

Wilk, Richard and Mac Chapin (1990). Ethnic Minorities in Belize. Mopan, Kekchi and Garifuna. *SPEAReports 1,* Belize City: SPEAR.

Williams, Eric E. (1970). *From Columbus to Castro: The History of the Caribbean, 1492–1969.* London: Deutsch.

Winzerling, E.O. (1946). *The Beginning of British Honduras, 1506–1765.* New York: North River Press.

Woodward, Ralph Lee (1999). *Central America. A Nation Divided.* Oxford: Oxford University Press.

Young, Colville N. (1973). *Belize Creole: A Study of the Creolized English Spoken in the City of Belize in its Cultural and Social Setting.* Ph.D. Dissertation., York University.

Young, Colville N. (1974). Pre-Emancipation Brazil and the Early Honduras Settlement – Study in Comparative Sociology. *Journal of Belizean Affairs.* June (3).

Young, Colville N. (1989). *Language and Education in Belize.* Belize City: National Printers Ltd.

Young, Thomas (1842). *Narrative of a Residence on the Mosquito Shore,* London: Smith, Elder&Co.

Abbreviations

AB   Archives of Belize, Belmopan
AGI   Archivo General de Indias, Sevilla
PRO CO   Public Record Office, Colonial Office Records, London
            America and the West Indies, Calender of State Papers,
            Colonial British Honduras

Primary Sources

Central Statistical Office

- *Belize – External Trade, 1980–1992.* Belmopan: Ministry of Finance, 1993.
- *Abstract of Statistics.* Belmopan: Ministry of Finance, 1995.